APPLIED MARKETING ANALYTICS USING R

Gokhan Yildirim & Raoul Kübler

S Sage

1 Oliver's Yard
55 City Road
London EC1Y 1SP

2455 Teller Road
Thousand Oaks
California 91320

Unit No 323-333, Third Floor, F-Block
International Trade Tower
Nehru Place, New Delhi - 110 019

8 Marina View Suite 43-053
Asia Square Tower 1
Singapore 018960

Editor: Matthew Waters
Assistant editor: Charlotte Hanson
Production editor: Nicola Marshall
Copyeditor: Richard Leigh
Proofreader: Richard Walshe
Marketing manager: Lucia Sweet
Cover design: Francis Kenney
Typeset by: C&M Digitals (P) Ltd, Chennai, India
Printed in the UK

Library of Congress Control Number: 2022949856

British Library Cataloguing in Publication data

A catalogue record for this book is available from the British Library

ISBN 978-1-5297-6873-2
ISBN 978-1-5297-6872-5 (pbk)

At Sage we take sustainability seriously. Most of our products are printed in the UK using responsibly sourced papers and boards. When we print overseas we ensure sustainable papers are used as measured by the Paper Chain Project grading system. We undertake an annual audit to monitor our sustainability.

CONTENTS

ACKNOWLEDGEMENTS

I warmly thank my industry partners for their input on producing practical, relevant, and rigorous content for the book. I am also grateful to my students. With them in mind, I tried to be clear when illustrating the key technical concepts.

I am particularly indebted to my co-authors who stimulated me and brought new ideas to my attention.

I also wish to thank my colleagues at Imperial College London for their useful suggestions on the creation of this book. Special thanks go to Britney Wang whose help with the software applications was enormous.

Finally, I would like to express my sincere appreciation to my wife, Asli, my children, Aras and Nehir, my parents, and my extended family for their constant support, encouragement, and sacrifices during the creation of this book.

Gokhan Yildirim

Writing a book is rather like a sailing trip. Without the right crew, you will never make it safe to shore. And in that sense, this book is like a sailing trip: driven by a wonderful crew, to whom I owe a lot.

Foremost, I must thank my many co-authors, project partners, and colleagues, who all contributed to this book by providing me with the knowledge, experience, and skills to navigate the seven seas of data analysis and helping me to develop the right skills and seamanship to start this endeavour. While I cannot name them all, I want to especially thank Koen Pauwels, who, besides being a mentor, became a close friend. Without your trust in me and your guidance, this ship would not even have left the shipyard!

I am, also particularly grateful to Lina Oechsner and Stefanie Dewender, who both significantly helped to keep this ship out of troubled waters by editing chapters, giving critical feedback, and helping with setting up the markdowns.

Last, I want to thank my family for their enduring support. I thank my parents for always keeping faith in me and giving me confidence and support whenever I had doubts. A big thank you to Köri, who always makes me smile.

And infinite thanks to my wife Melike, who constantly encourages and inspires me. Without you, I would have never dared to board this ship!

Raoul V. Kübler

Finally, we wish to thank Matthew Waters, Charlotte Hanson, and Nicola Marshall at Sage for all the excellent service they provided during the creation of this book.

ABOUT THE AUTHORS

Dr. Gokhan Yildirim is an associate professor of marketing at Imperial College Business School where he teaches on the full-time MBA, executive MBA, and MSc Business Analytics programmes. Gokhan's research is at the intersection of marketing effectiveness, metrics, and models. He quantifies how marketing actions impact offline and online consumer behaviour, and how changes in consumer attitudes in turn drive company performance. Specifically, his research concerns the short- and long-term effectiveness of digital and non-digital marketing activities, cross-channel marketing resource allocation, and consumer attitudinal metrics for guiding marketing decisions. He uses applied time-series econometrics and machine learning tools to offer managerial insights in these areas. Gokhan's academic work has appeared in leading journals of the field such as the *Journal of Marketing*, *Marketing Science*, and the *International Journal of Research in Marketing*. He is the recipient of prestigious research awards such as an Amazon award in advertising and the ISMS-MSI Gary Lilien Practice Prize award for outstanding implementation of marketing science concepts and methods.

Dr. Raoul Kübler is an associate professor of marketing at ESSEC Business School in Cergy/ Paris where he teaches on the Financial Times top 10 ranked Master in Management programme of ESSEC's Grande Ecole, as well as on the school's global MBA and executive MBA. Before joining ESSEC he worked from 2018 until 2022 as a junior professor at the University of Münster, and from 2012 until 2018 an assistant professor of marketing at Özyeğin University in Istanbul, Turkey. In his research, he examines how marketers can leverage user-generated content and social media data in combination with machine learning and artificial intelligence to derive better marketing decisions. His research focus is largely guided by his close collaboration with marketing professionals. He has consulted leading international companies such as TetraPak, Rausch AG Switzerland, Dr. Wolff Group, PepsiCo Turkey, Sisecam Turkey, Garanti Bank, GfK, and OD Yachting on digital marketing issues. Dr. Kübler's research is frequently published in leading international marketing and business journals such as the *Journal of Marketing*, the *Journal of the Academy of Marketing Science*, the *Journal of Interactive Marketing* and the *Journal of Cultural Economics*. Furthermore, Raoul has been ranked since 2018 within the top 10% of most successful business scholars in Germany, Switzerland, and Austria according to A+ publications, of which some have been awarded by institutions such as MSI, Marketing EDGE, and EMAC.

OVERVIEW

The marketing landscape is changing at an astonishing rate as a result of new emerging technologies, granular data availability, and ever-growing analytics tools. Indeed, today's marketing is no longer just an art; it requires the use of data and quantitative approaches to support strategic decisions in rapidly evolving offline and online environments. With the help of the latest artificial intelligence tools as well as other statistical and econometric models, marketers can now strengthen their decision-making with more accurate information and insights derived from the rich available data.

In combination with 'soft' skills (e.g. creativity, communication, and teamwork), coding, machine learning tools, big data analytics, and insight generation are now becoming the new 'must have' skill set for marketing graduates and practitioners. Taking a very hands-on approach with real-world datasets and cases, this textbook aims to help instructors, students, and practitioners explore a range of marketing phenomena using various applied analytics tools and frameworks. The textbook's practical orientation together with computer-based case studies and real-life examples will allow users to identify potential customers, boost their experience through improved targeting, turn customer engagement into sales, and derive useful and actionable managerial insights.

This textbook ties the theoretical marketing frameworks to real-world cases through computer-based applications and software code. It is particularly recommended to instructors who teach marketing analytics courses at bachelor's and postgraduate (MSc and MBA) levels and would like to adopt computer-supported case-based delivery in their teaching. Furthermore, we recommend the book to managers who are keen to extend their knowledge in the domain and gain a better understanding of how to set up and manage an analytics project, where to get data from, and how to use specific analytical models to answer contemporary marketing questions. The book provides such practitioners with easy-to-use tools and techniques that allow them to make evidence-based marketing decisions.

The structure and flow of the book reflect the traditional marketing strategy development process as mandated by the market-oriented leadership school. First the reader is introduced with the necessary processes and tools to identify and target suitable customer segments (Chapter 2). Then, the reader learns how to adapt the marketing activities to the targeted segments (Chapter 3) and evaluate the contribution of digital marketing touchpoints to consumer responses (Chapter 4) to increase customer acquisition. After the acquisition stage, marketers need to keep customers engaged to increase sales and turn one-time shoppers into loyal customers. The reader continues by learning how to benefit from user-generated data (Chapter 5) to gain more customer insights by enriching existing – commonly survey-based – marketing metrics with information obtained from online user chatter. Meanwhile, brand equity building may play an important role; to understand brand health and strategically guide brand management, marketers need to identify the relevant key performance indicators for their brand (Chapter 6). To refine information from the mined data, the reader learns how to use state-of-the-art text mining techniques (Chapter 7). As customer acquisition – and especially reacquisition – is among the most expensive and difficult tasks in marketing, managers are well advised to also monitor customer satisfaction and predict customer churn, to prevent customers from leaving the company early on (Chapter 8). Having established a strong and healthy brand, marketers need to be able to predict demand for future periods with the help of time-series models that account for marketing activities as well as market trends (Chapter 9). As an advanced market research technique, image-mining tools are introduced to turn user-generated visual data into meaningful information that can subsequently be fed into classic marketing analytics models (Chapter 10). The book closes with a discussion of data quality, data storage and data management questions as well as a profound ethical discussion of the potential impact of analytics on the various stakeholders and society at large (Chapter 11).

ENDORSEMENTS

There are good books on marketing principles, on analytical models, and on statistical software, but not on the combination of these three areas. This is where *Applied Marketing Analytics Using R* breaks new ground and offers exceptional value to the practice of marketing model building. The marketing decision areas are carefully selected, the modeling principles are well explained, and the case studies offer relevant applications of the R software modules. I recommend this book with enthusiasm!

Dominique M. Hanssens, Distinguished Research Professor of Marketing, UCLA Anderson School of Management, USA

Kuebler and Yildirim manage to mix tried-and-true marketing models with recent advances in machine learning to offer a coherent, practical, and down-to-earth toolbox for data-driven marketers. A must-have for modern marketing managers.

Arnaud De Bruyn, Ph.D., Professor of Marketing, ESSEC Business School, Author of *Principles of Marketing Engineering and Analytics*

This book brings a much-needed practical perspective to scientifically sophisticated marketing analytics. The authors Gokhan and Raoul truly represent the best of both worlds, being both accomplished marketing academics and practical data scientists. They start each chapter with a case study ranging from US banks to EU skincare, and UK airlines to Turkish kitchens and Finnish game developers. I love the natural flow of the book chapters, following the market orientation structure of segmentation, targeting, positioning and marketing mix modeling. At the same time, the authors demonstrate the value of adding the latest tools in attribution, online chatter and image mining. They explain every step both in the marketing strategy process and in the software installation and implementation. As to the latter, the R exercises give you hands-on experience in the latest in marketing analytics, which helps you optimize your decisions and shine in the marketplace.

Koen Pauwels, Distinguished Professor of Marketing at Northeastern University, Boston and co-director of its Digital, Analytics, Technology and Automation (DATA) Initiative.

Applied Marketing Analytics using R is an exceptional resource for individuals eager to achieve business success and students seeking an extensive exploration of marketing analytics and R. Unlike many purely academic books, Yildirim from Imperial College and Kubler from ESSEC seamlessly blend a rigorous academic perspective with a practical approach to solving real-world marketing problems. This comprehensive guide takes you through the entire A to Z process of marketing analytics, covering everything from fundamental data sets and visualization techniques to advanced statistical modelling and its business implications. The inclusion of insightful case studies further enhances the practicality of the book, offering valuable applications of marketing analytics. By delving into this book, marketing researchers can elevate their skills and expertise, making it an indispensable resource for anyone serious about pursuing analytics in the field of marketing. Overall, this book makes a significant contribution to the field and is highly recommended!

Shuba Srinivasan, Norman and Adele Barron Professor in Management, Professor, Marketing, Questrom School of Business, Boston University, USA

ONLINE RESOURCES

This textbook is accompanied by online resources to aid teaching and support learning. To access these resources, visit: **http://www.study.sagepub.com/yildirim**. Please note that lecturers will require a SAGE account in order to access the lecturer resources. An account can be created via the above link.

FOR LECTURERS

- **PowerPoints** that can be downloaded and adapted to suit individual teaching needs
- A **Teaching Guide** providing practical guidance and support and additional materials for lecturers using this textbook in their teaching
- A **Testbank** that can be used for both formative and summative student assessments

FOR STUDENTS

- Datasets, software code, and solutions (R markdowns, HTML files) that can be downloaded and used alongside exercises in the textbook

1

INTRODUCTION

Chapter contents

LEARNING OBJECTIVES

After your work on this chapter, you should be able to:

- define marketing analytics and its process
- describe potential areas of marketing analytics
- outline what is required for a successful marketing analytics team in an organization
- explain the common mistakes in implementing marketing analytics and how to avoid them
- install R and RStudio on your computer and run some of the basic functions.

This chapter provides an introduction to marketing analytics and familiarizes the reader with the software used throughout the book. The first part of the chapter explains what marketing analytics is about and why it is useful for businesses and customers. It focuses on how marketing analytics can help firms in supporting the customer value creation process and achieving or improving target performance levels. It also explains how to avoid some potential pitfalls in implementing model-based decision-making in marketing. The second part of the chapter deals with the installation of R, the free data analytics software package the book uses for computer applications. Specifically, the section shows the user step-by-step how to install R and RStudio, and perform some of the basic tasks such as installing and loading packages, creating R Markdown files and importing data to R.

WHAT IS MARKETING ANALYTICS ABOUT?

It is mind-blowing how much the world has changed in the last couple of decades and how marketing has evolved with it. In just a few short years, a range of technological innovations (e.g. IT infrastructures, cloud-based platforms, artificial intelligence (AI), and machine learning technologies) have dramatically transformed the marketing industry and contributed to companies' ever-growing databases. For example, Walmart, one of the world's biggest retailers, processes about 2.5 petabytes (i.e. 2.5 million gigabytes) of unstructured data every hour (Forbes, 2017). Facebook, the largest social networking site in the world, generates 4 petabytes of data per day (Smith, 2019). Many firms, indeed, have abundant information on their customers' profiles and choices (e.g. demographics, location-based real-time data, clickstream data, social media conversations, likes, comments, retweets, clicks, in-store visits, online and offline purchases). However, not all of them have the expertise and resources to act aptly on such information. How can marketing managers track and use consumer data in the age of AI to create better value for their firms? How can they utilize AI-based tools and techniques to gain a deep understanding of their customers and support their marketing mix decisions? How can they leverage text data, image data, or voice data to shape their product and marketing strategies? How can multiple data sources be integrated for better marketing insights? Addressing all these questions by means of quantitative approaches lies at the heart of marketing analytics. In other words, marketing analytics allows firms to make sense of consumer data, assess the effectiveness of their marketing actions, reach accurate insights on consumer behaviour,

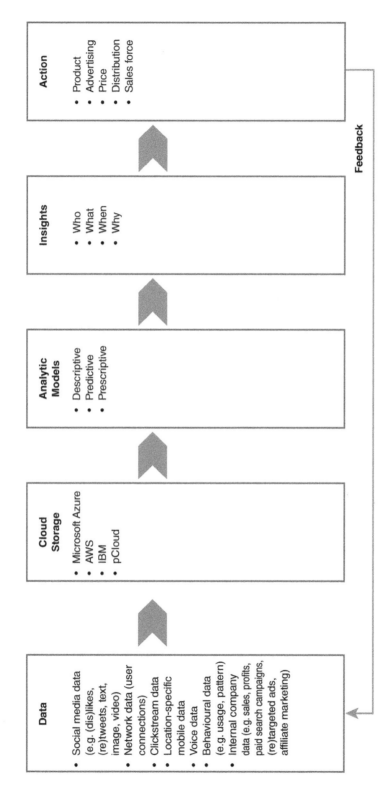

Data
- Social media data (e.g. (dis)likes, (re)tweets, text, image, video)
- Network data (user connections)
- Clickstream data
- Location-specific mobile data
- Voice data
- Behavioural data (e.g. usage, pattern)
- Internal company data (e.g. sales, profits, paid search campaigns, (re)targeted ads, affiliate marketing)

Cloud Storage
- Microsoft Azure
- AWS
- IBM
- pCloud

Analytic Models
- Descriptive
- Predictive
- Prescriptive

Insights
- Who
- What
- When
- Why

Action
- Product
- Advertising
- Price
- Distribution
- Sales force

Feedback

Figure 1.1   The process of marketing analytics

inform strategic marketing decisions, and eventually improve top- and bottom-line financial performance. Therefore, we can define marketing analytics as the process of collecting and analysing datasets in a systematic way to draw conclusions on marketing strategies and improve business outcomes with the help of analytic tools and techniques.

Figure 1.1 shows the main stages of the marketing analytics process. In today's digital world, consumers stay connected all the time through their devices (e.g. smartphone, tablet, desktop) and navigate across channels (e.g. social media, e-mail, websites). This results in enormous amounts of structured (e.g. impressions, clicks) and unstructured (e.g. user-generated content on social media) data. Firms typically store these data in cloud-based environments, and then feed them into analytic models (e.g. descriptive, predictive, and prescriptive models) to gain insights into the 'who' (who buys or clicks; consumer demographics and lifestyles), 'what' (what consumers bought), 'when' (when they clicked/bought), and 'why' (why they preferred one product over another) of consumer behaviour. Finally, insights are turned into marketing actions – product, advertising, price, distribution, and salesforce decisions – that are usually automated using AI systems such as chat-bots, robots, and other types of machine learning algorithms. Decisions taken by marketing managers, in turn, affect what consumers think, feel, and do in the marketplace. Consumer responses, then, generate new data points, and so the cycle continues.

It is important to note that the ultimate goal of marketing analytics is to help firms create value for their customers, clients, partners, and the society they are a part of. Thus, marketing analytics applications should not be seen as a standalone activity, rather as an important constituent of a value creation process of a firm. They should be performed continuously and in a structured way using the right toolkits.

What can a firm achieve with marketing analytics?

Research shows that companies that capitalize on marketing analytics perform better than those that do not, and that the benefits of adopting and implementing analytic models are enormous (Pauwels, 2015). If used appropriately, analytics can improve customer experience substantially and boost return on marketing investments by up to 20 per cent (Gordon and Perrey, 2015). For instance, L'Occitane, a French multinational retailer that sells organic cosmetics and well-being products, improved its revenues by 6.5 per cent by reallocating its customer relationship management (CRM) budget based on various analytic approaches (Valenti et al., 2021). Applying a new decision support tool, Mercedes-Benz optimized its advertising campaigns for four major new car launches in Germany and obtained an estimated savings of €2 million per campaign (Fischer, 2019). Georgia Aquarium, one of the most popular tourist destinations in the USA, wanted to increase site attendance without compromising visitor satisfaction (Kumar et al., 2015). Adopting various marketing science models, it was able to achieve a 10% increase in attendance and 12% increase in revenue. TGI Fridays, a global restaurant and bar chain, created more personal and memorable customer experiences thanks to its notable investment in AI technology and machine learning models (MarketingWeek, 2018). The company was able to combine social media mentions of its brand with online booking and card payment data in order to generate the most effective and targeted e-mail and social media content for each individual customer. These examples of how marketing analytics helps firms are numerous and can be extended to diverse product categories and industries. Some of the other practical uses of marketing analytics include:

- Segmentation by clustering individual-level data and exploring new customer groups
- Targeting the right audiences with the right messages in real time using online recommendation systems and/or geo-location mobile technologies
- Boosting customer engagement with personalized content
- Extracting social media data and summarizing user sentiment towards brands
- Deciding how much to spend on customer acquisition and retention activities
- Dividing up advertising budget across channels
- Understanding consumers' price sensitivity
- Assessing the effectiveness of ad campaigns and creating automated ads
- Analysing the consumer purchase journey and quantifying the contribution of marketing campaigns at different touchpoints (e.g. paid ads in social media, display ads, referral programs) to purchase outcomes
- Developing new products and making product modification decisions
- Predicting which consumers are likely to quit a service or cancel a subscription, also known as churn prediction
- Predicting future demand when consumer preferences are stable.

How do consumers benefit from marketing analytics?

There are countless benefits of marketing analytics that consumers enjoy. Perhaps the most significant one is convenience. In the past, consumers used to have a fragmented and often disrupted experience when interacting with brands. Thanks to AI-driven technologies, now consumers make purchases more seamlessly. For example, Amazon's search algorithms and one-click ordering system allow consumers to purchase all sorts of items, from a lawnmower to a chocolate bar, after an effortless journey, very quickly and easily. Also, the prevalence of deep learning models and image-based search tools enables consumers to spend less time searching for products and services that satisfy their needs. For instance, Tommy Hilfiger's image recognition app enables shoppers to upload an image of a product they want and search the exact or similar products. Services of this type reduce consumers' search costs and vastly enhance their experience. Moreover, consumers enjoy receiving attractive and relevant offers at different stages of their purchase journey. Machine learning models play a big role in such marketing programs. For instance, the UK-based online fashion retailer ASOS sends e-vouchers or free-delivery options to consumers who fill their online shopping basket but leave without a purchase. This kind of offer provides a great economic benefit to consumers. Also, personalized content delivered through online recommender algorithms significantly enriches the consumer experience. Netflix recommends movies based on viewers' past preferences and demographics, which creates a high level of viewer satisfaction and willingness to binge watch.

Some applications of marketing analytics help consumers avoid bad outcomes as well. For example, Barclays UK uses predictive models to detect fraudulent transactions among millions of data points. With such a service, customers can protect themselves against bad outcomes. Burberry, the luxury fashion house, allows its customers to use its image recognition tool to find out whether the product they are planning to purchase is authentic or fake.

Next, we will outline some of the important drivers for constructing a marketing analytics team and describe the most common challenges encountered by organizations.

How to build a marketing analytics team in an organization

A highly skilled marketing analytics team is an integral part of an organization that aims to improve business decisions and outcomes with data-driven approaches. Building a successful analytics team requires careful consideration on the following factors:

1. *Mindset.* You need the right mindset and must embrace the fact that analytics and AI-supported tools can resolve marketing issues and/or unearth new opportunities for growth.
2. *Key players.* A typical marketing analytics team consists of three essential roles:
    *   *Data analyst.* People working in this role are typically in charge of (i) collecting, integrating, and maintaining large-scale datasets, and (ii) developing algorithms, executing analytical models, and preparing data visualizations. This role is quite technical and requires advanced data, software, and programming skills.
    *   *Data translator.* This role plays a bridging role between data analysts and data directors. Data translators help analysts (i) look at the right marketing problems and how to approach them, (ii) define the scope of a project and outline the deliverables, and (iii) interpret the results and determine the next best course of action. Also, they generate project reports and communicate the results to marketing analytics directors. These people should have training in marketing analytics and possess some strong team and communication skills.
    *   *Marketing analytics director.* This is a leadership role that requires strong domain knowledge as well as strategic decision-making skills. Marketing analytics directors (i) ensure that analytics projects are aligned with the overall business objectives, (ii) prioritize projects and provide their team with a roadmap, (iv) inform the chief marketing officer about project findings/insights and recommend changes in marketing programs, (v) simplify complex analytics concepts for non-technical audiences and create a data-driven culture within an organization, (vi) manage the budget for analytics tools and systems, and (vii) ensure that team members are provided continuous and up-to-date educational courses.

How big the team should be, of course, depends on the size of the organization, the long-term needs, and other financial constraints.

Finally, to be able to get analytics projects up and running, the team should have access to data analytics software such as R, Python, MATLAB, or SAS along with high-powered computers.

What are the challenges?

No matter how great the marketing analytics team is, there will usually be some challenges in implementing the analytics projects within an organization:

1. *Culture*. Running analytics projects or experiments should not be a standalone activity. They should be run continuously and be part of the long-term value creation process of a firm. It is important to develop and maintain a data-driven culture within your organization to benefit from analytics projects.
2. *Disconnect between departments*. Different departments within the same organization (e.g. CRM and marketing departments) may not be aware that they run similar projects in the same time window. This leads to duplication of efforts across teams, culminating in waste of time and resources. Also, sometimes different departments use slightly different metrics and methodologies. This creates a lot of confusion. It becomes a lot harder to evaluate, understand, and communicate the results. Overall, teams' productivity suffers and less time is allocated for other opportunities.
3. *Relevant data*. Big data opportunities are ample. Marketers can track hundreds of metrics with thousands or even millions of data points. It is important to determine the relevant metrics for the problem at hand, instead of throwing them all at big data algorithms and predictive models in the hope that the perfect solution will be found. For example, marketers should ask themselves, 'is it brand awareness or brand preference that matters more in this context and what should I expect from the model?'
4. *Intangible metrics*. Marketing dashboards provide plenty of information on fast-moving online variables such as number of searches, clicks, visits, orders, and sales. However, intangible and slow-moving variables (e.g. brand awareness, image, and attitudinal data) are equally important but often absent. To fully grasp consumers' responses to their marketing campaigns, marketers should combine fast-moving online variables with slow-moving attitudinal data.
5. *Speed versus quality*. Real-time marketing mix decisions require fast data analysis, which sometimes may lead to bad outcomes. If the firm is discovering new problems to solve, it may take some time to identify the potential drivers of the problem and conduct the analysis. Hence, marketers' objective should be to make fast decisions without compromising on quality.
6. *Knowing the 'why'*. Predictive analytics is great at suggesting what a consumer will do next, but cannot reveal why and in what context. To uncover insights into the 'why' of consumer behaviour, big-data model findings should be complemented with field experiments.
7. *Analytics for business-to-business (B2B) companies*. Some key performance indicators of B2B companies are a bit hard to optimize with data (e.g. relationship ties). Metrics of this kind require a deep understanding of the customer.
8. *Risk-averse decisions*. In following marketing analytics approaches, marketers do what the data tell them to do. What is it that marketers lose when they become too data-driven? They no longer think outside the box and make risky decisions. This clearly is an obstacle for creating innovative ideas, products, or services. Thus, it is likely that data-driven approaches makes marketers risk-averse. Marketers should not let data-driven approaches take away their innovative product designs and creative programmes.

9.   *Driving markets.* Marketing managers should heed customers' needs and wants and develop market-driven products or services. Perhaps equally important is their vision and where they want to see their products in the future. Their role also requires them to create customer needs, and build clear and consistent brand identity. Therefore, marketers should be market-driven but also aim to drive the markets.

To summarize, analytic models should guide marketers to develop big-picture strategies rather than merely providing optimized short-term solutions. Combining analytics-based approaches with managerial intuition or judgement is key to growing the customer base, building and maintaining successful products.

Potential pitfalls and how to avoid them

When used inappropriately, marketing analytics may not be of great help to marketers or may even backfire by delivering biased or incorrect results, with fatal consequences in the long run. Therefore, it is important to understand why marketing analytics sometimes fails and how one can avoid the common pitfalls in implementing it.

Insufficient training and an underdeveloped statistical understanding often result in the choice of *inappropriate tools and methods*. Given that the internet has an overabundance of tutorials and packages, some users tend to simply rely on a quick Google search to find a suitable package for their marketing problem. While this may work in a few cases, most of the time the chosen package or a suggestion from an internet forum may lead to biased or incorrect results, as the chosen method is likely to be unsuitable for the type of data or problem. Marketing analysts, therefore, need to have a profound understanding of statistical methods to be able to judge the suitability of a specific method for the specific context and data application.

This becomes even more of an issue if managers use marketing analytics tools to prove their own expectations to be true rather than trying to fully understand a phenomenon. Such *confirmation biases* often result in the choice of rather poor methods or make managers stop analysing a problem once the desired results show up. Marketing analysts are, thus, well advised to try out different approaches and benchmark their results with different methods, types of datasets, and variables. Having an open mind and the will to discover and explain issues instead of confirming opinions formed pre-project is key. This can be achieved either by replicating studies in different contexts with different variables/metrics, or by comparing results of different types of analyses to confirm the reliability of the initial findings.

Another often underestimated issue is *data quality and data understanding*. Even the strongest methodological competence may not help if the data you have are not suitable to answer your question of interest. Data may originate from sources outside the company, which may prevent marketing analysts from understanding the quality of the data. Especially when it comes to secondary data sources (e.g. market research reports), it often remains unclear how the data were collected and how reliable they are. A key task in the process of data mining and data analysis is, thus, quality control, which often takes more time, energy, and resources than the main analysis. Being able to fully understand data composition, to identify outliers and other sources of biases, is therefore key to a successful analysis. Pre-analysis steps such as the visualization of the data structure, a visual inspection of the distribution of the data at hand, as well as an attempt to develop model-free evidence of the suspected effects with the help of tools such as correlation analysis, are tremendously helpful in developing an understanding of the data quality and structure, which in turn will help a marketing analyst to identify suitable tools and methods for further analyses.

Data quality may also depend on *data processing and data matching*. Very often marketing analysts need to employ various sources of data. This requires them to combine and match different datasets, which again provides a great deal of potential for mistakes. Proper data warehousing and data management through structured databases such as MySQL will help overcome data integration issues and ensure that the necessary data are provided in a clean and unbiased way once needed. Proper data warehousing and data storage should further prevent analysts from transferring datasets through different types of software and tools, which often brings the risk of data malfunctioning and errors, as different software solutions may manipulate data, or destroy the format of information matching such as time stamps or user IDs.

Even if data processing is flawless, *data sampling* may be another source of fatal errors and misinterpretation. Data may not originate from a representative sample. Hence, conclusions may not be generalizable to a specific group of interest. This may especially occur when data are outdated or when events and shocks have changed consumer behaviour in such a way that the existing data can no longer predict future behaviour. Data analysts are, thus, well advised to continuously question the suitability of their data sources to answer a specific question before even starting composing a dataset.

While exploring and understanding phenomena with the help of statistical and machine learning methods is a key goal in marketing research, marketing analysts also often need to develop models which make *predictions*. While common marketing research models are often judged on how well they explain a specific phenomenon, predictive models are often judged based on how successfully they predict the occurrence of a phenomenon (e.g. the number of customer churns in a specific period). When building predictive models, marketing analysts tend to fall into the so-called 'overfitting' trap. Their model fits a particular dataset incredibly well, but fails to perform well against future or unseen data. To prevent models from overfitting, marketing analysts are advised to not only focus on validation techniques but also monitor continuously the quality of their future predictions. We will explore the overfitting issue in greater depth later in the book. If models fail to correctly predict consumer actions, analysts should ask 'why' it happens, and look for alternative solutions, instead of defending their own efforts and outputs. For example, models can be recalibrated by incorporating new metrics, and new methods or data sources can be used until the model predictions become satisfactory.

GETTING STARTED WITH R

In this book, we will be applying various analytical tools to different datasets in order to explore some of the strategic marketing issues widely encountered by practitioners. To this end, we will use the software called R.

This section aims to prepare you for the upcoming data applications as there are a few things you should do and know before you can start using R for marketing analytics. Specifically, you will learn how to:

- install R and RStudio
- create and save your script files
- install and load R packages
- import (export) data to (from) R.

What is R?

R is a free, open-source software and programming language for statistical computing. R has become one of the dominant software packages for data analysis, and is widely used by leading organizations worldwide.

What is RStudio?

RStudio is a graphical front-end to R and provides a user-friendly environment for using R. We will be using RStudio throughout the book.

What is R Markdown?

R Markdown is a text formatting tool that allows you to write and run your own code. Using R Markdown, you can also make your analyses and prepare reports from those analyses in various file formats, including HTML (files that you can open using an internet browser), PDF, and Word. R Notebook is another document type, and can be perceived as a form of R Markdown. In the remainder of this book, we will use R Markdown for the data applications.

Why do I have to learn R for marketing analytics?

Marketers increasingly make use of larger and more varied data sources (e.g. text data), as well as more advanced algorithms (e.g. machine learning) to support their strategic decisions. These data and algorithms cannot be processed well by tools such as Excel and SPSS. Furthermore, leading companies are increasingly embracing a 'test-and-learn' culture, and adopt programming languages like R to make automated decisions, and improve efficiency and business outcomes.

What if I do not have any background in statistics or programming?

There is absolutely no need to worry about this. This book does not assume any background in statistics, programming, or R. It is designed for users without any quantitative background. It is important to note that we will be taking a practical approach to using R. The aim is to deliver R applications in an accessible way that allows you to solve marketing problems, not to convert you into a statistician or a programming expert. Thus, the focus will be on learning how to apply R codes in order to answer frequently asked marketing questions. You may initially find using R difficult and time-consuming, but after carefully working through the R applications you will become increasingly proficient, and develop new analytical skills along the way.

Installing R and RStudio

We will first install R, and then RStudio.

1. To install R, go to https://www.r-project.org/, and click on **download R**. See the screenshot in Figure 1.2.

Figure 1.2   Downloading R

2. You will land on the CRAN Mirrors page (see Figure 1.3). Scroll down the page and click on the URL associated with Imperial College London. If there is an available URL for your own country, you can click on it instead.

Figure 1.3   CRAN Mirrors

3. Select the appropriate operating system for your device (e.g. 'Download R for Windows'; see Figure 1.4).

Figure 1.4   Downloading R for various operating systems

4.   If you choose Windows, then on the next page you need to click on 'base'
      (see Figure 1.5).

Figure 1.5   Subdirectories for R

5.   Download the latest version of R (see Figure 1.6). On a Mac, you need to download the
      file with the .pkg extension under 'Latest Release'.

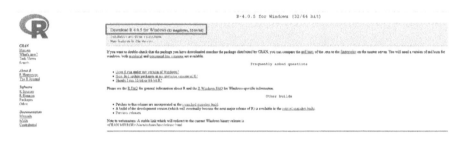

Figure 1.6   Downloading R for Windows

Once you download the .exe file to your computer, double-click on the file and follow the
instructions to complete the installation. You are done with the R installation.

If you already have R installed on your device, we would still recommend to download R
again if you do not have the latest version installed. This is because some of the functions
we will be using may not work on older versions of R. R will by default use the latest version
installed on your device, but you will still have the option of using earlier versions if you
wish to do so.

To download RStudio, follow the steps below:

1.   Go to https://posit.co/download/rstudio-desktop/. We will use the 'RStudio Desktop'
      Open Source License. Click on 'Download' for this version (see Figure 1.7).
2.   Under 'All installers', select the appropriate operating system for your device and
      download the appropriate file. Figure 1.8 shows the download file for Windows.

Download
RStudio Desktop

Used by millions of people weekly, the RStudio integrated
development environment (IDE) is a set of tools built to help you
be more productive with R and Python. It includes a console,
syntax-highlighting editor that supports direct code execution. It
also features tools for plotting, viewing history, debugging and
managing your workspace.

Select Your Operating System:

Figure 1.7 Free version of RStudio

OS	Download	Size	SHA-256
Windows 10/11	RSTUDIO-2022.12.0-353.EXE	202.76MB	FD8EA4B4
macOS 10.15+	RSTUDIO-2022.12.0-353.DMG	365.70MB	FD49E8B5

Figure 1.8 RStudio for different operating systems

Open the downloaded file and follow the instructions to complete the installation. You have
installed RStudio as well.

First steps in RStudio

Opening RStudio

From your start menu, you should now be able to find RStudio. Clicking on it will open
RStudio, at which point you should see a screen like the one in Figure 1.9. If you do not see a
window with a script file (the top left window), or if you want to open a new one, go to the
menu bar and click on **File>New File>R script**. Figure 1.10 shows these steps. Note that other
file types, *R Notebook* and *R Markdown*, are also accessed from here. In the *File* menu, you will
also find operations such as *Save, Save As, Import Dataset* etc.

Figure 1.9 RStudio main screen

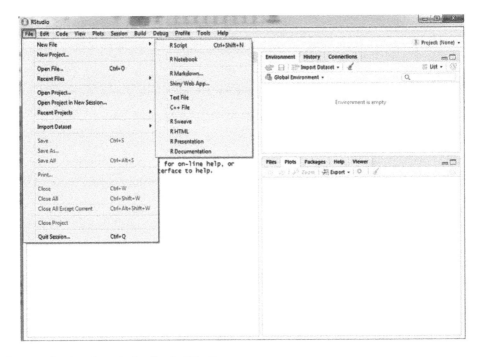

Figure 1.10 Opening a text editor in RStudio

When you write your code, you can run it by clicking on the *Run* button. Type the code shown in the top left window in Figure 1.11 in your text editor, highlight it, and run it.

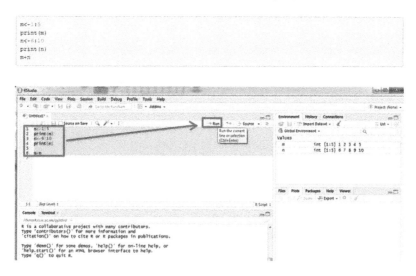

Figure 1.11   Running some code in RStudio

Figure 1.12   RStudio: code, environment, and output

Figure 1.12 shows what happens when we execute the code. The top left screen shows that we defined two vectors, **m** and **n**, and then summed them. Note that <- in R actually denotes the equality sign =. When we run the code, these vectors appear at the top right (*Environment*) panel. You can find all command results at the bottom left in the *Console* panel.

Setting your working directory

The working directory is where your files (e.g. your code and data) will be stored. Before continuing to work with RStudio, you should set up your working directory. We recommend creating a dedicated folder for all R materials on your computer, for instance 'R for Applied Marketing Analytics' (or any other name you would like to use).

Figure 1.13 shows the steps for setting up your working directory. You click on **Session** in the menu bar. Then you go to **Set Working Directory**, then **Choose Directory**, and finally choose the folder 'R for Marketing Analytics' that you just created on your computer.

Figure 1.13   Working directory

Note that you will have to set your working directory every time you start RStudio. To make this easier, you can set your working directory within your script file. You can copy the line of code that was generated just now into your console (the bottom left window in RStudio), starting with `setwd`, and paste this into your script file. Make sure not to include the > sign before `setwd` in the script file.

Saving your script

Code that you enter directly into the console will not be saved by R, so it is best to work in script files. Code that you enter into a script file can be saved as a reproducible record of your analysis.

Figure 1.14 shows how to save your script. Go to **File**, and click on **Save**. You can name your script (e.g. 'Introduction_to_R') and save it on your device (e.g. in your 'R for Applied Marketing Analytics' folder).

Figure 1.14 Saving an R script

Installing and loading packages

What are packages and why do I need them?

R automatically loads a number of functions to do basic operations, but packages provide extra functionality. They typically consist of a number of functions that can handle specific tasks. For example, a package could provide functions to run a machine learning algorithm, as we will do later on in this book.

How do I install packages?

To install a package, you need to type `install.packages("package name goes here")` in your script and run this line of code.

Let us try to install the popular `tidyverse` package, one of the packages we will be using in this book. Install the package by running the following line of code:

```
install.packages("tidyverse") # this line installs the tidyverse package
```

After installing a package, you will need to load it to make it work in R:

```
library(tidyverse) # this line loads the tidyverse package
```

It is worth noting the following:

- You only need to install packages once on your computer, but you need to load them every time you open R.

- After installing and loading the `tidyverse` package, you will be able to use the functions that are included in it.
- Installing a package will typically produce a lot of output in the console, which is not important in itself.
- Depending on your analysis, you will need to install and launch a different package.

Perhaps you noticed the hashtag symbol (#) in the above code. As you will gradually be working with more extensive files of code, it is very useful to annotate your script. This can help you identify and segregate distinct components of your code. You can annotate your script by using the hashtag symbol #.

How do I know if I have successfully installed a package?

You can check whether you have successfully installed a package by loading the package. If you try to load a package that has not been successfully installed, you will get an error in your console. Imagine you try to load a package called 'marketing':

Here, R is telling us that there is no package called 'marketing', because it is not downloaded (in fact, it does not exist). If you get this error while installing the `tidyverse` package, this means the installation was not successful.

```
library(marketing) # I am trying to load the (non-existent) package 'marketing'
Error in library(marketing) : there is no package called 'marketing'
```

What should I do if installation of a package in unsuccessful?

- Check carefully to make sure you have not made any spelling mistakes, have used quotation marks (" ") where appropriate, and have not used any capital letters as R is case sensitive.
- Alternatively, you can try to install the package manually, by clicking on the *Packages* tab in the bottom right panel of your screen. Click on *Install*, insert the name of the package under *Packages*, and click on *Install*. After installing packages manually, you still need to load them as before.
- For the remainder of this reading, successful installation of the `tidyverse` package is not needed, so for now, you can continue without having the package installed.

R Markdown

Of the text editors in R, R Markdown is one of the most popular. We provided a short introduction to it earlier in this chapter.

R Markdown will provide you with the tools to present your work and act as a notebook while you work. Suppose that you need to analyse a dataset in *CSV* format. Without *RStudio* and *R Markdown*, you would need to import the dataset into your program, then create an output, say a graph, then copy the graph, then perhaps edit it, and then insert it as an image into the presentation which you are preparing in, say, *MS PowerPoint* or *Keynote*. Whenever you made a change in your analysis and the resulting graph changed, you would need to repeat the same cycle again. This is exhausting. But *R Markdown* enables you to import your dataset, run your analysis, generate outcomes in multiple formats such as HTML, and finally make presentations in a single environment. More importantly, whenever you alter your analysis, it will be dynamically reflected in your outputs. Thus, you won't need to make further changes to your presentation.

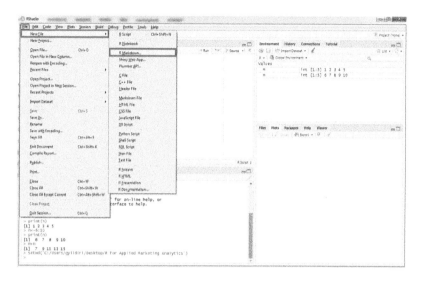

Figure 1.15 Opening an R Markdown

R Markdown can be found as shown in Figure 1.15. After clicking on *R Markdown* as shown, a dialogue box will appear so that you can choose the specifics of your R markdown (see Figure 1.16).

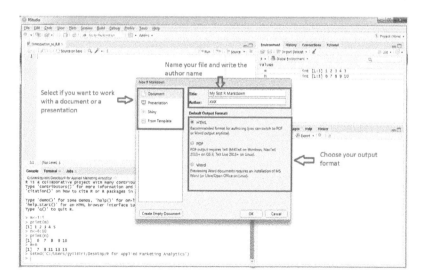

Figure 1.16 Choosing the specifics of an R markdown

First, type in the title of your file, and the author name. Click on *Document* to select it as the file type. Finally, choose *HTML* as the output format.

Your document will not be blank, but will have a certain structure. Figure 1.17 shows the sections of a standard *R Markdown* file.

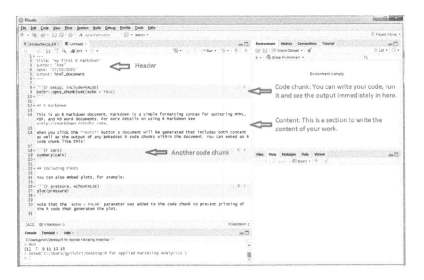

Figure 1.17   Sections of a standard R markdown

If you need a new code chunk, click on the *Insert* button as shown in Figure 1.18, and select the code chunk type you wish to insert. We insert an R code chunk.

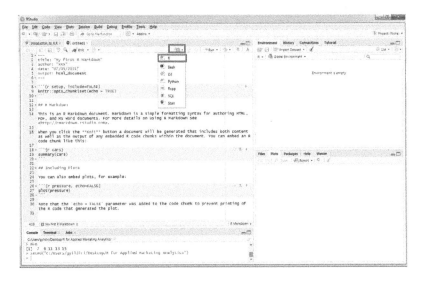

Figure 1.18   Inserting a new code chunk in R Markdown

Let us run the codes in the chunks (see Figure 1.19).

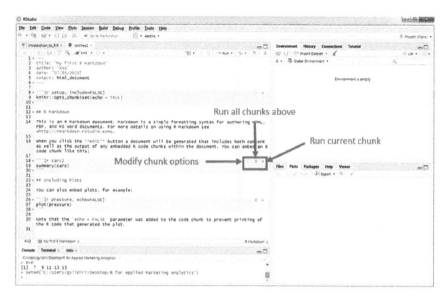

Figure 1.19   Running code chunks in R Markdown

The output will be illustrated just below the relevant chunk as shown in Figure 1.20.

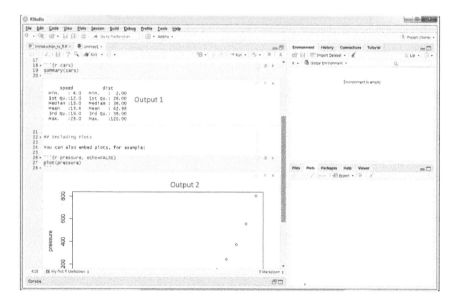

Figure 1.20   Running code chunks in R Markdown

Next, to generate an output file from all we have done in the *R Markdown* file, we click on *Knit*, and select *Knit to HTML* (see Figure 1.21).

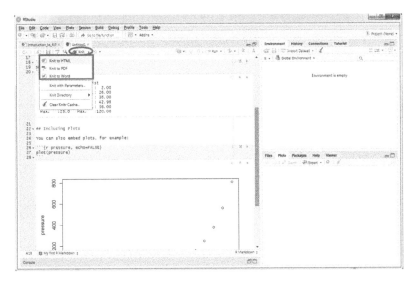

Figure 1.21   Knitting a document in R Markdown

An output document in a separate window will appear as displayed in Figure 1.22.

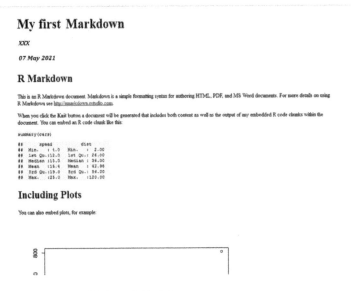

Figure 1.22   Generated HTML file from R Markdown

Before we can analyse data in R, we need to know how to import (export) a dataset to (from) R.

IMPORTING DATA TO R

The data can be kept in various forms. In this section, we will focus on the most widely used ones: Excel files and CSV files.

Importing an Excel file

First, open a new R Markdown file and insert a new code chunk. To import a dataset from an Excel file, we need the package called `readxl`. We type the following command within the chunk that we just created:

```
install.packages("readxl")
library(readxl)
```

The first statement is to install the package while the second one is to launch the package. Once you launch the package, then you are ready to import your data. The data you will import is called *data1*. Make sure that the data file is in the same directory as your R Markdown file.

Insert the following command in your code chunk and run as shown in Figure 1.23.

```
data<-read_excel("data1.xlsx")
```

Here, `read_excel` is a function from the `readxl` package. The argument it takes is the filename, *data1.xlsx*. `data` is the name you are giving to the file within R. You can choose any name you like.

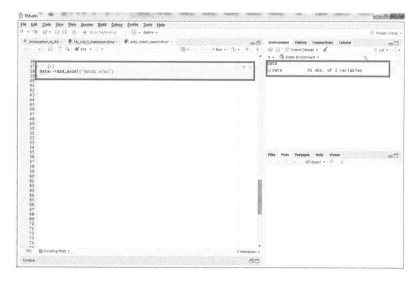

Figure 1.23   Importing data from Excel to R

Note that if you have missing values in the data, they are usually represented as blank cells. If the NAs are represented by something other than blank cells, you need to set the na argument in your chunk code as follows:

```
read_excel("data1.xlsx", na = "NA")
```

Now, let us have a first look at the data we have imported into R. We can do so by running the command as shown in Figure 1.24.

```
str(data)
```

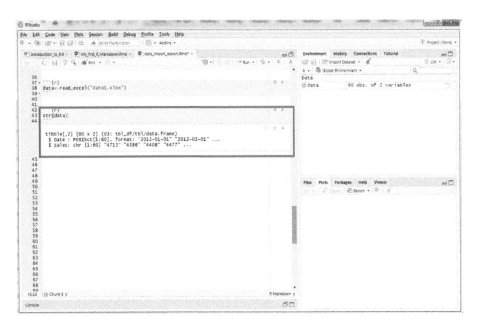

Figure 1.24 Imported data in R

As you can see from Figure 1.25, R tells us the data contains 60 observations of two variables: Date and Sales.

You can also have a look at the entire dataset, by running the command

```
View(data)
```

from your code chunk, or by clicking on the object data in your environment window (Figure 1.25).

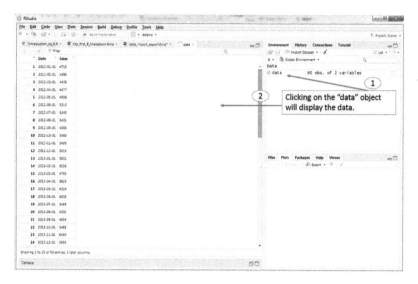

Figure 1.25   Viewing data in R

Importing CSV data

CSV stands for Comma Separated Values. In fact, CSV files are plain text files. They can be opened using programs like Notepad or Excel. To import a data file in CSV format, we need to insert a new code chunk in our R Markdown, then type the following command within the chunk. Figure 1.26 shows how the code looks in R Markdown.

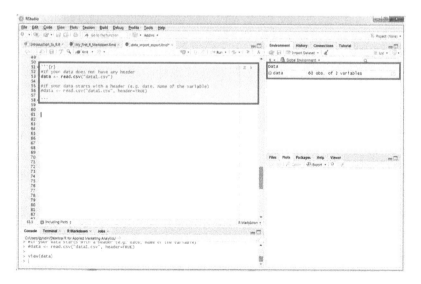

Figure 1.26   Importing a CSV data file to R

```
#If your data does not have any header
data <- read.csv("data1.csv")

#If your data starts with a header (e.g. date, name of the variable, use:
#data <- read.csv("data1.csv", header=TRUE)
```

These are all the important steps in getting R up and running. You are now ready to analyse your first dataset in the next chapter.

CHAPTER SUMMARY

In the first half of this chapter, we provided a big-picture overview of marketing analytics and described its role in influencing consumer behaviour and firms' financial performance. We listed some of the successful applications of marketing analytics, including customer segmentation, targeting consumers based on online recommendation systems, price sensitivity analysis and advertising budget allocation, churn predictions, demand forecasting, sentiment analysis, and the contribution of online touchpoints to purchase outcomes. Also, we highlighted the most common pitfalls that marketing practitioners should avoid when implementing the available toolkits and practices. We emphasized the fact that the success of marketing analytics initiatives lies in blending the 'science' of marketing with the 'art' of marketing well. Detecting the problems, approaching them with the right datasets, which tools and techniques to use, which variables to track and include in the models, how to interpret the results and translate them into insights and actions are all crucial for a successful application of marketing analytics.

In the second half of this chapter, we showed how to install R, the software used throughout the book. In particular, we learned how to set up a working directory, install and load packages, write code in R Markdown, and import data into R. We are now ready to apply various analytical models and learn how to transform marketing data into insights and actions through practical case studies.

REFERENCES

Fischer, M. (2019). Managing advertising campaigns for new product launches: An application at Mercedes-Benz. *Marketing Science*, 38(2), 343–359.

Forbes (2017). Really big data at Walmart: Real-time insights from their 40+ petabyte data cloud. https://www.forbes.com/sites/bernardmarr/2017/01/23/really-big-data-at-walmart-real-time-insights-from-their-40-petabyte-data-cloud/?sh=40dd54086c10

Gordon, J. and Perrey, J. (2015). The dawn of marketing's new golden age. https://www.mckinsey.com/business-functions/marketing-and-sales/our-insights/the-dawn-of-marketings-new-golden-age

Kumar, V., Sharma, A., Donthu, N. and Rountree, C. (2015). Implementing Integrated marketing science modeling at a non-profit organization: Balancing multiple business objectives at Georgia Aquarium. *Marketing Science*, 34(6), 804–814.

MarketingWeek (2018). What are the real customer benefits of AI? https://www.marketingweek.com/customer-benefits-ai/

Pauwels, K. (2015). Truly accountable marketing: The right metrics for the right results. *GfK Marketing Intelligence Review*, 7(1).

Smith, K. (2019) 53 incredible Facebook statistics and facts. *Brandwatch*. https://www.brandwatch.com/blog/facebook-statistics/

Valenti, A., Srinivasan, S., Yildirim, G. and Pauwels, K. (2021). Assessing direct mail and email effects for different customer segments of multichannel multinational retailers: Model and field experiment. *Gary Lilien ISMS-MSI Practice Prize Award Winner*, working paper.

FURTHER READING

Chapman, C. and Feit, E. (2015). *R for Marketing Research and Analytics*. Cham: Springer.

Hemann, C. and Burbary, K. (2018). *Digital Marketing Analytics: Making Sense of Consumer Data in a Digital World*, 2nd edn. Pearson Education.

James, G., Written, D., Hastie, T. and Tibshirani, R. (2017). *An Introduction to Statistical Learning: with Applications in R*. New York: Springer.

LaValle, S., Lesser, E., Shockley, R., Hopkins, M. S. and Kruschwitz, N. (2011). Big data, analytics and the path from insights to value. *MIT Sloan Management Review*, 52(2).

Mela, C. F. and Moorman C. (2018). Why marketing analytics hasn't lived up to its promise. *Harvard Business Review*, 30 May. https://hbr.org/2018/05/why-marketing-analytics-hasnt-lived-up-to-its-promise

2

CUSTOMER SEGMENTATION

Chapter contents

LEARNING OBJECTIVES

At the end of this chapter, you should be able to:

- understand the importance of segmentation, targeting, and positioning analysis in strategic marketing
- identify suitable segmentation variables and approaches
- identify suitable segments for your marketing activities
- apply *k*-means and *k*-nearest neighbour cluster analysis
- determine suitable clustering criteria and cluster sizes.

In marketing, we often have to deal with various groups of consumers with different types of interests and preferences. This can make marketing rather tricky, as we have to cater to different needs and thus need to adapt our value proposition accordingly. For example, we must think about what kind of value we can deliver to a customer, to make this customer buy our product instead of some other company's product. This again requires us then to think about the type of message we want to show to each type of customer. Additionally, this subsequently means that we have to select suitable communication channels for specific customer groups, and have to adapt our product portfolio, as well as our pricing strategy towards the interests and preferences of the different types of consumers we face. All these decisions require us to gain a profound understanding of the market. In fact, before we start developing our marketing strategy, we must understand the market. We commonly achieve this with the help of a customer segmentation, which aims to divide the general market into subgroups of similar customers from which we then select our target groups.

This chapter focuses on identifying and analysing these subgroups of similar customers within the customer base as a key task of strategic marketing. The chapter introduces you to the principles of segmentation, targeting, and positioning (STP) analysis as core functions of modern market-oriented leadership. It highlights the importance of suitable segmentation criteria and variables and teaches you how to apply common segmentation methods such as *k*-means and *k*-nearest neighbour cluster analysis to customer data. From a methodological point of view, you will be introduced to different distance measures, which will allow you to determine similarities and dissimilarities among different groups of consumers and customers.

We present a case study from a banking context to show how to apply modern segmentation methods in order to identify suitable customers for different financial services and products offered by a large bank.

━━━━━━ Case study ━━━━━━

Stratton AE Banking

Stratton AE Banking is a newly founded online bank in the US market. The e-banking service is a joint venture of a young fintech start-up and the long-standing New York Stratton & Fils private banking house. The joint venture was founded in 2020 and its digital private banking services have since enjoyed a measure of popularity. It profits from an AI-driven recommender engine that uses past investment information together with a market and finance machine learning engine to derive investment tips and portfolio suggestions for its customers. So far, the fintech start-up has been able to attract young investors and customers. After the joint venture with Stratton & Fils, the fintech hopes to also attract existing customers from the established bank.

However, the conservative bank management of Stratton & Fils is extremely worried about simply approaching all of its customers, as it fears that the data-driven and digital customer experience of Stratton AE Banking may disturb some of its long-standing customers and may harm its long-established and very intimate customer relations, which are believed to be an essential factor in the bank's history of success.

The management thus approaches you as the head of the data science team and asks you to conduct a segmentation analysis of the bank's existing customer base and to identify suitable customer segments which might be open to trying out the Stratton & Fils joint venture.

As a base for your segmentation analysis, the CRM manager provides you with data for the variables listed in Table 2.1.

Table 2.1   Stratton CRM data

Variable	Description	Measurement
Age	Customer Age	Age in Years
Income	Household Net Income	Net Income in USD
HouseholdSize	Number of People Living in Household	Integer number
CityAreaSize	City or Main Area Population	Integer number
MeanCityIncome	Average Income on ZIP-Code and Street Level	Average Income in USD
MeanCityHousePrice	Average House Prices on ZIP-Code and Street Level from last 5 years	Average Prices in USD
MeanCityHouseholdSize	Average Household Size on ZIP-Code and Street Level from last 10 years	Average Number Inhabitants
MeanCitySqFtPrice	Average Prizes per Square Foot on ZIP-Code and Street Level	Yes/No
NumbCars	Number of registered cars of customer	Number of Cars
InternetTrafficVolume	Volume of Internet Traffic per customer household	GB
MortgageVolume	Mortgage to be paid by Customer	USD
AccountSpending	Monthly average spending from bank account	USD

(Continued)

Table 2.1   (Continued)

Variable	Description	Measurement
CreditCardSpending	Monthly average spending from Credit Card	USD
HelpHotlineTime	Number of Minutes with Banking Hotline	Minutes
CustomerSince	Time since opening bank account	Months
GrocerySpending	Average grocery related spendings from bank account	USD
StockVolume	Stock Investment	USD
CreditVolume	Credits with the bank	USD
NASDAQInvest	Amount of money invested in NASDAQ listed companies	USD
USAXSFundInvest	Amount of money invested in Stratton owned share fund for mid-sized US companies	USD
BranchVisits	Number of recorded branch visits within the last 8 weeks	Integer number
AppLogins	Number of customer logins in mobile banking app within the last 8 weeks	Integer number
ATMVisitis	Number of times customer used an ATM service point within the last 8 weeks	Integer number
TimeOnlineBanking	Time logged into the Online Banking System	Minutes
ServiceFees	Extra Fees paid for banking services	USD
SocialMediaInter	Number of Finance Specific Social Media Profiles a customer follows	Integer number
Bitcoins	Number of Bitcoins hold by customer	Number
NFT	Number of NFTs bought by customer	Integer number

CUSTOMER SEGMENTATION AS A CORE FUNCTION OF MARKETING MANAGEMENT

Although often wrongfully confused with advertising, marketing is much more than communication. Instead, marketing must be understood as a central function and focus within the company that is responsible for identifying and managing customer values. This concept, often referred to as market-oriented leadership, postulates that a company's main goal should be to identify, manage, and maintain resources to create values for customers (Slater and Narver, 1998). Such values can originate from services, branding, or relationships as shown in Figure 2.1.

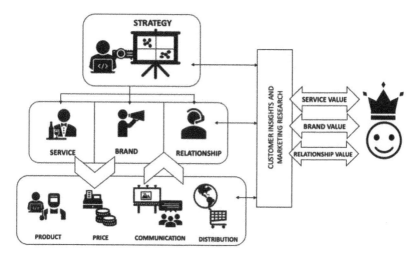

Figure 2.1   Concept of market-oriented leadership

The four classic marketing mix instruments of product, price, communication, and distribution thus play more of a tactical role, in which these tools are applied to create, foster, and maintain values for customers. Market orientation thus requires managers to first identify and understand customer preferences and then to cater to these needs and preferences to create value (Palmatier et al., 2006). This makes customer orientation fundamentally different from other strategy concepts such as product orientation or production orientation, where managers aim either to develop the best technological product (assuming customers always seek the best solution) or to offer the product for the lowest price (assuming that cost and price leadership are sustainable).

Try to identify reasons why product and production orientation may lead to fatal business outcomes (with examples) and explain how market orientation can address these risks.

Companies following a market-oriented leadership approach thus require a thorough understanding of their customers so that they can develop value bundles (Hennig-Thurau et al., 2013). Marketing research hence plays a key role in this approach and provides important information to all three domains. While it is needed at all stages, it plays an essentially important role right at the beginning of the value creation process, as it is responsible for generating initial customer insights on which all other planning and management activities then ground.

Given that customers and consumers do substantially differ in preferences, as well as in other important variables such as buying power, education, location, skills, buying frequency.

and many other factors, managers are well advised to first generate a general understanding of the heterogeneous consumers and customer groups which form markets (Smith, 1956). This becomes especially important as preferences may differ among subgroups of consumers. Before one thus observes a group of consumers to develop a marketing strategy as a foundation of value creation, one must first understand which different archetypes of consumer groups exist. This process is commonly known as consumer or customer segmentation. Segmentation refers to the task of dividing the whole market that consists of heterogeneous consumers into subgroups of similar (i.e. homogeneous) customers. The key aim of segmentation is thus to derive a set of groups that are very different from each other while containing very similar customers within each group (Plummer, 1974). This market segmentation then serves as a focal point of decision-making, as managers then need to inspect each identified segment and understand segment-specific preferences, so as to decide which segment(s) is (are) best suited for the company by judging the company's potential to deliver value to a segment as well as factors such as the segment size, the segment's profit potential, or the presence of potential competitors addressing a specific segment. The process of segment selection is commonly referred to as targeting. Once a company decides to target a specific segment, the process of value creation can be referred to as positioning, with the positioning strategy becoming a company's attempt to develop any sort of service, brand, or relationship value for the consumers in the targeted segment with the help of suitable product, price, communication, or distribution campaigns.

SEGMENTATION APPROACHES AND CRITERIA

Before focusing on the methodology, we might first ask ourselves which variables we should employ when attempting to cluster customers into subgroups. In marketing practice, we often see that companies use traditional and well-established socio-economic variables such as age, income, education, profession, and place of residence. While these variables are easy to track, rarely change, and show substantial variation among different types of customers, a common problem is that they hardly form any interpretable segments. Often we observe cluster analysis relying solely on socio-economic factors to derive no more than three different clusters: rich, middle-class, and poor customers. In addition, even if we develop more granular clusters, socio-economic variables often do not allow marketers to identify specific customer preferences, which in return would enable managers to develop a meaningful positioning strategy. A key reason for this is that socio-economic variables do not provide enough information to form truly homogeneous subgroups, and one risks ending up with clusters that contain people from a similar socio-economic background but who do not share any similar preferences or interests. Figure 2.2 underlines this issue. Assume we build a cluster of older white men who grew up in the UK, have an income of over £1 million a year, have been married twice, and prefer living in castles. You certainly have by now a concrete person in mind: HM King Charles III. But did you realize that the same criteria also fit Ozzy Osbourne, the self-styled Prince of Darkness?

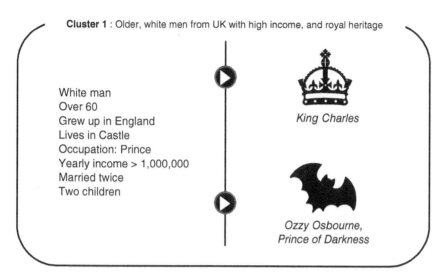

Cluster 1 : Older, white men from UK with high income, and royal heritage

White man
Over 60
Grew up in England
Lives in Castle
Occupation: Prince
Yearly income > 1,000,000
Married twice
Two children

King Charles

*Ozzy Osbourne,
Prince of Darkness*

Figure 2.2 Example of how socio-economic variables may mislead segmentation analysis

If both persons do not tell you anything, we suggest that you conduct a quick Wikipedia research, which will help you to realize that both princes certainly do not share too many preferences or interests with each other and should thus certainly not be in the same segment.

Instead of relying on demographic and socio-economic factors, one may employ so-called action–interest–opinion (AIO) segmentation approaches, also known as lifestyle segmentation. AIO often relies on preference- and interest-related variables to develop segments. While AIO segmentation is known for delivering more valid segments and higher return on marketing-investment rates, segmentation variable operationalization and measurement are trickier and more painful as variables such as interests, hobbies, leisure activities, attitudes, technology knowledge, and technology usage frequency are much harder to observe and measure. Often one may proxy AIO variables with the help of behaviour-based segmentation variables such as loyalty, usage frequency, category interest, product or category knowledge, or other consumer attitudes. While these measures are more suitable for consumer goods, one may similarly rely on measures such as technical knowledge and technology adaption, market power and market share, loyalty, sales team and buying team relations, as well as risk sensitivity in the case of B2B markets.

Screen the various variables in Table 2.1 and try to understand which variables are more and which are less suitable for a segmentation analysis.

DISTANCE AS A MEASURE OF SIMILARITY

To assign consumers into subgroups, we need to find a way to determine how similar or dissimilar consumers are. Similarity is commonly measured with the help of some kind of distance measure. Similar objects will have a smaller distance from each other, while larger distances indicate that objects are more dissimilar. Marketing research has relied on many different distance measures, depending on the type of variables and features used to describe objects or consumers. There are measures for calculating distances between objects based on continuous measurements of features of objects (e.g. measuring distance between bank customers based on their spending, credit volume, income, or mortgage volume), as well as distance measures that are based on categorical measurements of features (e.g. distance between customers based on whether they own a credit card, live in an urban area, their gender, or marital status). For a detailed discussion of different distance measures and their applicability to different types of variables, we recommend Backhaus et al. (2021, Chapter 8).

The most commonly used distance measure (at least in the case of continuous variables) is the Euclidean distance, given by

$$d(A,B) = \sqrt{\left(f_{1,A} - f_{1,B}\right)^2 + \left(f_{2,A} - f_{2,B}\right)^2 + \ldots + \left(f_{n,A} - f_{n,B}\right)^2}. \tag{2.1}$$

$d(A,B)$ measures the distance between customer A and customer B, while $f_{n,A}$ and $f_{n,B}$ represent the values of the n features for customers A and B. To illustrate the calculation of distance measures, let us have a look at four variables from our Stratton dataset for five different customers as depicted in Table 2.2.

Table 2.2 Extract of customer features

Customer	Age	Income (€)	Debt (€)	Household size
Hawkeye	32	45,000	25,000	1
Potter	64	75,000	10,000	3
Burns	49	42,000	20,000	5
Hotlips	33	22,000	2,000	1
Klinger	29	16,000	6,000	4

Let us now compare Hawkeye with Potter, Hotlips, Burns, and Klinger. To do so we simply put the corresponding values into formula (2.1), dividing the income by 1000 to facilitate comprehension:

$$d(Hawkeye, Potter) = \sqrt{(32-64)^2 + (45-75)^2 + (25-10)^2 + (1-3)^2} = 46.40,$$

$$d(Hawkeye, Hotlips) = \sqrt{(32-33)^2 + (45-22)^2 + (25-2)^2 + (1-1)^2} = 32.54,$$

$$d\left(Hawkeye, Burns\right) = \sqrt{\left(32-49\right)^2 + \left(45-42\right)^2 + \left(25-20\right)^2 + \left(1-5\right)^2} = 18.41,$$

$$d\left(Hawkeye, Klinger\right) = \sqrt{\left(32-29\right)^2 + \left(45-16\right)^2 + \left(25-6\right)^2 + \left(1-4\right)^2} = 34.93.$$

According to our chosen variables, Hawkeye is closest to Burns, and most distant from Potter. We can achieve the same with the help of R with the following code.

```
library(philentropy)
## Table Content

Hawkeye = c(32, 45, 25, 1)
Potter = c(64, 75, 10, 3)
Burns = c(49,42, 20, 5)
Hotlips = c(33, 22,2,1)
Klinger = c(29,16,6,4)

## Bind to Matrix
Table2_1 <- rbind(Hawkeye,Potter)
Table2_1 <- rbind(Table2_1, Burns)
Table2_1 <- rbind(Table2_1, Hotlips)
Table2_1 <- rbind(Table2_1, Klinger)

# Calculate Distance Matrix
distance(Table2_1, method = "euclidean")
```

We first create for each person a vector, and then combine the vectors into the matrix called Table2_1. We then use the distance function of the philentropy package to calculate all distances for all the consumers in our matrix. Figure 2.3 shows the output. Note that the function allows us to specify which distance measure we would like to use. If we do not have numerical information, we might wish to adapt the distance measure accordingly. You can use the help function of the package to get a list of all applicable distance measures.

```
Metric: 'euclidean'; comparing: 5 vectors.
          v1        v2        v3        v4        v5
v1  0.00000  46.40043  18.41195  32.542280  34.928498
v2 46.40043   0.00000  37.65634  61.951594  68.724086
v3 18.41195  37.65634   0.00000  31.559468  35.679126
v4 32.54228  61.95159  31.55947   0.000000   8.774964
v5 34.92850  68.72409  35.67913   8.774964   0.000000
>
```

Figure 2.3 Euclidean distance matrix

Looking at the output, how many groups of similar customers do you spot? How would you group them?

K-MEANS CLUSTER ANALYSIS

While the distances help us with understanding similarities and dissimilarities, they do not in themselves help us with forming subgroups, as we do not know what threshold determines similarity and dissimilarity. Hawkeye may be closest to Burns, but is 18 a great or small distance? Who should be paired with whom?

This implies that assigning consumers to homogeneous subgroups requires a lot of attention and balance, and more information than just similarity measures. In addition, it seems, even with our five customers, that grouping takes some time and effort and will certainly prevent us from forming larger groups or segmenting larger datasets with hundreds of thousands of customers.

Therefore, we need to find a method that uses intersubject distances to automatically form groups. Such methods are commonly referred to as cluster analysis. Cluster analysis is a well-known and well-established statistical method that has been used for the last 30–40 years in marketing research. With the advent of machine learning and AI applications, cluster analysis has enjoyed a resurgence in data science, where it is often referred to as unsupervised learning.

k-means cluster analysis uses distances to form clusters within data. Once the user has determined the number, k, of clusters the algorithm should define, the cluster randomly assigns k starting points within the data (step 1). It then calculates the distance from each observation in the data to each starting point. As illustrated in Figure 2.4, the algorithm then assigns each observation according to the distance to the closest starting point (step 2). This leads to an initial cluster solution. For each of these clusters the algorithm then calculates the new centre point of the cluster, called the centroid (step 3). The centroid can be interpreted as the mean of all observations within this cluster. Step 4 now repeats the procedure of step 2. The new centroids are used to again calculate all distances between all observations and all centroids. Then the observations are again assigned to the closest centroid. This may lead to changes in cluster membership and to new forms of clusters. In the next step (step 5), the algorithm calculates the resulting new centroids, recalculates the distances, and reassigns observations to clusters. The algorithm stops once no observation can be reassigned to another cluster or after a specified number of iterations.

k-means clustering can be considered as the workhorse of cluster analysis, as it is widely and frequently applied for segmentation and clustering purposes. A key reason for this is the simplicity of the algorithm, which is fast and cheap to carry out by computer. Despite its popularity, however, we have to also consider some of its caveats. First of all, the results of the algorithm often depend on the randomly assigned starting centroids. You may quickly realize that if we move the initial centroids in step 1 in Figure 2.4 to different places, the resulting cluster solutions may look different. This is something we have to be careful about when

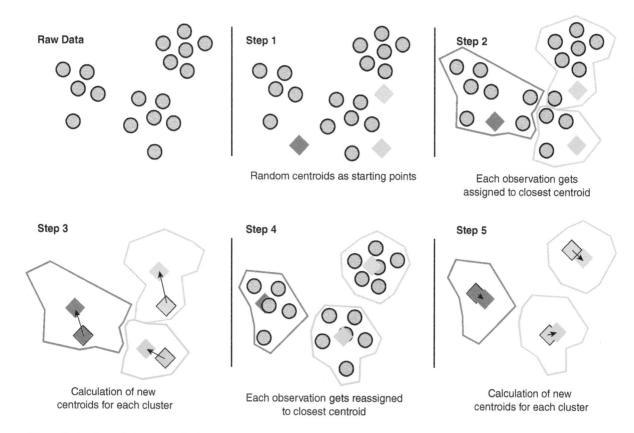

Figure 2.4 Steps in *k*-means cluster analysis

interpreting *k*-means output. Often it makes sense to rerun the algorithm several times, to see if it leads to robust results and if the clusters identified always converge to a similar solution. If this is not the case, it might not be a good idea to rely on the initial solution but to try out different settings to come to a robust solution.

Furthermore, another obstacle that can affect the final outcome is the number of clusters, which needs to be determined a priori. But how do we know how many clusters there are in our customer database before running the analysis?

Number of clusters

As pointed out above, the shape and appearance of clusters largely depends on the initial number of clusters we ask the *k*-means algorithm to find. It is thus recommended either to think conceptually about the number of clusters we expect to be present in the data or we can strategically handle, or to employ statistical measures to determine the 'optimal' number of clusters. For the latter, two different major approaches have been developed.

Before determining the best number of clusters, let us once more reflect on the main goal of cluster analysis: we want to obtain subgroups that are each homogeneous. That is, we try to maximize within-group homogeneity, which means we try to reduce the level of variance between members of a cluster. The overall level of within-cluster variance across all identified clusters can thus be used to describe the total degree of homogeneity obtained with a specific cluster solution. This gives us a chance to compare different cluster analyses with different numbers of clusters, as we can try to minimize the overall variance. The formal representation of this approach is expressed as

$$\min\left(\sum_{i=1}^{k} W(C_i)\right),$$ (2.2)

where C_i represents cluster i ($i = 1, ..., k$), and $W(C_i)$ the variance within cluster i. We can now estimate different cluster models with differing numbers of clusters. Using the within-cluster variance values, we can determine which solution works best and then focus on this cluster analysis. To do so, we first estimate n cluster solutions with cluster numbers from 1 to k. Then we can plot the within-cluster variance sums for each cluster solution.

Let us now apply this to our dataset. We first need to start some additional packages, which will help us to determine the right number of clusters.

One thing we ought to bear in mind before running a cluster analysis is scale heterogeneity. This is because k-means clustering is sensitive to data that include variables at different scale levels. Having variables at very different levels creates problems, which may ultimately lead to biased results. A quick fix is to adjust the variables so that they all share a similar range. This procedure is commonly referred to as standardization. There are different procedures to achieve this such as mean standardization or z-standardization. These procedures transform the series by, for example, subtracting the mean, μ, of a series from each value in the series and dividing the result by the standard deviation, σ:

$$(F2-3)z = \frac{x-\mu}{\sigma}$$

R can standardize all variables for us with the help of the scale() function as depicted below. When we now inspect the resulting new data frame scaled.crm with the head() function (as shown in Figure 2.5, with the first six observations for each variable), we will see that all variables now have a similar range. We can thus proceed with our analysis

```
scaled.crm = scale(BankinCRMData)
head(scaled.crm)
```

We can now start with the cluster analysis. Before we focus on identifying the optimal k with the help of the elbow measure, let us first try out different solutions with different numbers of clusters ourselves. To ensure that we start with the same centroids, we use the set.seed() function. This ensures that every time we run this code, we end up with the same results.

```
          Age      Income HouseholdSize CityAreaSize MeanCityIncome MeanCityHousePrize
[1,]  0.3576515 -0.1028962    -0.6110203    0.3617815     -1.1309409           1.271530
[2,]  0.1361200 -0.2651878     1.6529279    0.3520407     -0.1078328           1.270998
[3,]  2.6468104 -0.1251715    -1.3656697    0.3701496     -1.7221925           1.271494
[4,]  1.3176214 -0.2991988     0.1436291    0.3701496     -0.7011903           1.270582
[5,]  0.3576515 -0.2119217    -1.3656697    0.3500189     -1.9739204           1.270505
[6,] -0.2330992 -0.1816402     3.1622266    0.3681716     -1.1212168           1.271217
     MeanCityHouseHoldSize MeanCitySqFtPrice NumberCars InternetTrafficVolume MortageVolume
[1,]           -0.01716176       -0.62863020  0.6657393            -0.2889997     1.6471061
[2,]            1.47667561       -0.02266382  0.6657393            -0.9537126     1.2700695
[3,]           -0.01716176       -0.79901909 -0.4146800            -0.3192140     0.5749801
[4,]            0.72975692       -1.32689056 -1.4950993             0.1037852     1.3859733
[5,]            2.22359429       -1.31895578 -0.4146800            -0.8630700     1.0690862
[6,]           -0.01716176       -0.26404808 -0.4146800            -0.4702851     0.9330313
     AccountSpending CreditCardSpending HelpHotlineTime CustomerSince GrocerySpending StockVolume
[1,]      -0.3450280          0.8636732      -0.8632445     0.7723802     -0.34104672  -0.6842514
[2,]      -0.1509407         -0.6818782      -0.8427150     0.7723802      0.19341832  -0.5016177
[3,]      -0.3528008          0.5714726      -0.9302276     0.7723802      0.12646708  -0.6849314
[4,]      -0.2801354          0.2591261      -0.6214784     0.7723802      0.08311691  -0.5265523
[5,]      -0.1072321          0.2034089      -0.6937764     0.8184972     -0.75375557  -0.7384732
[6,]      -0.3513856         -0.1526760      -0.5917007     0.7723802      0.09847517  -0.3919688
     CreditVolume NASDAQInvest USAXSFundInvest BranchVisits AppLogins ATMVisits TimeOnlineBanking
[1,]   -0.4354132   -0.2353360      -0.3417909  -0.28345927 -1.319352  1.751956        -0.7152344
[2,]   -0.4407973   -0.2240967      -0.3244452   0.02716123 -1.059550  1.321701        -0.7897758
[3,]   -0.4507881   -0.2269506      -0.3549125  -0.28345927 -1.203885  1.321701        -0.9289516
[4,]   -0.4594416   -0.2294082      -0.3270950   0.02716123 -1.203885  1.321701        -0.8941460
[5,]   -0.4396339   -0.2268875      -0.3721992  -0.28345927 -1.146151  1.751956        -0.7894912
[6,]   -0.4472727   -0.2259212      -0.2313141   0.02716123 -1.232751  1.321701        -0.9766564
     ServiceFees SocialMediaInter  Bitcoins       NFTs
[1,]  0.02878044        0.4675133 -0.8542812 -0.4895549
[2,]  0.36121889        0.3502121 -0.8520388 -0.8611631
[3,]  0.44046295        0.5261639 -0.8076386 -0.8611631
[4,]  0.02794600        0.8780673 -0.8614570 -0.8611631
[5,]  0.52092062        0.8780673 -0.8349963 -1.2327713
[6,]  0.51830595        0.2915616 -0.8551782 -0.1179467
```

Figure 2.5 The first six observations for each variable of our standardized data frame

If you do not use set.seed() ahead of the cluster analysis, you will obtain different solutions, which will be close to each other but not identical. We can run a *k*-means cluster analysis with R's kmeans() function. We specify the dataset we want to cluster, and add the number of clusters we expect to find.

```
set.seed(123)
StrattonCluster_4k <- kmeans(scaled.crm, 4)
StrattonCluster_4k[["size"]]
sizes4k <- data.frame(Size = StrattonCluster_4k[["size"]],
                      Cluster = c("Cluster1", "Cluster2", "Cluster3", "Cluster4"))

ggplot(sizes4k, aes(x=factor(Cluster), y=Size)) +
  geom_col(fill=hcl(195, 100, 65)) +
  xlab("Cluster") + ylab("Size") + geom_text(aes(label=Size), vjust=0) +
  ggtitle("Cluster sizes k-means 4-cluster solution")
```

Once the algorithm has converged, we can extract the size information from the cluster solution. We combine this information in a new data frame with a column that names the four different clusters. We can then use ggplot to prepare a barplot chart that shows us the cluster sizes (Figure 2.6). Clusters 1 and 2 are smaller with 1000 and 1250 customers, while clusters 3 and 4 are substantially larger with 2996 and 5504 customers.

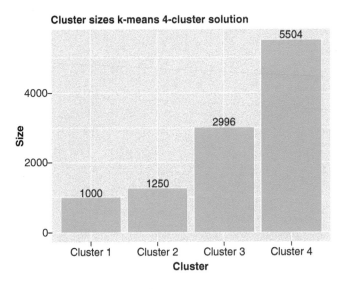

Figure 2.6 Cluster size plot for a *k* = 4 solution

We can now inspect the different clusters and check their mean values. We achieve this with the following code, which first matches the estimated cluster to each observation in our data frame. Subsequently, we use the group_by() command in dplyr to calculate the mean of each variable for each cluster. You can then inspect the resulting data frame. You will see that some of the clusters show substantially different mean values for specific variables, while in other cases the means do not vary across the clusters.

```
#Build Cluster Specific Means for all Variables
BankinCRMData$k4Cluster = StrattonCluster_4k[["cluster"]]

summarystats.percluster_4k = BankinCRMData %>% group_by(k4Cluster) %>%
  summarise_if(is.numeric, mean, na.rm = TRUE)

head(summarystats.percluster_4k)
```

Another approach to assessing the quality of our segmentation is to plot the different clusters. A key challenge here is dimensionality. Given that our clusters depend on a multitude of variables, we cannot plot them all together. To come to a solution that we can plot, we need to reduce the dimensions to two main factors, which then allows us to plot the points in two-dimensional space. A common technique to achieve this is principal component analysis (PCA), which reduces all variables to two main factors which we can then plot. The plot will then allow us to better see if clusters overlap or if we end up with a meaningful separation between the different identified clusters. R's `factoextra` package offers various functions which achieve this with a single command that does not require us to code the PCA or the plot. Instead, we simply use the following command, which produces the plot shown in Figure 2.7:

```
#Plot Clusters for 4k solution
library(factoextra)

fviz_cluster(StrattonCluster_4k, scaled.crm, ellipse.type = "norm")
```

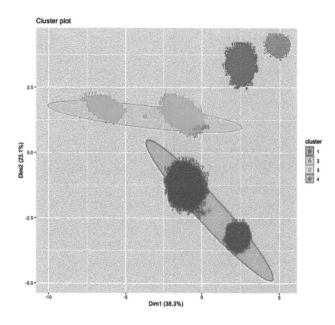

Figure 2.7 PCA reduced cluster plot of k-means cluster analysis for k = 4

A quick inspection of the plot already reveals that our k-means cluster approach is not optimal for k = 4, as two of the clusters (the larger ones, 3 and 4) appear to be separable into smaller subgroups.

 Repeat the k-mean analysis for a 3- and a 5-cluster solution. What do the cluster centres tell you, and which solution do you perceive to be best? Do the plots confirm your assumptions?

Trying out different solutions may be informative, but it may become evident that determining the right number of clusters can be tricky. Therefore, let us see what an elbow plot and a silhouette plot tell us. We can plot these with the nbclust function of the factoextra package. We specify the data frame and the type of cluster analysis we want to conduct, as well as the measure of interest and the maximum number of clusters we want to examine (here 15).

```
#Obtain Elbow and Silhouette and Plots to determine optimal k

factoextra::fviz_nbclust(na.omit(scaled.crm), kmeans, method =
"wss", k.max = 15)
factoextra::fviz_nbclust(na.omit(scaled.crm), kmeans, method =
"silhouette", k.max = 15)
```

Figure 2.8 shows the corresponding outputs.

The elbow plot (left) shows the total within sum of cluster variances for all estimated 15 solutions as specified in formula (2.1). The rule of thumb states that the optimal cluster number lies at the 'elbow' of the plot. So we have a problem, as the plot has no clear 'elbow'. Therefore, we employ a second method, the silhouette plot. The silhouette coefficient measures of how close an object is to its own cluster centroid, compared to those of other clusters. The coefficient ranges from –1 to +1. High values indicate strong separation, while low values indicate poor separation. We thus want to select the cluster solution with the highest silhouette coefficient. In our case, the plot suggests 8 clusters. Looking again at the elbow plot on the left, 8 may be a little high, especially as there could perhaps be said to be an 'elbow' around 6. The silhouette plot suggests that the 7-cluster solution is inferior to the 6- and 8-cluster solutions. We may thus enrich our insights by plotting all three solutions with the following command. The resulting plots are shown in Figure 2.9.

```
#Plot Cluster Solutions
#k6
StrattonCluster_6k <- kmeans(scaled.crm, 6)
fviz_cluster(StrattonCluster_6k, scaled.crm, ellipse.type = "norm")
#k7
StrattonCluster_7k <- kmeans(scaled.crm, 7)
fviz_cluster(StrattonCluster_7k, scaled.crm, ellipse.type = "norm")
#k8
StrattonCluster_8k <- kmeans(scaled.crm, 8)
fviz_cluster(StrattonCluster_8k, scaled.crm, ellipse.type = "norm")
```

Looking at the cluster plots, it appears that the 8-cluster solution does indeed provide the most meaningful separation, as the 6- and 7-cluster solutions either have totally overlapping clusters included ($k = 7$) or do not properly separate clusters ($k = 6$).

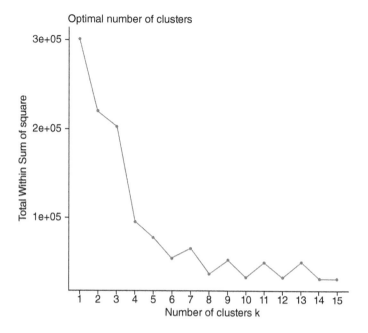

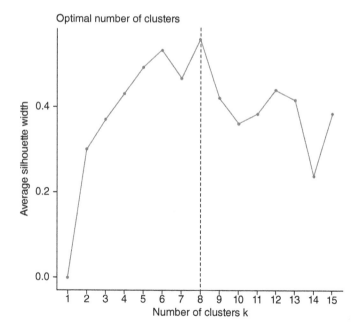

Figure 2.8   Elbow and silhouette plots

k = 6 solution

k = 7 solution

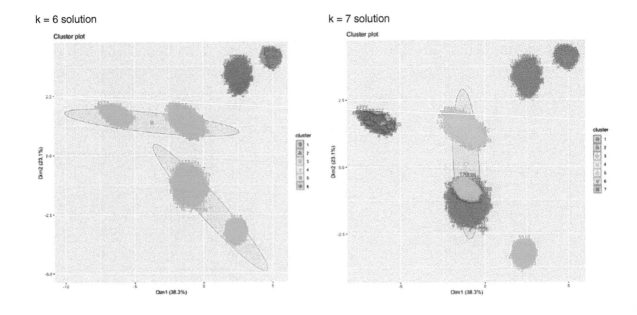

k = 8 solution

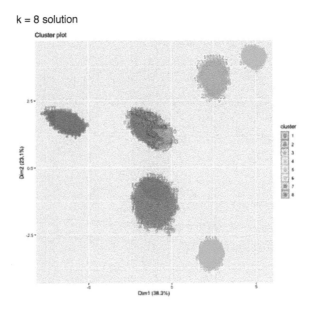

Figure 2.9   Plots for 6-,7-, and 8-cluster solutions

We shall thus continue with an 8-cluster solution for Stratton AE Banking. Nevertheless, keep in mind that despite indications coming from the total within sum of cluster variances, the silhouette coefficient, and cluster plots, selecting the final number of clusters should also take business factors into consideration such as the size of clusters, the interpretability of cluster centroids (centres), as well as the business potential of the identified clusters. This will become clearer if we now continue by looking in more detail at the 8-cluster solution.

Interpretation of output

Let us first start by looking in more detail at our 8-cluster *k*-means model. To obtain the cluster sizes we run the following code, which gives us the plot shown in Figure 2.10.

```
# 8 cluster k-means cluster size plot

sizes8k <- data.frame(Size = StrattonCluster_8k[["size"]],
                 Cluster = c("Cluster1", "Cluster2", "Cluster3", "Cluster4",
                             "Cluster5", "Cluster6", "Cluster7", "Cluster8"))

ggplot(sizes8k, aes(x=factor(Cluster), y=Size)) +
  geom_col(fill=hcl(195, 100, 65)) +
  xlab("Cluster") + ylab("Size") + geom_text(aes(label=Size), vjust=0) +
  ggtitle("Cluster sizes k-means 8-cluster solution")
```

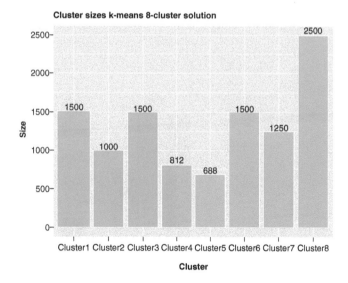

Figure 2.10   Cluster sizes for *k* = 8

To gain deeper insights into spending behaviour as well as the digital affinity of the different segments, we want to plot the means of the different variables. To achieve this we first again assemble a descriptive dataset with all variable means for each cluster with the help of the `group_by()` function in `dplyr`:

```
# Build Mean per Cluster DataFrame
BankinCRMData$k8Cluster = StrattonCluster_8k[["cluster"]]

summarystats.percluster_8k = BankinCRMData %>% group_by(k8Cluster) %>%
  summarise_if(is.numeric, mean, na.rm = TRUE)
```

We can now generate barplots of the different variables of interest and see if we find promising segments of Stratton & Fils customers who might be open to and suitable for Stratton AE Banking. Let us first focus on spending behaviour, as indicated by the service fee variable. Note that we have adapted some of the commands in `ggplot`. By leaving `geom_col()` blank we do not specify a colour and the plot remains in grey. In addition, we ask `ggplot` in `geom_text()` to add labels with the two-digit rounded values of `ServiceFees` in white and in font size 2. Using the `position_stack()` command, we put the values in the middle of the barplot. Figure 2.11 shows the resulting barplot.

```
#Barplot of Service Fees

ggplot(summarystats.percluster_8k, aes(x = factor(k8Cluster), y = ServiceFees)) +
  geom_col() +
  xlab("Clusters") + ylab("Spending") +
  geom_text(aes(label = round(ServiceFees, digits = 2)),
            size = 2, colour = "white",
            position = position_stack(vjust = 0.5)) +
  ggtitle("Average Spending in Service Fees per Cluster")
```

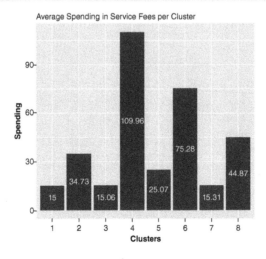

Figure 2.11 Barplot of service fee spending for each cluster

A visual inspection indicates that clusters 4 and 6 show the highest spending behaviour, with clusters 8 and 2 following, while the remaining clusters show rather low service fee spending. This makes at least the four high-spending segments attractive for Stratton AE Banking. However, to be sure that the rather novel and highly digital app service appeals to these segments, we need to understand how digitally active and interested these segments are. Following the AIO segmentation approach, we may rely on behavioural information from our data to identify the digitally active segments. Let us first focus on the latest developments in fintech such as Bitcoin and non-fungible token (NFT) investments. We can again compare the segment-specific means for both variables. This time we want to combine the Bitcoin and NFT plots in one plot. We can arrange this with the `facet_wrap()` function of `ggplot()`, which allows us to combine plots of different variables. The only 'complication' we need to address is that we need to rearrange the dataset we want to plot. We can again use `dplyr` for this. We first select the variables of interest (cluster, NFTs, and Bitcoins) and then transpose the data frame from a wide to a narrow format. We can then use `ggplot()` again. This time we use the `geom_bar` command instead of `geom_col`. The `facet_wrap` command will now tell `ggplot()` to make two plots and combine them under each other (`col = 1`). By setting scales to `"free_y"` we allow different y-axis levels, given that scales substantially vary across the two different variables. The resulting plot is shown in Figure 2.12.

```
#Barplots of Fintech investments

FinTech <- summarystats.percluster_8k %>% select(k8Cluster, NFTs, Bitcoins) %>%
  gather(key = "variable", value = "value", -k8Cluster)

ggplot(FinTech, aes(factor(k8Cluster), value))+
  geom_bar(stat='identity') + xlab("Clusters") +
  facet_wrap(~variable, ncol=1, scales = "free_y") +
  geom_text(aes(label = round(value, digits = 1)), size = 2, colour = "white",
          position = position_stack(vjust = 0.5)) +
  ggtitle("FinTech Cluster Means")
```

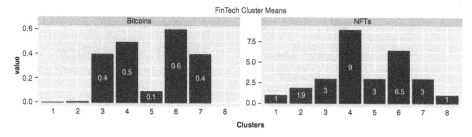

Figure 2.12 Fintech investments

We can see that clusters 4 and 6 show most activity in NFT acquisitions and are also most invested in Bitcoins, which makes them even more suitable for Stratton AE Banking. Let us now look at digital activities and compare digital and offline activities.

With the following code we can inspect the means for `BranchVisits`, `AppLogins`, `ATMVisits`, `TimeOnlineBanking`, `SocialMediaInter`, and `InternetTrafficVolume`. The resulting output is displayed in Figure 2.13. As you can see from `facet_wrap`, we now include two columns.

```
#Plots for Digital vs. Offline Life

DigLife = summarystats.percluster_8k %>%
  select(k8Cluster, BranchVisits, AppLogins,
    ATMVisits, TimeOnlineBanking, SocialMediaInter,
    InternetTrafficVolume) %>%
gather(key = "variable", value = "value", -k8Cluster)

ggplot(DigLife, aes(factor(k8Cluster), value))+
  geom_bar(stat='identity') + xlab("Clusters") +
  facet_wrap(~variable, ncol=2, scales = "free_y") +
  geom_text(aes(label = round(value, digits = 1)), size = 2, colour = "white",
            position = position_stack(vjust = 0.5)) +
  ggtitle("Digital Life vs. Offline Life Cluster Means")
```

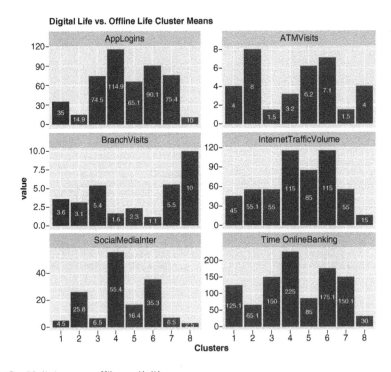

Figure 2.13 Digital versus offline activities

The plot further confirms the strong digital affinity of clusters 4 and 6. Both show the lowest number of branch and ATM visits, while showing strong activity in online baking, internet traffic, social media interest, and banking app logins.

While we can now be sure that customers from segments 4 and 6 have strong digital affinity and are thus likely to be interested in Stratton AE Banking, we should in the next step check the financial situation of these customers. Let us first focus on average age, income, and household sizes with the following code, giving us the plot shown in Figure 2.14.

```
#Plots for Socio Economic Factors

SocioEcon <- summarystats.percluster_8k %>%
  select(k8Cluster, Age, Income, HouseholdSize) %>%
  gather(key = "variable", value = "value", -k8Cluster)

ggplot(SocioEcon, aes(factor(k8Cluster), value))+
  geom_bar(stat='identity') + xlab("Clusters") +
  facet_wrap(~variable, ncol=1, scales = "free_y") +
  geom_text(aes(label = round(value, digits = 1)), size = 2, colour = "white",
        position = position_stack(vjust = 0.5)) +
  ggtitle("Socio-Economic Cluster Means")
```

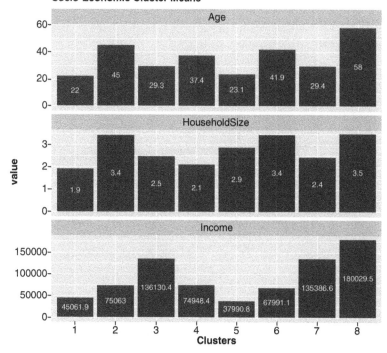

Figure 2.14   Socio-economic variables

The plots again reveal the problems with socio-economic clustering, as the results for age and household size do not vary too much across the eight clusters. We see some variation for income, where clusters 4 and 6 remain close to the total mean of the dataset, indicating that the users with digital affinity we identified are neither poor nor rich, making them still a suitable target group. Age-wise, we similarly see that both segments are mature adults in their late thirties or early forties. Given that the socio-economic information indicates that the users with digital affinity have stable incomes, we should in the next steps focus on spending and investment behaviour to understand whether these segments allow sufficient business volume and growth potential. We can thus compare the related variables with the following code, producing Figures 2.15 and 2.16.

```
#Plots for Spending and Investments

Invest <- summarystats.percluster_8k %>%
   select(k8Cluster, MortageVolume, StockVolume, NASDAQInvest, USAXSFundInvest) %>%
   gather(key = "variable", value = "value", -k8Cluster)

ggplot(Invest, aes(factor(k8Cluster), value))+
   geom_bar(stat='identity') + xlab("Clusters") +
   facet_wrap(~variable, ncol=2, scales = "free_y") +
   geom_text(aes(label = round(value, digits = 1)), size = 2, colour = "white",
             position = position_stack(vjust = 0.5)) +
   ggtitle("Investment Cluster Means")

Spending <- summarystats.percluster_8k %>%
   select(k8Cluster, AccountSpending, CreditCardSpending, GrocerySpending) %>%
   gather(key = "variable", value = "value", -k8Cluster)

ggplot(Spending, aes(factor(k8Cluster), value))+
   geom_bar(stat='identity') + xlab("Clusters") +
   facet_wrap(~variable, ncol=1, scales = "free_y") +
   geom_text(aes(label = round(value, digits = 1)), size = 2, colour = "white",
             position = position_stack(vjust = 0.5)) +
   ggtitle("Spending Cluster Means")
```

From the inspection of the two plots, it becomes evident that clusters 4 and 6 are more invested in stocks than their counterparts, and compared to the other clusters also have lower levels of mortgages. Looking at the types of investments, we see that cluster 4 is more invested in NASDAQ listed companies than all other clusters, while cluster 6 is strongly invested in Stratton's fund for small and medium-size US companies. Spending behaviour information tells us that both clusters are characterized by lower spending, with cluster 4 showing the

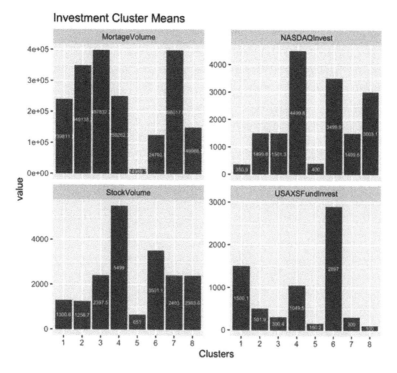

Figure 2.15 Investment behaviour

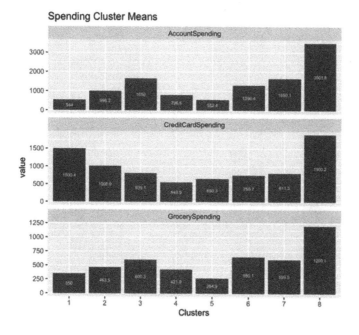

Figure 2.16 Spending behaviour

lowest credit card turnover of all clusters. In case of grocery expenditures, we see that cluster 6 has the second-highest average spending behaviour.

Finally, we can enrich our insights by looking at the living conditions of the different segments and see where the different segments are located. To achieve this, we compare residential information as shown in Figure 2.17, which results from the following code.

```
#Plots Residential Information

Life <- summarystats.percluster_8k %>%
    select(k8Cluster, CityAreaSize, MeanCitySqFtPrice, MeanCityHouseHoldSize, MeanCityIncome) %>%
    gather(key = "variable", value = "value", -k8Cluster)

ggplot(Life, aes(factor(k8Cluster), value))+
    geom_bar(stat='identity') + xlab("Clusters") +
    facet_wrap(~variable, ncol=2, scales = "free_y") +
    geom_text(aes(label = round(value, digits = 1)), size = 2, colour = "white",
              position = position_stack(vjust = 0.5)) +
    ggtitle("Life Conditions Cluster Means")
```

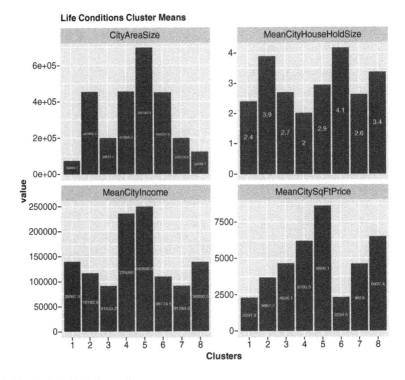

Figure 2.17 Residential information

From Figure 2.17 we learn that clusters 4 and 6 both prefer city areas with medium to lower levels of population. For cluster 4 the average household sizes in the residential areas are rather small, while for cluster 6 we observe larger compounds with on average four members living in one household. Looking at income distributions and the area's floor prices per square foot, we learn that people in cluster 4 live in rather richer neighbourhoods with higher floor prices, whereas cluster 6 members prefer middle-class neighbourhoods with affordable, low floor prices.

Combining the information at hand, how would you describe members of clusters 4 and 6, and how do you believe they differ from each other? Can you similarly come up with characterizations of other clusters?

Taking actions from insights

The results of the cluster analysis allow Stratton AE Banking to take several important marketing actions. First, a deep understanding of the different available market segments allows the joint venture to understand the different types of customers and to determine which segments in the existing customer base should constitute the base for future marketing activities. Spending behaviour as well as tech-savviness and a strong digital affinity make clusters 4 and 6 the most suitable starting points. Stratton AE Banking is thus well advised to use these clusters as target segments. To develop suitable positionings for each cluster and subsequently develop communication campaigns, one can use the further insights from the cluster analysis and the comparison of the cluster-specific means of the remaining variables. While both clusters show great interest in investments, they differ in investment focus. Cluster 4, which also exhibits the highest investment rates, is largely invested in NASDAQ listed shares, while the majority of cluster 6 customers prefer to invest in a Stratton & Fils stock fund with a focus on small and medium-size US companies. One may take this information as a first indication that cluster 6 members are more risk-averse than cluster 4 members. This information may be especially useful when deciding on communication content and creatives for the two clusters. In the case of cluster 4, communication might more accentuate the digital leadership of Stratton AE Banking's app. In contrast, communication targeting cluster 6 might place more emphasis on the safety and error resistance of AI and data-analytics-based banking. When it comes to the question where to target customers, the residential information helps planning with digital as well as offline marketing, indicating that bank branches in richer neighbourhoods should stock more information material for cluster 4 members, while branches in less upscale neighbourhoods should offer more information material for cluster 6 members.

Furthermore, the results of the cluster analysis can be used to also predict the interests and preferences of new customers. Here, one may use the existing information available and calculate the Euclidean distances (with the help of formula (2.1)) between the new customer and the centres (i.e. the means of each dimension) of each cluster. The customer is likely to belong to the cluster with the lowest distance.

CHAPTER SUMMARY

In this chapter, we discuss the essential role of customer segmentation, targeting, and positioning in marketing management. All three steps are the foundation of a sustainable marketing strategy as they allow managers to develop profound insights into the different types of customers and their preferences. Based on this information, managers must then decide which subgroup of consumers they want to address with their marketing activities to then subsequently align all marketing efforts with the respective segment's preferences. The empirical discovery of segments should be based on behavioural data obtained from consumer exploration. Often existing CRM data enriched with descriptive and additional consumer information can be the starting point of such a discovery expedition. Unsupervised machine learning, such as *k*-means cluster analysis, can then help marketers to identify segments of similar customers and assign consumers to clusters.

REFERENCES

Backhaus, K., Erichson, B., Gensler, S., Weiber, R. and Weiber T. (2021) *Multivariate Analysis: An Application-Oriented Introduction*. Wiesbaden: Springer Gabler.

Hennig-Thurau, T., Hofacker, C. F. and Bloching, B. (2013). Marketing the pinball way: Understanding how social media change the generation of value for consumers and companies. *Journal of Interactive Marketing*, 27(4), 237–41.

Palmatier, R. W., Dant, R. P., Grewal, D. and Evans, K. R. (2006). Factors influencing the effectiveness of relationship marketing: A meta-analysis. *Journal of Marketing*, 70(4), 136–53.

Plummer, J. T. (1974). The concept and application of life style segmentation: The combination of two useful concepts provides a unique and important view of the market. *Journal of Marketing*, 38(1), 33–7.

Slater, S. F. and Narver, J. C. (1998). Customer-led and market-oriented: Let's not confuse the two. *Strategic Management Journal*, 19(10), 1001–6.

Smith, W. R. (1956). Product differentiation and market segmentation as alternative marketing strategies. *Journal of Marketing*, 21(1), 3–8.

3

MARKETING MIX MODELLING

Chapter contents

LEARNING OBJECTIVES

At the end of this chapter, you should be able to:

- develop a sound understanding of how marketing mix modelling works
- build a marketing mix model using multiple regression
- apply marketing mix modelling to a real-world dataset to measure return on marketing investments and inform optimal marketing budget allocation decisions
- explain the drawbacks of marketing mix modelling and how they can be addressed by other potential modelling approaches.

This chapter focuses on marketing mix modelling (MMM). MMM is a tool widely used to assess the impact of marketing mix decisions (e.g. advertising, promotions, distribution, price, and salesforce) on performance metrics (e.g. web traffic, sales, revenues, and profits). It allows marketing managers to guide their resource allocation strategies by measuring the contribution of their marketing efforts to business performance outcomes.

The chapter begins with the description of a case study on marketing mix management problem faced by *FourTex*, an apparel brand. It introduces the methodological approach to address the managerial questions outlined in the case study. Then it provides an R application of MMM to FourTex. The software application demonstrates how to:

- assess the contribution of different advertising channels to web traffic performance
- perform return on marketing investment analysis
- allocate marketing budget optimally based on estimated elasticities.

Finally, we describe the limitations of the MMM and discuss some potential alternative approaches.

═══════════ Case study ═══════════

FourTex

FourTex is an apparel brand. Its products are targeted at the mass market with a focus on casual apparel for men and women. The brand's advertising is prominent and extensive, and is present on multiple channels such as television, radio, paid search, and social media.

Recently, digital marketing tools have extended FourTex's reach among potential customers. The marketing director, Hannah Schmidt, was so proud of her team's achievements. She was getting ready for a meeting with the management board to explain how successful their previous marketing campaigns had been, and hoping to get an additional budget in order to further improve the brand's online store visits and sales leads performance metrics.

The meeting did not go as planned. In a difficult conversation, the chief executive officer (CEO) of the company said: 'Mrs. Schmidt, you always ask for more money, but can rarely explain how much incremental value this money will generate.' As she left the meeting, Mrs. Schmidt felt that she was under enormous pressure to demonstrate the value of her marketing decisions.

Next day, she pulled some data from the company's database. Table 3.1 provides a brief description of the FourTex dataset.

Table 3.1   FourTex's marketing mix dataset

Marketing mix variable	Description	Channel
Google_AdWords	Cost of Google AdWords campaigns	Online
Facebook	Cost of sponsored ads delivered on Facebook	Online
TV	Cost of TV advertising	Offline
Radio	Cost of radio advertising	Offline
Traffic	Total number of visits to the website	Online

Being very keen to demonstrate the value of marketing, Mrs. Schmidt asked her analytics team to assess the impact of their Google AdWords, Facebook, TV, and radio ads on website traffic performance. She did not want to include the sales performance metric in the analysis because her campaigns last year aimed to increase conversion to the website rather than sales outcomes. Therefore, she thought that the relevant key performance indicator was *website traffic*.

Finally, Mrs. Schmidt prepared a checklist for the analytics team. She sought answers to the following questions:

- Which marketing mix instrument really drives the performance outcome, (i.e. website traffic)?
- What is the return on marketing investment?
- Should I keep pushing on with Google AdWords and Facebook ads? Should I stop advertising on TV and radio channels?

How can Mrs. Schmidt demonstrate the impact of her marketing mix decisions to the management board?

To address Mrs. Schmidt's questions, we will build a marketing mix model that gauges the effectiveness of her marketing mix decisions and estimates the contribution of each advertising vehicle to website traffic performance. To this end, we will briefly introduce the modelling approach, and then proceed to the R application.

MARKETING MIX MODELLING APPROACH

Mrs. Schmidt would like to quantify the contribution of her marketing decisions to the website traffic outcome. To help Mrs. Schmidt solve this problem, we will utilize the marketing mix modelling approach. In building a marketing mix model, we typically employ the multiple regression toolkit. The purpose of multiple regression analysis is to predict what the outcome variable (e.g. sales, profits, traffic) will be for a given value of input (e.g. advertising, promotion). In statistics, the outcome variable is called the *dependent variable*, whereas input variables are called *independent variables*.

Model formulation

More technically, suppose that we have multiple independent variables, x_1, x_2 ,..., x_p, in the model, and want to predict the outcome, y. We observe these variables over time ($t = 1,...,T$). We can write the multiple linear regression model in the following form:

$$y_t = \beta_0 + \beta_1 x_{1t} + \beta_2 x_{2t} + ... + \beta_p x_{pt} + \epsilon_t, \tag{3.1}$$

where

- β_0 is the intercept,
- $\beta_1, \beta_2 ,...., \beta_p$ are the coefficients (also known as slopes) for the independent variables $x_1, x_2 ..., x_p$,
- ϵ_t is the residual term.

Furthermore, we assume that the residuals are uncorrelated (independent), and follow a normal distribution with zero mean and constant variance.

Using equation (3.1), the expected value of y conditional on a set of values of $\mathbf{X}$, x_1, x_2, ..., x_p, is given by

$$E(y|\mathbf{X}) = \beta_0 + \beta_1 x_{1t} + \beta_2 x_{2t} + ... + \beta_p x_{pt}. \tag{3.2}$$

Once we estimate the intercept and slopes, the estimated regression function will be as follows:

$$\hat{y}_t = \hat{\beta}_0 + \hat{\beta}_1 x_{1t} + \hat{\beta}_2 x_{2t} + ... + \hat{\beta}_p x_{pt} . \tag{3.3}$$

From equation (3.3), the predicted residuals can be computed as

$$\hat{\epsilon}_t = y_t - \hat{y}_t. \tag{3.4}$$

In fact, the residuals can be thought of as prediction errors of our model estimates.

Coefficient interpretation

How can we interpret the estimated parameters? The intercept $\hat{\beta}_0$ captures baseline sales, that is, the estimated value of y (e.g. sales) when $\mathbf{X} = \mathbf{0}$ (i.e. no marketing effort). Each slope represents the estimated change in y per unit change in x_i. If the slope is positive, we say that there is a positive (negative) relationship, that is, when x_1 increases (decreases) by one unit, then y is expected to change by β_1. Note that this interpretation is for the model with variables where no data transformation has been applied. We will illustrate the coefficient interpretation of a model with log-transformed data in more depth in our software application.

Model estimation

To estimate the intercept and slope parameters, we use the ordinary least squares (OLS) estimation technique which minimizes the sum of squared residuals of the model.

In matrix notation, the model in equation (3.1) can be expressed as

$$
\begin{bmatrix} y_1 \\ y_2 \\ \vdots \\ y_T \end{bmatrix} = \begin{bmatrix} 1 & \cdots & x_{1p} \\ 1 & \cdots & x_{2p} \\ \vdots & \ddots & \vdots \\ 1 & \cdots & x_{Tp} \end{bmatrix} \begin{bmatrix} \beta_0 \\ \beta_1 \\ \vdots \\ \beta_p \end{bmatrix} + \begin{bmatrix} \epsilon_1 \\ \epsilon_2 \\ \vdots \\ \epsilon_T \end{bmatrix}. \tag{3.5}
$$

We can reduce the above matrix–vector notation to a compact form as follows:

$$
y = \mathbf{X}\beta + \epsilon. \tag{3.6}
$$

Then we obtain the parameters of the model by minimizing the sum of squared residuals (*SSR*):

$$
\hat{\beta} = \arg \min_{\beta} SSR(\beta), \tag{3.7}
$$

where

$$
SSR(\beta) = \| y - \mathbf{X}\beta \|^2 = \sum_{t=1}^{T} \left(y_t - \beta_0 - \sum_{j=1}^{p} x_{tj}\beta_j \right)^2.
$$

Taking the partial derivatives with respect to β yields the OLS estimates

$$
\hat{\beta} = (\mathbf{X}'\mathbf{X})^{-1}\mathbf{X}'y. \tag{3.8}
$$

Next, we turn to the FourTex case study and implement the marketing mix model with R.

MODEL APPLICATION WITH R

Before we roll out the analyses, we should make sure that all our files are organized and our R environment is set up. We encourage the reader to follow the instructions below and to consult the R Markdown and HTML files that are available on the website of this book.

Preparation and set-up

Begin with the following steps:

- Create a folder on your computer and name the folder (e.g. *fourtex*).
- Download the data to the folder you just created.
- Open RStudio and launch a new R Markdown file from the *File* tab (see Figure 3.1).

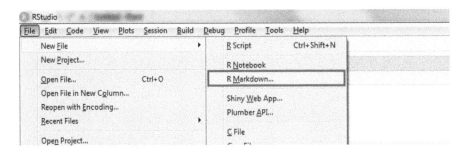

Figure 3.1   Opening an R Markdown file from RStudio

You can change the text at the top of the page as shown in the following code chunk.

```
---
title: "Marketing Mix Modelling"
author: "Case study: FourTex"
output:
  html_document:
    df_print: paged
  pdf_document: default
---
```

- Using the *File* tab, save your R Markdown file to your folder. You can give any name to your file (e.g. *mmm_fourtex*).
- Set the working directory.
- Click on the icon shown in Figure 3.2 to create a new code chunk.

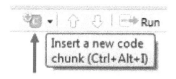

Figure 3.2   Creating a new code chunk

The code chunk is where you put your R code. Run only part of the following code chunk, depending on the operating system of your device.

```
```{r warning=FALSE}
# Run the following codes depending on the operating system on your
laptop/PC.

# If you are using iOS, and your 'fourtex' folder is created on your
'Desktop' on your Mac, you will need to set your working directory
to the 'FourTex' folder in the following way:

setwd("~/Downloads/fourtex")

# If you are using Windows, and your 'fourtex' folder is created in
your H drive, you need to set your working directory to the 'fourtex'
folder in the following way:

#setwd("H:/downloads/fourtex")
```
```

To avoid running code that is not applicable and receiving error messages, add # before each line of non-applicable code. For example, if you are using a Mac computer, you need to put # before the code setwd("H:/downloads/fourtex") .

We are now ready load the dataset to R, and perform some exploratory data analysis to get a feel for the data.

Exploratory data analysis

The following code chunk will load the data to your R environment. To run this code in your R Markdown file, make sure that you have downloaded the data file called *data_fourtex* to your working directory.

```
```{r}
data<- read.csv(file = "data_fourtex.csv",header = TRUE)
str(data)
```
```

When you run the code by clicking on the arrow at the right-hand corner of the chunk, the output in Figure 3.3 will appear. The dataset has six variables and 57 time-series observations for each variable. In the output, we also see the variable names, data type (e.g. numeric or integer), and a few observations from each variable.

```
'data.frame':   57 obs. of  6 variables:
 $ week_beg      : chr  "06/07/2020" "13/07/2020" "20/07/2020" "27/07/2020" ...
 $ Google_Adwords: num  94017 93635 112239 121250 130471 ...
 $ Facebook      : int  82950 66150 94650 96450 114600 119550 106350 116550 90150 82650 ...
 $ TV            : num  0 0 0 0 0 0 0 0 0 0 ...
 $ Radio         : num  0 0 0 0 0 ...
 $ traffic       : int  6719812 6186229 6790416 7146957 7815741 8444791 8267982 7059093 6137780 6356676 ...
```

Figure 3.3 Code output

If you check the environment tab from the top right-hand corner of your RStudio screen, you will see that the dataset is loaded (see Figure 3.4). You can click on data and observe its elements.

Figure 3.4 Environment tab

Next, we would like to retrieve each of the variables from the dataset and place it separately in the environment tab. The following code chunk does this task.

```
```{r eval=TRUE, echo=TRUE}
# Retrieve the variables
google_adwords<-data$Google_Adwords
facebook<-data$Facebook
tv<-data$TV
radio<-data$Radio
traffic<-data$traffic
```
```

The environment tab lists the retrieved variables as 'Values'. R knows the variables we want to work with. However, it does not know that they are time-series variables. So, we should make sure they can be recognized as time-series data by using the `ts()` function as in the following code chunk.

```{r}
# Make the data time series data in R
# Frequency=52
google_adwords <- ts(google_adwords,frequency = 52, start=c(2020,28))
facebook <- ts(facebook,frequency = 52, start=c(2020,28))
tv <- ts(tv,frequency = 52, start=c(2020,28))
radio <- ts(radio,frequency = 52, start=c(2020,28))
traffic <- ts(traffic,frequency = 52, start=c(2020,28))
```

Note that the dataset runs on a weekly basis. We set the frequency of the data to 52 weeks. However, not all the years have 52 weeks. Normally, the year has 365.25/7=52.18 weeks, on average. This allows for a leap year every fourth year. Therefore, some years may have 53 weeks. This is not an issue for our data as we have 57 observations spanning 2 years. None of them covers 53 weeks.

Data plots

To get a feel for the data patterns, we need to perform a visual inspection through time-series plots. As an example, we may want to sum up online spending variables to find the total online spending, then do the same for offline spending variables.

```{r}
online_total<-google_adwords +facebook
offline_total<-tv+radio
```

Next, we plot the time-series data on total online spending, total offline spending, and traffic. The following code chunk produces the time-series plots.

```{r}
#par(mfrow=c(1,3))
plot(traffic, col="blue", main="Online traffic")
plot(online_total, col="darkgreen", main="Online spending")
plot(offline_total, col="red", main="Offline spending")
```

When we run the code chunk, three windows appear (Figure 3.5). When we click on the first window, we get the plot for the online traffic variable. The second and third windows show us the online spending and the offline spending plots, respectively.

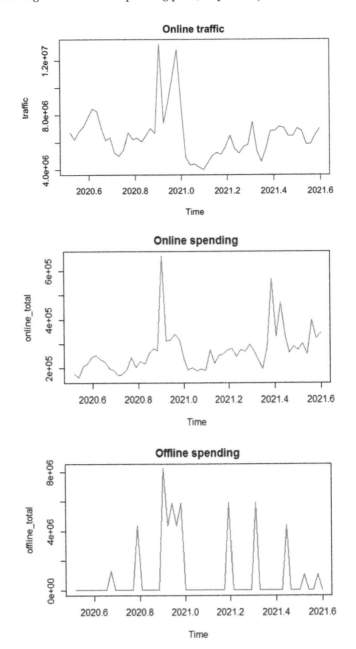

Figure 3.5 Time-series plots

Looking at the plots in Figure 3.12, what do you observe? Do increases and decreases in online traffic coincide with online and offline advertising spending? Do you see any seasonality or trend patterns?

In addition to simple time-series plot analysis, we may want to explore how much the brand spent on online and offline ads over the data period. The R code for this is given below and the corresponding pie chart output is shown in Figure 3.6. We see from the pie chart that FourTex spent 77% of its budget on offline ads, while 23% of the budget went on online ads.

```{r}
### Media spending share
sum_online<-sum(online_total)
sum_offline<-sum(offline_total)
total_spend<-sum_online+sum_offline

online_share<-sum_online/total_spend
offline_share<-sum_offline/total_spend

### Pie-Chart for Media Spending Share
slices<-c(online_share, offline_share)
lbls<-c("Online", "Offline")
pct<-round(slices*100)
lbls<-paste(lbls, pct) # add percent data to labels
lbls<-paste(lbls, "%", sep="") # add % sign to labels
par(mfrow=c(1,1))
pie(slices, labels=lbls, col=rainbow(length(lbls)), main="Ad Spending
Share" )
```

Ad Spending Share

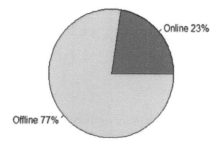

Figure 3.6   Ad spending share

Marketing mix modelling

Having explored the main features of the data, we are ready to investigate the drivers of web traffic performance. We will develop a multiple regression model that uses the `traffic` data as dependent variable (i.e. outcome or response variable) and `Google_AdWords`, `Facebook`, `TV`, and `Radio` as independent variable (i.e. predictors).

Diminishing returns

At this point, an important decision we need to make is what functional form to use in the model. Shall we assume a linear or a nonlinear relationship? The marketing literature suggests that the relationship between advertising and performance variables mostly follows a diminishing returns pattern (Hanssens et al., 2001, 2014), as illustrated in Figure 3.7.

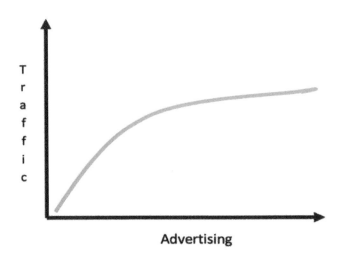

Figure 3.7 Diminishing returns

This plot tells us that initially spending more and more money on advertising is beneficial, but after a certain point the additional value gained from an extra spending will be very small. How can we introduce this type of nonlinearity into the model? A typical approach is to use a log–log model specification.[1] The log–log regression model suggests that log transformation is performed on both sides of the equation.

Turning to our data application, with the log–log specification our marketing mix model becomes

---

[1]A semi-log model can also be used to allow for a diminishing returns pattern. The semi-log model suggests that log transformation is performed for the independent variable(s) but not for the dependent variable. Another alternative approach would be to take the square root of the independent variable(s). To decide which transformation suits best, one can try all alternative specifications and compare the model fit statistics.

$$\ln(\textit{Traffic}_t) = \beta_0 + \beta_1 \ln(\textit{Traffic}_{t-1}) + \beta_2 \ln(\textit{Adwords}_t) + \beta_3 \ln(\textit{Facebook}_t) + \beta_4 \ln(\textit{TV}_t) + \beta_5 \ln(\textit{Radio}_t) + \epsilon_t \quad (3.9)$$

where ln stands for the natural logarithm.

> Did you notice that we added the lagged traffic variable as an additional predictor to our model? Do you think including the first lagged traffic variable in the model makes sense? Why?

To estimate the log–log model in equation (3.9), we need to log-transform our variables. The following code chunk shows how to do so.

```{r}
lngoogle_adwords<-log(google_adwords+1)
lnfacebook<-log(facebook+1)
lnTV<-log(tv+1)
lnradio<-log(radio+1)
lntraffic<-log(traffic+1)
```

Did you notice that we added +1 to the original variables? The reason for doing this is that some variables include zero observations, and the logarithm of zero (ln 0) is undefined. Therefore, we should add a small number to be able to take the logarithm.

We have all the variables to be used in the model, except the first lagged traffic variable, $\ln\textit{Traffic}_{t-1}$. The following code chunk creates this variable.

```{r}
#Creating Lagged Traffic Variable
m <- 1 # one lag
#number of observations
n <- length(traffic)
#Build Lag
L1.lntraffic <- c(rep(NA,m), lntraffic[1:(n-m)])
```

Finally, using the following code, we run our model.

```{r}
#Fit a Regression
options(scipen=999)
```

```
#regression1 <- lm(traffic~L1.traffic+google_adwords+facebook+tv+radio)
regression1 <- lm(lntraffic~L1.lntraffic+lngoogle_adwords+lnfacebook+
lnTV+lnradio)
summary(regression1)
```

Normally, R reports the numbers in scientific format (e.g. 1E-05). The first line of the code, options(scipen=999), allows us to see the numbers in a non-scientific format. The second line defines our regression model: the traffic variable is explained by all the marketing variables and past traffic performance. Note that in coding a regression model in R, the dependent variable always precedes the tilde symbol ~ , and the predictors come after that symbol. Finally, the third line puts the regression summary output in R Markdown.

Model output

The R output of our model is shown in Figure 3.8. We will take a closer look at the model output and learn about its key components.

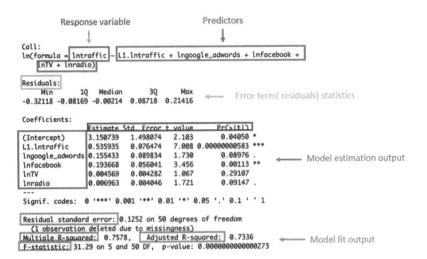

Figure 3.8   Marketing mix model output

Residuals

Recall that residuals represent the 'unexplained' part of the model, that is, the impact of other factors that are not explicitly included in the model. The descriptive statistics (e.g. min, max) of residuals are reported at the top of the model output.

Coefficient estimates

We can write down the estimated coefficients of this marketing mix model as an equation:

$$\ln(\textit{Traffic}_t) = 3.151 + 0.536 \ln(\textit{Traffic}_{t-1}) + 0.155 \ln(\textit{Adwords}_t) + 0.194 \ln(\textit{Facebook}_t) + 0.005 \ln(\textit{TV}_t) + 0.007 \ln(\textit{Radio}_t) \tag{3.10}$$

In Figure 3.8, the standard error of each coefficient shows at what precision level we have estimated that particular coefficient, that is, it represents the uncertainty surrounding that coefficient. The t-value is obtained by dividing the coefficient by its standard error. The p-value, $\Pr(>|t|)$, is computed based on the t-value, and helps us understand whether the coefficient is statistically significant. Note that significance codes are also provided in the table. For example, lagged traffic is a strong indicator of the next period's traffic as it is highly significant (the p-value is close to zero). The effect of Facebook ads is significant at the 0.1% level while Google AdWords and radio effects are significant at the 10% level. Finally, the effect of TV ads is not statistically significant.

How to interpret the estimated coefficients

We start with the interpretation of the autoregressive coefficient. The estimated effect size is 0.536. If web traffic performance gains a certain momentum today, we would expect that it will carry over into future periods with an attrition rate of 0.464 (1 – 0.536). This implies that some FourTex customers make repeat web visits because the brand or advertising has gained a place in their memories, while others stop visiting after some time because their ad or site memory decays rather quickly.

Next, we look at the advertising media effects. Since this is a log–log model output, the estimated coefficients of the advertising variables can be interpreted as elasticities: the expected percentage change in the response variable with respect to a percentage change in a predictor variable, holding other predictors of the model constant.

To understand this better, let us focus on the effect of Google AdWords. Take two values of Google AdWords at two consecutive periods: A1 and A2. Holding the other variables fixed in equation (3.10), we obtain the following:

$$\textit{lnTraffic}(A2) - \textit{lnTraffic}(A1) = 0.155 \, (\textit{lnAdwords}(A2) - \textit{lnAdwords}(A1)). \tag{3.11}$$

Using the properties of logarithms, we can simplify equation (3.11) as follows:

$$\ln\left(\frac{\textit{Traffic}(A2)}{\textit{Traffic}(A1)}\right) = 0.155 \ln\left(\frac{\textit{Adwords}(A2)}{\textit{Adwords}(A1)}\right). \tag{3.12}$$

Simplifying the equation in (3.12) further, we get

$$\frac{\textit{Traffic}(A2)}{\textit{Traffic}(A1)} = \left(\frac{\textit{Adwords}(A2)}{\textit{Adwords}(A1)}\right)^{0.155}. \tag{3.13}$$

This result suggests that as long as the ratio of the two Google AdWords spending levels, $\frac{Adwords(A2)}{Adwords(A1)}$, stays the same, the expected ratio of the response variable, $\frac{Traffic(A2)}{Traffic(A1)}$, stays the same. In other words, percentage increases in Google AdWords lead to constant percentage changes in traffic. For example, when we increase Google AdWords by 10%, we expect a roughly 1.5% increase in Traffic ($1.10^{0.155} = 1.015$).

 What is your interpretation of the estimated coefficients of the other advertising variables, Facebook, TV, and radio?

R-squared

R-squared, also known as coefficient of determination, measures the proportion of variation in the response variable explained by the independent variables. In our case, the model we built explains 76% of the variation in logged traffic (Multiple R-squared in the regression output).

Adjusted R-squared

It is possible to increase *R*-squared by adding more and more variables to the regression equation. However, the model's explanatory power can be increased just by chance when we add more variables to the model. To see whether a new variable will improve the model, the adjusted *R*-squared value should be checked. From the regression output, we see that the adjusted *R*-squared is 0.73. That means that our model did not suffer much from adding more variables (76% for *R*-squared compared to 73% for adjusted *R*-squared).

Residual standard error

The residual standard error (also known as the standard error of regression) is a measure of the accuracy of predictions. To put it differently, it shows the average distance that the observed values deviate from the regression line. So, the lower the standard error of regression, the better. One can use this statistic to compare the model fits of alternative models.

F-test

We use the *F*-test to assess whether a linear regression with predictor variables is favoured over a simple average value of the response variable. The computed *F*-statistic is 31.29, with a p-value of 2.73×10^{-14}. This is a very small number, far less than the threshold of 0.05 for a 95% level of statistical significance. Thus, we can conclude that the model we estimated is favoured over a simple mean of the traffic variable.

Model fit

Having estimated the parameters, we can obtain the model fit plot to see visually whether our model captures the patterns in the traffic data. Running the following code chunk gives us the model fit plot in Figure 3.9.

```r
```{r}
# Model fit plot
fitted_traffic<-ts(regression1$fitted.values, frequency = 52,
start=c(2020,28))
plot(lntraffic, type="l", col="blue", main="Web Traffic",lwd=2)
lines(fitted_traffic, type="b", col="red")
legend("topleft", lty=1, col=c("blue", "red"),
       c("Logged Traffic Data","Fitted"))
```
```

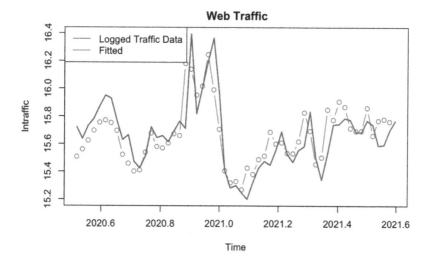

Figure 3.9   Model fit plot

   Do you think the model predicted well the web traffic performance of FourTex?

Model diagnostics

Having estimated our marketing mix model, it is usually good practice to perform model diagnostic checks on the estimated residuals (Franses, 2005; Esteban-Bravo et al., 2017). In the marketing mix model above, we assume that residuals are uncorrelated (i.e. independent), have zero mean and constant variance. If the model passes these diagnostics, we conclude that the model is not misspecified and can be used to make statistical inferences and predictions. For a detailed review on how to conduct model diagnostic tests, see Chapter 9 on demand forecasting.

Next, we turn our attention to the following questions that are central to the case study:

- What drives the web traffic performance?
- What is the traffic return on marketing investment?
- What is the optimal budget allocation?

What drives web traffic performance?

What is contribution of marketing to web traffic performance? How much traffic was generated thanks to TV, radio, Facebook, and Google AdWords? To see this, first we need to convert the elasticities to unit effects using the following formula:

$$\theta_i = \beta_i \frac{\bar{y}}{\bar{x}_i}, \quad i = \{Adwords, Facebook, TV, Radio\}, \tag{3.14}$$

where θ_i denotes the unit effect for advertising media i, β_i is the estimated elasticity for media i, $\bar{y}$ is baseline (average) traffic, and $\bar{x}_i$ is baseline advertising for media i. Readers interested in learning how to derive this formula are referred to the appendix to this chapter.

For example, for Google AdWords, equation (3.14) can be expressed as follows:

$$\theta_{AdWords} = \beta_{AdWords} \frac{Baseline\ Traffic}{Baseline\ AdWords}. \tag{3.15}$$

The following code chunk retrieves the coefficients (elasticities) from our log–log model output and then computes the unit effects using equation (3.14).

```r
#Retrieve each model coefficient:
beta_adwords<-summary(regression1)$coefficients[3,1]
beta_facebook<-summary(regression1)$coefficients[4,1]
beta_tv<-summary(regression1)$coefficients[5,1]
beta_radio<-summary(regression1)$coefficients[6,1]

#Calculate the baseline (average) traffic:
average_traffic<-mean(traffic)

#Calculate the baseline (average) advertising spending for each media:
average_adwords<-mean(google_adwords)
average_facebook<-mean(facebook)
average_tv<-mean(tv)
average_radio<-mean(radio)

# Finally, calculate the unit effects:
theta_adwords<-beta_adwords*(average_traffic/average_adwords)
theta_facebook<-beta_facebook*(average_traffic/average_facebook)
```

```
theta_tv<-beta_tv*(average_traffic/average_tv)
theta_radio<-beta_radio*(average_traffic/average_radio)

```

Next, we compute the contribution of each advertising media to the overall traffic performance using the formula

$$Contribution_i = \theta_i \sum_{t=1}^{T} x_t^i, \quad i = \{Adwords, Facebook, TV, Radio\},$$ (3.16)

where θ_i indicates the estimated unit effect for advertising media i, and x_t^i is the spending of advertising media i at time t.

For example, for Google AdWords, we multiply the estimated unit effect of Google AdWords, $\theta_{AdWords}$, (6.44 from equation (3.15)) by the sum of Google AdWords spending. We compute the contribution of the other advertising media in the same way. The following code chunk performs this task.

We can show these media contributions graphically as well. We will use barplots for this.

```{r}
#How much traffic we got thanks to TV, Adwords etc.?
sum_adwords<-sum(google_adwords)
sum_facebook<-sum(facebook)
sum_tv<-sum(tv)
sum_radio<-sum(radio)


#Each media's contribution to traffic
adwords_contribution<-theta_adwords*sum_adwords
facebook_contribution<-theta_facebook*sum_facebook
tv_contribution<-theta_tv*sum_tv
radio_contribution<-theta_radio*sum_radio

print(adwords_contribution)
print(facebook_contribution)
print (tv_contribution)
print (radio_contribution)

```

To obtain the barplots, we need to install the ggplot2 package. If you have previously installed ggplot2 on your computer, you can add a hashtag symbol, #, and then run the following code to load the package.

```{r}
# Note: If you have not installed the 'ggplot2' package to your computer
before,
# remove the hashtag symbol, #, and run the code.
#install.packages("ggplot2")
library(ggplot2)
```

We need to plug in the necessary input for the barplot. The following code chunk shows the
R code for this.

```{r}
# Bar plot information
media_contribution<-c(adwords_contribution,facebook_contribution,
                      tv_contribution, radio_contribution)
media_contribution=round(media_contribution, digits=0)
media_names<-c("AdWords","Facebook","TV","Radio")
df<-data.frame(media_names,media_contribution)
head(df)
```

Here, the first and second lines produce the *media contribution* column using the calculated
contribution of each media. The third line of the code rounds off the numbers to integers (zero
decimal places). The fourth line tells R the names of the variables. The fifth line combines the
media contribution and media names together and creates a *data frame* called df. Finally, the last
line, head(df), shows the data in R Markdown. The output of the code is shown in Figure 3.10.

	media_names <chr>	media_contribution <dbl>
1	AdWords	57994699
2	Facebook	72261042
3	TV	1704751
4	Radio	2597922

4 rows

Figure 3.10   Media contribution data for the barplot

We will use this information to create a barplot of the web traffic contribution of each media.
The following code chunk generates this bar chart.

```{r}
barp_plot1<-ggplot(data=df,aes(x=media_names,y=media_contribution)) +
  geom_bar(stat="identity", color="black",
         fill=c("Red","Orange","Blue","Green")) +
```

```
    geom_text(aes(label=media_contribution), vjust=-0.3, size=3.5)+
    labs(title="Contribution to Traffic", x="Media", y="Contribution") +
    theme_minimal()
#bar_plot1
# change the order of the bars
barp_plot1 + scale_x_discrete(limits=c("Facebook","AdWords","Radio","TV"))

` ` `
```

The first line of the code tells R to use the function `ggplot()`, which is characterized by data, x-axis, and y-axis inputs. The second and third lines (`geom_bar()`) dictate the shape and colour details of the bars in the plot. The fourth line (`geom_text()`) adds the data labels to the bars. The fifth line provides the `title` of the plot, and labels for the horizontal and vertical axes. The last line suggests that there will be minimal effect on the background of the plot. Note that the + sign at the end of a line tells us that the code continues.

Running the code above generates the barplot in Figure 3.11. This barplot suggests that most of the traffic is driven by Facebook and Google AdWords campaigns, with Facebook being the leading contributor. Radio and TV contribute very little.

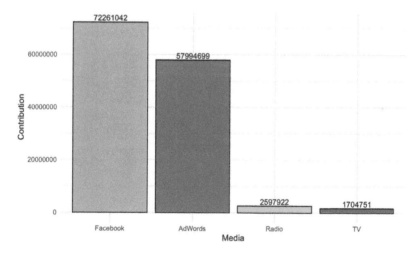

Figure 3.11 The contribution of marketing to web traffic performance

Sometimes, it is difficult to communicate large numbers displayed above the bars. To avoid this, we can compute the contribution of each traffic driver in percentage terms.

Install and launch the `formattable` package, which will help us use the percentage format. If you have installed `formattable` to your computer previously, you can add a hashtag symbol, #, and then run the following code.

```{r}
#Contribution in %.
#install.packages("formattable")
library(formattable)
```

Next, we compute the media contributions in percentage terms. Running the following code chunk provides the output in Figure 3.12.

```{r}
#Calculate each media's contribution as %.
allmedia_contribution<-adwords_contribution++facebook_contribution+
  tv_contribution+radio_contribution

adwords_pct<-adwords_contribution/allmedia_contribution
facebook_pct<-facebook_contribution/allmedia_contribution
tv_pct<-tv_contribution/allmedia_contribution
radio_pct<-radio_contribution/allmedia_contribution

## all media in a vector (contribution in %)
pct_contribution<-c(adwords_pct,facebook_pct,tv_pct, radio_pct)
pct_contribution<-percent(pct_contribution)        # this line writes
the numbers in %


media_names<-c("Adwords", "Facebook","TV","Radio")
df2<-data.frame(media_names,pct_contribution)
head(df2)

```

	media_names <chr>	pct_contribution <S3: formattable>
1	Adwords	43.10%
2	Facebook	53.70%
3	TV	1.27%
4	Radio	1.93%

4 rows

Figure 3.12   Data for the barplot with percentages

Finally, the following R code generates the barplot with media contribution in percentage terms.

```r
```{r}
barp_plot2<-ggplot(data=df2,aes(x=media_names,y=pct_contribution)) +
  geom_bar(stat="identity", color="black",
           fill=c("Red","Orange","Blue","Green")) +
  geom_text(aes(label=pct_contribution), vjust=-0.3, size=3.5)+
  labs(title="Contribution to Traffic in %", x="Media", y="Contribution
(%)") +
  theme_minimal()
#barp_plot2
# change the order of the bars
barp_plot2 + scale_x_discrete(limits=c("Facebook",
"Adwords","Radio","TV"))

```
```

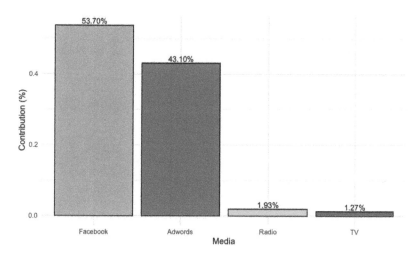

Figure 3.13 Barplot with percentages

The plot in Figure 3.13 tells us that 53.7% of the web traffic is driven by Facebook, 43.1% is driven by Google AdWords, 1.9% by radio, and 1.3% by TV.

Return on marketing investment

Does performance increase most with a £1 reduction in TV ads or by increasing social media ads by £1? Financially oriented marketing executives are very often concerned about the return on marketing investment. That is, they would like to know how much they earn with respect to how much they spend. Usually, the return metric is sales, revenues, or profits. However, it can also be something non-financial, such as customer engagement, web traffic, or store traffic. For FourTex, we focus on the traffic return on marketing investment (TROMI).

The first input we need is the cost data. We obtain it using the following code chunk.

```r
#Calculate the cost of each media
cost_adwords<-sum(google_adwords)
cost_facebook<-sum(facebook)
cost_tv<-sum(tv)
cost_radio<-sum(radio)
cost_total<-cost_adwords+cost_facebook+cost_tv+cost_radio

cost<-c(cost_adwords,cost_facebook,cost_tv,cost_radio)
cost=round(cost, digits=0)
```

We run the following code to get the input for the barplot of traffic contribution and cost incurred (see Figure 3.14).

```r
# Traffic Contribution vs. Cost
df3<-data.frame(traf_cost=rep(c("Traffic","Cost"), each=4),
                media_names=rep(c("Adwords","Facebook","TV","Radio"),2),
                values=c(media_contribution, cost))
head(df3)
```

	traf_cost <chr>	media_names <chr>	values <dbl>
1	Traffic	Adwords	57994699
2	Traffic	Facebook	72261042
3	Traffic	TV	1704751
4	Traffic	Radio	2597922
5	Cost	Adwords	8999557
6	Cost	Facebook	6437100

6 rows

Figure 3.14   Input for traffic versus cost plot

Next, we run the following code chunk to see the traffic return and cost data together in a barplot (see Figure 3.15).

```{r}
barp_plot3<-ggplot(data = df3, aes(x = media_names,y = values,fill = traf_
cost)) +
                     geom_bar(stat = "identity", color = "black",
position = position_dodge()) +
    labs(title = "Traffic vs. Media Cost", x = "Media", y = "Traffic and Cost") +
theme_minimal()

bar_plot3<-barp_plot3 + scale_x_discrete(limits = c("Facebook",
"Adwords", "TV","Radio"))
bar_plot3
```

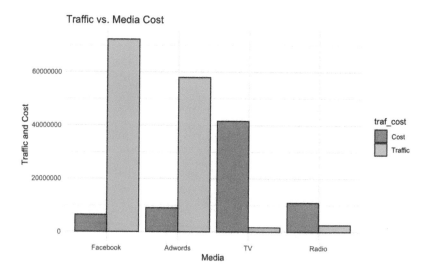

Figure 3.15 Plot of traffic against media cost

 Have a look at the barplot in Figure 3.34. What is your conclusion about traffic generated and cost incurred? Which media returns the most and which the least?

Instead of showing cost and return data together, we can compute the TROMI, and show the results in percentages. We just need to divide the traffic contribution of each media by the cost of each media, as in the following code chunk.

```{r}
# Calculate the traffic return for each media
roi_adwords=adwords_contribution/cost_adwords
roi_facebook=facebook_contribution/cost_facebook
roi_tv=tv_contribution/cost_tv
roi_radio=radio_contribution/cost_radio

```

Next, we get the input for the TROMI barplot via the following code chunk.

```{r}
# TROMI plot input
roi<-c(roi_adwords, roi_facebook, roi_tv,roi_radio)
# Round off the numbers.
roi=round(roi, digits=0)
media_names<-c("Adwords", "Facebook","TV","Radio")
df4<-data.frame(media_names,roi)
head(df4)
```

Finally, we obtain the barplot for the TROMI analysis using the following code.

```{r}
# TROMI bar plot
bar_plot4<-ggplot(data = df4, aes(x = media_names,y = roi)) +
   geom_bar(stat = "identity", color = "black",
            fill = c("Red","Orange","Blue","Green")) +
   geom_text(aes(label = roi), vjust = -0.3, size = 3.5) +
   labs(title = "Traffic Return on Marketing Investment", x = "Media",
y = "TROMI") +
   theme_minimal()
bar_plot4<-bar_plot4 + scale_x_discrete(limits=c("Facebook", "Adwords",
"Radio","TV"))
bar_plot4

```

In a nutshell, the barplot in Figure 3.16 suggests that for every £1 spent on Facebook, the expected number of web visits is 11. For every £1 spent on Google AdWords campaigns, we expect six web visits to occur.

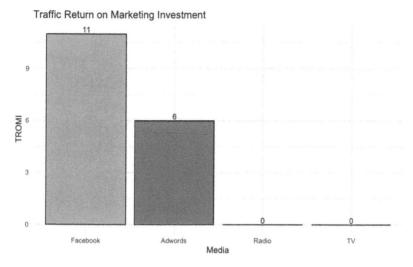

Figure 3.16 Barplot for traffic return on marketing investment

 Are you surprised that the TROMI for TV and radio is zero? Why do you think that the company invested in TV and radio channels even though their traffic return is almost null?

Next, we explore what Mrs. Schmidt should do with regard to her next budget allocation strategies.

Marketing budget allocation

Marketing analysts follow two main approaches to guide their resource allocation strategies. One of them is normative decision-making based on constrained optimization models (e.g. profit maximization subject to budget constraints). The other is elasticity-based allocation. In this R application, we will allocate the marketing budget of FourTex by making use of the elasticities obtained from the log–log regression model above.

Before diving into the optimal resource allocation, let us see what the current budget allocation looks like. Running the following code yields the output in Figure 3.17.

```{r}
#Actual Budget Spending
costshare_adwords<-cost_adwords/cost_total
costshare_facebook<-cost_facebook/cost_total
costshare_tv<-cost_tv/cost_total
costshare_radio<-cost_radio/cost_total
```

```
# Input for the pie-chart
slices_actual<-c(costshare_adwords, costshare_facebook,costshare_
tv,costshare_radio )
lbls_actual<-c("Adwords", "Facebook", "TV", "Radio")
pct_actual<-round(slices_actual*100)
lbls_actual<-paste(lbls_actual, pct_actual)      # add data to labels
lbls_actual<-paste(lbls_actual, "%", sep= "")    # add % sign to labels

# Get the pie-chart
pie(slices_actual, labels = lbls_actual, col = rainbow(length(lbls_
actual)), main = "Actual Ad Spending")

```
```

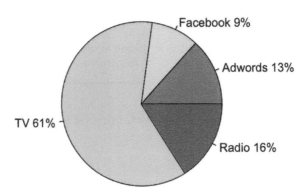

Figure 3.17   Current budget allocation of FourTex

The pie chart in Figure 3.17 tells us that 61% of the marketing budget was used for TV ads, while 16% of the budget went on radio campaigns, 13% on Google AdWords, and 9% on Facebook. Given our findings on the media elasticities, how would you spend the budget? Would you spend so much money on TV ads to boost web traffic?

For the optimal allocation, we will use the estimated coefficients (βs) from the log–log regression model. Recall that those coefficients are elasticities.

We calculate the optimal allocation for each media using the following formula:

$$Optimal\ Allocation_i = \frac{\beta_i}{\sum_i \beta_i}, \quad i = \{Adwords,\ Facebook, TV,\ Radio\}. \tag{3.17}$$
```

As an example, for Google AdWords, we have

$$Optimal\ Allocation_{AdWords} = \frac{\beta_{AdWords}}{\beta_{AdWords} + \beta_{Facebook} + \beta_{TV} + \beta_{Radio}}.$$ (3.18)

Let us now do this in R.

```{r}
#The sum of all elasticities
beta_allmedia<-beta_adwords+beta_facebook+beta_tv+beta_radio

#Optimal resource allocation
optim_adwords<-beta_adwords/beta_allmedia
optim_facebook<-beta_facebook/beta_allmedia
optim_tv<-beta_tv/beta_allmedia
optim_radio<-beta_radio/beta_allmedia

```

When we run the code chunk above, we can see the computed allocation at the top right of the screen in the environment tab. Now following running the code chunk we can get the pie chart in Figure 3.18, which shows the allocation with percentages.

```{r}
## Pie-chart ingredients
optimal_spend<-c(optim_adwords,optim_facebook,optim_tv,optim_radio)
optimal_spend=round(optimal_spend, digits=2)
optimal_spend

slices_optim<-c(optim_adwords, optim_facebook,optim_tv,optim_radio)
lbls_optim<-c("Adwords", "Facebook", "TV","Radio")
pct_optim<-round(slices_optim*100)
lbls_optim<-paste(lbls_optim, pct_optim)        # paste variable
names to data labels
lbls_optim<-paste(lbls_optim, "%", sep="")       # add % sign to labels

# Get the pie-chart
pie(slices_optim, labels=lbls_optim, col=rainbow(length(lbls_optim)),
main="Optimal Budget Allocation" )

```

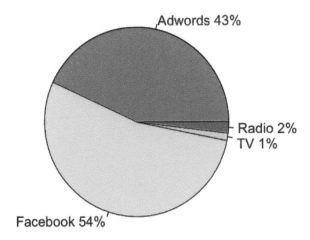

Optimal Budget Allocation

Adwords 43%

Radio 2%
TV 1%

Facebook 54%

Figure 3.18 Visualization of optimal budget allocation

What is your conclusion? Is the optimal allocation different from the actual spending? How do you suggest FourTex should deploy their marketing resources to boost the web traffic performance? Would the optimal allocation be different for a different performance metric (e.g. sales)?

To summarize, through the case study on FourTex, we have explored how to:

- assess the contribution of different advertising channels to web traffic performance
- perform return on marketing investment analysis
- allocate marketing budget optimally based on estimated elasticities.

Limitations

Although the marketing mix model that we have developed in this chapter is a useful tool for marketers, it has some limitations. We discuss these limitations below.

Functional form. The log–log model we developed in this chapter allows for a diminishing returns pattern. However, the relationship between website traffic performance and advertising media can be characterized by different nonlinear approximations as well (e.g. an S-shape pattern). The decision on the exact functional form can be made by examining the scatterplots of the variables as well as the model fit statistics. Depending on the type of nonlinearity observed in the data, one can opt for different data transformation techniques.

Synergy effects: According to Naik and Raman (2003), an advertising activity serves a dual purpose: it increases sales and enhances the effectiveness of other advertising media. For example, while consumers watch TV, they browse social mobile apps on their devices. This implies that when consumers are exposed to TV commercials, they may remember the sponsored advertisement images from social media (e.g. Facebook or Twitter) they have recently viewed. This kind of media reinforcement suggests that one media may strengthen the impact of other media. In marketing, this effect is called *synergy*. The central idea behind synergy effects is that the combined impact of advertising media (e.g. TV ads and Facebook ads) exceeds the sum of their independent effects (i.e. $\beta_3 Facebook_t + \beta_4 TV_t$). Although our computer application did not include any synergy effects, marketers are advised to inspect some potential synergy effects in their datasets and model them by generating interaction terms (e.g. $Facebook_t \times TV_t$).

Long-term effects.: The marketing literature demonstrates that the consumer response to advertising campaigns may be delayed (Hanssens, 2018). In other words, the impact of advertising on traffic performance may not be immediate. We call this a *delay or lagged effect*. Thus, an advertising campaign run today is expected to be remembered by customers over the next periods. Our marketing mix model, however, did not account for the impact over time (or dynamic impact) of advertising. In addition to modelling contemporaneous effects, one can include lagged variables in the model (e.g. $Facebook_{t-1}$, $Facebook_{t-2}$, TV_{t-1}, TV_{t-2}), and compute the long-term or cumulative effects. Autoregressive distributed-lag (models can accommodate such effects (Hendry et al., 1984; Hanssens et al., 2001). Alternatively, considering the theoretical foundation of the well-established Koyck model (Koyck, 1954; Franses, 2021), one can use the estimated coefficients in equation (3.10) to compute the long-term effects. For example, the long-term effect for Facebook ads, $\varphi_{Facebook}$, is calculated as

$$\varphi_{Facebook} = \frac{\beta_3}{1-\beta_1} = \frac{0.194}{1-0.536} = 0.42. \tag{3.19}$$

If more than one lag is used for the lagged dependent variable, the denominator term should include the sum of all the autoregressive coefficients instead of β_1.

Finally, multi-equation time-series models (e.g. vector autoregressive models) can be used to infer the long-term effects of the marketing variables (Dekimpe and Hanssens, 1999). These dynamic models are flexible in capturing not only the immediate and lagged response to marketing variables, but also the complex feedback loops (e.g. TV ads→Facebook ads→web traffic). The impulse-response functions derived from such dynamic system models allow managers to evaluate the wear-in, wear-out as well as short- and long-term effects of their marketing actions (Pauwels, 2018; Wang and Yildirim, 2022).

Segment-specific effects. Our marketing mix model used aggregate-level data on FourTex's marketing activities and web traffic performance. Thus, the estimated advertising effects are not segment- or individual-specific. However, some managers may be interested in exploring the responsiveness of different segments to advertising campaigns, and measuring the return on marketing investment at the segment or individual level. A practical approach to address this is to determine the distinct segments (clusters) in the dataset using clustering techniques (e.g. *k*-means algorithm, latent class segmentation), apply the marketing mix model to each segment, and obtain the effects at the disaggregate level.

Intermediate metrics, While bottom-line-oriented managers typically assess marketing effectiveness using the observable metrics (e.g. web traffic, sales, profits), some marketers may use different performance metrics such as brand awareness, consideration, and liking (Pauwels et al., 2013). These metrics are often considered as *intermediate* performance metrics and help managers track the state of mind of consumers (Srinivasan et al., 2016). Our model did not include such intermediate metrics as the dataset we use for FourTex did not cover such information. However, in Chapter 6 of this book, we will delve into consumer attitudinal metrics, and learn how they can be utilized to assess the impact of marketing.

Endogeneity. One of the assumptions that we made in our model is that there is no correlation between the advertising variables and the residuals term, that is, that advertising media are strictly exogenous. However, this assumption may sometimes fail due to the following factors:

i. *Omitted variable bias.* It is possible that advertising spending decisions are made strategically based on future web traffic expectations. For example, in the FourTex case study, Mrs. Schmidt may adjust her TV ad spending around special events in the UK, or she may decide to advertise only the successful products in her social media campaigns. When managers adapt their decisions in response to factors that are unobserved by the analyst (Papies et al., 2017), then we say that the model suffers from endogeneity, and that the estimated effects are inconsistent or biased. The common approach to address this type of endogeneity in marketing mix models is the use of instrumental variables. Since this is beyond the scope of this book, we refer the interested reader to our references on this issue.

ii. *Simultaneity.* When advertising media and web traffic performance variables are co-determined, an endogeneity issue arises. For example, advertising spending on Google AdWords and Facebook may influence web traffic performance, and the brand manager may decide how much to spend on AdWords and Facebook campaigns based on the observed web traffic performance. When simultaneity-induced endogeneity occurs, the OLS estimates become biased, which in turn may result in erroneous conclusions on return on media calculations. The common approach to address this type of endogeneity is to employ multi-equation dynamic models (e.g. vector autoregressive models, vector error correction models). We refer the reader to Dekimpe and Hanssens (1999), Lütkepohl (2005), and Srinivasan (2022) for in-depth applications of these models.

CHAPTER SUMMARY

Marketing mix modelling has become one of the most frequently used analytical approaches by marketers in recent years. This approach uses aggregate-level data on marketing mix actions (e.g. advertising, promotions, distribution, price, and salesforce) and performance metrics (e.g. traffic, sales, revenues, profits), and enables marketers to understand what parts of their marketing strategy generate the desired outcomes and which decisions need to be optimized.

In this chapter, we presented a case study on marketing mix management problem faced by FourTex, an apparel brand. Then we introduced the multiple regression toolkit to tackle the managerial questions outlined in the case study. Finally, we demonstrated the data application of the marketing mix modelling approach to FourTex, using R. Through the case study, we explored how to:

- assess the contribution of different advertising channels to web traffic performance
- perform return on marketing investment analysis
- allocate the marketing budget optimally based on estimated elasticities.

REFERENCES

Dekimpe, M. G. and Hanssens, D. M. (1999). Sustained spending and persistent response: A new look at long-term marketing profitability. *Journal of Marketing Research*, 36, 397–412.

Esteban-Bravo, M., Vidal-Sanz, J. M. and Yildirim, G. (2017). Can retail sales volatility be curbed through marketing actions? *Marketing Science*, 36(2), 232–253.

Franses, P. H. (2005). On the use of econometric models for policy simulation in marketing. *Journal of Marketing Research*, 42, 4–14.

Franses, P. H. (2021). Marketing response and temporal aggregation. *Journal of Marketing Analytics*, 9, 111–117.

Hanssens D. M. (2018). Return on media models. In C. Homburg, M. Klarmann and A. E. Vomberg (eds), *Handbook of Market Research*. Cham: Springer.

Hanssens, D. M., Parsons, L. J. and Schultz, R. L. (2001). *Market Response Models: Econometric and Time-Series Research*, 2nd edn. Boston: Kluwer Academic Publishers.

Hanssens, D. M., Pauwels, H. K., Srinivasan S., Vanhuele, M. and Yildirim, G. (2014) Consumer attitude metrics for guiding marketing mix decisions. *Marketing Science*, 33(4), 534–50.

Hendry, D. F., Pagan, A. R. and Sargan, J. D. (1984). Dynamic specification. In Z. Griliches and M. D. Intriligator (eds), *Handbook of Econometrics* (Vol. 2, pp. 1023–1100). Amsterdam: Elsevier.

Koyck, L. M. (1954). *Distributed Lags and Investment Analysis*. Amsterdam: North-Holland.

Lütkepohl, H. (2005). *New Introduction to Multiple Time Series Analysis*. Berlin: Springer.

Naik, P. A. and Raman, K. (2003). Understanding the impact of synergy in multimedia communications. *Journal of Marketing Research*, 40(4), 375–388.

Papies, D., Ebbes, P. and van Heerde, H. J. (2017). Addressing endogeneity in marketing models. In P. S. H. Leeflang, J. E. Wieringa, T. H. A. Bijmolt, and K. H. Pauwels (eds), *Advanced Methods for Modeling Markets*. Cham: Springer.

Pauwels, K. H. (2018). Modeling dynamic relations among marketing and performance metrics. *Foundations and Trends in Marketing*, 11(4), 215–301.

Pauwels, K., Erguncu, S. and Yildirim, G. (2013). Winning hearts, minds and sales: How marketing communication enters the purchase process in emerging and mature markets. International *Journal of Research in Marketing*, 30(1), 57–68.

Srinivasan, S. (2022). Modeling marketing dynamics using vector autoregressive (VAR) model. In C. Homburg, M. Klarmann and A. Vomberg (eds), *Handbook of Market Research*. Cham: Springer.

Srinivasan, S., Rutz, O. and Pauwels, K. (2016). Paths to and off purchase: Quantifying the impact of traditional marketing and online consumer activity. *Journal of the Academy of Marketing Science*, 44(4), 440–453.

Wang, W. and Yildirim, G. (2022). Applied time-series analysis in marketing. In C. Homburg, M. Klarmann and A. E. Vomberg (eds), *Handbook of Market Research*. Cham: Springer.

APPENDIX

Unit effects and elasticities

Here we demonstrate how unit (marginal) effects and elasticities are interrelated. Suppose that we have the following log–log model:

$$\ln(y) = \beta_0 + \beta_1 \ln(x_1) + \varepsilon. \tag{3A.1}$$

Note that we omit the subscript t to keep the notation simple. Solving for y, we get:

$$y = e^{\beta_0 + \beta_1 \ln(x_1) + \varepsilon}. \tag{3A.2}$$

Next, we differentiate y with respect to x_1:

$$\frac{dy}{dx_1} = \frac{\beta_1}{x_1} e^{\beta_0 + \beta_1 \ln(x_1) + \varepsilon}. \tag{3A.3}$$

Since $y = e^{\beta_0 + \beta_1 \ln(x_1) + \varepsilon}$, we can express equation (3A.3) as follows:

$$\frac{dy}{dx_1} = \frac{\beta_1}{x_1} y. \tag{3A.4}$$

Rearranging the terms, we get the unit (marginal) effects

$$\frac{dy}{dx_1} = \beta_1 \frac{y}{x_1}, \tag{3A.5}$$

where y and x_1 can be replaced by average values over a range. It is straightforward to see that β_1 is elasticity:

$$\beta_1 = \frac{dy}{dx_1} \frac{x_1}{y}. \tag{3A.6}$$

4

ATTRIBUTION MODELLING

Chapter contents

LEARNING OBJECTIVES

At the end of this chapter, you should be able to:

- define what attribution is and explain why it is important in digital marketing
- explain the commonly used attribution models, including single-touch, Markov chain, and Shapley value-based approaches
- apply the attribution models in R to an individual-level consumer dataset
- outline the challenges in implementing the attribution models.

This chapter focuses on attribution modelling, one of the fundamental analytical approaches used in digital marketing. Attribution models enable marketers to evaluate the impact of various digital touchpoints along the customer journey using customer data at the individual level, uncover important insights into digital consumer behaviour, and customize future marketing communications to each individual.

To introduce the chapter, we utilize a brief case study on KNC, a company that sells beauty items. The case highlights the importance of attribution modelling from a managerial standpoint. Then we describe attribution modelling and give an overview of the most widely used attribution models in practice. Next, we use R to demonstrate how the attribution models can be applied to the case study. Finally, we discuss the challenges in implementing attribution models and provide the key conclusions of the chapter.

═══════════ Case study ═══════════

KNC

'Let's show a bird's-eye view of our digital channel performance from this year first. Here we could have a bar chart on *the* number of online purchases and some advertising data on mobile, paid search, affiliations, and social media activities. And some correlations here as well. What do you think?' said Levi.

'Perhaps Prisha will ask about the overall improvement compared to last year, right? So, let's add the same figures from last year and make a comparison here too,' responded Emma.

Levi and Emma, the marketing science team members at KNC – a European firm that sells trendy and quality make-up and skincare products at affordable prices for students and young professionals – sat round a modern-look, high-gloss conference table to discuss what to include in their presentation deck prior to their meeting with Prisha, the chief marketing officer (CMO) of KNC.

'I am sure that during the meeting, she will ask about each channel's contribution to final purchases. This is quite critical for next year's budget request. How about drilling down to the individual-level data and running some attribution models?' said Levi.

Emma nodded in agreement and said, 'We can show the results from the 'first-touch' and 'last-touch' heuristics, and let her decide which model to use for budget-related decisions. Most brands use the "last-touch" model, anyway.'

After a long day at work, Levi and Emma agreed on what to cover in their presentation for the CMO: an overview of digital channel performance and some detailed results from attribution modelling.

Meeting with the CMO

 'Well, these were the results from the first-touch attribution model. Now, the results from the last-touch model [Figure 4.1]. This model gives full credit to the last digital channel that consumers interacted with right before making a purchase. According to this attribution model, the least effective digital channel is "paid search". It contributes a mere 12 per cent to conversions. The most effective is mobile. It contributes 39 per cent. Affiliations surprisingly account for 27 per cent in sales conversions. Social media has a moderate impact: its contribution is 22 per cent. Therefore, we propose to reduce our efforts for paid search campaigns and increase our investments in mobile,' said Emma.

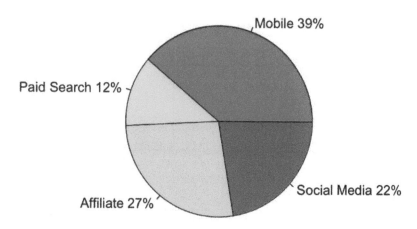

Figure 4.1 Last-touch attribution model for KNC

Prisha interrupted the presentation and said, 'I am a little bit puzzled here, Emma. It is hard to believe that the social media channel has a lower impact on consumer purchases than affiliates. Most of our targeted consumers are young adults who spend considerable time on social networks. These results are not convincing enough.'

Pointing to the title [below] of an online article from her laptop screen (Hercher, 2021), Prisha continued: 'Look at this.'

(Continued)

Goodbye, Last-Click Attribution: Google Ads Changes Default To Data Modeling

'Google won't use the last-click attribution as the default conversion model. I am not sure what exactly they mean by "data modelling", but they seem to be right in ditching the last-touch model. It is very clear that assigning full credit for a sale to the last digital channel in the consumer's path to purchase may mislead us.'

Meanwhile, as a recently graduated marketing analyst, Levi opens his laptop, digs up his analytics course content and rediscovers that there are other approaches to attribution modelling.

Inspired by his class materials, Levi responded to Prisha: 'Well, we can use more advanced models – for example, Markov chain models – to get a better picture of attribution across digital channels. Also, we can use the Shapley value-based modelling approach to quantify the effect of a channel removal. What would happen if we turn off a channel? Perhaps by turning off a particular channel we would not lose much on conversion rates...'

'Excellent suggestions,' said Prisha. 'My gut feeling is telling me that the model should assign different weights to all the touchpoints on the customer journey. Why don't you start right now? I will discuss our digital marketing budget with the board next week. So, we need to be quick on this.'

Before we delve into the attribution modelling and address the issue outlined in the case study, we will define what attribution means in the context of digital marketing and provide an overview of the common attribution models used in practice. Finally, we will show the R application of the attribution models for the case study.

INTRODUCTION

Over the past few decades, digital technology has advanced very quickly, making it easier than ever for firms to track online consumer data at the individual level. When a firm knows a specific consumer's online journey (e.g. what a consumer searched online, which affiliate website they visited, which banner ad they viewed, which social media ad they clicked on), it can use attribution modelling approach to (i) understand which touchpoints contribute to purchases made by that customer, and (ii) customize future messages to that customer to enrich their experience (e.g. which banner ad or landing page to show next). A touchpoint is defined as any point of contact where a customer interacts with a firm along their journey (de Haan, 2022).

Figure 4.2 illustrates a customer's journey over multiple touchpoints. On day 1, using her desktop computer, the customer lands on an affiliate's webpage that provides a link to KNC. A few days later, the customer sees a sponsored ad from KNC on her Instagram page (social media). The same day, the customer gets back to her desktop computer and searches for cosmetics on Google, and then clicks on KNC's pay-per-click (paid search) campaign. Finally, she decides to buy a bundle of skincare products from KNC.

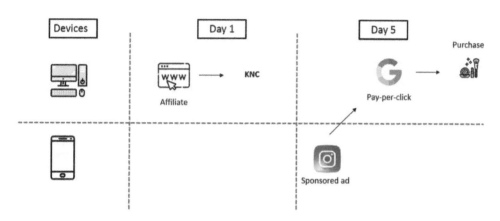

Figure 4.2 Illustration of an online customer journey

This journey is also known as the 'path to purchase' (Xu et al., 2014). In this illustration, the affiliate website, sponsored ad on Instagram and pay-per-click campaign on Google are all the touchpoints that the customer has encountered before making her purchase decision. Which touchpoints have influenced the customer's purchase decision? Which touchpoint(s) should get the credit for the sale? What is the incremental value of a touchpoint? These are important questions that form the basis for attribution modelling.

What is attribution?

Attribution is defined as the identification of a set of customer touchpoints that contribute to a desired outcome (e.g. purchase) and the assignment of credit to each of the touchpoints on the customer journey (Kannan et al., 2016). In attribution modelling, our aim is, therefore, to find the best allocation of credit for the touchpoints via analytical tools.

OVERVIEW OF ATTRIBUTION MODELS

Turning to our example in Figure 4.2, did the final purchase occur because of the affiliated marketing that started the journey? Or was it the pay-per-click campaign that triggered the purchase decision? Should the sponsored ad on Instagram get any credit for the sale? Perhaps a combination of these touchpoints led to the purchase decision. To address these allocation questions, marketers typically adopt two types of attribution models: single-touch and multi-touch attribution models.

Single-touch attribution models assign the full credit to a single touchpoint. In the first-touch attribution model, 100% credit is given to the first touchpoint on the customer journey. In Figure 4.2, affiliate marketing gets the full credit for the purchase outcome if we follow the first-touch model. However, in the last-touch attribution model, 100% credit is given to the last touchpoint. In Figure 4.2, Google's pay-per-click campaign gets the full credit for the purchase outcome if we follow the last-touch model.

Multi-touch attribution models assume that all touchpoints contribute to the purchase outcome (Shao and Li, 2011). Figure 4.3 visualizes various multi-touch attribution models used in practice. According to the *bathtub* attribution approach, the first and last touchpoints are most heavily weighted. In *even-split (linear)* attribution, all touchpoints receive an equal share. *Time-decay* attribution suggests that the touchpoint which is closest to the purchase outcome gets the highest credit and other touchpoints get credit with a decaying pattern, that is, more recent touchpoints to the purchase outcome receive higher credit than the more distant touchpoints. Finally, more advanced approaches such as *Shapley value-based* and *Markov chain* models use data-driven rather than rule-based approaches. Markov models account for complex customer paths and adjust the weights of the touchpoints on the basis of path dependencies, while the Shapley model looks for a fair partition of the outcome among the customer touchpoints via channel removal effects. Therefore, these models usually provide more accurate predictions of customers' path-to-purchase behaviour (Abhishek et al., 2012). Below we explain these models in detail.

Markov chain model

Markov chain or Markovian graph-based models allow us to explore the dependencies in the customer's path to purchase. Figure 4.4 provides a simple example of a Markov chain. At the start of her journey, the customer uses an affiliate website as the first touchpoint. Then she switches between the touchpoints and discovers various potential cosmetics to buy. Her last touch, Google's pay-per-click campaign, is likely to lead to a purchase. In this illustration, The recursive arrow, ⌒↘, denotes the own-state dependence of a touchpoint, while the double-edged arrows signify the interplay of touchpoints.

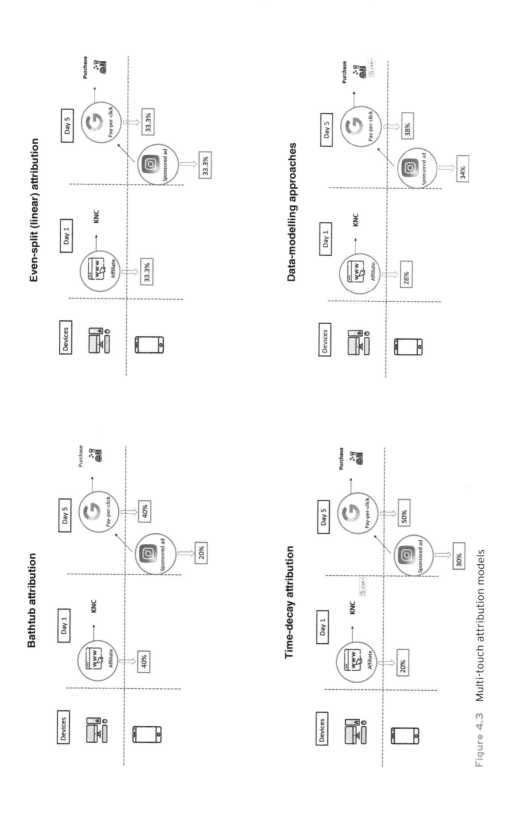

Figure 4.3   Multi-touch attribution models

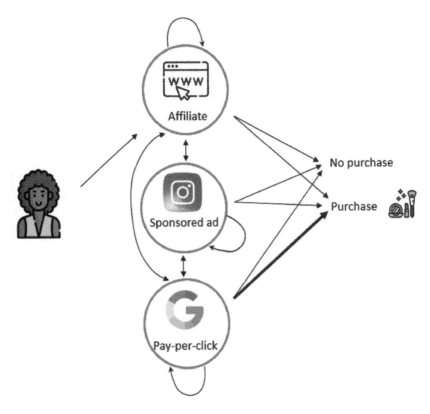

Figure 4.4 An example of a Markov chain

In essence, the Markov chain model is a probabilistic model that represents the dependencies between touchpoints over time. Hence, it helps us estimate the likelihood of a particular path converting to a purchase (Anderl et al., 2016).

Mathematically, we define a Markov chain with (i) a set of states $S = \{s_1, s_2, ...,s_n\}$ where n is the maximum number of states, and (ii) a transition matrix W represented by $w_{ij} = P(X_t = s_j | X_{t-1} = s_i)$ where X is a random variable that displays the state variable s. So, w_{ij} shows the probability of the customer being in state j given that she was in state i in the previous period. Furthermore, w_{ij} lies between 0 and 1, and the sum of the transition probabilities for each state should sum to 1, that is, $\sum_j w_{ij} = 1$ for all i.

Given the generic formulation of a Markov chain, how do we construct the state space with three touchpoints, similar to our example in Figure 4.4? Obviously, we include the three touchpoints (affiliate, sponsored ad on Instagram, Google's pay-per-click campaign) in the state space. In addition, we include three more state variables: *start*, *conversion*, and *null*: *start* is the initial touchpoint of the journey, *conversion* is the state where a purchase occurs, and *null* is the state where the journey has not ended in a purchase (Anderl et al., 2016). Thus, we can write the state space as

$$S = \{affiliate, Instagram, Google, start, conversion, null\}. \tag{4.1}$$

The concept of transition probability that we introduced above is based on the first-order Markovian process in which the current state depends only on the previous state. However, customers' online activities may suggest a longer memory, entailing a higher-order Markov chain model. When we fit a kth-order Markovian model, the transition probabilities become

$$P(X_t = s_t | X_{t-1} = s_{t-1}, ..., X_{t-k} = s_{t-k}). \tag{4.2}$$

Fitting a higher-order Markov model gives us some flexibility. However, it comes at a price: the parameter space grows very quickly as we increase the order. Therefore, with large datasets, setting the order to a small number (e.g. 3 or 4) helps increase model efficiency.

To summarize, the Markov chain model takes into account the dynamics between touchpoints and offers insights into the path dependence of customer journeys. These are important aspects that one should be aware of when developing an attribution model.

Shapley value-based attribution model

Another approach to understanding the importance of a touchpoint on the customer's journey is to remove that touchpoint from the sequence and check how much the conversion probability changes.[1] We will use the Shapley value-based approach to examine the potential impact of touchpoint removal on the outcome of the customer journey.[2]

The Shapley value-based attribution model was first introduced as a concept in cooperative game theory (Shapley, 1953). The aim of the Shapley model is to find how much each member of a team contributes to the end result of a game. The model has been used in a wide range of applications since it was developed, including feature selection in machine learning and teamwork assessment in organizations. In digital advertising, we use the Shapley value-based approach to quantify the attribution of a customer touchpoint to a conversion. Touchpoints in a customer journey can be thought of as players that jointly produce an output (e.g. purchase). Thus, using the Shapley model, we can attribute the model prediction (i.e. conversion probability) to each of the customer touchpoints.

---

[1]Removal of a touchpoint may push customers to other existing channels and therefore cause a significant change in the sequential steps of the customer journey. In practice, such actions should be taken only after a careful strategic analysis.
[2]Markov chain models can also be used to find the removal effects of customer touchpoints (see de Haan, 2022).

How to compute Shapley values

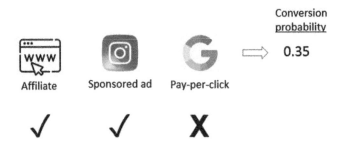

Figure 4.5 Touchpoint removal effect

Suppose that for a certain customer we predict the conversion probability to be 0.35. The customer used the affiliate website and the sponsored ad on Instagram but did not encounter the pay-per-click campaign (see Figure 4.5). Furthermore, we find that the average conversion probability for this customer is 0.70. We wonder how much each touchpoint value contributes to the prediction of 0.35 compared to the average prediction of 0.70. Using the Shapley value-based approach, we would like to explain the difference in conversion probability (i.e. 0.70 – 0.35). For example, it could be that the affiliate website contributes 0.10, the Instagram ad contributes 0.25, and Google's campaign contributes nothing. In this example, the affiliate website and Instagram ad were in a coalition or a subset. To compute the marginal contribution of Google's pay-per-click campaign, we consider all the possible subsets. These are: (i) no touchpoint, (ii) affiliate, (iii) Instagram ad, and (iv) affiliate and Instagram ad.[3] For each of these subsets, we compute the conversion probabilities with and without the Google campaign and take the difference to obtain the marginal contribution. Finally, the Shapley value for Google's pay-per-click campaign is the average of marginal contributions.

In a more general form, the Shapley value, $\phi_j(v)$, is defined as follows (Molnar, 2022):

$$\phi_j(v) = \sum_S \frac{|S|!(n-|S|-1)!}{n!}\left(v\left(S \cup \{j\}\right) - v\left(S\right)\right), \quad j = 1,2,\ldots,n. \tag{4.3}$$

This equation shows that the customer journey has n touchpoints, $j = 1,2,\ldots,n$. S is the subset of customer touchpoints, $v(S)$ is the predicted conversion probability achieved by subset S, and $v(S \cup \{j\})$ is the predicted conversion probability when the touchpoint j joins the subset S. Thus, for a given touchpoint j, we take the sum over all the subsets S that exclude touchpoint j, and compute the contribution ϕ of touchpoint j via the value function v.

---

[3] In this example, each touchpoint takes either a 'yes' or 'no' value. In other applications, each of these touchpoints may have different values. For instance, 'affiliate website' may be a touchpoint with more than two values: affiliate 1, affiliate 2, affiliate 3, and so on. In such cases, subsets should be formed considering all the possible values of each touchpoint.

It is important to note that the touchpoint effects that we find through the Shapley model are not causal because (i) some consumers in the dataset may already have a higher tendency to purchase, and (ii) touchpoints do not typically occur at random (de Haan, 2022). To find the causal effect of a touchpoint, firms are encouraged to run field experiments where consumers are randomly assigned to control and treatment groups. Hoban and Bucklin (2015) provide more details on the causal effects and attribution models.

Reviewing these models, one may ask how to choose an attribution model. To decide a suitable attribution model, firms can consider either their strategic objectives (e.g. increasing brand awareness in social media) or model performance (e.g. predictive ability) along with the use of managerial intuition.

Next, we demonstrate the R applications of the attribution models covered in this chapter to the KNC case study.

MODEL APPLICATIONS WITH R

This section guides the reader through the R application. Although we present the step-by-step instructions alongside the software screenshots here, we encourage the reader to go through these notes together with the R Markdown file which is provided on the website of the book.

The R application below helps us address the following questions on the KNC case study:

- Taking a path-to-purchase view, which customer touchpoint contributes to conversion?[4]
- Should KNC give up on paid search and put more effort into mobile marketing?
- Which attribution modelling approach should the KNC marketing analysts, Levi and Emma, adopt in the future?

Preparation and set-up

Before we roll out the analyses, we need to make sure that all our files are organized, and our R environment is set up. To do so, we follow the steps below:

- Create a folder and set the working directory to that folder on our device.
- Install and load the R packages needed for this application.
- Download the dataset to our working directory.

Create a folder and set a working directory

We create a folder on our computer and name it *attribution*. Then we launch RStudio and open a new R Markdown file. From the upper left menu of our RStudio screen, we choose *File>New File>R Markdown*.

---

[4]In this R application, the words 'channel' and 'touchpoint' are used interchangeably.

Next, we set the working directory in our R Markdown file. The following code chunk shows how to set the working directory.

```
```{r warning=FALSE}
# Run the following codes depending on the operating system on your
laptop/PC.

# If you are using iOS and your 'attribution' folder is created under
'Downloads' on your Mac' you will need to first set your working
directory to the 'attribution' folder:

setwd("~/Downloads/attribution")

# If you are using Windows and your 'attribution' folder is created in
your H drive, you will need to first set your working directory to
the 'attribution' folder:

#setwd("H:/downloads/attribution")
```
```

Depending on the operating system of our device, we run only part of the code from the above code chunk. To avoid running the codes that are not applicable and receiving error messages, we add the # symbol before each line of non-applicable codes. For example, if we use a Mac computer, we need to put # before the code `setwd("H:/downloads/attribution")`.

Install and load R packages

The next step is to install the R packages. The following code chunk does this task.

```
```{r, eval=TRUE, error=FALSE, warning=FALSE, message=FALSE}

if (!require("knitr")) install.packages("knitr", repos = "http://
cran.us.r-project.org")
if (!require("kableExtra")) install.packages("kableExtra",repos = "http://
cran.us.r-project.org")
if (!require("readxl")) install.packages("readxl",repos = "http://
cran.us.r-project.org")
if (!require("dplyr"))install.packages("dplyr", repos = "http://
cran.us.r-project.org")
if (!require("ChannelAttribution")) install.packages("ChannelAttribution",
repos = "http://cran.us.r-project.org")
if (!require("devtools")) install.packages("devtools",repos = "http://
cran.us.r-project.org")
```
```

```
if (!require("reshape2")) install.packages("reshape2",repos = "http://
cran.us.r-project.org")
if (!require("ggplot2")) install.packages("ggplot2",repos = "http://
cran.us.r-project.org")
if (!require("ggthemes")) install.packages("ggthemes",repos = "http://
cran.us.r-project.org")
if (!require("ggrepel")) install.packages("ggrepel",repos = "http://
cran.us.r-project.org")
if (!require("RColorBrewer")) install.packages("RColorBrewer",repos = "http://
cran.us.r-project.org")
if (!require("markovchain")) install.packages("markovchain",repos ="http://
cran.us.r-project.org")


```
```

Once the packages are installed on our computer, we should load them into R with the following code chunk.

```
```{r, eval=TRUE, error=FALSE, warning=FALSE, message=FALSE}

library(knitr)
library(kableExtra)
library(readxl)
library(dplyr)
library(ChannelAttribution)
library(devtools)
library(reshape2)
library(ggplot2)
library(ggthemes)
library(ggrepel)
library(RColorBrewer)
library(markovchain)


```
```

Next, we will load the dataset.

Consumer path-to-purchase data

The dataset of this case study is available on the book's website. The file is named *knc_attribution* and is stored in CSV format. We run the following code chunk to load the dataset into R.
```

```r
```{r}
# load the dataset

attribution<- read.csv(file = "knc_attribution.csv",header = TRUE)
```
```

In the upper right corner of the RStudio screen, we click on 'attribution' and see the data spreadsheet as shown in Figure 4.6.

users_id	channel1	channel2	channel3	channel4	channel5	channel6	channel7	channel8	channel9	channel10	channel11
1	1	mobile	paid_search	paid_search	paid_search	affiliate	mobile	paid_search	paid_search	social_media	mobile	social_media
2	2	paid_search	mobile	mobile	paid_search	affiliate	paid_search	mobile	paid_search	mobile	mobile	paid_search
3	3	social_media	social_media	mobile	affiliate	social_media	paid_search	mobile	mobile	affiliate		
4	4	mobile	affiliate	mobile	social_media	affiliate	mobile	social_media	mobile			
5	5	paid_search	paid_search	affiliate	paid_search	mobile	paid_search	paid_search	affiliate	mobile	affiliate	paid_search
6	6	mobile	mobile	social_media	social_media	affiliate	affiliate	paid_search	mobile	social_media	affiliate	affiliate
7	7	paid_search	mobile	paid_search	mobile	paid_search	paid_search	social_media	affiliate	paid_search	mobile	mobile
8	8	affiliate	paid_search	paid_search	mobile	affiliate	social_media	mobile	paid_search	social_media	mobile	paid_search
9	9	affiliate	paid_search	affiliate	paid_search	social_media	mobile	social_media	paid_search	social_media	affiliate	social_media
10	10	affiliate	paid_search	affiliate	paid_search	affiliate	affiliate	affiliate	affiliate	affiliate	mobile	affiliate
11	11	affiliate	paid_search	affiliate	social_media	social_media	mobile	mobile	paid_search	mobile		
12	12	social_media	paid_search	social_media	paid_search	mobile	affiliate	paid_search	mobile	paid_search	social_media	affiliate
13	13	paid_search	social_media	mobile	social_media	social_media	affiliate					
14	14	paid_search	paid_search	social_media	mobile	mobile	mobile	paid_search	affiliate	affiliate	paid_search	mobile
15	15	mobile	social_media	affiliate	paid_search	social_media	mobile	affiliate	paid_search	paid_search	mobile	
16	16	mobile	paid_search	paid_search	paid_search	affiliate	mobile	paid_search	paid_search	social_media	mobile	social_media
17	17	paid_search	mobile	mobile	paid_search	affiliate	social_media	mobile	paid_search	mobile	mobile	paid_search
18	18	social_media	social_media	mobile	affiliate	social_media	paid_search	mobile	mobile	affiliate		
19	19	mobile	affiliate	mobile	social_media	affiliate	mobile	social_media	mobile			
20	20	paid_search	paid_search	affiliate	social_media	mobile	paid_search	paid_search	affiliate	mobile	affiliate	paid_search
21	21	mobile	mobile	social_media	social_media	affiliate	affiliate	paid_search	mobile	social_media	affiliate	affiliate
22	22	paid_search	mobile	paid_search	mobile	paid_search	paid_search	social_media	affiliate	paid_search	mobile	mobile
23	23	affiliate	paid_search	paid_search	mobile	affiliate	social_media	mobile	paid_search	social_media	mobile	paid_search

Showing 1 to 23 of 105 entries, 48 total columns

Figure 4.6 Attribution data

A close look at the data suggests that we have 105 unique online consumer journeys, of which 89 turned into purchases. This corresponds to a conversion rate of 85%. Note that this figure is quite high. We typically observe such high conversion rates around heavy promotional times.

Next, we would like to see the variables of the dataset and their descriptions. The following code chunk gives the output in Figure 4.7.

```r
```{r echo=FALSE}
var_desc<- data.frame(
  Variable = c("users_id", "channeln", "user_purchase", "null_purchase"),
  Description = c("Unique user ID", "Online advertising (i.e., mobile,
paid search, affiliate, and social media) exposure path, with channel1
referring to the first exposure, channel2 the second, …, channeln the
nth (maximum number of exposure = 45).", "Consumer final conversion
indicator, which takes value of 1 if a specific consumer made purchase
```
```

```
(i.e., converted) at the end of her path, and 0 otherwise.", "The
opposite of 'user_purchase', taking value of 1 if there is no purchase
and 0 otherwise.")
  )

var_desc %>%
  kbl() %>%
  kable_styling

```
```

Variable	Description
users_id	Unique user ID
channeln	Online advertising (i.e., mobile, paid search, affiliate, and social media) exposure path, with channel1 referring to the first exposure, channel2 the second, ..., channeln the nth (maximum number of exposure = 45).
user_purchase	Consumer final conversion indicator, which takes value of 1 if a specific consumer made purchase (i.e., converted) at the end of her path, and 0 otherwise.
null_purchase	The opposite of 'user_purchase', taking value of 1 if there is no purchase and 0 otherwise.

Figure 4.7   Variable descriptions

Having had a glimpse of the data, we can start running the attribution models. We will begin with the Markov chain modelling approach.

Markov chain approach

To estimate the Markov model, first we will prepare the data.

Data preparation

To estimate a Markov chain model, we use the ChannelAttribution package in R. We start by knitting consumer advertising exposures into a desired *sequenced path* format for the analysis. The following code generates *conversion sequences* for all consumers.

```{r}

# Construct conversions sequences for all visitors

attribution[is.na(attribution)] <- " "

attribution$path = paste(attribution$channel1,attribution$channel2,a
ttribution$channel3,attribution$channel4,attribution$channel5,attrib
ution$channel6,attribution$channel7,attribution$channel8,attribution
```
```

```
$channel9,attribution$channel10,attribution$channel11,attribution$c
hannel12,attribution$channel13,attribution$channel14,attribution$c
hannel15,attribution$channel16,attribution$channel17,attribution$c
hannel8,attribution$channel9,attribution$channel20,attribution$chan
nel21,attribution$channel22,attribution$channel23,attribution$chan
nel24,attribution$channel25,attribution$channel26,attribution$chann
el27,attribution$channel28,attribution$channel29,attribution$channe
l30,attribution$channel31,attribution$channel32,attribution$channel
33,attribution$channel34,attribution$channel35,attribution$channel3
6,attribution$channel37,attribution$channel38,attribution$channel39
,attribution$channel40,attribution$channel41,attribution$channel42,
attribution$channel43,attribution$channel44,attribution$channel45,
sep=">")

path <- gsub("\\s.*","", attribution$path)
attribution$cleaned_path <-gsub("\\W$","", path)
```
```

If we look at the dataset again, we see that there is a new variable created, called cleaned_path.
Now let us look at the paths of the first five consumers in our dataset. The following code
chunk produces the output in Figure 4.8.

```{r}

# take a look at the data

data_view <- attribution [1:5,50]
data_view %>%
  kable() %>%
  kable_styling()

```

Figure 4.8 Examples of consumer journeys
```

We can already observe some heterogeneity across consumers in terms of starting touchpoint (i.e. first touch), ending touchpoint before (non-)conversion (i.e. last touch), and composition and length of paths.

For model estimation, we decide to take the first 80 consumers in the dataset as our training set and keep the remaining 25 observations for the test set. The following code chunk shows the data split into training and test sets.

```{r}
# define training and testing set

attribution_train <-attribution[1:80,]
attribution_test <-attribution[81:105,]

```

As a final preparatory step, we need to create a *channel stack*, through which we summarize consumer paths and calculate the total number of conversions (frequency) and non-conversions for each path pattern. The following code chunk helps us generate the channel stack output in Figure 4.9.

```{r}
channel_stack = attribution_train %>%
  group_by(cleaned_path) %>%
  summarize(conversion = sum(user_purchase),non_conversion =
sum(null_purchase)) %>%

collect()

# Take a look at the prepared dataset

data_view <- channel_stack [1:10,]
data_view %>%
  kable() %>%
  kable_styling()

```

cleaned_path
affiliate>mobile>affiliate>social_media>social_media>mobile>mobile>mobile>mobile>>>>>>>>mobile>mobile>>>>>>>>>>>>
affiliate>paid_search>affiliate>paid_search>affiliate>affiliate>affiliate>affiliate>affiliate>mobile>affiliate>paid_search>paid_se
affiliate>paid_search>affiliate>paid_search>mobile>mobile>paid_search>paid_search>mobile>affiliate>affiliate>paid_search>
affiliate>paid_search>affiliate>paid_search>social_media>mobile>social_media>paid_search>social_media>affiliate>social_n
affiliate>paid_search>affiliate>social_media>social_media>mobile>mobile>paid_search>mobile>>>>>>>>paid_search>mobil
affiliate>paid_search>paid_search>mobile>affiliate>social_media>mobile>paid_search>social_media>mobile>paid_search>m
mobile>affiliate>mobile>social_media>affiliate>mobile>social_media>mobile>>>>>>>>mobile>>>>>>>>>>>>>>>>>>>>>>
mobile>mobile>affiliate>paid_search>affiliate>mobile>affiliate>paid_search>paid_search>mobile>>>>>>>>paid_search>paid_
mobile>mobile>social_media>social_media>affiliate>affiliate>paid_search>mobile>social_media>affiliate>affiliate>mobile>p
mobile>paid_search>affiliate>paid_search>mobile>mobile>affiliate>paid_search>paid_search>mobile>>>>>>>>paid_search>p

Figure 4.9   Channel stack

Now we are ready to estimate the Markov chain model with the cleaned version of our data.

Markov chain modelling

To estimate the Markov chain model, we use the `markov_model` function. Specifically, we estimate a third-order Markov model so that the *memory* of the chain goes back to the most recent three states. Our assumption here is that consumer journeys typically cannot be restricted to the most recent state, that is, consumers have a longer memory. Recall that first-order Markov model assumes that the current state is only determined by the previous or the most recent state. The following code chunk estimates the third-order Markov chain model and generates the output shown in Figure 4.10.

```{r}
# Third-order Markov chain model

markov = markov_model(channel_stack, "cleaned_path", "conversion",
order=3)

table_markov<-data.frame(channel = markov$channel_name,total_conversions
=round(markov$total_conversions), percent =
round(markov$total_conversions/sum(attribution_train$user_purchase),3))

table_markov
```

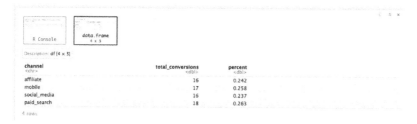

Figure 4.10   Third-order Markov chain model estimation

The results based on Markov chain model tell us quite a different story compared to what the KNC analysts found using the last-touch heuristic. The Markov chain model informs us that:

- The four touchpoints do not differ dramatically from each other in effectiveness in driving conversions.
- Both social media advertising and affiliate advertising contribute around 24% to conversion, while both paid search and mobile channels contribute around 26%.

To further make sense of what we have found, we can obtain the transition probabilities between all states through the following code chunk.

```{r}
# Transition Matrix of order 3

trans_3rd_order<-transition_matrix(attribution_train, var_path =
"cleaned_path", var_conv = "user_purchase", var_null = "null_purchase",
order=3, sep=">", flg_equal=TRUE)

```

To build the transition matrix of the third-order Markov model, we obtain the transition prob-abilities to *conversion state* using three-channel paths. The following code chunk performs this task and yields the output in Figure 4.11. For example, we can see that consumers with social media > paid search > affiliate as last three channel exposures have the highest conversion probability ($p = 0.455$).

```{r echo=FALSE}

markov_result <-
data.frame(channel_3rd_order=c("social_network>paid_search>affiliate",
"mobile>social_media>mobile", "mobile>mobile>mobile",
"mobile>mobile>affiliate", "paid_search>affiliate>mobile",
```

```
"social_media>affiliate>social_media","social_media>social_media>affiliate",
"social_media>social_media>mobile", "social_media>mobile>affiliate",
"mobile>mobile>paid_search", "mobile>paid_search>paid_search",
"paid_search>paid_search>mobile", "mobile>paid_search>mobile",
"paid_search>paid_search>social_media","paid_search>mobile>paid_search"),
transition_probability=c(0.455, 0.273, 0.250, 0.238, 0.227, 0.200, 0.190,
0.161, 0.156, 0.125, 0.116, 0.100, 0.097, 0.09,0.086) )


markov_result


` ` `
```

channel_3rd_order <chr>	transition_probability <dbl>
social_network>paid_search>affiliate	0.455
mobile>social_media>mobile	0.273
mobile>mobile>mobile	0.250
mobile>mobile>affiliate	0.238
paid_search>affiliate>mobile	0.227
social_media>affiliate>social_media	0.200
social_media>social_media>affiliate	0.190
social_media>social_media>mobile	0.161
social_media>mobile>affiliate	0.156
mobile>mobile>paid_search	0.125

1-10 of 15 rows

Figure 4.11   Three-channel transition probabilities

We can imagine that such a path might appropriately describe teenagers' consumer behaviour online. They are attracted by fancy social network advertising on Instagram or Facebook. Then they click on paid search advertising to get further information about the product. Later, they are further enticed by repeatedly browsing on affiliate websites, and finally decide to purchase the latest beauty product of KNC.

> **Question**. Considering the Markov transition matrix and path-to-conversion output in Figure 4.11, can you try to infer why we have such different conclusions about *social media* and *affiliate* channel contributions based on Markov chain and last-touch modelling approaches?

Visualizations

Markov graph

A Markov graph helps us further understand the paths that consumers in our dataset have taken towards conversion and non-conversion. We could plot a Markov graph for the third-order Markov chain model that we have just estimated. However, due to the complexity in the visual representation of the third-order model, here we obtain a graph of the first-order Markov chain model to illustrate how to interpret such graphs from Markov chain models.

Running the following code chunks gets us a nice-looking Markov graph (Figure 4.12).

```r
```{r}

# Estimate a first-order Markov Model to plot Markov graph for
illustration

trans_1st<-transition_matrix(attribution_train, var_path = "
cleaned_path", var_conv = "user_purchase", var_null = "null_purchase",
order=1, sep=">", flg_equal=TRUE)

trans_matrix_1st <-trans_1st$transition_matrix

df_dummy <- data.frame(channel_from = c('(start)', '(conversion)',
'(null)'),channel_to = c('(start)', '(conversion)', '(null)'),
transition_probability = c(0,1,1))

trans_matrix_1st <-rbind(trans_matrix_1st, df_dummy)

trans_matrix_1st$channel_from <-factor(trans_matrix_1st$channel_from,
levels = c('(start)', '(conversion)', '(null)', '1','2','3','4'))
trans_matrix_1st$channel_to <-factor(trans_matrix_1st$channel_to,
levels =c('(start)', '(conversion)', '(null)', '1','2','3','4'))

trans_matrix_1st <-dcast(trans_matrix_1st, channel_from~channel_to,
value.var = 'transition_probability')

trans_matrix_final <- matrix(data = as.matrix(trans_matrix_1st[, -1]),
nrow = nrow(trans_matrix_1st[, -1]), ncol=ncol(trans_matrix_1st[,-1]),
dimnames = list(c(as.character(trans_matrix_1st[,1])),
c(colnames(trans_matrix_1st[,-1])))))

trans_matrix_final[is.na(trans_matrix_final)] <-0
trans_matrix1 <- new("markovchain", transitionMatrix =
trans_matrix_final)

```

```{r fig, fig.height = 15, fig.width = 10, fig.align = "center"}

# Plot the Markov graph
plot(trans_matrix1, edge.arrow.siz=0.01, main="Markov Graph",
fill=c("yellow") )

```
```

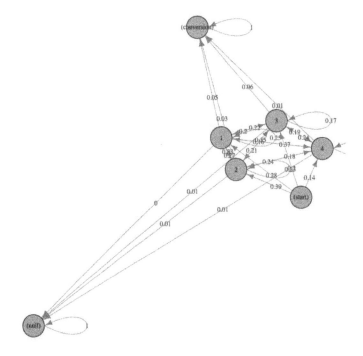

Figure 4.12 Markov graph

In the Markov graph:

- Nodes 1, 2, 3, and 4 refer to mobile, paid search, affiliate, and social media advertising, respectively.
- The 'conversion' and 'null' nodes refer to conversion and non-conversion, respectively.
- The 'start' node represents a starting point for all paths, as requested by the plotting package that we use.
- Arrows point from the 'departure' node (i.e. the $(n-1)$th channel) to the 'arrival' node (i.e. the nth channel).
- The numeric value along an arrow pointing from node i to node j is the transition probability of a customer exposed first to channel i and then to channel j.

Looking at the graph, the probability of purchase for a consumer with a simple path of *start* > *paid_search* > *conversion* is 0.41 × 0.03 = 0.0123, since the transition probability from *start* to *paid search* is 0.41, and that from *paid search* to *conversion* is 0.03.

Transition heatmap

We may also want to create a *heatmap* for the transition matrix of our estimated Markov model. The following code chunk generates the heatmap output in Figure 4.13.

```r
```{r}

df_plot_trans <-trans_1st$transition_matrix
# If you prefer a map with 3rd order Markov chain, you may simply run the
following line of code instead of the one above:
#df_plot_trans <-trans_3rd_order$transition_matrix

# Start setting up plotting index

cols <- c("#e7f0fa", "#c9e2f6", "#95cbee", "#0099dc", "#4ab04a",
"#ffd73e", "#eec73a",
          "#e29421")
t <- max(trans_1st$transition_matrix$transition_probability)

ggplot(df_plot_trans, aes(y = channel_from, x = channel_to, fill =
transition_probability)) +
        theme_minimal() +
        geom_tile(colour = "white", width = .9, height = .9) +
        scale_fill_gradientn(colours = cols, limits = c(0, t),
                             breaks = seq(0, t, by = t/4),
                             labels = c("0", round(t/4*1, 2),
round(t/4*2, 2), round(t/4*3, 2), round(t/4*4, 2)),
                             guide = guide_colourbar(ticks = T, nbin =
50, barheight = .5, label = T, barwidth = 10)) +
        geom_text(aes(label = round(transition_probability, 2)), fontface
 = "bold", size = 4) +
        theme(legend.position = 'bottom',
              legend.direction = "horizontal",
              panel.grid.major = element_blank(),
              panel.grid.minor = element_blank(),
              plot.title = element_text(size = 14, face = "bold", vjust =
2, color = 'black', lineheight = 0.8),
              axis.title.x = element_text(size = 12, face = "bold"),
              axis.title.y = element_text(size = 12, face = "bold"),
              axis.text.y = element_text(size = 12, face = "bold", color
= 'black'),
              axis.text.x = element_text(size = 12, angle = 90, hjust =
0.5, vjust = 0.5, face = "plain")) +
        ggtitle("Transition matrix heatmap")

```
```

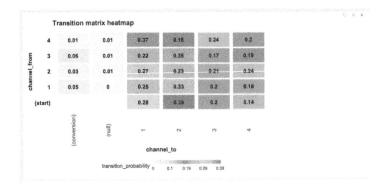

Figure 4.13 Transition matrix heatmap

In the transition matrix heatmap, the rows represent the *starting point* and the columns represent the *end point* of each one-step transition. From this heatmap, we can reach the same conclusions as from the Markov graph. Note that there are no rows representing *conversion* or *null* states in the matrix because in our setting there are no paths starting from a *conversion* or starting from a *non-conversion* state. That is also why the cells referring to the transition from *start* to *conversion* and *null* are empty.

Model comparison

We would like to see the difference in outcomes of the traditional heuristic approaches (i.e. first touch, last touch) and the model-based approach (i.e. Markov chain). We first use the `heuristic_models` function to obtain results for the heuristic models. The following code chunk performs this task and obtains the output in Figure 4.14.

```{r warning=FALSE}
# Heuristic Models

heuristic_models(channel_stack, "cleaned_path", "conversion", NULL, sep = ">")

```

Description: df [4 × 4]

channel_name <chr>	first_touch <dbl>	last_touch <dbl>	linear_touch <dbl>
affiliate	14	23	14.80225
mobile	17	24	19.23514
social_media	8	4	14.13698
paid_search	28	16	18.82563

4 rows

Figure 4.14 Heuristic models

Note that the output of `heuristic_models` also includes the linear touch model. As explained previously in the chapter, the linear (even-split) touch model is a simple heuristic model that assumes that each channel contributes to final conversion equally. We do not discuss this specific model in this chapter as it is not of interest to KNC.

Next, we summarize the model results of all three models into one table by running the following code chunk.

```{r}
table_summary <- data.frame(Item = c("Mobile","Paid Search",
"Affiliate", "Social Media"), First_Touch = round(c(17, 28, 14, 8)/67,3),
Last_Touch= round(c(26, 15, 18, 8)/67,3), Markov_Chain = c(0.260, 0.245,
0.238, 0.257))


table_summary

```

Description: df [4 x 4]

Item <chr>	First_Touch <dbl>	Last_Touch <dbl>	Markov_Chain <dbl>
Mobile	0.254	0.388	0.260
Paid Search	0.418	0.224	0.245
Affiliate	0.209	0.269	0.238
Social Media	0.119	0.119	0.257

4 rows

Figure 4.15 Model comparison

Figure 4.15 suggests that one can reach very different conclusions by adopting the first-touch, last-touch, and Markov chain approaches. Such difference is even clearer if we contrast model results by plotting a bar chart. The following code chunk plots the bar chart in Figure 4.16.

```{r}

# create a dataset
method <- c(rep("First Touch",4), rep("Last Touch",4), rep("Markov
chain",4))
channel <- rep(c("Mobile", "Paid Search", "Affiliate", "Social Media"),
3)
value <- c(0.254, 0.418, 0.209, 0.119, 0.388, 0.224, 0.269,
0.119,0.260,0.245, 0.238, 0.257)
```

```
data <- data.frame(method,channel,value)
# Stacked + percent
ggplot(data, aes(fill=channel, y=value, x=method)) +
    geom_bar(position="fill", stat="identity")

```
```
```

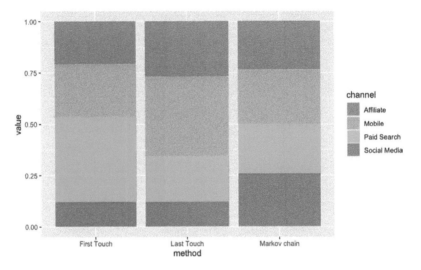

Figure 4.16 Model comparison using a bar chart

While the first-touch model guides KNC to invest more in paid search and less in social media, the last-touch model would suggest that mobile advertising has a strong influence. Finally, the Markov graph approach suggests that the contributions made by all four touchpoints are actually quite similar.

Which model should KNC choose?

There are two strategies available for KNC when deciding which model to choose:

1. KNC should try to make sense of these results first. Prisha can combine the model-based evidence with her managerial intuition. Given her concerns about single-touch-based models, Prisha is advised to make her next budget allocation decisions based on the Markov chain model output. At the end of the experimental period, she can assess whether there is a significant improvement in conversion rates.
2. An alternative approach would be to assess the predictive power of attribution models by using a larger dataset. Research on attribution models demonstrates that Markov

chain models provide a fairer allocation of weights to channels and perform better than heuristic (e.g. first-touch and last-touch) methods in predicting conversion rates because they take into account the interplay across touchpoints and sequentiality in a customer journey (Anderl et al., 2016). In the appendix to this chapter, we illustrate how the predictive performance of these models can be assessed using the current dataset. In our illustration, the Markov model performs better than heuristic methods. However, we take those results with a pinch of salt because some paths to purchase occur only a few times in the test set, which may make conversion probabilities less reliable.

What if a touchpoint were removed from the path to purchase?

What would happen to the conversion rate if a particular channel were removed from the path to-purchase? To address this question, we will use the Shapley value-based approach. This allows us to evaluate the relative importance of a customer touchpoint to conversion.

Using mobile marketing as an example, we will calculate the drop in conversion probability. The scale of the drop will be the importance of mobile marketing in converting customers. Specifically, we will calculate the following:

$$\frac{No.\ of\ conversions}{No.\ of\ observations} - \frac{No.\ of\ conversions_{nomobile}}{No.of\ observations_{nomobile}}.$$

We do the same for each of the four touchpoints in the dataset.

The following code chunk searches whether each of the paths contains mobile, paid search, affiliate, and social media or not. Then it generates four indicator variables.

```{r}
# Search if each of the paths contains mobile, paid search, affiliate,
and social media or not, and generate four indicator variables.

channel_stack$with_mobile =
grepl(x=channel_stack$cleaned_path,pattern="mobile")
channel_stack$with_paid_search =
grepl(x=channel_stack$cleaned_path,pattern="paid_search")
channel_stack$with_affiliate =
grepl(x=channel_stack$cleaned_path,pattern="affiliate")
channel_stack$with_social_media =
grepl(x=channel_stack$cleaned_path,pattern="social_media")

channel_stack$no_mobile_conversion<-ifelse
(channel_stack$with_mobile=="FALSE", channel_stack$conversion,0)
channel_stack$no_mobile_count<-ifelse
(channel_stack$with_mobile=="FALSE",channel_stack$conversion+
channel_stack$non_conversion,0)
```

```
channel_stack$no_paidsearch_conversion<-ifelse
(channel_stack$with_paid_search=="FALSE", channel_stack$conversion,0)
channel_stack$no_paidsearch_count<-ifelse
(channel_stack$with_paid_search=="FALSE", channel_stack$conversion+
channel_stack$non_conversion,0)

channel_stack$no_affiliate_conversion<-ifelse (
channel_stack$with_affiliate=="FALSE", channel_stack$conversion,0)
channel_stack$no_affiliate_count<-ifelse (
channel_stack$with_affiliate=="FALSE", channel_stack$conversion+
channel_stack$non_conversion,0)

channel_stack$no_social_media_conversion<-ifelse
(channel_stack$with_social_media=="FALSE", channel_stack$conversion,0)
channel_stack$no_social_media_count<-ifelse
(channel_stack$with_social_media=="FALSE", channel_stack$conversion+
channel_stack$non_conversion,0)

```
```

Next, we compute the Shapley values for each customer touchpoint and convert them to proportions See the code chunks below.

```{r}
# get Shapley values for each touchpoint

shapley_mobile<-(sum(channel_stack$conversion)/105)-(67-
sum(channel_stack$no_mobile_conversion))/(105-
sum(channel_stack$no_mobile_count))
shapley_paidsearch<-(sum(channel_stack$conversion)/105)-(67-
sum(channel_stack$no_paidsearch_conversion))/(105-
sum(channel_stack$no_paidsearch_count))
shapley_affiliate<-sum(channel_stack$conversion)/105-(67-
sum(channel_stack$no_affiliate_conversion))/(105-
sum(channel_stack$no_affiliate_count))
shapley_socialmedia<-sum(channel_stack$conversion)/105-(67-
sum(channel_stack$no_social_media_conversion))/(105-
sum(channel_stack$no_social_media_count))

shapley_mobile
shapley_paidsearch
```
```

```
shapley_affiliate
shapley_socialmedia
```

```
```{r}
# converting Shapley values to percentage terms

shapley_mobile_pct<-
shapley_mobile/(shapley_mobile+shapley_paidsearch+shapley_affiliate
+shapley_socialmedia)
shapley_paidsearch_pct <-
shapley_paidsearch/(shapley_mobile+shapley_paidsearch+shapley_affiliate
+shapley_socialmedia)
shapley_affiliate_pct<-
shapley_affiliate/(shapley_mobile+shapley_paidsearch+shapley_affiliate
+shapley_socialmedia)
shapley_socialmedia_pct<-
shapley_socialmedia/(shapley_mobile+shapley_paidsearch+shapley_affiliate
+shapley_socialmedia)

shapley_mobile_pct
shapley_paidsearch_pct
shapley_affiliate_pct
shapley_socialmedia_pct

```
```

```
[1] 0.3238919
[1] 0.3238919
[1] 0.1058878
[1] 0.2463284
```

Figure 4.17   Shapley values

The output from the Shapley model in Figure 4.17 suggests that the impact of mobile and paid search advertising is the largest because they are associated with the largest drop in conversion percentage, followed by social media, and then affiliate. Thus, removing mobile and paid search channels would not be an appropriate action for KNC. Our further advice to Prisha is that she needs to evaluate the strategic implications of a channel removal very carefully with a forward-looking perspective because consumers may be pushed to other touchpoints (e.g. paid search), which may result in higher costs to KNC. Finally, the conclusions from the Shapley model are not causal. To understand the causal impact of a channel removal, randomized field experiments should be undertaken, in which consumers are randomly assigned to control and treatment groups.

Overall, the marketing group at KNC should proceed as follows:

- KNC should analyse and predict consumer conversion by switching from first- and last-touch heuristic approaches to the Markov chain model.
- Instead of downgrading their emphasis on affiliate and social media advertising, KNC should keep investing in all of the customer touchpoints.
- KNC can use the Shapley value-based modelling approach to quantify the potential impact of a channel removal on consumers' purchases. However, the removal of a channel (e.g. social media) may result in significant changes in the customer journey. Consumers may be pushed to other touchpoints (e.g. paid search) that might be more costly to the firm. Therefore, the findings from the Shapley model should always be combined with a careful strategic analysis. For instance, even though the model finds zero contribution for the social media channel, the manager may still want to be present on social media to increase brand awareness in the market.
- KNC should bear in mind that results obtained from these models do not imply causality. To understand the causal impact of a touchpoint on the relevant performance metrics, KNC should run randomized field experiments.

Challenges with attribution

The implementation of attribution models presents a number of challenges as well. For example, it is difficult to account for the fact that each customer may use multiple devices (de Haan et al., 2016). Furthermore, the evolution of data privacy and regulations (e.g. Apple ITP, GDPR) makes it very difficult to track all the touchpoints of a user and obtain representative individual-level data to draw conclusions on the effectiveness of digital advertising channels. Finally, adopting the attribution modelling approach requires a strong cross-functional collaboration (e.g. data input from finance, marketing, and operations) within an organization, which may sometimes be difficult.

CHAPTER SUMMARY

In this chapter, we focused on one of the essential digital marketing tools for marketers: attribution modelling. Attribution models, in general, allow marketers to (i) assess the contribution of different digital touchpoints along the customer's journey using individual-level data, (ii) tailor future marketing communications to each individual consumer, and (iii) uncover new insights into digital consumer behaviour.

We began the chapter with a mini case study on KNC, a firm that sells beauty products. The case study illustrated the importance of attribution modelling from a managerial point of view. Next, we defined attribution modelling and described the main attribution models used in practice. Finally, we demonstrated the application of the attribution models with R to the case study.

There are a few important takeaways from this chapter. First, single-touch heuristic attribution models (e.g. first-touch, last-touch) ignore the fact that all the touchpoints on a customer journey may have an impact on the final outcome. Thus, we need more advanced models (e.g. Markov chain) that can capture the dynamics of the customer journey better and produce a fairer allocation of weights to different touchpoints. Second, it is always possible to build a more sophisticated attribution model (e.g. increasing the order for Markovian models) that mimics the customer journey. However, we should always remind ourselves that attribution models are simple illustrations of complex customer journeys. If we increase the complexity of the model, we are likely to lose out on efficiency, which is crucial for large datasets. Third, we can use the Shapley value-based approach to understand the impact of touchpoint removal on the outcome of the customer journey. Nevertheless, we should be aware of the fact that the findings from this method mostly do not have causal meanings. To make causal interpretations, we should use randomized field experiments (Li and Kannan, 2014). However, the decision on conducting experiments sometimes may not be a smooth choice. Removal of a touchpoint (e.g. a banner ad) may result in significant changes in the customer journey. Consumers may be pushed to other touchpoints (e.g. Google's pay-per-click campaigns) that might be more costly to the firm. Fourth, findings from data-driven models should always be supported by a careful strategic analysis. For instance, even though the model finds zero contribution for a social media ad, the manager may still want to be present on social media to increase brand awareness in the market. Finally, the examples we discussed in this chapter use a purchase metric as the outcome variable. Marketers can pick different outcome variables depending on their objectives (e.g. awareness, engagement, web traffic, retention, acquisition).

Although attribution models are very useful, embarking on them without due consideration may sometimes do more harm than good. Before diving directly into attribution modelling, we suggest that firms should first determine what their strategic goal is, what they would like to achieve at the end, and relate their data to decision-making.

REFERENCES

Abhishek, V., Fader, P. S. and Hosanagar, K. (2012) Media exposure through the funnel: A model of multi-stage attribution. http://ssrn.com/abstract=2158421

Anderl, E., Becker, I., Von Wangenheim, F. and Schumann, J. H. (2016) Mapping the customer journey: Lessons learned from graph-based online attribution modeling. *International Journal of Research in Marketing*, 33(3), 457–474.

De Haan, E. (2022) Attribution modeling. In C. Homburg, M. Klarmann and A. Vomberg (eds), *Handbook of Market Research*. Cham: Springer.

De Haan, E., Thorsten W. and Pauwels, K. (2016) The effectiveness of different forms of online advertising for purchase conversion in a multiple-channel attribution framework. *International Journal of Research in Marketing*, 33(3), 491–507.

Hercher, J. (2021). Goodbye, last-click attribution: Google Ads changes default to data modeling. *Adexchanger*, 27 September. https://www.adexchanger.com/online-advertising/goodbye-last-click-attribution-google-ads-changes-default-to-data-modeling/

Hoban, P. R. and Bucklin, R. E. (2015) Effects of internet display advertising in the purchase funnel: Model-based insights from a randomized field experiment. *Journal of Marketing Research*, 52(3), 375–393.

Kannan, P. K., Reinartz, W. and Verhoef, P. C. (2016) The path to purchase and attribution modeling: Introduction to special section. *International Journal of Research in Marketing*, 33(3), 449–456.

Li, H. A. and Kannan, P. K. (2014) Attributing conversions in a multichannel online marketing environment: An empirical model and a field experiment. *Journal of Marketing Research*, 51(1), 40–56.

Molnar, C. (2022) *Interpretable Machine Learning: A Guide for Making Black Box Models Explainable*, 2nd edn. https://christophm.github.io/interpretable-ml-book/

Shao, X., and Li, L. (2011) Data-driven multi-touch attribution models. In C. Apté, J. Ghosh and P. Smyth (eds), *Proceedings of the 17th ACM SIGKDD International Conference on Knowledge Discovery and Data Mining* (pp. 258–264). ACM.

Shapley, L. S. (1953) A value for n-person games. In H. W. Kuhn and A. W. Tucker (eds), *Contributions to the Theory of Games* (AM-28, Vol. II, pp. 307–317). Princeton, NJ: Princeton University Press.

Xu, L., Duan, J. A. and Whinston, A. B. (2014) Path to purchase: A mutually exciting point process model for online advertising and conversion. *Management Science*, 60(6), 1392–1412.

APPENDIX

Predictive comparison of attribution models

Here we examine whether the Markov chain model outperforms the other two heuristic models (i.e. first-touch and last-touch) in terms of predictive accuracy. It is important to mention that we do not include the Shapley value-based in the prediction exercise because the model essentially explores 'what-if' scenarios.

To compare the predictive power of the attribution models, we pull out the last 25 observations from the dataset and use them as a test set, `attribution_test`.

First-touch model

For the first-touch model, the idea of prediction is quite straightforward. We need to extract the first channel exposure of each consumer in the test set and refer back to what we obtained from the training set about conversion probability of each channel type. The following code chunk helps us get the first-touch model estimation results in Figure 4A.1.

```
```{r warning=FALSE }

# recall estimation results from First Touch model

table_summary2 <- data.frame(Item = c("Mobile", "Paid Search",
```
```

```
"Affiliate", "Social Media"), First_Touch = round(c(17, 28, 14, 8)/67,3))

table_summary2

```
```

Description: df [4 x 2]
```

Item <chr>	First_Touch <dbl>
Mobile	0.254
Paid Search	0.418
Affiliate	0.209
Social Media	0.119

4 rows

Figure 4A.1   First-touch model estimation results

Depending on what the first touch of each consumer in the test set is, we can simply take the corresponding estimated probability of conversion as the predicted outcome.

Next, we use the model estimation results to obtain the model predictions. The following code chunk gives us the predicted conversion probabilities in Figure 4A.2.

```
```{r warning=FALSE}

# Get the first channel exposure of each consumer in the test set
attribution_test$first_touch <-attribution_test$channel1

# Predict based on training set result
attribution_test$first_touch_prediction <-
ifelse(attribution_test$first_touch=="mobile", 0.254,
ifelse(attribution_test$first_touch=="paid_search",0.418,
ifelse(attribution_test$first_touch=="affiliate", 0.209,0.119)))

# Compare prediction with actual purchase based on first-touch model

first_touch<-data.frame(user_id = attribution_test$users_id, first_touch
 = attribution_test$first_touch, user_purchase =
attribution_test$user_purchase, predicted_conversion_probability =
attribution_test$first_touch_prediction)

first_touch

```
```

user_id <int>	first_touch <chr>	user_purchase <int>	predicted_conversion_probability <dbl>
81	mobile	1	0.254
82	mobile	1	0.254
83	paid_search	1	0.418
84	affiliate	1	0.209
85	social_media	1	0.119
86	affiliate	0	0.209
87	paid_search	0	0.418
88	paid_search	0	0.418
89	mobile	0	0.254
90	paid_search	1	0.418

Description: df [25 × 4]

1-10 of 25 rows   Previous 1 2 3 Next

Figure 4A.2 First-touch model predictions

Here we spot some issues with predictions from the first-touch model. For example, for consumers 87 and 88, the predicted conversion probabilities are high (0.418 for both consumers). However, when we look at the actual data, we see that they did not purchase at all.

Last-touch model

We follow the same procedure as we did for the first-touch model above. The following code chunk retrieves the last-touch model estimation results and produces the output in Figure 4A.3.

```{r}

table_summary3 <- data.frame(Item = c("Mobile", "Paid Search",
"Affiliate", "Social Media"), Last_Touch = round(c(26, 15, 18, 8)/67,3))

table_summary3

```

Description: df [4 × 2]

Item <chr>	Last_Touch <dbl>
Mobile	0.388
Paid Search	0.224
Affiliate	0.269
Social Media	0.119

4 rows

Figure 4A.3 Last-touch model estimation results

The following code chunk generates the last-touch model predictions and yields the output in Figure 4A.4.

```r
```{r}

for(i in 1:25){
  s <- 45-sum(attribution_test[i,]==" ")
  attribution_test$channel_n[i] <- attribution_test[i,s+1]}

# Get the last channel exposure of each consumer in the testing set
attribution_test$last_touch <-attribution_test$channel_n

# Predict based on training set result
attribution_test$last_touch_prediction <-
ifelse(attribution_test$last_touch=="mobile", 0.388,
ifelse(attribution_test$last_touch=="paid_search",0.224,
ifelse(attribution_test$last_touch=="affiliate", 0.269,0.119)))

# Compare prediction with actual purchase based on last-touch model

last_touch<-data.frame(user_id = attribution_test$users_id, user_purchase
= attribution_test$user_purchase, predicted_conversion_probability =
attribution_test$last_touch_prediction)

last_touch

```
```

Description: df [25 × 3]

user_id <int>	user_purchase <int>	predicted_conversion_probability <dbl>
81	1	0.119
82	1	0.119
83	1	0.119
84	1	0.269
85	1	0.119
86	0	0.119
87	0	0.119
88	0	0.119
89	0	0.119
90	1	0.119

1-10 of 25 rows   1   2   3   Next

Figure 4A.4 Last-touch model predictions

From these results, we understand that the last-touch model is able to predict purchases to a certain extent, but definitely not perfectly.

Markov chain model

To get predictions using Markov model, we refer to the third-order Markov transition matrix. Similar to the rationale in first-touch model prediction, we extract all the paths that lead to conversion and retrieve their corresponding transition probabilities to conversion. We then match these paths with the last three channel exposures of each customer in the test set to obtain the predictions.

The following code chunk is run to see the number of conversions in the test set. From the output of this code, we understand that in the test set there are 16 conversions out of 25 observations.

```r
```{r}


# Take a look at the total number of conversions in the test set
testing_conversion <- sum(attribution_test$user_purchase)
testing_conversion


```
```

Next, we turn to Markov model predictions. By running the following code chunk we create the variable `last_three_channels` in the test set, representing the last three touchpoints that each consumer interacted with along their journey.

```r
```{r warning=FALSE}
for(i in 1:25){
  s <- 45-sum(attribution_test[i,]==" ")
  attribution_test$channel_n[i] <- attribution_test[i,s+1]
  attribution_test$channel_n_1[i] <- attribution_test[i,s]
  attribution_test$channel_n_2[i] <- attribution_test[i,s-1]

attribution_test$last_three_channels[i] <-
paste(attribution_test$channel_n_2[i], attribution_test$channel_n_1[i],
attribution_test$channel_n[i], sep = ">")
}
```
```

Now we simply need to match the last three exposures of consumers in the test set with their corresponding conversion probability, if any. The following code chunk performs the matching.

```r
```{r}


# Matching Markov model estimation and actual data in the test set to
create predictions

merged_attribution <- merge(attribution_test, markov_result, by.x
 ="last_three_channels", by.y = "channel_3rd_order", all.x = TRUE,
all.y=FALSE)


```
```

After matching, we can summarize the results on actual versus predicted values by listing customers in the test set together with their actual conversion (user_purchase) and predicted conversion probability (predicted_conversion_probability), and order the new dataset by predicted probability in descending order. To this end, we run the following code chunk and obtain the output in Figure 4A.5.

```{r}

performance <-data.frame(users_id = merged_attribution$users_id,
user_purchase = merged_attribution$user_purchase,
predicted_conversion_probability =
merged_attribution$transition_probability)

performance[is.na(performance)] <- 0
markov_prediction <- performance[order(-
performance$predicted_conversion_probability),]

markov_prediction

```

Description: **df** [25 × 3]

	users_id <int>	user_purchase <int>	predicted_conversion_probability <dbl>
1	81	1	0
2	82	1	0
3	83	1	0
4	85	1	0
5	86	0	0
6	87	0	0
7	88	0	0
8	89	0	0
9	90	1	0
10	91	0	0

1–10 of 25 rows   Previous 1 2 3 Next

Figure 4A.5   Actual versus predicted values from Markov chain model

Predictive performance comparison across models

To determine which model performs best in predicting consumer conversion, we compare predicted conversion probabilities for each consumer with the actual conversion data. Specifically, we need to compare model performance in terms of accuracy and efficiency in identifying consumers with a high likelihood of conversion.

To do this, we need to take the following steps:

- Rank the data by predicted conversion probability (i.e. `predicted_conversion_probability`) in descending order. Note that an observation with non-conversion (i.e. `user_purchase = 0`) might correspond to a positive or even high predicted probability of conversion. This tends to happen if our prediction model performs poorly.
- Starting from the first observation of ranked data, count the cumulative number of actual conversions. The 'quicker' the cumulative count reaches the total number of conversions (16 in this case), the more capable the model is in identifying promising consumers through their channel exposure paths.

The following code executes these steps for the first-touch model and gives the output in Figure 4A.6.

```{r}

# sort data in descending order

first_touch_prediction <- first_touch[order(-
first_touch$predicted_conversion_probability),]
first_touch_prediction

```

	user_id <int>	first_touch <chr>	user_purchase <int>	predicted_conversion_probability <dbl>
3	83	paid_search	1	0.418
7	87	paid_search	0	0.418
8	88	paid_search	0	0.418
10	90	paid_search	1	0.418
12	92	paid_search	0	0.418
13	93	paid_search	1	0.418
14	94	paid_search	1	0.418
22	102	paid_search	1	0.418
23	103	paid_search	1	0.418
1	81	mobile	1	0.254

Description: df [25 × 4]

1–10 of 25 rows   1   2   3   Next

Figure 4A.6 First-touch model: predicted cumulative conversions

We immediately notice that the second and third consumers did not make a purchase (i.e. *user_purchase*=0). However, the model predicts conversion probabilities (41.8%) for both of them.

Knowing that the first channel exposure for both consumers is *paid search*, we can explain the discrepancy between actual and predicted data in the following way. Model estimation using the training set gives us a high transition probability from *paid search* to *conversion*, whereas in the test set consumers do not behave homogeneously with those in the training set.

Now let us count the cumulative number of *actual* conversions based on the ordered data, using the following code chunk.

```{r}

first_touch_prediction$cumu_conversion_ft <-
cumsum(first_touch_prediction$user_purchase)


# take a look at the first five rows of the data with cumulative count
first_touch_prediction[1:5,]


```

Description df [5 × 5]

	user_id	first_touch	user_purchase	predicted_conversion_probability	cumu_conversion_ft
	<int>	<chr>	<int>	<dbl>	<int>
3	83	paid_search	1	0.418	1
7	87	paid_search	0	0.418	1
8	88	paid_search	0	0.418	1
10	90	paid_search	1	0.418	2
12	92	paid_search	0	0.418	2

5 rows

Figure 4A.7   First-touch model: actual versus cumulative conversions

The output displayed in Figure 4A.7 suggests that among the first five customers with highest predicted conversion probabilities, there are only two customers (83 and 90) who actually made purchases. This means that, using the top 20% of valuable customers (in terms of conversion potential) based on our prediction, we can capture only two out of 16 total conversions in the test set. This corresponds to 12.5% of actual purchases.

> **Question.** Do you think this is a satisfactory performance? Why or why not? (*Hint*: think of what the output would look like if we made predictions via randomly selected data.)

For the last-touch model, we follow the same steps as we did above with the first-touch model. See the following code chunk and the corresponding output in Figure 4A.8.

```{r}
last_touch_prediction <- last_touch[order(-
last_touch$predicted_conversion_probability),]
last_touch_prediction

last_touch_prediction$cumu_conversion_lt <-
cumsum(last_touch_prediction$user_purchase)


# take a look at the first five rows of the data with cumulative count
last_touch_prediction[1:5,]


```

data.frame 25 x 3 | data.frame 5 x 4

Description: df [5 × 4]

	user_id <int>	user_purchase <int>	predicted_conversion_probability <dbl>	cumu_conversion_lt <int>
4	84	1	0.269	1
1	81	1	0.119	2
2	82	1	0.119	3
3	83	1	0.119	4
5	85	1	0.119	5

5 rows

Figure 4A.8 Last-touch model: predicted cumulative conversions

Next, we look at the Markov model predictions. As with first- and last-touch models, we need to calculate the cumulative *actual* conversions that the Markov model can capture. We do so with the following code chunk.

```
```{r}
markov_prediction$cumu_conversion_mm <-
cumsum(markov_prediction$user_purchase)

# take a look at the first five rows of the data with cumulative count

markov_prediction[1:5,]

```
```

Description: df [5 × 4]

	users_id <int>	user_purchase <int>	predicted_conversion_probability <dbl>	cumu_conversion_mm <int>
1	81	1	0	1
2	82	1	0	2
3	83	1	0	3
4	85	1	0	4
5	86	0	0	4

5 rows

Figure 4A.9 Markov model: predicted versus actual cumulative conversions

From the output in Figure 4A.9, it seems that the Markov chain model performs much better than the first-touch model. For the first five customers with highest predicted conversion probabilities, four have actually made purchases in real life.

Question. Comment on the prediction performance of the Markov model compared to the first-touch model.

Model performance visualization

Finally, it is always a good idea to visualize the results on models' predictive power so that Levi and Emma can make more informed decisions.

As described above, we can plot the cumulative actual conversions captured by each model on one graph.

In the following code chunk, `Cumu_Markov` and `Cumu_First_Touch` are the cumulative number of actual conversions captured by Markov and first-touch predictions, respectively. `Observation` identifies the observation with the nth highest predicted conversion probability ($n = 1,2,...,25$).

```{r}
# prepare a dataset for plotting

plot_raw <- data.frame(Observation= 1:25, Cumu_Markov =
markov_prediction$cumu_conversion_mm, Cumu_First_Touch =
first_touch_prediction$cumu_conversion_ft, Cumu_Last_Touch =
last_touch_prediction$cumu_conversion_lt)


plot_raw

```

Running the above code gives us the input for model visualization (see Figure 4A.10).

Description: df [25 x 4]

Observation	Cumu_Markov	Cumu_First_Touch	Cumu_Last_Touch
1	1	1	1
2	2	1	2
3	3	1	3
4	4	2	4
5	4	2	5
6	4	3	5
7	4	4	5
8	4	5	5
9	5	6	5
10	5	7	6

1–10 of 25 rows   1 2 3 Next

Figure 4A.10   Input for model visualization

Finally, using the above input, we visualize the predictive performance of these models. Running the following code chunk yields the plot shown in Figure 4A.11.

```{r}

plot_markov <-
c(plot_raw$Cumu_Markov[5]/16,plot_raw$Cumu_Markov[10]/16,plot_raw$Cumu_
Markov[15]/16,plot_raw$Cumu_Markov[20]/16,plot_raw$Cumu_Markov[25]/16)

plot_first_touch <-
c(plot_raw$Cumu_First_Touch[5]/16,plot_raw$Cumu_First_Touch[10]/16,
plot_raw$Cumu_First_Touch[15]/16, plot_raw$Cumu_First_Touch[20]/16,
plot_raw$Cumu_First_Touch[25]/16)

plot_last_touch <-
c(plot_raw$Cumu_Last_Touch[5]/16,plot_raw$Cumu_Last_Touch[10]/16,
plot_raw$Cumu_Last_Touch[15]/16, plot_raw$Cumu_Last_Touch[20]/16,
plot_raw$Cumu_Last_Touch[25]/16)

plot <- data.frame(Markov = plot_markov, First_Touch =
plot_first_touch,Last_Touch = plot_last_touch, Observation =
c(5,10,15,20,25)/25 )

ggplot(plot,aes(x=Observation))+
  geom_line(aes(y=Markov), color = "darkred") +
              geom_line(aes(y=First_Touch), color="blue") +
  geom_line(aes(y=Last_Touch), color="orange")+
  xlab('% of Observations') +
  ylab('Cumulative % of Actual Conversions Captured') +
  scale_color_discrete(name = "Model Approach", labels = c("Markov",
"First Touch"))

```

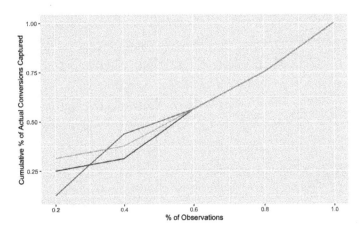

Figure 4A.11   Model performance visualization

The dark red line in the plot represents the Markov model, while the blue line refers to the first-touch model and the orange line refers to the last-touch model.

The horizontal axis refers to the *percentage of ranked observations*. We have 25 predicted observations in total. The first 20% means the first five observations with highest predicted conversion probability.

The vertical axis refers to the *percentage of actual conversions captured* by our model using a specific percentage of ranked observations. For example, a Y% capture with X% observations means that our model can capture Y% of actual sales by using the first X% of ranked observations.

Figure 4A.11 further shows that, within the first 20% of observations (i.e. the first five observations with highest likelihood of conversion), the Markov model is able to capture 25% of the actual conversions (i.e. 4 out of 16) already while the first-touch model can only capture 12.5% (i.e. 2 out of 16). The last-touch model's performance is slightly better than that of Markov chain model. One can argue that Markov chain model performs relatively better but its predictive accuracy is not high. Tweaking the Markov model further (e.g. trying higher-order models) with a more balanced and larger dataset, we can better understand how much can be gained from this model in practice.

5

USER-GENERATED DATA ANALYTICS

Chapter contents

LEARNING OBJECTIVES

At the end of this chapter, you should be able to:

- have a clear understanding of the pros and cons of various user-generated data sources
- extract user-generated data from Google and online review websites
- explain information and derive actionable marketing insights from user-generated data.

The focus of this chapter is on how marketers can leverage user-generated data (UGD) from various platforms to gain customer- and brand-specific insights. Marketing research has shown UGD to be a powerful and essential source of information, which can be used to measure customer mindset metrics (see also Chapter 6 of this book on how to analyse customer mind-set metrics) such as brand image, buying consideration, and customer satisfaction (Kübler, Colicev, and Pauwels, 2020). In addition, marketers may similarly use UGD to understand innovation and market potential while developing new products and discover sources of dis-satisfaction to overhaul and solve issues. UGD is thus often perceived as an alternative to, addition to, or sometimes even replacement for common – often survey-based – marketing and customer research tools.

We begin this chapter with a practical case study that highlights the key questions that can be addressed with the help of user-generated content. Then we continue with an overview of the key sources for user-generated content and discuss different approaches and methodologies, which help to translate unstructured information such as text into data that can be analysed with the help of statistical models to then derive actionable insights. Next, we provide various R applications of crawling and text mining relevant to the case study. Finally, we outline the limitations of UGD and discuss some potential alternative approaches as well as latest development in the field.

━━━━━━ Case study ━━━━━━

Leviev Air I

Leviev Air is a recently founded private airline in the UK. The airline intends to offer private business trips with its recently acquired fleet of 50 private jets. It targets business professionals and intends to win customers from the established airline market by offering a better service experience for business class travellers at a similar or only slightly higher price level.

The investor pitch went well, and the company was able to acquire not only sufficient funding but also adequate jets. However, the company board struggles with Leviev Air's positioning in the market. While the targeted segment of business professionals is clear, it remains largely unclear how to attract these high-profile customers and how to make business class travellers switch from established airlines to Leviev Air.

To decide on which values to provide to potential clients and to understand which benefits to communicate to Leviev Air's potential customer base, the executive board asks you to conduct some thorough market research. The executives want especially to learn which factors business travellers pay attention to and which factors business travellers dislike most with the leading airlines in the field. Unfortunately, Leviev's initial business plan neglected to include a budget for a commercial market research company. Thus, running costly surveys or focus group interviews will not be feasible.

The next day you pull together a checklist to develop substantial business intelligence in the area. By answering the following points with the help of UGD you try to narrow down the positioning strategy for Leviev Air:

- Which airlines do potential customers in the UK frequently use?
- What alternatives do potential customers seek?
- Which general pain points do customers see with existing airlines?
- What common problems occur for which competitor?
- Which positive factors do potential customers have in mind when choosing an airline?
- Which factors need to be satisfied when looking for an airline?
- Which factors should Leviev Air emphasize when trying to convince business customers to switch from established airlines to their new service?

To answer the questions, we will first try to gain a deeper understanding of potential data sources of UGD and how to collect data from these sources. Subsequently we will learn how to automatically extract information from the various sources with the help of the R framework. We will then apply text mining tools in R to transform the unstructured data into a more suitable format. Finally, we will apply statistical tools to gain reliable information and use these insights to take decisions for Leviev Air.

THE POTENTIAL OF USER-GENERATED DATA

Modern communication technologies and the digital transformation provide marketers with a rich data environment. Today, we produce and store more data each day than humankind did altogether within the previous 2000 years. A substantial part of these data is actively created by users, sharing information about what they like and dislike, which products they consider, how satisfied they are with a product or service, and how likely they are to recommend it to their peers. In addition, this data source has become a focal information point for decision-making. The majority of internet users confirm that, before making a decision, they first look up what other users write or think about a product. While 'user-generated content' is often used as a synonym for online reviews and social media communication in forms of texts, images, and videos, it is important to remark that user-generated data actually comprise more information as they originate from more sources than just review pages and social media networks. Saura et al. (2021) define it as any data source that 'includes forms of information and data that users generate individually as a result of interacting with the elements that make up any digital market (actions, experiences, feelings, comments, reviews, and so forth)'. User-generated data are thus data that have been consciously (social media and reviews) or unconsciously (web search queries, bidding behaviour) created by internet users and that can give us information about a user's preferences. UGD thus provide us with rich opportunities to better understand consumers and to predict customer behaviour. Companies can, for example, use auction data from ebay.com to understand consumer's willingness to pay for products. A recent case from the toy industry highlights this potential. An action figure company planned a new toy set and forecasted a demand of approx. 250,000 units. After production the units went on sale shortly before Christmas at a unit price of €19.99. Demand was huge and shortly after market introduction the toy set was sold out. Given the high demand for the toy set, some parents preferred to sell their kid's toys before Christmas on ebay.com as the average sales price of €55 on the online auction platform exceeded by far the initial retail price. In other words, ebay.com auction prices indicated that the toy company misinterpreted their customer's willingness to pay by €35 and in total forwent €8.75 million in revenue (250,000 × €35). The case underlines how secondary data sources can be used to gain consumer insights and derive important and actionable information such as willingness to pay and demand.

To understand whether a marketing campaign has increased brand knowledge or the awareness of a product or service, marketers can use classic search engine trend data as provided by, for example, Google Trends. Similar to the variable website visits in the marketing mix modelling example in Chapter 4, marketers may use search volume data to see whether awareness of a brand changes over time and how much marketing activities affect search volume. Skiera and Ringle (2017) provide a great case study. They use clickstream data to reveal customer perceptions of companies. They are able to build complete brand landscapes by simply analysing consumers' browsing behaviour and observing which brand and product websites consumers frequently visited. Such an approach may be especially helpful when trying to depict and understand consumer choice behaviour and when trying to analyse the formation of a consideration set.

Besides such 'behavioural' data, consumers reveal preferences also in a more direct and active way on social media in the form of chatter. This information may provide marketers with reliable and valid information about consumer preferences, but may similarly also help marketers to understand, track, and monitor consumer mindset metrics such as brand image, consideration, customer satisfaction, perceived product quality, or brand loyalty. Recent research shows how online chatter can be used to replace image data (Kübler, Colicev, and Pauwels, 2020), forecast sales and investor reactions (Colicev et al. 2020), voting behaviour (Kübler, Pauwels, and Manke, 2020), as well as stock performance (Nofer and Hinz, 2015). Finally, consumer reviews provide rich information about customer satisfaction and dissatisfaction and provide marketers with the necessary knowledge about which factors consumers value and which they do not.

DERIVING A POSITIONING STRATEGY WITH THE HELP OF UGD

To help develop a positioning strategy for Leviev Air, we follow a multi-step process in which we first determine which airlines business travellers currently use and which service factors they include in their choice process. To then understand which factors business passengers appreciate with these airlines and which factors these passengers dislike, we further analyse airline reviews from a public airline rating website. Based on this information, we then derive the positioning strategy of Leviev Air, which will try to deliver a meaningful solution to common airlines' pain points while offering a similar service in the domain of positively rated factors.

UNDERSTANDING THE AIRLINE CHOICE PROCESS WITH GOOGLE TRENDS DATA

To gain a better understanding of which airlines business travellers in the UK consider we turn to Google Trends. This service allows users to examine search histories. Users can rely on Google's own web interface to search and export data. This is a great way to familiarize yourself with the general possibilities of Google Trends and what kind of data one can obtain from this source. Figure 5.1 provides a screenshot of the service.

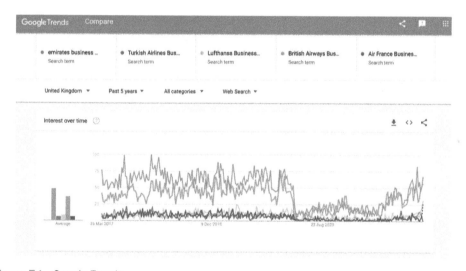

Figure 5.1   Google Trends

While the web interface is well suited for a first inspection, accessing Google Trends directly through R is easier, more comfortable, and less prone to error. To be able to conduct Google Trends inquiries with R we need to install and load the gTrendsR package.

With the help of the gTrendsR package we can now check which business class airlines are most popular and compare search volume over time for the business class airlines we are interested in. To do so, we use the following code:

```
web.trends.businessclass = gtrends(c("British Airways Business Class",
"Emirates Business Class", "Lufthansa Business Class",
"Air France Business Class", "Turkish Airlines Business Class"),
gprop = "web", geo="GB", time = "2017-03-05 2022-03-04")
time_trend. web.trends.businessclass =
web.trends.businessclass$interest_over_time
```

The code allows us to access the Google Trends application programming interface (API). APIs are common access points which are implement in all established online platforms. Through these access points app developers can request data directly from the platform and use the data to deliver their own service. Some platforms require developers to register and authenticate, others provide open access. The gtrends() function does not require any authentication and allows us to get the search result data stored in the web.trends.businessclass data frame. gtrends() requires the same input as the web interface. We specify the search requests we are interested in, the type of Google Search we require (here web search; alternatively we could also rely on news, images, and YouTube searches to access the search results from these categories), the relevant country (here the UK), and the time frame for which we want results.

To see the frequency of searches over time, we can simply plot the content of the data frame with the following code. The result should look like Figure 5.2.

```
plot(web.trends.businessclass)
```

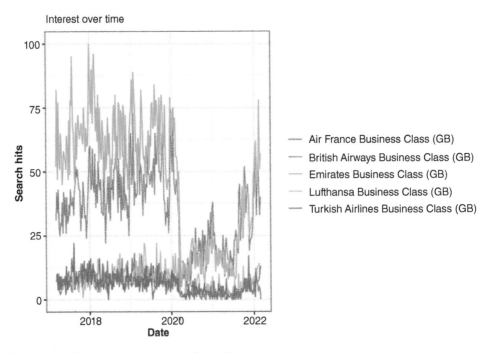

Figure 5.2 Plot of search volume business classes

A quick inspection of the plot shows that we have replicated with R the plot we would usually obtain from Google's web interface. At second glance you may discover that the vertical axis does not display the number of web searches. Instead, it ranges from 0 to 100. This is because Google Trends only provides us with relative search results by indexing the day with the highest search volume as 100. Consequently, all other days are reported as a measure relative to the day with the highest volume. If we have multiple search terms – as in our example – the 100 will be set for the keyword with the highest search volume. In fact, this means that we cannot compare search volume data from different search terms if we extract them separately. However, there is an easy workaround. We may simply check which search term enjoys the highest interest and include this term in all searches as a reference. So, we ensure that all the data we obtain from Google Trends are relative to this search term and we can thus compare results across different searches. This is especially helpful, as Google Trends only allows us to compare up to five search terms per call. Let us assume we also want to have search results for other airlines such as KLM, United, Singapore Airlines, and SAS. If we simply looked for these four airlines, Google would index the 100 to the search term with the most interest in this call. To make the results comparable, we include Emirates in our search, as this is the airline that apparently enjoys most interest and will thus serve for both calls as a reference mark. We can extract these data with the following command and then plot the new time series. Figure 5.3 shows the result.

```
web.trends.businessclass2 = gtrends(c("Emirates Business Class",
"KLM Business Class", "Singapore Airlines Business Class",
"United Airlines Business Class","SAS Business Class"),
gprop = "web", geo="GB", time = "2017-03-05 2022-03-04")

plot(web.trends.businessclass2)
```

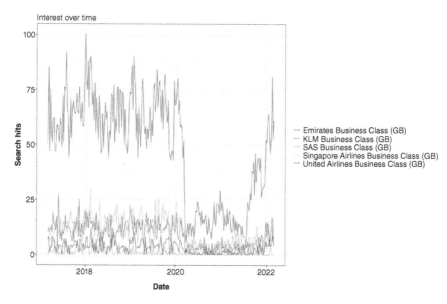

Figure 5.3   Results from second web search

Using the `summary()` function you can inspect the two objects in your environment window and you will see that they consist of different lists and elements.

```
summary(web.trends.businessclass)
summary(web.trends.businessclass2)
```

We can see that both objects consist of the multiple data frames, which include the information we usually obtain from the different windows within the Google Trends webpage. Besides the interest over time, we can check for interest in different regions and cities, and furthermore explore other related search terms, which are frequently used together with our search terms.

Let us have a look at the other search terms. We create a new data frame and store the other search terms in it with the following code:

```
webtrends1 = web.trends.businessclass[["related_queries"]]
webtrends2 = web.trends.businessclass2[["related_queries"]]
```

We can now combine the two data frames. However, keep in mind that `webtrends1` and `webtrends2` share the results for Emirates, and that as we included the airline in both searches we need to filter our Emirates-related queries from one of the two, as we otherwise would have double information in the joined data frame. We can use `dplyr`'s `filter()` function to filter out Emirates results from `webtrends2` and then combine the two data frames. To achieve this we use the following code.

```
webtrends2.filtered = webtrends2 %>% filter(keyword != "Emirates
Business Class")
webtrends.total = rbind(webtrends1, webtrends2.filtered)
```

With the `filter()` command in combination with `!=` we tell R to only include rows from the `webtrends2` data frame, which do not include the terms 'Emirates Business Class' in the column keyword. We then use the `rbind()` command to simply put the filtered `webtrends2` data frame below the `webtrends1` data frame and store these in the new data frame. `webtrends.total`, which now includes all related search queries. We can do the same for the web search results with the following code.

```
web.search1 = web.trends.businessclass[["interest_over_time"]]
web.search2 = web.trends.businessclass2[["interest_over_time"]]
web.search2.filtered = web.search2 %>% filter(keyword != "Emirates
Business Class")
web.search.total = rbind(web.search1, web.search2.filtered)
```

Both data frames – `web.search.total` and `webtrends.total` – now feature valuable information we can use for determining key insights for our campaign. Let us now focus on the related search queries.

> Inspect the data frame with `glimpse(webtrends.total)`. What kind of information might be useful for developing a positioning strategy? What do you learn from the information about the business class market? What implications may this have for Leviev Air?

To develop a systematic understanding of which search terms are frequently used we could try to produce a word cloud with the help of the related query keywords.

```
library(wordcloud)
library(tidytext)

tidy_keywords <- webtrends.total %>% unnest_tokens(word, value)
tidy_keywords %>% count(word) %>% with(wordcloud(word, n, min.
freq = 3, max.words = 90))
```

We need to load two more packages, which are used for text processing and designing word clouds: `tidytext` and `wordcloud`. We then use the `unnest_tokens()` function from `tidytext` to split the search queries in the value column of the `webtrends.total` data frame into single observations. By doing so we can then count how many times a query is posted and use this information to then produce a word cloud that includes all search queries which have been used at least three times. The results should look similar to the word cloud displayed in Figure 5.4. If yours deviates, do not worry: given that we are looking for different time frames, any deviation may be due to changes in search volume and search types.

Figure 5.4   Word cloud with the most often searched terms

What kind of additional information does the word cloud provide? How does this information deviate from your previous inspection? What can we take away from the frequencies?

It appears that consumers compare different types of airlines and business class settings in terms of different aircraft. Furthermore, we can identify the two most frequently discussed airplanes: the Airbus A380 and the Boeing 777. In addition, we get a quite good impression of the different types of airlines consumers tend to consider when they need to buy a ticket.

This is in line with classic decision theory and the classic decision funnel model often used in marketing theory. Here we assume that consumers' need recognition leads to information searches. To obtain information which may help to come to a purchase decision, consumers form a consideration set, which commonly consists of three to six alternatives.

It might thus be interesting for us to see which airlines are commonly searched with other airlines to understand the different types of consideration set compositions. This may point us towards different passenger types, which may then ultimately help us to derive implications for Leviev Air. To come to this point we use dplyr's filter function to create separate data frames for each airline, containing only the airline-specific queries. We can then plot these as separate word clouds with the following code.

 From inspecting the related search queries of each airline, which airlines seem to share similar customers, and which seem to stand out?

```
Emirates.Queries = webtrends.total %>% filter(keyword == "Emirates
Business Class")
tidy_keywords.Emirates <- Emirates.Queries %>%
  unnest_tokens(word, value) %>%
  count(word) %>%
  with(wordcloud(word, n, min.freq = 3, max.words = 90))

BritishAirways.Queries = webtrends.total %>% filter(keyword ==
"British Airways Business Class")
tidy_keywords.British <- BritishAirways.Queries %>%
  unnest_tokens(word, value) %>%
  count(word) %>%
  with(wordcloud(word, n, min.freq = 3, max.words = 90))

Lufthansa.Queries = webtrends.total %>% filter(keyword == "Lufthansa
Business Class")
tidy_keywords.Lufthansa <- Lufthansa.Queries %>%
  unnest_tokens(word, value) %>%
  count(word) %>%
  with(wordcloud(word, n, min.freq = 3, max.words = 90))
```

```
AirFrance.Queries = webtrends.total %>% filter(keyword == "Air
France Business Class")
tidy_keywords.AirFrance <- AirFrance.Queries %>%
  unnest_tokens(word, value) %>%
  count(word) %>%
  with(wordcloud(word, n, min.freq = 3, max.words = 90))


Turkish.Queries = webtrends.total %>% filter(keyword == "Turkish
Airlines Business Class")
tidy_keywords.Turkish <- Turkish.Queries %>%
  unnest_tokens(word, value) %>%
  count(word) %>%
  with(wordcloud(word, n, min.freq = 3, max.words = 90))


KLM.Queries = webtrends.total %>% filter(keyword == "KLM Business Class")
tidy_keywords.KLM <- KLM.Queries %>%
  unnest_tokens(word, value) %>%
  count(word) %>%
  with(wordcloud(word, n, min.freq = 3, max.words = 90))


Singapore.Queries = webtrends.total %>% filter(keyword ==

"Singapore Airlines Business Class")
tidy_keywords.Singapore<- Singapore.Queries %>%
  unnest_tokens(word, value) %>%
  count(word) %>%
  with(wordcloud(word, n, min.freq = 3, max.words = 90))


United.Queries = webtrends.total %>% filter(keyword == "United
Airlines Business Class")
  tidy_keywords.United <- United.Queries %>%
  unnest_tokens(word, value) %>%
  count(word) %>%
  with(wordcloud(word, n, min.freq = 3, max.words = 90))


SAS.Queries = webtrends.total %>% filter(keyword == "SAS Business
Class")
tidy_keywords.SAS <- SAS.Queries %>%
  unnest_tokens(word, value) %>%
  count(word) %>%
  with(wordcloud(word, n, min.freq = 3, max.words = 90))
```

The resulting word clouds are displayed in Figure 5.5.

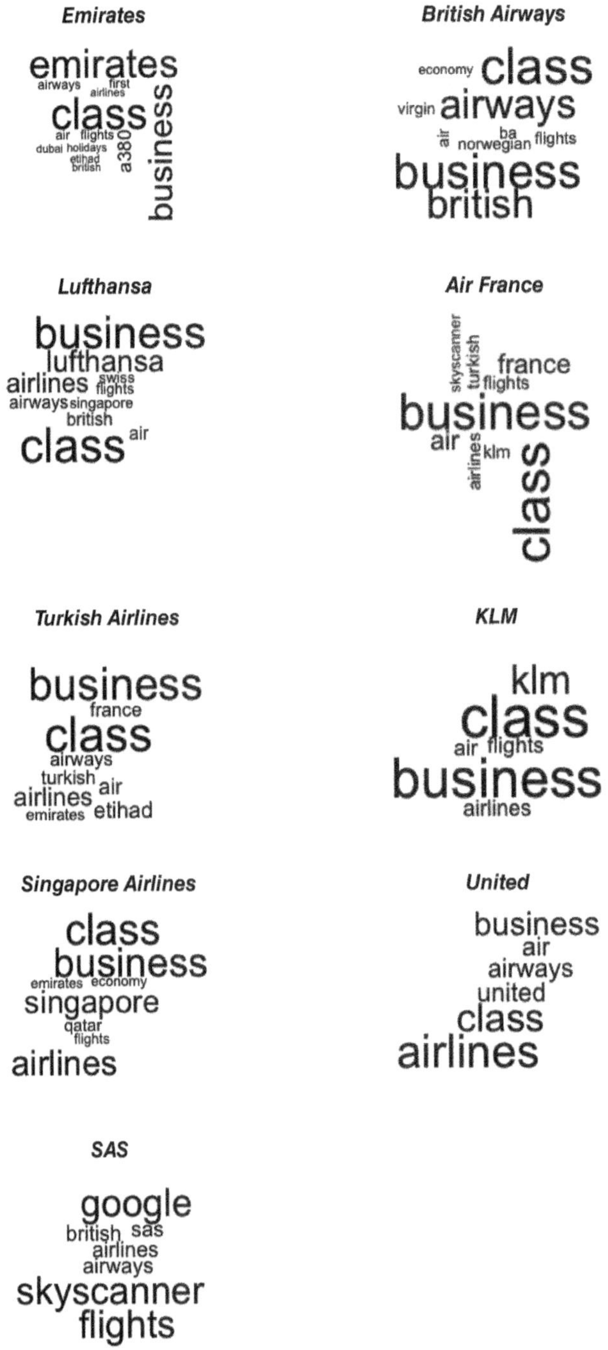

Figure 5.5   Airline-specific search query word clouds

ENRICHING INSIGHTS WITH THE HELP OF AIRLINE REVIEWS: A CRAWLING EXERCISE

As we now have a clearer understanding of the consideration set of business travellers, we can continue to gather information about what customers like and dislike about the different airlines. As pointed out at the beginning of the chapter, there are different sources of UGD to measure and understand customer satisfaction. A key source, however, are user reviews. In the case of the airline market there are different websites that collect user reviews and ratings. As we are targeting business class travellers, price comparison sites for low-cost travel such as Kayak and Skyscanner may be less suitable. Instead we use a general airline review page: Skytrax Airline Quality. You can find the webpage at the following address: https://www.airlinequality.com.

Just browse through the webpage and check the different airlines and the corresponding reviews. The website provides many useful and interesting insights, which we may use as a base for our analysis.

Besides the general numerical rating of the flight experience on the upper left-hand side, we also get information on the purpose of the flight, the type of passenger, the category booked, the destinations, and ratings for a variety of sub-characteristics such as comfort, cabin staff service quality, satisfaction with food and beverages, as well as general information on whether the reviewer recommends the airline or not.

While we can quickly inspect some of the reviews, a thorough inspection seems quite impossible due to time constraints. Similarly, copying and pasting reviews from the website would take a significant amount of time and would certainly be prone to error, potentially jeopardizing our data quality. But what if we could automatically extract the information from the webpage? To see if and how this is feasible, let us inspect the website and the code behind it more thoroughly. We can do this with most web browsers. Simply highlight the element you are interested in and right-click on it. You will find an option that says 'Show Source Code' or 'Inspect Element'. If you do this for the review headline and the main review text, for example, you will discover something like the examples shown in Figure 5.6.

Figure 5.6   Source code for reviews

Looking at the highlighted areas in the code, you will recognize that some of the text you see on the webpage is always preceded by the same code. For the general headline of the review we see for both examples the HTML code `<div class="text_header">` in front of the written text. In the case of the review text it is `<div class="text_content">`. Without diving too deeply into HTML and webpage coding, we can conclude that a website's code needs these tags to place content always at the same place and to ensure that the page is consistent in design and appearance. We can take advantage of this and tell R to go through the website code, look up where the two tags appear in the code, and then always copy and paste for us the text that comes behind these tags. Doing so, we are able to quickly store the information in a data frame, which we then can analyse later on. As R is working not only much quicker than us, but also more reliably, this approach ensures that we can extract any sort of information from a webpage if we know the corresponding HTML code that embeds the information we are interested in.

At the beginning, inspecting webpages may feel uncomfortable or chaotic. Instead of relying on your browser's inspection tools, you may similarly employ other plug-ins such as the SelectorGadget (https://selectorgadget.com). The tool is a plug-in for Chrome and helps you find the tags you need to extract data from a website.

 Use your browser or selectorgadget to identify the tags for the overall rating score on the top left.

We can now use this information to set up our first crawler. To achieve this we use another package in R called `rvest`. After installing and loading the package, we can use the following code to conduct our first crawling attempt.

```
install.packages("rvest")
library(rvest)
link = "https://www.airlinequality.com/airline-reviews/emirates/
page/1/?sortby=post_date%3ADesc&pagesize=100"
Review.Title.Emirates <- read_html(link) %>%
    html_nodes(".text_header") %>%
    html_text()
```

As you can see, we have now crawled all the review titles for Emirates that are available on the site. We have already learned that there are 100 reviews listed on a page at a time; however, looking at `Review.Title.Emirates`, we see that there are 103 lines. If we take a closer look at the text vector, we see that the `.text_header` element also appears in the context of the headers for the embedded ads – so not only above the reviews we are interested in. In this case, if we save all `.text_header` elements, we would be saving information with them that is neither needed nor otherwise useful for further analysis. To solve the problem, we need to take another look at the structure of the website. We noticed that each review is located in a review 'tile', of which there are exactly 100 on the page. So in our command, we can tell R to first find all the tiles on the page and then list only the .text_header elements that are in the tiles. So, using the SelectorGadget, we look for the name of the element that marks the tiles in the source code (.comp_media-review-rated) and include that in our code. It will look like this:

```
Review.Title.Emirates <- read_html(link) %>%
    html_nodes(".comp_media-review-rated") %>%
    html_node (".text_header") %>%
    html_text() %>%
    unlist()
```

As you can see, we now have 100 rows in the corresponding vector. We can now finally develop a crawler that extracts the review title, the review text, the overall airline rating, the seat category, the type of aircraft, and the route the passenger was booked on.

```
#Title
Review.Title.Emirates <- read_html(link) %>%
   html_nodes(".comp_media-review-rated") %>%
   html_node (".text_header") %>%
   html_text() %>%
   unlist()


#ReviewText
Review.Text.Emirates <- read_html(link) %>%
   html_nodes(".comp_media-review-rated") %>%
   html_node(".text_content") %>%
   html_text() %>%
   unlist()


#Rating
Rating.Emirates <- read_html(link) %>%
   html_nodes(".comp_media-review-rated") %>%
   html_nodes(".rating-10") %>%
   html_node("span:nth-child(1)") %>%
   html_text() %>%
   unlist()


#Seat Type
Seattype.Emirates <- read_html(link) %>%
   html_nodes(".querylist") %>%
   html_nodes(xpath = ".//article[contains(@class, 'comp comp_media-
```

```
        review-rated list-item media position-content review-')]") %>%
        html_node(".cabin_flown+ .review-value") %>%
        html_text() %>%
        unlist()


    #Aircraft Type
    Aircraft.Emirates <- read_html(link) %>%
        html_nodes(".querylist") %>%
        html_nodes(xpath = ".//article[contains(@class, 'comp comp_media-
        review-rated list-item media position-content review-')]") %>%
        html_node(".aircraft+ .review-value") %>%
        html_text() %>%
        unlist()


    #Route
    Route.Emirates <- read_html(link) %>%
        html_nodes(".querylist") %>%
        html_nodes(xpath = ".//article[contains(@class, 'comp comp_media-
        review-rated list-item media position-content review-')]") %>%
        html_node(".route+ .review-value") %>%
        html_text() %>%
        unlist()


    Emirates.Skytrax = data.frame(Review.Title.Emirates = Review.Title.
    Emirates, Review.Text.Emirates = Review.Text.Emirates, Rating.
    Emirates = Rating.Emirates, Seat.Type.Emirates = Seattype.Emirates,
    Emirates.Aircaft = Aircraft.Emirates, Route.Emirates = Route.
    Emirates)g.Emirates)
```

The crawler is now extracting all information for the 100 first reviews. If you would like to have more reviews you need to adapt the link so that it also leads to the second page of reviews. Inspecting the review page links, we see that the page numbers are basically an element in the URL. So far we have used the link for the first page with the first 100 reviews:

https://www.airlinequality.com/airline-reviews/emirates/page/1/?sortby=post_date%3ADesc&pagesize=100

To access the second page we simply need to exchange the 1 in the URL by a 2:

https://www.airlinequality.com/airline-reviews/emirates/page/2/?sortby=post_date%3ADesc&pagesize=100

If we want to access, say, the reviews between 1800 and 1900, we use 19:

https://www.airlinequality.com/airline-reviews/emirates/page/19/?sortby=post_
    date%3ADesc&pagesize=100

You get the idea. To make things easier we can, instead of typing in each link separately, use R's `loop` function and ask R to go from 1 to 21 to extract all 2000 reviews from Emirates in one step with the following code.

```
Emirates.SkyTraxFull = data.frame()
page = 1
endpage = 22


while(page < endpage){

link = paste0("https://www.airlinequality.com/airline-reviews/emirates/
page/",page,"/?sortby=post_date%3ADesc&pagesize=100", sep="")
#Title
Review.Title.Emirates <- read_html(link) %>%
  html_nodes(".comp_media-review-rated") %>%
  html_node (".text_header") %>%
  html_text() %>%
  unlist()


##ReviewText
Review.Text.Emirates <- read_html(link) %>%
  html_nodes(".comp_media-review-rated") %>%
  html_node(".text_content") %>%
  html_text() %>%
  unlist()

#Rating
Rating.Emirates <- read_html(link) %>%
  html_nodes(".comp_media-review-rated") %>%
  html_nodes(".rating-10") %>%
  html_node("span:nth-child(1)") %>%
  html_text() %>%
  unlist()

#Seat Type
Seattype.Emirates <- read_html(link) %>%
  html_nodes(".querylist") %>%
```

```
  html_nodes(xpath = ".//article[contains(@class, 'comp comp_media-
  review-rated list-item media position-content review-')]") %>%
  html_node(".cabin_flown+ .review-value") %>%
  html_text() %>%
  unlist()

#Aircraft Type
Aircraft.Emirates <- read_html(link) %>%
  html_nodes(".querylist") %>%
  html_nodes(xpath = ".//article[contains(@class, 'comp comp_media-
  review-rated list-item media position-content review-')]") %>%
  html_node(".aircraft+ .review-value") %>%
  html_text() %>%
  unlist()

#Route
Route.Emirates <- read_html(link) %>%
  html_nodes(".querylist") %>%
  html_nodes(xpath = ".//article[contains(@class, 'comp comp_media-
  review-rated list-item media position-content review-')]") %>%
  html_node(".route+ .review-value") %>%
  html_text() %>%
  unlist()

Emirates.Skytrax = data.frame(Review.Title.Emirates = Review.Title.
Emirates, Review.Text.Emirates = Review.Text.Emirates, Rating.Emirates =
Rating.Emirates, Seat.Type.Emirates = Seattype.Emirates, Emirates.Aircaft =
Aircraft.Emirates, Route.Emirates = Route.Emirates)
Emirates.SkyTraxFull = rbind(Emirates.SkyTraxFull, Emirates.Skytrax)
page = page +1
}
```

As you can see, we are now using the two variables page and endpage in a loop. R will execute the code between the {} brackets as long as the rule stated in the while command is fulfilled. In our case this means it will run through the code as long as the condition page < endpage is fulfilled, that is, until page takes the value 22. As you can see, the last thing R does while going through the loop is to add 1 to the value stored in the variable page. So every time R passed one loop, page grows by 1. Meanwhile, at the beginning of the while command you can see that we have adapted the link information. We now use R's paste0 command to construct a link that in each loop has a different page number in it and will thus collect reviews from different pages each time. Keep in mind that executing the code above will take some time, as the crawler will have to access the website 21 times and download all the information. So don't worry if R is busy for a couple of minutes!

Did you realize that not only is the review page number an element of the URL but also the airline name? This should make it easy for you to adapt our code to any airline within minutes. Just try it out!

As we are only interested in business class reviews we can now again filter the `Seat.Type` variable and only take business class trip reviews.

```
Emirates.BusinessClass = Emirates.SkyTraxFull %>%
filter(Seat.Type.Emirates == "Business Class")
```

To understand which things customers do like and do not like, it makes sense to split the data frame further into one data frame with reviews from only satisfied and one data frame with reviews from only dissatisfied customers.

Which variable might be best to indicate satisfaction?

There might be different ways to measure satisfaction. On the one hand, the website also allows us to explore whether the customer would recommend the service or not. However, this may take additional time and may require us to develop more sophisticated code. Instead, we may simply rely on the numerical information at our disposal in the form of the overall airline rating: dissatisfied customers will obviously give lower ratings than satisfied ones. While it seems obvious that satisfaction correlates with ratings, the question remains as to which numerical ratings express dissatisfaction and which display satisfaction. Given that the numerical rating spans from 1 to 10, we can conduct a brief digression and focus on the net promoter score (NPS), which is a common tool in strategic marketing and customer satisfaction measurement. You may previously have been asked the question, 'On a scale from 1 to 10, how likely are you to recommend our service to a friend of colleague?' Commonly these questions are asked by customer services right after you had a service encounter. Introduced by Reichheld and Covey (2006), the NPS was intended to deliver a single measure of customer satisfaction that is supposedly tied to company performance. The idea was to develop an item that can be easily tracked and included in the company's return on investment measurement. Since its introduction the NPS has been heavily criticized (e.g. Baehre et al., 2022), although people agree on its general ability to measure satisfaction. Only customers with a recommendation score over 8 are considered to be satisfied, while anyone with a NPS score below 7 is considered to be a dissatisfied customer.

Using this concept, we can filter our business class data frame with the following code.

```
Emirates.BusinessClass$Rating.Emirates = as.numeric(Emirates.
BusinessClass$Rating.Emirates)
```

```
Emirates.BC.Satisfied = Emirates.BusinessClass %>% filter(Rating.
Emirates > 8)
Emirates.BC.Dissatisfied = Emirates.BusinessClass %>% filter(Rating.
Emirates < 7)
```

The first line of the code is used to tell R that the information in the column `Rating.Emirates` is numeric as R does not yet recognize this and treats the variable as character (i.e. text). Then we again use the `filter()` function in `dplyr` to split the data frame.

As we can see, we end up with more dissatisfied than satisfied passengers, which is already great information for Leviev Air. But perhaps this is not very much surprising, as we know from previous research that users tend more often to complain online than to praise a company (Kübler, Colicev, and Pauwels, 2020).

We can now repeat this exercise for all other relevant airlines in our sample with the following code. Note that we now introduce an `airline` variable. You can look up the corresponding values by checking www.airlinequality.com for each airline. In addition, remember to adapt the number of pages. In addition, we introduce the command `Sys.sleep()` which asks R to wait for a specified time before repeating the loop. We use a value of 1.5 seconds to mimic human browsing behaviour and to prevent the webpage from banning our IP address.

```
Airline.SkyTraxFull = data.frame()
airline = "british-airways"
airline2 = paste0(airline, "/page/", sep ="")
page = 1
endpage = 36
link1 = paste0("https://www.airlinequality.com/airline-reviews/", airline2, sep="")
while(page < endpage){

  link = paste0(link1, page,"/?sortby=post_date%3ADesc&pagesize=100", sep="")
  #Title
  Review.Title.Airline <- read_html(link) %>%
    html_nodes(".comp_media-review-rated") %>%
    html_node (".text_header") %>%
    html_text() %>%
    unlist()

  ##ReviewText
  Review.Text.Airline <- read_html(link) %>%
    html_nodes(".comp_media-review-rated") %>%
    html_node(".text_content") %>%
    html_text() %>%
    unlist()

  #Rating
  Rating.Airline <- read_html(link) %>%
```

```
    html_nodes(".comp_media-review-rated") %>%
    html_nodes(".rating-10") %>%
    html_node("span:nth-child(1)") %>%
    html_text() %>%
    unlist()

  #Seat Type
  Seattype.Airline <- read_html(link) %>%
    html_nodes(".querylist") %>%
    html_nodes(xpath = ".//article[contains(@class, 'comp comp_
    media-review-rated list-item media position-content review-')]") %>%
    html_node(".cabin_flown+ .review-value") %>%
    html_text() %>%
    unlist()

  #Aircraft Type
  Aircraft.Airline <- read_html(link) %>%
    html_nodes(".querylist") %>%
    html_nodes(xpath = ".//article[contains(@class, 'comp comp_media-
    review-rated list-item media position-content review-')]") %>%
    html_node(".aircraft+ .review-value") %>%
    html_text() %>%
    unlist()

  #Route
  Route.Airline <- read_html(link) %>%
    html_nodes(".querylist") %>%
    html_nodes(xpath = ".//article[contains(@class, 'comp comp_media-
    review-rated list-item media position-content review-')]") %>%
    html_node(".route+ .review-value") %>%
    html_text() %>%
    unlist()

  Airline.Skytrax = data.frame(Review.Title.Airline = Review.Title.
  Airline, Review.Text.Airline = Review.Text.Airline, Rating.Airline =
  Rating.Airline, Seat.Type.Airline = Seattype.Airline, Airline.Aircaft =
  Aircraft.Airline, Route.Airline = Route.Airline)
  Airline.SkyTraxFull = rbind(Airline.SkyTraxFull, Airline.Skytrax)
  page = page +1
  Sys.sleep(1.5)

}
BritishAirways.Skytrax = Airline.SkyTraxFull
BritishAirways.BusinessClass = BritishAirways.SkyTraxFull %>%
```

```
filter(Seat.Type.Airline =="Business Class" )
BritishAirways.BusinessClass$Rating.Airline =
as.numeric(BritishAirways.BusinessClass$Rating.Airline)
BritishAirways.BC.Satisfied = BritishAirways.BusinessClass %>%
filter(Rating.Airline > 8)
BritishAirways.BC.Dissatisfied = BritishAirways.BusinessClass %>%
filter(Rating.Airline < 7)
```

 Repeat this exercise for Lufthansa, Singapore Airlines, Qatar Airlines, and Turkish Airlines.

While our Google Trends analysis has already helped us to understand which airlines are considered in the premium segment, it might now be interesting to see which of these airlines have more or less satisfied and dissatisfied customers, as this may help us with targeting potential Leviev Air clients.

We can use the following code to obtain some initial information.

```
Airlines = c("Emirates", "Qatar", "Singapore", "Lufthansa", "British
Airways", "Turkish Airlines")

Number.Reviews = c(
    nrow(Emirates.BusinessClass),
    nrow(Qatar.BusinessClass),
    nrow(Singapore.BusinessClass),
    nrow(Lufthansa.BusinessClass),
    nrow(BritishAirways.BusinessClass),
    nrow(THY.BusinessClass))

Number.Dissatisfied = c(
    nrow(Emirates.BC.Dissatisfied),
    nrow(Qatar.BC.Dissatisfied),
    nrow(Singapore.BC.Dissatisfied),
    nrow(Lufthansa.BC.Dissatisfied),
    nrow(BritishAirways.BC.Dissatisfied),
    nrow(THY.BC.Dissatisfied))
Satisfaction.Rates = data_frame(Airline = Airlines, N_Reviews =
Number.Reviews, N_Dissatisfied = Number.Dissatisfied)
Satisfaction.Rates = Satisfaction.Rates %>% mutate(
    N_Satisfied = N_Reviews - N_Dissatisfied) %>% mutate(
    Share_Satisfied = N_Satisfied/N_Reviews,
    Share_Dissatisfied = N_Dissatisfied/N_Reviews)
```

The resulting `Satisfaction.Rates` data frame provides us with the total and relative numbers of satisfied and dissatisfied business class travellers for each premium airline. We can plot the satisfaction and dissatisfaction shares with the following code:

```
ggplot(Satisfaction.Rates, aes(x= reorder(Airline,Share_
Dissatisfied), y = Share_Dissatisfied)) +
    geom_bar(stat = "identity", position = position_stack()) +
    labs(y="Share of Dissatisfied Users", x="Airline", title = "Rate
    of Dissatisfied User Reviews per Airline") + ylim (0,1)

ggplot(Satisfaction.Rates, aes(x= reorder(Airline,Share_
Dissatisfied), y = Share_Satisfied)) +
    geom_bar(stat = "identity", position = position_stack()) +
    labs(y="Share of Satisfied Users", x="Airline", title = "Rate of
    Satisfied User Reviews per Airline") + ylim (0,1)
```

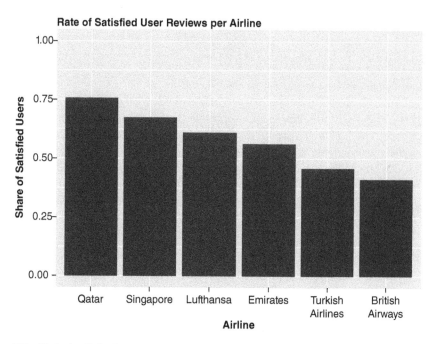

Figure 5.7 Plot of satisfaction shares per airline

From the resulting satisfaction plot in Figure 5.7 we learn that Qatar Airways and Singapore Airlines have the most satisfied business class travellers, while Turkish Airlines and British Airways share the least satisfied business class travellers. In between we find Lufthansa and Emirates. While the two worst airlines provide the opportunity to attract many dissatisfied customers, the two best airlines may allow us to investigate which things passengers really appreciate.

For the latter purpose, we use again word clouds to investigate the reviews from the satisfied Qatar Airways and Singapore Airlines customers for often occurring terms and words.

```
tidy_keywords.Qatar<- Qatar.BC.Satisfied %>%
   unnest_tokens(word, Review.Text.Airline) %>% count(word) %>%
   with(wordcloud(word, n, min.freq = 15, max.words = 30, random.order = FALSE))
```

A quick inspection of the plot, as shown in Figure 5.8, reveals that the word cloud does not provide any useful information.

Figure 5.8   Simple word cloud of Qatar Airways reviews

There are two reasons for this. First of all, we only see frequently occurring words such as 'the', 'two', 'of', and 'and'. In linguistics these words are often referred to as stopwords. Only by removing these words are we able to find frequently occurring and relevant words. In addition, we must realize that looking at single words makes it hard to interpret the meaning. Therefore, we do not use the token function at the word level, but at the bigram level. A bigram is a combination of words that occur together. With the following code we can print the bigram word clouds that do not feature any stopwords.

```
data("stop_words")
pal <- brewer.pal(8,"Dark2")

tidy_keywords.ngramQatar<- Qatar.BC.Satisfied %>%
   unnest_tokens(word, Review.Text.Airline, token = "ngrams", n = 2) %>%
   separate(word, c("word1", "word2"), sep = " ") %>%
   filter(!word1 %in% stop_words$word,
          !word2 %in% stop_words$word) %>%
   count(word1, word2, sort = TRUE) %>% unite(bigram, word1, word2, sep = " ") %>%
   with(wordcloud(bigram, n, min.freq = 15, max.words = 30, random.
   order = FALSE, colors=pal))
```

```
tidy_keywords.ngramSingapore<- Singapore.BC.Satisfied %>%
  unnest_tokens(word, Review.Text.Airline, token = "ngrams", n = 2) %>%
  separate(word, c("word1", "word2"), sep = " ") %>%
  filter(!word1 %in% stop_words$word,
         !word2 %in% stop_words$word) %>%
  count(word1, word2, sort = TRUE) %>% unite(bigram, word1, word2, sep = " ") %>%
  with(wordcloud(bigram, n, min.freq = 5, max.words = 30, random.order =
  FALSE, colors=pal))
```

Figure 5.9 shows the two resulting word clouds. As you can see, we use a colour palette to make things a bit clearer.

Figure 5.9   Word clouds of most frequent bigrams in Qatar Airways and Singapore Airlines reviews by satisfied customers

An inspection of the plots reveals that for both airlines, customers especially value on-board service and crew friendliness, as well as flat bed seats. In the case of Qatar Airways we see that the airport lounge is often highlighted. Singapore Airlines customers often especially highlight the food quality and often refer to the lobster thermidor on the menu.

We can now repeat this with the reviews of dissatisfied customers from British Airways and Turkish Airlines. The resulting plots are in Figure 5.10.

Figure 5.10 Word clouds of most frequent bigrams in Turkish Airlines and British Airways reviews by dissatisfied customers

An inspection reveals that customers are especially dissatisfied with the service on the ground and staff behaviour, as well as the seat quality. In case of Turkish Airlines we find in addition that customers were unhappy about the entertainment system on board and the chaotic boarding system, while in the case of British Airways customers were especially displeased with Heathrow airport and long waiting lines.

Leviev Air is thus well advised either not to start from Heathrow, or to ensure that boarding is easy and pleasant. Furthermore, it may be beneficial for Leviev Air to accentuate seat comfort, pleasant staff behaviour, and to ensure the highest service quality onboard and on the ground.

To finally understand on which routes Leviev faces the best potential to acquire dissatisfied customers from British Airways and Turkish Airlines, we should try and see on which routes we observe the most dissatisfied reviews. We can do this with the following code.

```
Dis.routes.THY = THY.BC.Dissatisfied %>%
    group_by(Route.Airline) %>%
    summarise(Number = n(),
            Airline = "THY") %>% filter(Number > 2) %>% drop_na()

Dis.routes.BA = BritishAirways.BC.Dissatisfied %>%
    group_by(Route.Airline) %>%
    summarise(Number = n(),
            Airline = "B.A.") %>% filter(Number > 2) %>% drop_na()
```

We use the `group_by()` function in `dplyr` with the `summarize` command to count how many times a route was mentioned in the corresponding data frames. In addition, we only want to look at routes which are mentioned more than twice. Furthermore, we use `tidyr`'s `drop_na` to exclude all reviews in which no route was provided.

A quick inspection of the two resulting data frames shows that for Turkish Airlines the route between Istanbul and London is most often mentioned, which is not surprising as Istanbul is the home airport of Turkish Airlines. In the case of British Airways we can again use barplots to see which destinations most often cause trouble and are thus especially suitable for Leviev Air to conquer market share. We use the following code to obtain Figure 5.11.

```
ggplot(Dis.routes.BA, aes(x= reorder(Route.Airline,-Number), y = Number))
    + geom_bar(stat = "identity", position = position_stack()) +
    labs(y="N", x="Route", title = "Number of times a route is
    mentioned in a negative review") + theme(axis.text.x=element_
    text(angle=90, hjust=1))
```

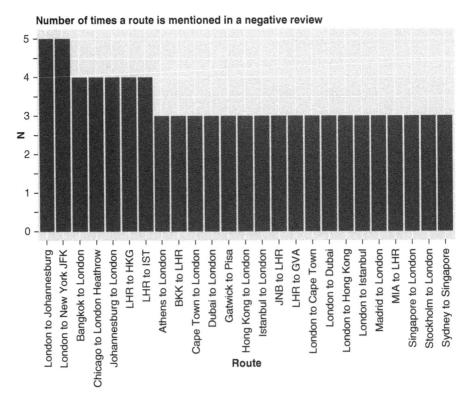

Figure 5.11 Frequencies of routes

It looks like British Airways business class passengers are especially unhappy on flights to and from Johannesburg, Hong Kong, New York, Chicago, and Bangkok.

Leviev Air can now take these insights as a starting point for its launch campaign. One way to leverage these insights could be a search engine advertising campaign in which Leviev uses keywords related to the routes identified with high volume of dissatisfied customers. Meanwhile, Leviev Air might also accentuate its priority service, high service quality, and its full bed seats and on-board entertainment service.

CHAPTER SUMMARY

In this chapter, we discussed how user-generated data may enrich the market research efforts of marketing managers and how to access information and insights which might otherwise not be accessible at all. We discovered different suitable sources of user-generated content and developed an understanding of how to judge and rate sources of UGD for marketing decision-making. Furthermore, we learned how to use the structure of website code to automatically extract large sources of content from online sources and then use this content to derive customer insights with the help of simple but meaningful frequency analysis.

REFERENCES

Baehre, S., O'Dwyer, M., O'Malley, L. and Lee, N. (2022) The use of Net Promoter Score (NPS) to predict sales growth: Insights from an empirical investigation. *Journal of the Academy of Marketing Science*, 50(1), 67–84.

Colicev, A., Malshe, A., Pauwels, K. and O'Connor, P. (2018) Improving consumer mindset metrics and shareholder value through social media: The different roles of owned and earned media. *Journal of Marketing*, 82(1), 37–56.

Kübler, R. V., Colicev, A. and Pauwels, K. H. (2020) Social media's impact on the consumer mindset: When to use which sentiment extraction tool? *Journal of Interactive Marketing*, 50, 136–55.

Kübler, R., Pauwels, K. and Manke, K. (2020) How social media drove the 2016 US presidential election: A longitudinal topic and platform analysis. https://papers.ssrn.com/sol3/papers.cfm?abstract_id=3661846

Nofer, M. and Hinz, O. (2015) Using Twitter to predict the stock market. *Business & Information Systems Engineering*, 57(4), 229–42.

Reichheld, F. F. and Covey, S. R. (2006) *The Ultimate Question: Driving Good Profits and True Growth*. Boston: Harvard Business School Press.

Saura, J. R., Ribeiro-Soriano, D. and Palacios-Marqués, D. (2021) From user-generated data to data-driven innovation: A research agenda to understand user privacy in digital markets. *International Journal of Information Management*, 60, 102331.

Skiera, B. and Ringel, D. M. (2017). Using big search data to map your market: Marketing in a digital age. *IESE Insight*, 32, 31–7. https://www.marketing.uni-frankfurt.de/fileadmin/user_upload/dateien_abteilungen/abt_marketing/Bilder/Professor_Skiera/Slides/Skiera-Ringel-2017-IESE-Insights-Map-your-Market.pdf

6

CUSTOMER MINDSET METRICS

Chapter contents

LEARNING OBJECTIVES

At the end of this chapter, you should be able to:

- explain the importance of consumer attitude metrics for assessing brand performance
- outline the effectiveness criteria for attitude metrics and describe how to build share in customers' hearts and minds
- apply the analytical models in R to a real-world consumer attitude dataset to gain some actionable insights into marketing mix decisions and financial performance.

Long-term-oriented brand managers tend to spend a substantial amount of their budget on building and improving customers' 'hearts and minds' (Pauwels et al., 2013; Wall Street Journal 2018). To measure the impact of such brand-building activities, they often collect data on customer mindset metrics (e.g. awareness, consideration, and liking), also known as brand health indicators (Bruce et al., 2012). In contrast, bottom-line-oriented managers (e.g. chief financial officers) assess marketing effectiveness using measures such as 'advertising elasticity' and 'return on sales'. How can brand managers justify the economic value of their long-term brand-building activities to the firm? To address this strategic managerial question, this chapter provides some guidance to brand managers on the use of customer attitude information to create long-lasting financial performance.

The chapter begins with a practical case study from a fast-moving consumer goods brand. Next, it develops a theoretical framework that outlines the connection between marketing mix actions, customer mindset metrics, and financial performance. Finally, the software application showcases how to implement analytic tools, allowing brand managers to develop some actionable guidelines and improve their marketing mix decisions based on the diagnostic value of the customer mindset metrics.

Case study

Zanten shampoo

Watching the dark clouds over the city of London from her office, Bo Zhang, the chief marketing officer of shampoo brand Zanten, had many thoughts about what to say at tomorrow's six-monthly meeting regarding the somewhat radical changes she was planning to make with her next advertising and promotion decisions.

The next day, Zhang and the chief executive officer, Anne Comstock, met over Zoom to discuss the most recent performance outcomes and decide the best possible moves for the future. Zhang began to talk excitedly:

'I am very proud of my team. They have run very successful marketing campaigns over the past few months on social media, giving us a strong position in consumers' hearts. See how we outperform our closest competitor in terms of brand liking.' Sharing her screen, she showed Anne Figure 6.1.

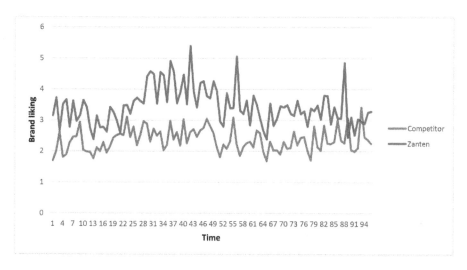

Figure 6.1   Brand liking of Zanten versus competitor

Zhang continued with a quiet voice: 'However, I must admit that the gains in brand liking have not yet been translated into higher revenues. But I believe that these gains in consumer heart share will soon result in better financial performance. We just need to promote ourselves more heavily or increase our advertising substantially, and also believe in ourselves.'

The CEO thanked Zhang and said 'These analytic insights are great. But there is another pressing issue that we are facing now. The fierce competition is putting a lot of pressure on our margins. As a result, we may need to be a bit careful about how we spend our budget. Therefore, it is extremely important that you justify how these positive changes in consumers' attitudes will turn into better sales performance.'

Moving forward

After the meeting, Zhang continued her deliberations on how to allocate marketing resources that would provide noticeable and long-lasting improvements not only in customers' attitudes but also in the brand's sales performance. With one eye on her marketing dashboard on her laptop, she called her analytics team.

'I would like you to prepare a report that provides some concrete directions on how the effectiveness of advertising and promotional campaigns can be improved by examining customer mindset metrics,' she said. 'I would like to know (1) to what extent the advertising and promotional campaigns run in recent years have affected consumers' attitudes towards the brand and (2) whether the changes in consumers' perceptions have yielded any significant improvement in our brand's sales performance.'

To help Zhang, the marketing analytics team gathered data from various sources. Table 6.1 summarizes the variables of the dataset.

(Continued)

Table 6.1 Dataset description

Variable	Description	Source
Advertising	Monthly total spending on advertising media	Internal database
Promotion	Monthly total spending on promotional campaigns	
Price	Average price paid by end consumer	
Mindset metrics		
Aided awareness (% aware)	'Which of the following brands have you heard of?' (Respondent is given a list of brands, and responds YES or NO to each.) % aided awareness is the percentage of respondents responding YES for the particular brand.	Online survey conducted by a market research company
Brand consideration (% considering buying)	'Which of these brands would you consider buying?' (Respondent is given a list of brands, and responds YES or NO to each.) % score is the percentage of respondents responding YES for the particular brand.	
Brand liking (average liking)	'Please indicate how much you like brand X.' (1: I don't like it at all, 7: I like it a lot)	
Sales	Brand sales volume (in millilitres)	Internal database

The options on the table

Moving forward, Zhang has to decide on her promotion and advertising spending choices, and ponders two options:

1   Quintupling advertising spending
2   Doubling promotion

Which of these options should Zhang propose to Comstock? How would these decisions influence the hearts and minds of consumers, and the sales performance of the company?

To address these questions, we will first develop a conceptual framework that establishes the link between marketing mix actions, customer mindset metrics, and sales performance. In doing so, we will propose four effectiveness criteria that allow us to understand this link: potential, stickiness, responsiveness, and conversion. Then we will present the model application to the aforementioned dataset using R.

CUSTOMER MINDSET METRICS

Customer mindset metrics such as brand awareness, consideration, and liking show how effectively marketing programmes capture customers' 'hearts and minds' (Srinivasan et al., 2010; Wall Street Journal, 2018). These metrics are critical for marketing managers, who often spend a significant portion of their budget on developing and refining such attitudinal constructs (Bruce et al., 2012; Hammett, 2018; Keller, 1993; Avagyan et al., 2022). Yet marketing managers struggle to guide their future resource allocation strategies using the informational value of these customer mindset metrics (Forbes, 2018; Hanssens et al., 2014).

Suppose that a marketing manager has run various social media marketing campaigns and collected data on customer mindset metrics. How should the brand manager act on the informational value that these metrics provide? Which marketing mix action (e.g. price, advertising, promotion, distribution) should be prioritized to improve them? Which effectiveness criteria should be used to find out whether marketing efforts will pay off in terms of lifting consumers' attitudes and generating sales?

To answer these questions, we need a conceptual framework that reveals how marketing actions influence firm performance through changes in consumer attitudes. Figure 6.2 shows that marketing actions may create an impact on a brand's performance without making significant changes in customers' hearts and minds, that is, the brand harvests consumers' established attitudes. We call this a 'transaction route' which shows the direct effects of marketing actions on brand performance. Also, marketing actions may build customer attitudes first, and then changes in customers' hearts and minds convert into sales. We call this a 'mindset route'. This route shows the indirect effects of marketing actions on brand performance.

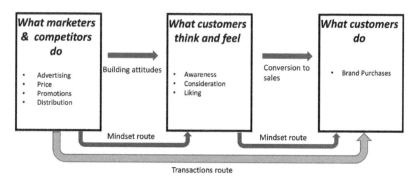

Figure 6.2   Conceptual framework (adapted from Hanssens et al., 2014)

Overall, this framework explains the channels of marketing influence through building consumer attitudes and/or through leveraging the brand's existing health.

Four criteria

What determines the relevance of customer mindset metrics to guiding marketing mix decisions? We propose four criteria to capture the properties of attitudinal metrics and their relationship to sales performance.

Potential

Does the metric have room to grow? Suppose that a brand manager has run various social media campaigns and collected data on customer mindset metrics. The data reveal that brand liking stands at 15% while brand consideration stands at 80%. Of these two metrics, brand liking has the higher potential because the remaining distance to the maximum is larger for this metric (85% versus 20%).

A marketing campaign that aims to improve brand liking will have more impact potential if brand liking at the outset is 15% as opposed to, say, 80%. To quantify the 'potential' of a customer mindset metric, we use the following formula:

$$Potential_t = \frac{\bar{A} - A_{t-1}}{\bar{A}},$$ (6.1)

where $\bar{A}$ is the maximum level of the customer attitude metric A, and A_{t-1} is the level of the attitude metric from the previous period. For example, if the maximum liking score is 100% and previous liking, A_{t-1}, is 15%, then the potential is 85%. The equation holds regardless of the scale used. If brand managers ignore the potential of a customer mindset metric, they may overspend on a saturated metric and obtain lower returns.

Stickiness

This criterion refers to the staying power of a change in the customer mindset metric. It measures whether an increase in a customer mindset metric is long-lasting. If a marketing campaign increases the stickiness of a mindset metric, that campaign is likely to generate higher sales in the long term. Stickiness can be modelled as follows:

$$A_t = c + \sum_{i=1}^{p} \varphi_i A_{t-i} + \epsilon_t,$$ (6.2)

where t is the time index, A denotes the mindset metric, c is a constant term, i is the time gap (also known as the lag indicator), p is the maximum number of lags, A_{t-i} is the past mindset metric at lag I, and φ_i is the associated coefficient. Finally, ϵ is a residual term that follows a normal distribution with zero mean ($\mu = 0$), and constant variance (σ^2). Furthermore, we assume that residuals are uncorrelated, that is, the residual at one period is not related to the residual at another period.

The model in equation (6.2) is basically a univariate time-series process with p lags. It is also known as pth-order autoregression, denoted by AR(p) (Wang and Yildirim, 2022). Stickiness is quantified as the sum of the autoregressive coefficients, i.e. $\sum_{i=1}^{p} \varphi_i$.

Let us take an example. Suppose that the following AR(2) process captures the univariate dynamics of the *brand consideration* metric:

$$Cons_t = c + \varphi_1 Cons_{t-1} + \varphi_2 Cons_{t-2} + \epsilon_t .$$ (6.3)

Furthermore, assume that the model is estimated with the following coefficients:

$$\widehat{Cons}_t = 10.2 + 0.60\, Cons_{t-1} + 0.15\, Cons_{t-2} ,\tag{6.4}$$

where $\widehat{Cons}_t$ is the predicted brand consideration at time t. Summing the autoregression coefficients, the stickiness is measured as 0.75. The stability of the model requires that the sum of the autoregressive coefficients should be less than 1 in absolute value. This is also consistent with the well-established memory decay effects in consumer psychology (Burke and Srull, 1988).

Responsiveness

This criterion captures the short-term impact of a marketing mix action (e.g. advertising) on customer mindset metrics. It shows the power of marketing in lifting customers' attitudes. To quantify responsiveness, we use the following multiplicative response model (Hanssens et al., 2001):

$$A_t = \alpha A_{t-1}^{\gamma} X_{1t}^{\beta_1} X_{2t}^{\beta_2} X_{3t}^{\beta_3} e^{u_t} ,\tag{6.5}$$

where t is the time index, A is a customer mindset metric, X_1, X_2, X_3 are marketing mix variables (e.g. price, advertising, promotions), and β_1, β_2, β_3 are the corresponding coefficients that measure responsiveness. α is a constant, and γ is the autoregression coefficient for the mindset metric from the previous period (A_{t-1}). The residuals, u_t, are assumed to be uncorrelated and distributed as normal with zero mean ($\mu = 0$), and constant variance (σ^2).

The advantage of the multiplicative model in equation (6.5) is that it allows for diminishing returns to scale. Taking the logarithm of both sides, the model becomes log-linear. This specification allows us to interpret the estimated βs as elasticities. For example, if A is awareness, X_2 is advertising spending and the estimated β_2 is 0.3, it suggests that a 1% increase in advertising spending results in a 0.3% increase in awareness.

Conversion

This criterion shows whether an increase in a customer mindset metric translates into sales performance. In other words, it indicates the extent to which changes in an attitudinal metric convert into sales performance. If brand managers view customer mindset metrics as the ultimate performance metrics but ignore sales conversion, they run the risk of practising silo marketing.

We model sales conversion using the following multiplicative funnel model:

$$S_t = \omega S_{t-1}^{\rho} A_t^{\theta_1} C_t^{\theta_2} L_t^{\theta_3} e^{v_t} ,\tag{6.6}$$

where t is the time index, S denotes sales, A, C, L are customer mindset metrics of awareness, consideration, and liking, respectively. ω is a constant, ρ is the autoregression coefficient for past sales performance (S_{t-1}), and θ_1, θ_2, θ_3 are the coefficients of the mindset metrics A, C, L, respectively. The residuals, v_t, are assumed to be uncorrelated and distributed as normal with zero mean ($\mu = 0$), and constant variance (σ^2).

It is worth noting that in practice mindset metrics often move more slowly than sales performance, and their effect on sales may be lagged. If this pattern is observed in the data, the subscript t of the mindset metrics should be replaced by $t - k$, where k is the number of lags.

Marketing investment appeal

How should one combine the four criteria discussed above to evaluate the investment appeal of a given mindset metric? First, we need to calculate the long-run (LR) impact of each marketing mix element i for each mindset metric k, by combining the three criteria of potential, responsiveness, and long-run stickiness, as follows:

$$LR\ impact_k^{(i)} = Potential_k \times Responsiveness_k^{(i)} \times \frac{1}{1 - Stickiness_k}, \qquad \forall k \in K, \tag{6.7}$$

where the term $Potential_k \times Responsiveness_k^{(i)}$ measures the short-term response, and the term $1/(1 - Stickiness_k)$ is the long-run multiplier.

Finally, to obtain the investment appeal for marketing mix element i, we multiply the long-run impact by the conversion factor of mindset metric k and sum across k:

$$Appeal^{(i)} = \sum_{k=1}^{K} LR\ impact_k^{(i)} \times Conversion_k. \tag{6.8}$$

Having reviewed the customer mindset metrics and discussed the four criteria, we will next apply the model in R to the dataset of the case study and evaluate the options for Zanten's brand manager.

MODEL APPLICATION WITH R

Before we start, we need to do some preparatory work. The reader is encouraged to follow the R Markdown and HTML files that are available on the website of the book.

Preparation and set-up

The following first steps should be familiar:

- Create a folder (e.g. *mindset*) and set the working directory to that folder on your device.
- Download the dataset needed for this R application onto your working directory. The dataset for this application, *mindset_shampoo.xlsx*, is available on the website of this book.
- Load the dataset to R for analysis as we proceed.

In order to load the datasets into R, we need to run only a part of the code chunk below, depending on the operating system of your device. To avoid running code that is not applicable and receiving error messages, add # before each line of inapplicable code in the chunk. For example, if you are using a Mac, you need to put # before `setwd("H:/Downloads/mindset")`.

```r
```{r}
# Run the following codes depending on the operating system on your
laptop/PC.

# If you are using iOS and your 'mindset' folder is created under
'Downloads' on your Mac, you will need to first set your working
directory to the 'mindset' folder:

setwd("~/Desktop/mindset")

# If you are using Windows and your 'mindset' folder is created in
your H drive, you will need to first set your working directory to
the 'mindset' folder:

# setwd("H:/Downloads/mindset")

```
```

Next, install and load the packages that are needed to run the code for this application.

```r
```{r include=FALSE}
#Before we load the dataset, we need to install and load a few packages.

if(!require(knitr)) install.packages("knitr",repos = "http://cran.
us.r-project.org")
if(!require(readxl)) install.packages("readxl",repos = "http://cran.
us.r-project.org")
if(!require(tseries)) install.packages("tseries",repos = "http://
cran.us.r-project.org")
if(!require(vars)) install.packages("vars",repos = "http://cran.
us.r-project.org")
if(!require(R6)) install.packages("R6",repos = "http://cran.us.r-
project.org")
if(!require(tidyverse)) install.packages("tidyverse",repos =
"http://cran.us.r-project.org")

library(knitr)
library(readxl)
```
```

```
library(tseries)
library(vars)
library(R6)
library(tidyverse)

```

We are now ready to proceed with the analysis.

Data

First, we will load the dataset into R with the following code chunk.

```
```{r warning=FALSE}
# load the dataset
data_shampoo<-read.csv("mindset_shampoo.csv")

```

We can preview the dataset and a get a feel for how the variables of the data look. We run the following code chunk and obtain the output in Figure 6.3.

```
```{r warning=FALSE}

# Take a look at the data

head(data_shampoo)

```

	time	consideration	liking	awareness	promotion	advertising	price	vol
1	1	14.26	5.136	26.78	2.39	449.572	4.349	1280.44
2	2	16.77	5.010	29.93	4.90	483.416	4.406	1129.63
3	3	17.17	4.901	29.63	3.80	374.110	4.203	1059.38
4	4	16.46	5.094	27.11	2.94	567.110	4.145	933.61
5	5	18.43	4.944	31.77	2.81	418.777	4.212	826.36
6	6	15.54	4.991	30.26	4.33	847.159	4.141	999.60

6 rows

Figure 6.3 Previewing the data

Next, we will calculate our four criteria: potential, stickiness, responsiveness, and conversion. Finally, by aggregating the results of all these stages, we will evaluate the appeal of our marketing mix decisions.

The four criteria

Potential

For awareness and consideration, we need to calculate the average level of awareness and consideration for this shampoo brand and then calculate the potential by deducting 1 from them.

For liking, things are slightly more complicated since those values are measured on a seven-point scale. Therefore, we need to first convert those values into percentages (e.g. if liking is 3.5 out of 7, then it is actually 50% of the full score and the value should be 50) and then take the average and calculate the corresponding potential.

The R codes below calculate the potential criteria and generate the output in Figure 6.4. We get that potential is 0.725 for awareness, 0.825 for consideration and 0.263 for liking.

```r
```{r}

# Calculate potential for awareness and consideration
potential_awareness <- (100-mean(data_shampoo$awareness))/100

potential_consideration <- (100-mean(data_shampoo$consideration))/100

# Calculate potential for liking

data_shampoo$liking_transformed <- data_shampoo$liking/7
potential_liking <- 1- mean(data_shampoo$liking_transformed)
```
```

potential	value
awareness	0.7252698
consideration	0.8252083
liking	0.2630961

3 rows

Figure 6.4 Potential

```r
```{r echo=FALSE}
table_potential<-data.frame(
  potential=c("awareness", "consideration","liking"), value =
c(potential_awareness, potential_consideration, potential_liking)
)

table_potential
```
```

Judging from what you have now, which mindset metric should you put more effort into? Why?

Stickiness

As discussed earlier in this chapter, stickiness can be modelled by a simple univariate AR(p) process on the attitude metric, where stickiness is quantified as the sum of the AR coefficients (see equation (6.2)). The code below calculates stickiness and gives the output in Figure 6.5. It is important to note that the order of lag for these AR models is determined by model fit statistics such as the Akaike information criterion or the Bayesian information criterion.

```r
```{r warning=FALSE}
#awareness
ar1 <- ar(data_shampoo$awareness, aic = TRUE)
ar1

#consideration
ar2 <- ar(data_shampoo$consideration, aic = TRUE)
ar2

#liking
ar3 <- ar(data_shampoo$liking, aic = TRUE)
ar3

```
```

```
Call:
ar(x = data_shampoo$awareness, aic = TRUE)

Coefficients:
     1       2       3
0.4524  0.0459  0.2660

Order selected 3  sigma^2 estimated as  8.621

Call:
ar(x = data_shampoo$consideration, aic = TRUE)

Coefficients:
     1       2       3
0.3028  0.3121  0.1591

Order selected 3  sigma^2 estimated as  5.564

Call:
ar(x = data_shampoo$liking, aic = TRUE)

Coefficients:
     1       2       3
0.4287  0.1136  0.2224

Order selected 3  sigma^2 estimated as  0.03379
```

Figure 6.5 Stickiness

From these results, we can calculate the stickiness of our mindset metrics by summing their AR coefficients as follows.

```r
```{r}
stick_awareness <- ar1$ar[1] + ar1$ar[2]+ar1$ar[3]
stick_consideration <- ar2$ar[1] + ar2$ar[2]+ar2$ar[3]
stick_liking <- ar3$ar[1] + ar3$ar[2]+ar3$ar[3]

```
```

To summarize, the stickiness measures for the awareness, consideration, and liking metrics are 0.764, 0.774, and 0.765, respectively.

Responsiveness

Using equation (6.5), we estimate the log-linear model for each mindset metric and sales to get responsiveness measures. The code below performs this estimation.

```
```{r warning=FALSE}
#We start by generating lagged variables for each mindset metric and
sales

data_shampoo$lag_aware<-lag(data_shampoo$awareness)
data_shampoo$lag_aware[1]<-0
data_shampoo$lag_liking <-lag(data_shampoo$liking)
data_shampoo$lag_liking[1]<-0
data_shampoo$lag_consideration <-lag(data_shampoo$consideration)
data_shampoo$lag_consideration[1]<-0
data_shampoo$lag_sales <-lag(data_shampoo$vol)
data_shampoo$lag_sales[1]<-0

#Now estimate the log-linear model

response_aware <- lm(log(data_shampoo$awareness+1)~log(lag_
aware+1)+log(data_shampoo$price+1)+log(data_
shampoo$promotion+1)+log(data_shampoo$advertising+1), data =
data_shampoo)

response_consideration <- lm(log(data_shampoo$consideration+1)
~log(lag_consideration+1)+log(data_shampoo$price+1)+log(data_
shampoo$promotion+1)+log(data_shampoo$advertising+1), data = data_
shampoo)

response_liking <- lm(log(data_shampoo$liking+1)~log(lag_
liking+1)+log(data_shampoo$price+1)+log(data_
shampoo$promotion+1)+log(data_shampoo$advertising+1), data =
data_shampoo)

response_sales <- lm(log(data_shampoo$vol+1)~log(lag_
sales+1)+log(data_shampoo$price+1)+log(data_
shampoo$promotion+1)+log(data_shampoo$advertising+1), data =
data_shampoo)
```
```

```
#Summarize all the regression results here:

summary(response_aware)
summary(response_consideration)
summary(response_liking)
summary(response_sales)

```

Figure 6.6 displays the R output for the responsiveness models.

We run the following code chunk to summarize the responsiveness coefficients.

```
```{r echo=FALSE}
table_response_aware<-data.frame(round(response_
aware$coefficients,4))
table_response_liking<-data.frame(round(response_
liking$coefficients,4))
table_response_consideration<-data.frame(round(response_consideratio
n$coefficients,4))
table_response_sales<-data.frame(round(response_
sales$coefficients,4))

table_response_aware
table_response_consideration
table_response_liking
table_response_sales

```

The R output in Figure 6.7 shows the responsiveness coefficients of each mindset metric to marketing mix variables (i.e. price, promotion, and advertising).

Conversion

To estimate the conversion model in equation (6.6), we run the following code. Note that we take the logarithm of both sides of the equation and estimate a log-linear model.

```
```{r}

conversion <- lm(log(data_shampoo$vol+1)~log(lag_sales+1)+log(data_
shampoo$awareness)+log(data_shampoo$consideration)+log(data_
shampoo$liking), data = data_shampoo)
summary(conversion)

```

Responsiveness of awareness to marketing mix decisions

```
## Call:
## lm(formula = log(data_shampoo$awareness + 1) ~ log(lag_aware +
##     1) + log(data_shampoo$price + 1) + log(data_shampoo$promotion +
##     1) + log(data_shampoo$advertising + 1), data = data_shampoo)
##
## Residuals:
##      Min       1Q   Median       3Q      Max
## -0.34958 -0.05989  0.01399  0.09772  0.17647
##
## Coefficients:
##                                   Estimate Std. Error t value Pr(>|t|)
## (Intercept)                       2.950944   0.553568   5.331 7.06e-07 ***
## log(lag_aware + 1)                0.046713   0.032299   1.446   0.152
## log(data_shampoo$price + 1)      -0.082973   0.331404  -0.250   0.803
## log(data_shampoo$promotion + 1)   0.021483   0.014737   1.458   0.148
## log(data_shampoo$advertising + 1) 0.052073   0.007739   6.729 1.45e-09 ***
## ---
## Signif. codes:  0 '***' 0.001 '**' 0.01 '*' 0.05 '.' 0.1 ' ' 1
## Residual standard error: 0.1104 on 91 degrees of freedom
## Multiple R-squared:  0.4273, Adjusted R-squared:  0.4021
## F-statistic: 16.97 on 4 and 91 DF,  p-value: 1.98e-10
```

Responsiveness of consideration to marketing mix decisions

```
## Call:
## lm(formula = log(data_shampoo$consideration + 1) ~ log(lag_consideration +
##     1) + log(data_shampoo$price + 1) + log(data_shampoo$promotion +
##     1) + log(data_shampoo$advertising + 1), data = data_shampoo)
##
## Residuals:
##      Min       1Q   Median       3Q      Max
## -0.34442 -0.06840 -0.00619  0.08660  0.32549
##
## Coefficients:
##                                   Estimate Std. Error t value Pr(>|t|)
## (Intercept)                       1.862814   0.654452   2.846  0.00546 **
## log(lag_consideration + 1)        0.099604   0.044201   2.253  0.02663 *
## log(data_shampoo$price + 1)       0.280150   0.401082   0.698  0.48665
## log(data_shampoo$promotion + 1)   0.066172   0.018268   3.622  0.00048 ***
## log(data_shampoo$advertising + 1) 0.017685   0.009394   1.883  0.06295 .
## ---
## Signif. codes:  0 '***' 0.001 '**' 0.01 '*' 0.05 '.' 0.1 ' ' 1
## Residual standard error: 0.1344 on 91 degrees of freedom
## Multiple R-squared:  0.3412, Adjusted R-squared:  0.3123
## F-statistic: 11.79 on 4 and 91 DF,  p-value: 9.312e-08
```

Responsiveness of liking to marketing mix decisions

```
## Call:
## lm(formula = log(data_shampoo$liking + 1) ~ log(lag_liking +
##     1) + log(data_shampoo$price + 1) + log(data_shampoo$promotion +
##     1) + log(data_shampoo$advertising + 1), data = data_shampoo)
##
## Residuals:
##       Min        1Q    Median        3Q       Max
## -0.070126 -0.026017 -0.002351  0.021598  0.074947
##
## Coefficients:
##                                    Estimate Std. Error t value Pr(>|t|)
## (Intercept)                        1.454127   0.160915   9.037 2.65e-14 ***
## log(lag_liking + 1)               -0.001644   0.018375  -0.089   0.9289
## log(data_shampoo$price + 1)        0.178931   0.097082   1.843   0.0686 .
## log(data_shampoo$promotion + 1)    0.019200   0.004330   4.434 2.58e-05 ***
## log(data_shampoo$advertising + 1)  0.002394   0.002274   1.053   0.2952
## ---
## Signif. codes:  0 '***' 0.001 '**' 0.01 '*' 0.05 '.' 0.1 ' ' 1
## Residual standard error: 0.03251 on 91 degrees of freedom
## Multiple R-squared:  0.3293, Adjusted R-squared:  0.2996
## F-statistic: 11.16 on 4 and 91 DF,  p-value: 2.078e-07
```

Responsiveness of sales to marketing mix decisions (i.e. transactions route)

```
## Call:
## lm(formula = log(data_shampoo$vol + 1) ~ log(lag_sales + 1) +
##     log(data_shampoo$price + 1) + log(data_shampoo$promotion +
##     1) + log(data_shampoo$advertising + 1), data = data_shampoo)
##
## Residuals:
##      Min       1Q   Median       3Q      Max
## -0.89143 -0.18286  0.02051  0.15740  0.68007
##
## Coefficients:
##                                   Estimate Std. Error t value Pr(>|t|)
## (Intercept)                       6.23503    1.41066    4.420 2.72e-05 ***
## log(lag_sales + 1)                0.06423    0.03900    1.647   0.1030
## log(data_shampoo$price + 1)      -0.27759    0.85154   -0.326   0.7452
## log(data_shampoo$promotion + 1)   0.29700    0.04117    7.214 1.57e-10 ***
## log(data_shampoo$advertising + 1) 0.05965    0.01996    2.989   0.0036 **
## ---
## Signif. codes:  0 '***' 0.001 '**' 0.01 '*' 0.05 '.' 0.1 ' ' 1
## Residual standard error: 0.2847 on 91 degrees of freedom
## Multiple R-squared:  0.59, Adjusted R-squared:  0.5719
## F-statistic: 32.73 on 4 and 91 DF,  p-value: < 2.2e-16
```

Figure 6.6 Responsiveness

Responsiveness of awareness

Description: **df [5 × 1]**

	round.response_aware.coefficients..A. <dbl>
(Intercept)	2.9509
log(lag_aware + 1)	0.0467
log(data_shampoo$price + 1)	-0.0830
log(data_shampoo$promotion + 1)	0.0215
log(data_shampoo$advertising + 1)	0.0521

5 rows

Responsiveness of consideration

Description: **df [5 × 1]**

	round.response_consideration.coefficients..A. <dbl>
(Intercept)	1.8628
log(lag_consideration + 1)	0.0996
log(data_shampoo$price + 1)	0.2801
log(data_shampoo$promotion + 1)	0.0662
log(data_shampoo$advertising + 1)	0.0177

5 rows

Responsiveness of liking

Description: **df [5 × 1]**

	round.response_liking.coefficients..A. <dbl>
(Intercept)	1.4541
log(lag_liking + 1)	-0.0016
log(data_shampoo$price + 1)	0.1789
log(data_shampoo$promotion + 1)	0.0192
log(data_shampoo$advertising + 1)	0.0024

5 rows

Responsiveness of sales

Description: **df [5 × 1]**

	round.response_sales.coefficients..A. <dbl>
(Intercept)	6.2350
log(lag_sales + 1)	0.0642
log(data_shampoo$price + 1)	-0.2776
log(data_shampoo$promotion + 1)	0.2970
log(data_shampoo$advertising + 1)	0.0596

5 rows

Figure 6.7 Summary of responsiveness coefficients

```
Call:
lm(formula = log(data_shampoo$vol + 1) ~ log(lag_sales + 1) +
    log(data_shampoo$awareness) + log(data_shampoo$consideration) +
    log(data_shampoo$liking), data = data_shampoo)

Residuals:
     Min      1Q  Median      3Q     Max
-0.66869 -0.15410  0.01979 0.20478 0.73796

Coefficients:
                                  Estimate Std. Error t value Pr(>|t|)
(Intercept)                       -1.89070    1.24620  -1.517  0.13269
log(lag_sales + 1)                 0.11209    0.03832   2.925  0.00435 **
log(data_shampoo$awareness)        0.80095    0.25293   3.167  0.00210 **
log(data_shampoo$consideration)    0.42672    0.30376   1.405  0.16349
log(data_shampoo$liking)           2.81405    0.99745   2.821  0.00587 **
---
Signif. codes:  0 '***' 0.001 '**' 0.01 '*' 0.05 '.' 0.1 ' ' 1

Residual standard error: 0.2943 on 91 degrees of freedom
Multiple R-squared:  0.5616,    Adjusted R-squared:  0.5423
F-statistic: 29.14 on 4 and 91 DF,  p-value: 1.35e-15
```

Figure 6.8   Conversion

From Figure 6.8, we can conclude that brand liking converts into sales at a higher rate (2.81) than awareness (0.80) and consideration (0.43).

The following code chunk combines all the results together to gain a clear understanding of the measures on potential, stickiness, responsiveness, and conversion. Figure 6.9 shows these results.

```r
```{r echo=FALSE}
table_final<-data.frame(
  Item = c("beginning level", "potential", "stickiness",
"responsiveness to advertising", "responsiveness to promotion",  "conversion"),
awareness=c(round(mean(data_shampoo$awareness)/100,3),round(1-
mean(data_shampoo$awareness)/100,3),round(stick_awareness,3),
      round(response_aware$coefficients[5],3),
      round(response_aware$coefficients[4],3),round(conversion$coefficients[3],3)),
consideration=c(round(mean(data_shampoo$consideration)/100,3),
round(1-mean(data_shampoo$consideration)/100,3),  round(stick_
consideration,3),round(response_consideration$coefficients[5],3),
round(response_consideration$coefficients[4],3),round(conversion$
coefficients[4],3)), liking = c(round(mean(data_shampoo$liking_
transformed)/100,3),  round(1- mean(data_shampoo$liking_
transformed),3),  round(stick_liking,3),round(response_liking$
coefficients[5],3),  round(response_liking$coefficients[4],3),
round(conversion$coefficients[5],3)))

table_final
```
```

Description: **df [6 × 4]**

Item <chr>	awareness <dbl>	consideration <dbl>	liking <dbl>
beginning level	0.275	0.175	0.007
potential	0.725	0.825	0.263
stickiness	0.764	0.774	0.765
responsiveness to advertising	0.052	0.018	0.002
responsiveness to promotion	0.021	0.066	0.019
conversion	0.801	0.427	2.814

6 rows

Figure 6.9 Summary of analysis of the four criteria

Appeal

Finally, the appeal of each marketing mix action (i.e. promotion and advertising) is calculated using equations (6.7) and (6.8). The code below calculates the appeal of advertising and promotion decisions, and produces the output in Figure 6.10.

```{r echo=FALSE}

#Calculate appeal from model estimations. Note that we do not multiply
potential here since the responsiveness we get from the model already
incorporates potential.

appeal_adv_awareness <- round(table_final[2,"awareness"]*table_
final[4,"awareness"]*(1/(1-table_final[3,"awareness"]))*table_
final[6,"awareness"],3)
appeal_promo_awareness <- round(table_final[2,"awareness"]*table_
final[5,"awareness"]*(1/(1-table_final[3,"awareness"]))*table_
final[6,"awareness"],3)
appeal_adv_consideration<- round(table_
final[2,"consideration"]*table_final[4,"consideration"]*(1/(1-table_
final[3,"consideration"]))*table_final[6,"consideration"],3)
appeal_promo_consideration<- round(table_
final[2,"consideration"]*table_final[5,"consideration"]*(1/(1-table_
final[3,"consideration"]))*table_final[6,"consideration"],3)
appeal_adv_liking <- round(table_final[2,"liking"]*table_
final[4,"liking"]*(1/(1-table_final[3,"liking"]))*table_
final[6,"liking"],3)
appeal_promo_liking <-round(table_final[2,"liking"]*table_
final[5,"liking"]*(1/(1-table_final[3,"liking"]))*table_
final[6,"liking"],3)

appeal_table<-data.frame(
```

```
   Item = c("appeal_advertising", "appeal_promotion"),
   awareness=c(appeal_adv_awareness,appeal_promo_awareness),
   consideration=c( appeal_adv_consideration, appeal_promo_consideration),
   liking = c( appeal_adv_liking,appeal_promo_liking))


   appeal_table


   ```
```

Description **df [2 x 4]**

Item <chr>	awareness <dbl>	consideration <dbl>	liking <dbl>
appeal_advertising	0.128	0.028	0.006
appeal_promotion	0.052	0.103	0.060

2 rows

Figure 6.10   Appeal of advertising and promotion

What is your takeaway from the output in Figure 6.10? Which marketing tool (i.e. promotion or advertising) is more effective for the marketing manager of Zanten to improve consumer awareness, consideration, and liking? If you were the manager of this shampoo brand, what type of marketing strategy would you adopt?

What-if analysis

Given that this chapter focuses on the value of marketing activities through customer mindset metrics on brand sales, we would like to evaluate the impact of a change in a marketing mix variable (e.g. advertising and promotion) on long-term sales, and decompose such effect into gain/loss due to mindset metrics and gain/loss due to transactions.

In particular, we will evaluate the two alternative options for Zhang, the marketing manager of Zanten, mentioned earlier: quintupling advertising spending and doubling promotion.

Quintupling advertising spending

Suppose that Zhang decides to quintuple advertising spending from £100,000 to £500,000 without making any further changes for the other marketing mix decisions. Let us visualize the calculations using a table. The following code chunk generates Table 6.2.

```
   ```{r echo=FALSE}


   table_whatif<-data.frame(
```

```
  Item = c("Advertising", "Promotion", "Awareness", "Consideration",
"Liking", "Sales"), Start=round(c(100,100, mean(data_
shampoo$awareness)/100, mean(data_shampoo$consideration)/100,
mean(data_shampoo$liking_transformed),mean(data_shampoo$vol)),3),
New=round(c( 500, 100, new_awareness, new_consideration, new_liking,
new_sales ),3), Gain = round(c(400, 0, gain_awareness, gain_
consideration, gain_liking, gain_sales ),3), LRGain = c( "/", "/",
lrgain_awareness, round(lrgain_consideration,3), round(lrgain_
liking,3), round(lrgain_sales,3) ), contribution =c("/", "/",
round(contribution_awareness,3),round(contribution_consideration,3),
round(contribution_liking,3),"/"))

table_whatif

```
```

Table 6.2 Quintupling advertising spending

Item	Start	New	Gain	LRGain	Contribution
Advertising	100	500	400	/	/
Promotion	100	100	0	/	/
Awareness	0.275	?	?	?	?
Consideration	0.175	?	?	?	?
Liking	0.737	?	?	?	?
Sales	1800.391	?	?	?	/

The cells with question marks are the ones that we need to fill in. We proceed as follows:

1. First, we derive the new level of each mindset metric and sales based on the changes that we decide to make to the marketing mix decisions (i.e. advertising).
2. Then, by comparing the new and the old levels, we can derive immediate or short-run gain for each metric and sales.
3. Next, with the help of carryover parameters from responsiveness models, we transform those short-run gains into corresponding long-run gains.
4. Finally, to decompose the long-run gain in sales and attribute it to gains due to mindset metrics and gains due to transaction, we calculate how much the long-run gains from step 3 translate into an actual increase in sales.

New values

The 'Start' column in Table 6.2 summarizes all the base values for each item. For example, the average level of awareness, expressed in percentage terms, is 27.5%, leaving a 72.5% potential.
```

We need to decide what happens to all the mindset metrics and sales after we quintuple advertising (from £100,000 to £500,000). First, we need to determine the new level of each metric and sales after the change to the marketing mix. More specifically, the change to marketing mix exerts its impact on each metric through short-run responsiveness. Therefore, we need to go back to our previous analysis and use the model parameters in responsiveness models.

For mindset metric M_i ($i = 1,2,3$ in our case), we apply the formula

$$New_{M_i} = Start_{M_i} \times \left(Advertising_{new} / Advertising_{old}\right)^{Responsiveness\,Advertising\,M_i} . \tag{6.9}$$

The following code chunk computes the new values.

```r
#Note that we do not include short run impact of change in promotion
on each mindset metric because there is no change (100/100=1)

new_awareness <- round((1-table_potential[1,"value"])*(table_
whatif[1,"New"]/table_whatif[1,"Start"])^(table_
final[4,"awareness"]),3)
new_consideration <- round((1-table_potential[2,"value"])
*(table_whatif[1,"New"]/table_whatif[1,"Start"])^table_
final[4,"consideration"],3)
new_liking <- round((1-table_potential[3,"value"])*
(table_whatif[1,"New"]/table_whatif[1,"Start"]) ^ table_
final[4,"liking"],3)
#the responsiveness of sales to advertising can be found in the
"response_sales"
new_sales <- round(mean(data_shampoo$vol)*(table_
whatif[1,"New"]/table_whatif[1,"Start"])^as.numeric(response_
sales$coefficients[5]),3)
```

Short-run gain

We derive the gain (loss if negative) in each mindset metric and sales by simply calculating the growth rate. The code below calculates the short-run gains.

```r
#Calculate long run gain for each mindset metric and sales

lrgain_awareness <- round(gain_awareness/(1-as.numeric(response_
aware$coefficients[2])),3)
```

```
lrgain_consideration <-round(gain_consideration/(1-as.
numeric(response_consideration$coefficients[2])),3)
lrgain_liking <- round(gain_liking/(1-as.numeric(response_
liking$coefficients[2])),3)
lrgain_sales <- round(gain_sales/(1-as.numeric(response_
sales$coefficients[2])),3)

```

```{r}
#Calculate gain (from "start" to "new")
gain_awareness <- round((new_awareness/(1-table_potential[1,"value"]))
       -1,3)
gain_consideration <- round((new_consideration/(1-table_
potential[2,"value"]))-1,3)
gain_liking <-round( (new_liking/(1-table_
potential[3,"value"]))-1,3)
gain_sales <-round((new_sales/mean(data_shampoo$vol))-1,3)

```

Long-run gain

We can now translate the short-run gain into long-run gain for each metric and sales performance. To do this, we need to make use of the carryover effect (i.e. the autoregression coefficient) we get from our responsiveness models. Again, for each mindset metric M_i and also for sales, we use the following formula:

$$LR\ Gain_{M_i} = \frac{Gain_{M_i}}{1 - Carryover_{M_i}}.$$

(6.10)

The code chunk below shows how we implement the formula in R.

Contribution

In the final step of the what-if analysis, we evaluate the contribution of mindset metrics to long-term sales. To do so, we need to refer to the conversion model:

$$Contribution_{M_i} = LR\ Gain_{M_i} \times Conversion_{M_i}.$$

(6.11)

The R following code calculates the contribution of each mindset metric to long-run sales.

```{r}
#Calculate conversion, i.e., decompose the gain and attribute to
awareness, consideration, and liking

contribution_awareness <- round(lrgain_awareness * table_final[6,
"awareness"],3)
contribution_consideration <-round(lrgain_consideration * table_
final[6, "consideration"],3)
contribution_liking <- round(lrgain_liking * table_final[6,
"liking"],3)

```

Finally, we insert the estimated values in Table 6.2 and calculate the decomposition effects by running the following code chunk.

```{r echo=FALSE}

table_whatif<-data.frame(
  Item = c("Advertising", "Promotion", "Awareness", "Consideration",
"Liking", "Sales"), Start=round(c(100,100, mean(data_
shampoo$awareness)/100, mean(data_shampoo$consideration)/100,
mean(data_shampoo$liking_transformed),mean(data_shampoo$vol)),3),
New=round(c( 500, 100, new_awareness, new_consideration, new_liking,
new_sales ),3), Gain = round(c(400, 0, gain_awareness, gain_
consideration, gain_liking, gain_sales ),3), LRGain = c( "/", "/",
lrgain_awareness, round(lrgain_consideration,3), round(lrgain_
liking,3), round(lrgain_sales,3) ), contribution =c("/", "/",
round(contribution_awareness,3), round(contribution_consideration,3),
round(contribution_liking,3),"/"))

table_whatif

```

Table 6.3   Decomposition of effects

Item	Start	New	Gain	LRGain	Contribution
Advertising	100	500	400	/	/
Promotion	100	100	0	/	/

(Continued)

Table 6.3   (Continued)

Item	Start	New	Gain	LRGain	Contribution
Awareness	0.275	0.299	0.088	0.089	0.074
Consideration	0.175	0.180	0.024	0.030	0.014
Liking	0.737	0.739	0.003	0.003	0.008
Sales	1800.391	1981.787	0.097	0.108	/

By summing $Contribution_{awareness}$, $Contribution_{consideration}$ and $Contribution_{liking}$, we can get the total long-run gain in sales that originates from improvement in mindset metrics. A close look at Table 6.3 suggests that there is a 10.8% gain in sales. We observe that:

- Long-term sales gain = 10.8%
- Sales gain due to mindset metrics = 9.6% (0.074 + 0.014 + 0.008 = 0.096)
- Sales gain due to transactions = 108% – 9.6% = 1.2%.

Therefore, we can tell that by quintupling advertising, there is a significant improvement in mindset metrics, and such improvement can contribute to a 9.6% increase in sales. The eventual net effect on long-run sales is a 10.8% increase, and this is due to a 1.2 per cent increase in sales due to transactions.

Next, we will examine the scenario in which the brand manager of Zanten doubles the promotion spending.

Doubling promotion spending

Suppose that the marketing manager of Zanten doubles the promotion spending from £100,000 to £200,000 and does not make further changes in the marketing mix. What would be the impact on long-term sales? Let us visualize the calculations by using a table. The following code chunk generates Table 6.4.

```r
```{r echo=FALSE}

table_whatif2<-data.frame(
 Item = c("Advertising", "Promotion" ,"Awareness",
 "Consideration", "Liking", "Sales"), Start=c(100,100,
 round(mean(data_shampoo$awareness)/100,3), round(mean(data_
 shampoo$consideration)/100,3), round(mean(data_shampoo$liking/7),3
 ),round(mean(data_shampoo$vol),3)), New=c( 100, 200, "?" ,"?" ,"?"
 ,"?" ), Gain = c(0, 100, "?" ,"?" ,"?" ,"?" ), LRGain = c( "/", "/",
 "?" ,"?" ,"?" ,"?" ), Contribution =c("/", "/", "?", "?", "?", "/"))

table_whatif2

```
```

Table 6.4 Doubling promotion spending

Item	Start	New	Gain	LRGain	Contribution
Advertising	100	100	0	/	/
Promotion	100	200	100	/	/
Awareness	0.275	?	?	?	?
Consideration	0.175	?	?	?	?
Liking	0.737	?	?	?	?
Sales	1800.391	?	?	?	/

Table 6.4 shows the calculations we need to carry out. The cells with question marks are the ones we need to fill in. We proceed as follows:

1. Calculate the new level of each mindset metric and sales based on the changes that we decide to make to the marketing mix (i.e. doubling promotion spending).
2. Then, by comparing the new and the old levels, we will calculate the short-run gain for each mindset metric and sales.
3. Next, with the help of carryover parameters from responsiveness models, we will transform those short-run gains into corresponding long-run gains.
4. Finally, we will decompose the long-run sales gain into transaction and mindset routes.

New values

The 'Start' column in Table 6.4 summarizes the base values for each metric. For example, the average level of awareness, expressed in percentage terms, is 27.5%, leaving a 72.5% potential.

Next, we will see what happens to all the mindset metrics and sales after we double the promotion spending. To this end, we will determine the new level of each metric and sales after the change to promotion. We need to use the model parameters from the responsiveness models. For mindset metric M_i ($i = 1,2,3$ in our case), we apply the formula

$$New_{M_i} = Start_{M_i} \times \left(Promotion_{new} / Promotion_{old}\right)^{Responsiveness\, Promotion\, M_i} \tag{6.12}$$

The following R code calculates the new values.

```{r}
#Note that we do not include short run impact of change in ads on
each mindset metric and sales because there is no change (100/100=1)

new_awareness2 <- round((1-table_potential[1,"value"]) *
(table_whatif2[2,"New"]/table_whatif2[2,"Start"])^(table_
final[5,"awareness"]),3)
new_consideration2 <- round((1-table_potential[2,"value"])
*(table_whatif2[2,"New"]/table_whatif2[2,"Start"])^table_
```

```
final[5,"consideration"],3)
new_liking2 <- round((1-table_potential[3,"value"])*
(table_whatif2[2,"New"]/table_whatif2[2,"Start"]) ^ table_
final[5,"liking"],3)
#the responsiveness of sales to advertising can be found in the
"response_sales"
new_sales2 <- round(mean(data_shampoo$vol)*(table_
whatif2[2,"New"]/table_whatif2[2,"Start"])^as.numeric(response_
sales$coefficients[4]),3)

` ` `
```

Short-run gain

We calculate the short-run gain of each mindset metric and sales by simply calculating the growth rate. The following code chunk calculates the short-run gain.

```
` ` `{r}
#Calculate gain (from "start" to "new")
gain_awareness2 <- round((new_awareness2/(1-table_
potential[1,"value"]))-1,3)
gain_consideration2 <- round((new_consideration2/(1-table_
potential[2,"value"]))-1,3)
gain_liking2 <-round( (new_liking2/(1-table_
potential[3,"value"]))-1,3)
gain_sales2 <-round((new_sales2/mean(data_shampoo$vol))-1,3)

` ` `
```

Long-run gain

We can now translate the short-run gain into long-run gain for each metric and sales performance, using equation (6.10). The following code calculates the long-run gains.

```
` ` `{r}
#Calculate long-run gain for each mindset metric and sales

lrgain_awareness2 <- round(gain_awareness2/(1-as.numeric(response_
aware$coefficients[2])),3)
lrgain_consideration2 <-round(gain_consideration2/(1-as.
numeric(response_consideration$coefficients[2])),3)
lrgain_liking2 <- round(gain_liking2/(1-as.numeric(response_
liking$coefficients[2])),3)
```

```
lrgain_sales2 <- round(gain_sales2/(1-as.numeric(response_
sales$coefficients[2])),3)
```

```
```
```

## Contribution

In the final step of the what-if analysis, we evaluate the contribution of mindset metrics to long-term sales. To do so, we use the estimated parameters from the conversion model and apply the formula in equation (6.11). The following code performs this task.

```
```{r}
#Calculate conversion, i.e., decompose the gain and attribute to
awareness, consideration, and liking

contribution_awareness2 <- round(lrgain_awareness2 * table_final[6,
"awareness"],3)
contribution_consideration2 <-round(lrgain_consideration2 * table_
final[6, "consideration"],3)
contribution_liking2 <- round(lrgain_liking2 * table_final[6, "liking"],3)
```

```
```
```

Finally, we insert the estimated values in Table 6.4 and calculate the decomposition effects by running the following code chunk.

```
```{r echo=FALSE}
table_whatif2<-data.frame(
  Item = c("Advertising", "Promotion", "Awareness", "Consideration",
"Liking", "Sales"), Start=round(c(100,100, mean(data_
shampoo$awareness)/100, mean(data_shampoo$consideration)/100,
mean(data_shampoo$liking/7),mean(data_shampoo$vol)),3), New=round(c(
100, 200, new_awareness2, new_consideration2, new_liking2,
new_sales2 ),3), Gain = round(c(0, 100, gain_awareness2, gain_
consideration2, gain_liking2, gain_sales2 ),3), LRGain = c( "/",
"/", lrgain_awareness2, round(lrgain_consideration2,3), round(lrgain_
liking2,3), round(lrgain_sales2,3) ), contribution =c("/", "/",
round(contribution_awareness2,3),round(contribution_consideration2,3),
round(contribution_liking2,3),"/"))

table_whatif2
```

```
```
```
```

Table 6.5   Decomposition of effects

Item	Start	New	Gain	LRGain	Contribution
Advertising	100	100	0	/	/
Promotion	100	200	100	/	/
Awareness	0.275	0.279	0.016	0.017	0.014
Consideration	0.175	0.183	0.047	0.052	0.022
Liking	0.737	0.747	0.014	0.014	0.039
Sales	1800.391	2211.931	0.229	0.245	/

By summing $Contribution_{awareness}$, $Contribution_{consideration}$, and $Contribution_{liking}$, we can get the total long-run gain in sales that originates from improvement in mindset metrics. The results in Table 6.5 suggest that there is a 24.5% gain in sales. We observe that:

- Long-term sales gain = 24.5%
- Sales gain due to mindset metrics 7.5% (0.014 + 0.022 + 0.039)
- Sales gain due to transactions = 24.5% – 7.5% = 17%.

Recall that quintupling advertising expenditure resulted in a 10.8% increase in brand sales. The above analysis shows that doubling promotion results in a 24.5%% increase in sales. Therefore, we can conclude that doubling promotion seems to be more effective in driving up sales. However, doubling promotion generates less improvement in consumer mindset metrics. If the ultimate objective of the marketing manager is to 'build a brand', then gains in mindset metrics should be more important. Therefore, depending on the strategic objective of the brand, the marketing manager of Zanten may want to give more importance to one of these two strategies.

To summarize, marketing managers can conduct such scenario analyses, compare the estimated long-run effects, and make evidence-based decisions to win their customers' hearts and minds and boost sales.

CHAPTER SUMMARY

In this chapter, we discuss the role of customer mindset metrics – awareness, consideration, and liking – in guiding marketing mix decisions. These metrics are important intermediary performance indicators and allow brand managers to establish an actionable connection between marketing activity and financial performance. We conclude that the relative importance of customer mindset metrics is determined by four criteria: potential, stickiness, responsiveness, and conversion. Using these criteria and harnessing the data on customer mindset metrics, brand managers can assess the investment appeal of their marketing mix decisions, and make evidence-based decisions.

REFERENCES

Avagyan, V., Yildirim, G., Koca, E. and Srinivasan, S. (2022) The role of customer mindset metrics in optimal advertising. Working paper. http://proceedings.emac-online.org/pdfs/A2020-63170.pdf

Bruce, N., Peters, K. and Naik, P. (2012) Discovering how advertising grows sales and builds brands. *Journal of Marketing Research*, 49(6), 793–806.

Burke, R. R. and Srull, T. K. (1988) Competitive interference and consumer memory for advertising. *Journal of Consumer Research*, 15(1), 55–68.

Forbes (2018), Retailers and brands measure customer engagement all wrong. https://www.forbes.com/sites/nikkibaird/2018/08/21/retailers-and-brands-measure-customer-engagement-all-wrong/#32f949b23f91

Hammett, E. (2018) Revealed: The world's most valuable brands. *Marketing Week*, 29 May. https://www.marketingweek.com/2018/05/29/worlds-most-valuable-brands-2018/

Hanssens, D. M., Parsons, L. J. and Schultz, R. L. (2001) *Market Response Models: Econometric and Time Series Analysis*, 2nd edn. Boston: Kluwer Academic Publishers.

Hanssens, D. M., Pauwels, K., Srinivasan, S., Vanhuele, M. and Yildirim, G. (2014) Consumer attitude metrics for guiding marketing mix decisions. *Marketing Science*, 33(4), 534–50.

Keller, K. L. (1993) Conceptualizing, measuring, and managing customer-based brand equity. *Journal of Marketing*, 57(1), 1–22.

Pauwels, K., Erguncu, S. and Yildirim, G. (2013) Winning hearts, minds and sales: How marketing communication enters the purchase process in emerging and mature markets. *International Journal of Research in Marketing*, 30(1), 57–68.

Srinivasan, S,, Vanhuele, M. and Pauwels, K. (2010) Mindset metrics in market response models: An integrative approach. *Journal of Marketing Research*, 67(August), 672–84.

Wall Street Journal (2018) Assessing brand health risk. https://deloitte.wsj.com/cmo/2018/01/11/assessing-brand-health-risk/

Wang, W. and Yildirim, G. (2022) Applied time-series analysis in marketing. In C. Homburg, M. Klarmann and A. E. Vomberg (eds), *Handbook of Market Research*. Cham: Springer.

7

TEXT MINING

Chapter contents

LEARNING OBJECTIVES

At the end of this chapter, you should be able to:

- understand the value contribution of text mining in marketing
- apply sentiment analysis and text mining in marketing
- understand the difference between top-down and bottom-up sentiment analysis
- conduct sentiment as well as topic analysis
- harvest relevant information from textual data to depict segments and industry trends
- apply topic models to textual data to identify and track latent topics within textual data to gain a better understanding of consumer satisfaction and consumer preferences.

In the previous chapter, we saw how user-generated data can be used to generate important and valuable insights for our decision-making. Still, we were mostly focusing on numbers and how much people talk about something. But we have not yet leveraged the full potential of user-generated data as we have not explored in detail what users write and what we can learn from such textual data. This chapter will close this gap and will teach you how to access information encoded in text. We will see that automated text analysis – powered through different text mining tools – can reveal important consumer patterns and provide essential information for marketers. In addition, we can use insights to automate user-generated data analysis processes and to automatically feed information from textual data into our own database. Text mining tools are thus essential for creating monitoring tools, which allow us to identify trends, track brand knowledge and brand equity, and control how our own marketing resonates within consumers' minds. The chapter will enable you to measure emotions and sentiment in textual data and to identify latent topics within text, to inform your decision-making.

━━━━━━━━ Case study ━━━━━━━━

Leviev Air II

After an initial meeting in which you presented your first insights from the user-generated data research project, the question arises whether one can find more insights from the reviews and review headlines of the different airlines. The board is especially interested to learn if there are general patterns and topics passengers talk about when it comes to travelling by air. The board is also interested in finding a way to measure brand equity and customer satisfaction in order to develop an industry dashboard that tracks brand equity and customer satisfaction for the most prominent airlines.

Ideally, you would come up with an approach that allows brand equity to be tracked from various user-generated content sources such as airline reviews, but also social media networks such as Twitter or Instagram.

The next day you sit down and pull all the reviews available for all the major airlines flying from London Heathrow and start running your analysis to answer the following questions:

- Which airlines get more reviews than others?
- Which issues garner most praise from customers when flying?
- Which common issues do customers complain about most when flying?
- How does sentiment relate to customer experience?
- How do passengers use emotions in their feedback when talking about different airlines?
- Can we leverage the review data to build a brand equity measure?
- Can we develop our own text-sentiment classifier to harvest airline sentiment from social media?

THE POWER OF TEXT

The growth of user-generated data not only provides opportunities but also brings challenges for researchers. Given that UGD are mostly unstructured, we cannot immediately rely on traditional statistical tools to infer information from this rich data source. Instead, we have to use a set of methodologies which help us to measure how favourably or unfavourably people write about something, what kind of topics people write on, or what kind of emotions are embodied in a piece of text. This procedure is commonly referred to as text mining. Text mining shares a long and fruitful history in many different disciplines such as informatics, computer sciences, linguistics, and marketing. Given its multidisciplinary heritage, text mining also goes under different names, and is often also referred to as natural language processing (NLP) or textual data mining. The key idea behind text mining is to transform textual data into numerical information that can then be processed by algorithms to subsequently extract underlying insights as well as to measure, track, understand, and interpret the reasons for and drivers of consumer behaviour and relate them to a company's marketing actions (see, for example, Berger et al., 2020). Text mining can thus help develop a better understanding of customers, discover customer preferences, and many other tasks in marketing. In addition, text mining has been applied in many other contexts: in finance it has been used to analyse investor sentiment with the goal of building better stock portfolios (e.g. Nofer and Hinz, 2015; Tirunillai and Tellis, 2012); in political research to investigate how people write about candidates with the aim of predicting election outcomes (e.g. Kübler et al., 2020); and in health sciences to predict the number of Covid-19 infections with the help of Twitter data (Skiera et al., 2020)

APPLICATIONS OF TEXT MINING IN MARKETING

In marketing, text mining has found a fast-growing supporter base that relies on rich user-generated datasets to gain customer insights and to better plan and manage marketing actions. Applications of text mining thus complement the whole customer journey and accompany the full decision funnel.

Online reviews as well as chatter in various online forums and social media networks have been shown to be important sources of information about consumer preferences (Archak et al., 2011; Decker and Trusov, 2010) which can provide substantial information for new product developments and innovation (Joung et al., 2018). Meanwhile, similar data have been used to map consumer brand perceptions and depict consideration sets and brand landscapes (Netzer et al., 2012). Companies can thus rely on UGD in written form to identify and trace consumer preferences (as an alternative to established experimental approaches such as conjoint analysis) and to understand how similar or distinct consumers perceive different brands and products to be. Both insights may be especially helpful when it comes to product development as well as brand positioning, where it is essential to gain a better understanding of the consumer perspective.

When it comes to brand building and developing brand positioning, as well as affecting choice behaviour, marketers need to keep track of classic consumer mindset metrics connected to the decision funnel (Chapter 6). Traditionally this is achieved with the help of panel survey data, which commonly originates from large research panels operated by companies such as YouGov or Nielsen. A representative set of consumers is frequently polled about how much they know about specific brands, what they associate with brands, and how satisfied they are with the brand. While classic survey research is widely applied and these measures are well-accepted metrics in the marketing domain, we also know that surveys have several flaws with regard, for example, to social desirability biases, interviewer effects, strategic answering behaviour, and other response errors. As an alternative to – or enrichment of – these traditional survey measures, marketers may thus similarly use user-generated content to measure and track mindset metrics. Brand knowledge may, for example, be approximated by the number of followers a brand has on various platforms. Meanwhile, brand-related sentiment (i.e. brand equity) may be measured by the average daily sentiment expressed in social media posts mentioning a brand, while brand satisfaction and brand recommendation may similarly be computed by the ratio of positive and negative comments each day (Kübler et al., 2020).

Investigating the dataset

To see how Leviev Air can leverage insights from the textual dataset, let us first explore the dataset in general and get a general feel for what kind of data we have in front of us. We can load the CSV with the corresponding reviews and other variables from our working directory with the following command:

```
Airline_Reviews_Leviev <- read_csv("airlinereviews.csv")
```

The dataset consists of 24,391 reviews from 16 different major airlines and thus provides a sufficient level of information to base our analysis on. To explore the number of reviews per airline we can use the following code that will give us a pie chart and the relative share of reviews for each airline.

```
numb.rev.airline = Airline_Reviews_Leviev %>% group_by(Airline) %>%
summarise(NumberofReviews = n())

piepercent<- paste(round(100*numb.rev.airline$NumberofReviews/
sum(numb.rev.airline$NumberofReviews), 1), "%", sep="")

pie(numb.rev.airline$NumberofReviews, labels = piepercent, main =
" Proportion of reviews, by airline",
col = rainbow(length(numb.rev.airline$NumberofReviews)))

legend("topright", c("Air Canada", "Air France", "Alitalia", "British
Airways", "Emirates", "Etihad Airways","Iberia", "Lufthansa", "Qatar
Airways", "Singapore Airlines", "Southwest Airlines", "Swiss Air","Thai
Airways", "Turkish Airlines", "United Airlines", "Virgin Atlantic"),
cex = 0.5, fill = rainbow(length(numb.rev.airline$NumberofReviews)))
```

The resulting plot is shown in Figure 7.1.

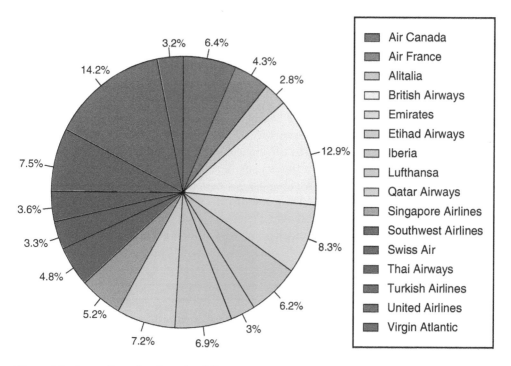

Figure 7.1 Proportion of reviews, by airline

The pie chart reveals that we have some airlines with substantially more reviews (United and British Airways) and other airlines with rather fewer reviews (Alitalia, Thai Airways, Iberia, and

Virgin Atlantic). Still, if we calculate the total number of observations, we see that no airline has fewer than 680 reviews (2.8% of 24,391).

To further understand how satisfied passengers are and to ensure that we base our analysis equally on positive and negative reviews, let us use the overall rating score each review comes with. The following code allows us to inspect boxplots for the overall rating for each airline.

```
library(ggplot)
library(tidyverse)
library(RColorBrewer)
library(scales)
library(ggthemes)


Airline_Reviews_Leviev %>%
  ggplot(aes(x=Airline,y=overall_rating, fill=Airline)) +
  geom_boxplot() + geom_jitter(width=0.05,alpha=0.05) +
  scale_fill_tableau(palette = "Tableau 20") +
  theme(axis.text.x = element_text(angle = 90)) +
  ggtitle("Boxplots of Overall Ratings, by Airline")
```

We use again `ggplot` together with `dplyr` (included in the `tidyverse` package) to prepare the boxplot as shown in Figure 7.2. In addition, we use `RColorBrewer` and `ggthemes` to allow us to use a non-standard colour representation that matches the colour coding of other popular data visualization tools such as Tableau.

Boxplots allow us to easily understand the central tendency, spread, and skewness of numerical data. A boxplot thus shows the median value and indicates outliers, as well as the quartiles and the range between these. Looking at Air France, for example, we can see that the median rating is somewhere close to 5.0. The upper quartile is around 7.8 (close to the median rating of Thai Airways). The lower quartile goes almost down to 2. The 'blurry' dots represent the values of the different reviews of each airline and we can thus also understand how many positive and negative reviews airlines got and how the distribution of ratings looks.

Look at the different boxplots of the airlines and compare them. What does the size of the box (how long the box is) tell you?

To better understand and inspect the mean ratings we can also use a bar chart (Figure 7.3), which we obtain with the following code. Note that we use the `reorder()` function to put the airlines in ascending order of mean rating.

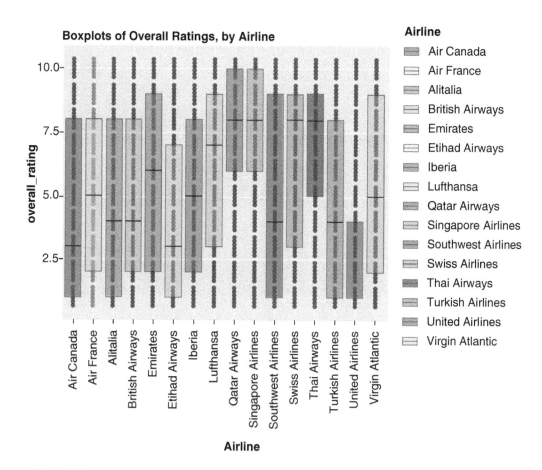

Figure 7.2   Boxplots of overall ratings, by airline

```
meanrating.airline = Airline_Reviews_Leviev %>% group_by(Airline) %>%
summarise(MeanRating = mean(overall_rating, na.rm=TRUE))

meanrating.airline %>% ggplot(aes(reorder(Airline,MeanRating), MeanRating)) +
   geom_col() +
   xlab("Airlines") + ylab("Mean Rating") +
   geom_text(aes(label = round(MeanRating, digits = 2)),
             size = 2, colour = "white",
             position = position_stack(vjust = 0.5)) +
   theme(axis.text.x = element_text(angle = 90)) +
   ggtitle("Mean ratings, by airline")
```

Both the boxplots and the bar chart indicate that we have enough variation in our reviews to continue with our analysis. We can thus start with trying to understand how favourably (or unfavourably) passengers write about an airline.

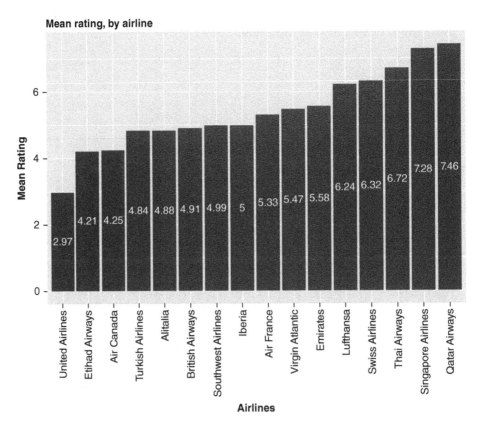

Figure 7.3 Bar chart of mean ratings, by airline

Sentiment analysis

To infer how positive or negative a written text is, we can employ sentiment analysis. Sentiment analyses have been an essential tool in many different research domains, ranging from linguistics via computer sciences to marketing research. The key goal is to develop an understanding of whether a text contains a specific emotion or sentiment. Methods and approaches to infer sentiment from text can generally be divided into two groups: top-down and bottom-up sentiment analysis (for more details on the two groups and their application in marketing research, see Humphreys and Wang, 2018).

Top-down sentiment analysis commonly relies on a bag-of-words approach, where one assumes that a document – from which we intend to measure sentiment – is composed of different words. The bag represents the document containing different words. To infer sentiment, we now look at each word and try to see if it relates to some sentiment category of interest. To achieve this, we need to use so-called 'dictionaries' (often also called 'lexica'). These feature lists of, for example, positive and negative words.

Bottom-up sentiment classifiers rely on a different approach. Here we use pre-labelled texts (which we know are positive or negative, for example). With the help of machine learning models (e.g. support vector machines or neural networks) we then try to learn which words determine whether a document is pre-labelled to be positive or negative, that is, the probabilities that a document is positive (or negative) given the occurrence of a specific word. The trained machine learning models can then be used to classify new text (where we do not know the sentiment). While top-down sentiment classifiers are easy to use and quick to apply, they are not as accurate and flexible as bottom-up approaches, although the latter cost more time and energy to develop. This price, however, also comes with the benefit of flexibility, as one can use company- or industry-specific training data to develop a customized sentiment classifier. Figure 7.4 summarizes the benefits and downsides of each approach.

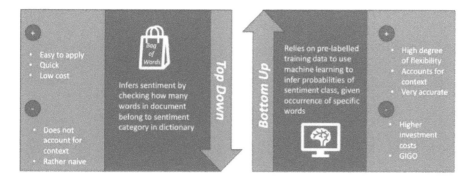

Figure 7.4 Top-down versus bottom-up sentiment analysis

Top-down analysis

As pointed out above, top-down sentiment analysis relies on dictionaries (i.e. word lists) to count words which belong to a pre-determined category such as positive or negative sentiment. With the increasing popularity of text mining and the availability of social media chatter and text data from various online sources, the number of available dictionaries has substantially increased, and one can choose from many different options. The most common (commercial) alternative is still the Linguistic Inquiry and Word Count (LIWC) software that is frequently used in marketing practice and marketing research to measure various constructs such as anxiety, inclusive and exclusive language patterns, or positive and negative emotions. While LIWC is certainly among the most established dictionaries, other dictionaries provide similar insights and are in addition freely available as R packages.

When it comes to measuring consumer emotions in text, the EmoLex – often also referred to as NRC – dictionary by Mohammad and Turney (2013) is of great help. EmoLex has been applied in various marketing contexts, as it allows the user to track not only positive and negative sentiment, but also subdimensions of emotions such as fear, anger, disgust, and sadness on the negative side, and joy, trust, anticipation, and surprise on the positive side.

The dictionary thus also accounts for the well-established circumplex model of human affect, as introduced by Russel (1980) and visualized in Figure 7.5.

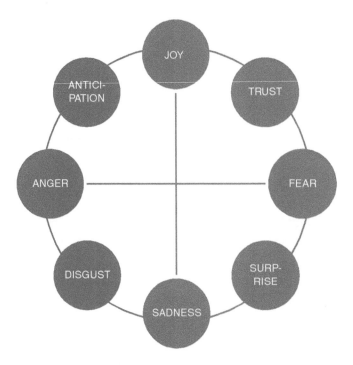

Figure 7.5 Circumplex emotion model

Especially when one tries to understand what causes negative sentiment, focusing on these sub-dimensions proves to be helpful, as negative sentiments caused by fear may call for a totally different company reaction than negative sentiment that is largely caused by disgust. Similarly, it may be interesting to marketers to understand if, for example, specific communication efforts or a particular campaign visual causes trust or joy, as both positive emotions may lead to completely different brand associations. To summarize, the EmoLex NRC dictionary can be very helpful for marketers to track specific emotions in consumer conversations and relate these to their own marketing activities, to control or monitor how their own actions affect public opinion.

In R the EmoLex dictionary is implemented in various packages. We recommend using the tidy-text package, as it enables very good text handling and has furthermore been shown to be superior in terms of speed and computational requirements. After loading the package, we can now use the EmoLex NRC lexicon to gain a first understanding of which airlines face which types of emotions, by looking at the mean emotion levels for each airline. We start with the following code.

```
library(tidytext)

AirlineReviews_Words <- Airline_Reviews_Leviev %>% mutate(ReviewNumb = 1:24391) %>%
    unnest_tokens(word, review_text)
```

Looking at the AirlineReviews_Words data frame we have created, you will quickly realize that we added now two more columns to the initial data frame. ReviewNumb simply contains a number from 1 to 24391 which is assigned to each review. With `unnest_tokens()` we have additionally created a separate row for each word in a review. Screening through the data frame, you can see that we now have 93 rows for review 1, which corresponds to the total number of words written in review 1. If you look at the different words in the `word` column, you will quickly realize that the majority of words listed do not have a real emotional meaning. For example, we cannot infer anything from words such as 'and', 'the', or 'that'. These words are, however, frequently used and thus complicate sentiment measurement, as our computer needs to also read through them while trying to find words from the emotion lists. To help, we can simply delete all words which do not provide too much meaning, using another dictionary. Words without much meaning potential are commonly referred to as stopwords. There are many stopword lists one can use (or adapt by adding other words as necessary). In `tidytext`, we can achieve this by simply applying the following command.

```
AirlineReviews_Words <- AirlineReviews_Words %>%
    anti_join(stop_words, by = "word")
```

By including `anti_join()` we simply tell R to look up all words in the `stop_words` list and drop rows which contain a stopword from the data frame. Looking into our environment, we can now see that the data frame has substantially shrunk, and now 'only' incorporates 1,476,635 rows. This will make it much easier for our computer to count the emotion words.

```
AirlineReviews_Sentiment <- AirlineReviews_Words %>%
    inner_join(get_sentiments("nrc")) %>%
      count(Airline, index = ReviewNumb, sentiment) %>%
    pivot_wider(names_from = sentiment, values_from = n, values_fill = 0)
```

The resulting data frame now shows how many times a word from each emotion category appears in each review. We can take this information and now calculate the airline-specific mean emotion values.

```
AirlineReviews_Sentiment_Means = AirlineReviews_Sentiment %>%
    group_by(Airline) %>% summarise(
      MeanAnger = mean(anger),
      MeanDisgust = mean(disgust),
      MeanFear = mean(fear),
      MeanSadness = mean(sadness),
      MeanNegative = mean(negative),
      MeanAnticipation = mean(anticipation),
      MeanSurprise = mean(surprise),
      MeanTrust = mean(trust),
      MeanJoy = mean(joy),
      MeanPositive = mean(positive)) %>%
  mutate(MeanSentiment = MeanPositive - MeanNegative)
```

We can now take this data frame to plot the values for each airline. To ensure a good overview, we can also split the frame into three new frames, for the positive and the negative emotions, as well as for the general sentiment scores.

```
#Plot of Positive Emotions


AirlineReviews_PosMeansWide <- AirlineReviews_Sentiment_Means %>%
  select (Airline, MeanJoy, MeanAnticipation, MeanSurrise, MeanTrust) %>%
  gather (key = "variable", value = "value", -Airline)


AirlineReviews_PosMeansWide %>%
  ggplot (aes (x=Airline,y=value, fill=Airline))+
  scale_fill_tableau(palette = "Tableau 20") +
  geom_col() + geom_jitter (width = 0.05, alpha = 0.05) +
  geom_text (aes(label = round(value, digits = 2)),
            size = 2, colour = "white",
            position = position_stack(vjust = 0.5)) +
  theme (axis.text.x = element_text (angle = 90)) + facet_wrap (~variable, ncol = 2) +
  ggtitle ("Mean Values of Positive Emotions, by Airline")

#Plot of Negative Emotions


AirlineReviews_NegMeansWide <- AirlineReviews_Sentiment_Means %>%
  select (Airline, MeanAnger, MeanDisgust, MeanFear, MeanSadness) %>%
  gather (key = "variable", value = "value", -Airline)


AirlineReviews_NegMeansWide %>%
  ggplot (aes (x=Airline,y=value, fill=Airline))+
  geom_col() + geom_jitter (width = 0.05, alpha = 0.05) +
  scale_fill_tableau(palette = "Tableau 20") +
  geom_text (aes(label = round(value, digits = 2)),
    size = 2, colour = "white",
    position = position_stack(vjust = 0.5)) +
  theme (axis.text.X = element_text (angle = 90)) + facet_wrap (~variable, ncol = 2) +
  ggtitle ("Mean Values of Negative Emotions, by Airline")

#Plot of General Sentiment
AirlineReviews_SentimentMeansWide <- AirlineReviews_Sentiment_Means %>%
  select (Airline, MeanPostitive, MeanNegative, MeanSentiment) %>%
  gather (key = "variable", value = "value", -Airline)
```

```
AirlineReviews_SentimentMeansWide %>%
  ggplot (aes (x=Airline,y=value, fill=Airline))+
  scale_fill_tableau(palette = "Tableau 20") +
  geom_col() + geom_jitter (width = 0.05, alpha = 0.05) +
  geom_text (aes(label = round(value, digits = 2)),
              size = 2, colour = "white",
              position = position_stack(vjust = 0.5)) +
  theme (axis.text.x = element_text (angle = 90)) + facet_wrap (~variable, ncol = 1) +
  ggtitle ("Mean Values of Sentiment Scores, by Airline")
```

The resulting plots are shown in Figure 7.6.

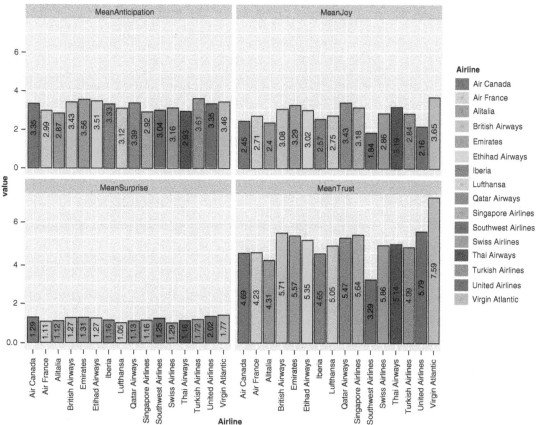

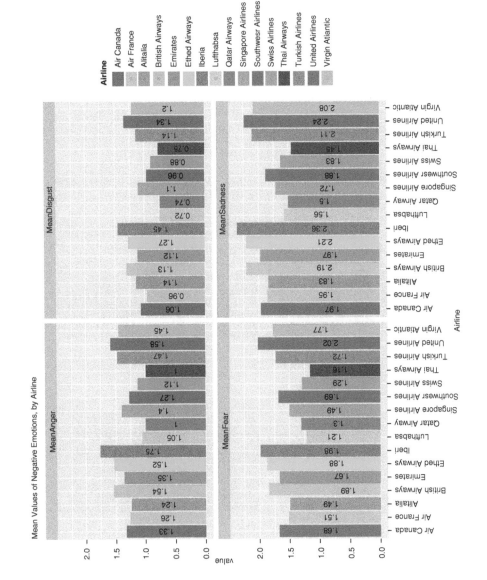

Mean Values of Negative Emotions, by Airline

Airline: Air Canada, Air France, Alitalia, British Airways, Emirates, Ethed Airways, Iberia, Lufthabsa, Qatar Airways, Singapore Airlines, Southwesr Airlines, Swiss Airlines, Thai Airways, Turkish Airlines, United Airlines, Virgin Atlantic

MeanAnger

Airline	value
Air Canada	1.33
Air France	1.26
Alitalia	1.24
British Airways	1.54
Emirates	1.35
Ethed Airways	1.52
Iberi	1.75
Lufthabsa	1.05
Qatar Airway	1
Singapore Airlines	1.4
Southwesr Airlines	1.27
Swiss Airlines	1.12
Thai Airways	1
Turkish Airlines	1.47
United Airlines	1.58
Virgin Atlantic	1.45

MeanDisgust

Airline	value
Air Canada	1.06
Air France	0.96
Alitalia	1.14
British Airways	1.13
Emirates	1.12
Ethed Airways	1.27
Iberi	1.45
Lufthabsa	0.72
Qatar Airway	0.74
Singapore Airlines	1.1
Southwesr Airlines	0.96
Swiss Airlines	0.88
Thai Airways	0.75
Turkish Airlines	1.14
United Airlines	1.34
Virgin Atlantic	1.2

MeanFear

Airline	value
Air Canada	1.68
Air France	1.51
Alitalia	1.49
British Airways	1.89
Emirates	1.67
Ethed Airways	1.88
Iberi	1.98
Lufthabsa	1.21
Qatar Airway	1.3
Singapore Airlines	1.49
Southwesr Airlines	1.69
Swiss Airlines	1.29
Thai Airways	1.16
Turkish Airlines	1.72
United Airlines	2.02
Virgin Atlantic	1.77

MeanSadness

Airline	value
Air Canada	1.97
Air France	1.95
Alitalia	1.83
British Airways	2.19
Emirates	1.97
Ethed Airways	2.21
Iberi	2.36
Lufthabsa	1.56
Qatar Airway	1.5
Singapore Airlines	1.72
Southwesr Airlines	1.88
Swiss Airlines	1.83
Thai Airways	1.45
Turkish Airlines	2.11
United Airlines	2.24
Virgin Atlantic	2.08

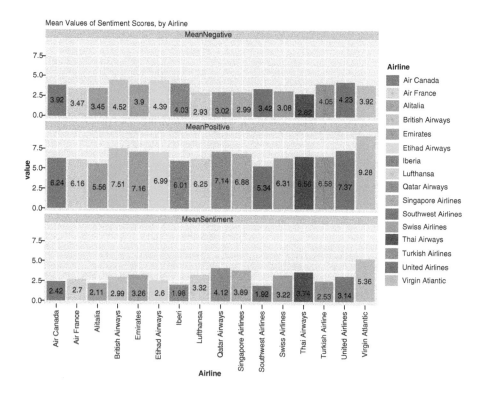

Mean Values of Sentiment Scores, by Airline

We can also use the emotion information to see how different airlines are from each other. Do you remember the concept of Euclidean distance, which we discussed in Chapter 2? We can simply calculate the distance across all airlines based on the mean emotions.

```
# Calculate Emotions Distances

Airlines_MeanEmotions = AirlineReviews_Sentiment_Means[,1:10]
EmotionDistance_Airlines = as.matrix(dist(Airlines_MeanEmotions))
rownames(EmotionDistance_Airlines) <- AirlineReviews_Sentiment_Means$Airline
```

We can then use a method called *multidimensional scaling* (MDS) to plot the airlines in a two-dimensional space, based on the Euclidean distances we just calculated. The resulting plot can be seen in Figure 7.7.

```
# Plot Airlines in 2-dimensional space

MDS_Emotions <- cmdscale(EmotionDistance_Airlines,eig=TRUE, k = 2)
x <- MDS_Emotions$points[,1]
```

```
y <- MDS_Emotions$points[,2]
plot(x, y, xlab ="Dimension 1", yla = "Dimension 2",
      main = "MDS Airlines by Emotions in Reviews", type ="n")
text(x, y, labels = row.names(EmotionDistance_Airlines), cex =.7)
```

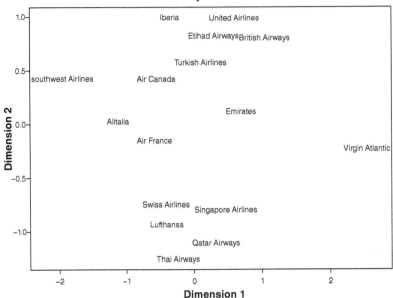

Figure 7.7 MDS plot

A key issue with MDS is that it does not automatically provide us with an interpretation of the x- and y-axes. Still, looking at the different groups of airlines, we may be able to make sense of the dimensions and come up with an interpretation of why certain airlines are closer or farther apart from each other.

Looking at the different groups of airlines in the plot, what do you think it means if an airline is more towards the bottom? What does it mean if an airline is more towards the right than the left of the plot?

Rule-based top-down analysis

While basic dictionaries such as LIWC and NRC provide a quick and reliable way to capture words expressing different forms and levels of sentiment, they often face the problem that they do not take into account the context in which a word occurs. This can quickly become an issue, as in the following example:

> I did not like the airline there was no good service and no one cared about us

If we ignore the negation, the review actually consists of several words which are commonly assigned to a positive sentiment such as 'like', 'good', and 'care'. Many dictionaries would thus come to the wrong conclusion, by simply counting the occurrence of words which belong to a positive sentiment category.

Similarly, reviews may be ambiguous, with different types of sentiment being assigned to two different entities as in the following example:

> It was a shitty holiday with a lot of rain and a bad hotel, but Alitalia was great and we love the service.

Here the negative sentiment targets the weather and the hotel, while it explicitly spares the corresponding airline. Again simply counting the occurrence of words does not help, as the total number of negative sentiment words is twice the number of positive words.

Furthermore, the way people write may also indicate something about the strength of emotion involved. Take the following two reviews:

> I love Alitalia

> I LOVE Alitalia!!!!

You will certainly agree that the latter expresses more emotion than the former, as the love for Alitalia is expressed in capital letters and further emphasized by four exclamation marks. Again, simply counting the occurrence of positive words would lead to a wrong result, as both reviews only consist of one positive word ('love').

It is also worth observing that digital communication is changing and that consumers adapt their linguistic styles. Often emotions are expressed not only by words, but also by symbols. Think about emojis, emoticons (e.g. ☺), or common abbreviations such as 'lol' (laughing out loud) or 'rofl' (rolling on floor laughing), which have made their way into our everyday online conversations. Most established dictionaries do not yet list these new terms and will thus ignore them.

However, there are some dictionaries which have lately been developed that are able to deal with negations and context, while also being able to account for symbol usage in text. These dictionaries have often been developed with an eye on online and social media conversations and are also able to cope with rather short sentences. One of the most common dictionaries that combines all these abilities is VADER (which stands for Valence Aware Dictionary and sEntiment Reasoner). VADER is a rule-based dictionary, which means that it takes context into account and checks to see if a word stands together with a negation, or if a sentiment is reinforced by, for example, exclamation marks or being written in caps (Hutto and Gilbert, 2014). While VADER was initially developed for Python, there is now a package available that allows us to use VADER in R. Given the rule implementation, the benefit of accounting for context comes of course at a cost: time. Applying VADER to larger sets of reviews of comments will take substantially longer than NRC, for example. Still, the results are often worth the wait. Let us now see how well VADER performs. We first load the package and build vectors with our special sentences.

```
# VADER Test

library(vader)

Clear_Review = "It was a shitty holiday with a lot of rain and a bad airline"
Negations_Review = "I did not like the airline there was no good
service and no one cared about us."
Ambiguous_Review = "It was a shitty holiday with a lot of rain and a bad
hotel, but Alitalia was great and we love the service."
Symbolic_Review = "Alitalia is my <3!!!! Always :-D"
NoExclamation_Review = "I love Alitalia"
Exclamation_Review = "I LOVE Alitalia!!!!"
```

We can now use the following code to calculate the sentiment of each sentence.

```
# VADER Test
Sentiment_Clear_Review = get_vader(Clear_Review, incl_nt = T, neu_set =
T, rm_qm = F)
Sentiment_Negations_Review = get_vader(Negations_Review, incl_nt =
T, neu_set = T, rm_qm = F)
Sentiment_Ambiguous_Review = get_vader(Ambiguous_Review, incl_nt =
T, neu_set = T, rm_qm = F)
Sentiment_Symbolic_Review = get_vader(Symbolic_Review, incl_nt =
T, neu_set = T, rm_qm = F)
Sentiment_NoExclamation = get_vader(NoExclamation_Review, incl_nt =
T, neu_set = T, rm_qm = F)
Sentiment_Exclamation = get_vader(Exclamation_Review, incl_nt =
T, neu_set = T, rm_qm = F)

# Combine Scores in new DataFrame

VADER = bind_rows(Sentiment_Clear_Review, Sentiment_Negations_
Review, Sentiment_Ambiguous_Review,
Sentiment_Symbolic_Review, Sentiment_NoExclamation,
Sentiment_Exclamation)

Text_vader = c(Clear_Review, Negations_Review, Ambiguous_Review,
Symbolic_Review, NoExclamation_Review, Exclamation_Review)

VADER$Text = Text_vader
```

If we now compare the compound results in the VADER data frame, we can see that the rule-based dictionary was able to account for all specifics in our specially composed sentences. In addition, we can see how it assigns a sentiment score to each word in the sentences (word_scores) as well as the general positive and negative sentiment.

word_scores	compound	pos	neu	neg	but_count	Text
[0, 0, 0, -2.6, 1.7, 0, 0, 0, 0, 0, 0, 0, -2.5, 0]	-0.66	0.13	0.529	0.341	0	It was a shitty holiday with a lot of rain and a bad airli...
[0, 0, 0, -1.11, 0, 0, 0, 0, 0, -1.406, 0, 0, 0, 0, -1.33]	-0.705	0	0.672	0.328	0	I did not like the airline there was no good service an...
[0, 0, 0, -1.3, 0.85, 0, 0, 0, 0, 0, 0, 0, -1.25, 0, 0...]	0.895	0.371	0.502	0.127	1	It was a shitty holiday with a lot of rain and a bad hot...
[0, 0, 0, 0, 0, 2.3]	0.667	0.472	0.528	0	0	Alitalia is my <3!!!! Always :-D
[0, 3.2, 0]	0.637	0.677	0.323	0	0	I love Alitalia
[0, 3.933, 0]	0.796	0.753	0.247	0	0	I LOVE Alitalia!!!!

Figure 7.8 VADER compound scores

Bottom-up analysis

While top-down sentiment analysis relies on pre-curated lists which commonly originate from previous research studies and are the result of thorough qualitative research work, bottom-up sentiment analysis tries to 'build' its own dictionaries with the help of supervised machine learning. Here, we use textual data, where we already know the sentiment, to infer probabilities that the occurrence of words (or word combinations) represents a positive or negative sentiment (or any other category we are interested in such as satisfaction, recommendation, or disgust). The textual data from which we infer the probabilities is commonly referred to as training data. Training data can be obtained from various sources. For example, one may use human coders to classify a set of texts into the categories of interest (i.e. positive or negative sentiment) and use these texts as training data. Often, this is achieved with the help of platforms such as Amazon M-Turk or Clickworkers.com, where you can hire subjects to classify your texts. A key challenge here is of course the amount and quality of training data, as reliable and valid sentiment classifiers require a substantial amount of training input. Human coding thus often comes at substantial costs (and usually also requires some time). Therefore, we often see projects relying on other types of training sets such as online reviews where the textual data are commonly accompanied by an overall rating, which already gives us some information about the general sentiment or satisfaction level of the corresponding text. Given that we already have overall rating scores, we can follow the latter approach and split our own review dataset into two subsets, containing only negative and positive reviews.

```
# Building Training Data Set
library(tm)
library(SnowballC)


Negative_Reviews = Airline_Reviews_Leviev %>% filter(overall_rating < 2)
Positive_Reviews = Airline_Reviews_Leviev %>% filter(overall_rating > 8)


set.seed(123)
```

```
Negative_Reviews_Sample = sample_n(Negative_Reviews, 2000)
Positive_Reviews_Sample = sample_n(Positive_Reviews, 2000)

BottomUpDF = data.frame(sentiment = "positive", text = Positive_Reviews_
Sample$title)
BottomUpDF = rbind(BottomUpDF, data.frame(sentiment = "negative",
text = Negative_Reviews_Sample$title))
```

Once we have the sets of positive and negative reviews, we can randomly extract 2000 positive and 2000 negative reviews, which will then serve as our training data. Of course, you can use more (or less) data, according to the computational power available. Another trick here to save computational power and not to overburden our laptops is to use only the title of the reviews and not the whole review text, as we can assume that the title will perfectly summarize the review and thus contain the main sentiment.

Once we randomly selected the reviews, we bind them together in the data frame `BottomUpDF`, which now contains the titles as well as telling us whether the title originates from the 'positive' or 'negative' sentiment set. We can then continue to further prepare the textual information and to make life a bit easier for our computers, by converting all text to lower case (otherwise the algorithm would treat airline and Airline as two different words), removing any punctuation (as elements such as commas do not provide much meaning), removing all stopwords from the corpus, and stemming all words to their common form, which again helps remove redundancies in the data and make the set slimmer. Finally, we can use the `removeSparseTerms` function to identify words which occur only rarely and which will thus not provide too much information (here we drop words which only occur in 0.5% of all documents; feel free to try out other cut-off values).

The resulting `tSparse` data frame now has a column for each word included in our training dataset, and indicates for each document (row) if a word occurs or not (1/0). A matrix of this kind is commonly referred to as a document term matrix. Finally, we use `prop.table` to show us the distribution of positive and negative review titles in our dataset. The output indicates that we have a perfectly balanced training dataset that consists of 50% negative and 50% positive review titles.

```
# Cleaning and Preparing Data Set

corpus = Corpus(VectorSource(BottomUpDF$text))
corpus = tm_map(corpus, PlainTextDocument)
corpus = tm_map(corpus, tolower)
corpus = tm_map(corpus, removePunctuation)
corpus = tm_map(corpus, removeWords, c("cloth", stopwords("english")))
corpus = tm_map(corpus, stemDocument)
frequencies = DocumentTermMatrix(corpus)
sparse = removeSparseTerms(frequencies, 0.995)
```

```
tSparse = as.data.frame(as.matrix(sparse))
colnames(tSparse) = make.names(colnames(tSparse))
tSparse$sentiment = BottomUpDF$sentiment

#Show distribution of Positive and Negative Training Data
prop.table(table(tSparse$sentiment))
```

We can now start to train a basic machine learning model that allows us to determine whether a new review (or any other airline-specific text) is positive or negative.

To be able to later assess the quality of our sentiment classifier, we have to again split our training dataset into the 'real' training set and a test set. The test set will allow us later to determine how accurate our sentiment predictions are, as we can first predict the sentiment with the help of the sentiment classifier, and compare the predictions with the known sentiment. Commonly, one uses 20% to 30% of the training data to compose a test set and the remaining 70% to 80% of the training set to train the classifier. We use an 80–20 split here, but feel free to try out other splits.

```
# Split set in final training and in test set
library(caTools)

set.seed(100)
split = sample.split(tSparse$sentiment, SplitRatio = 0.8)
trainSparse = subset(tSparse, split==TRUE)
testSparse = subset(tSparse, split==FALSE)
```

We can now start to use the `trainSparse` set to develop our classifier. We will employ a common classification algorithm, called random forest (for more information on machine learning classifiers see Chapter 8 below, or see Kübler et al., 2017). The algorithm will try to infer for each word in our document term matrix the probability that this word occurs in a positive or negative review title. Given that the `randomForest()` function requires factors as input, we also adapt our matrix accordingly, before training the model with the following code. Don't worry if this takes a while.

```
# Train Random Forest
library(randomForest)

set.seed(100)
trainSparse$sentiment = as.factor(trainSparse$sentiment)
testSparse$sentiment = as.factor(testSparse$sentiment )

RF_model = randomForest(sentiment ~ ., data=trainSparse)
```

Our classifier is now basically ready. Nevertheless, we need to understand how well it predicts. So, we need to go ahead and predict the sentiment of all review titles in our test set to see how many times the model correctly predicts negative and positive titles. We can achieve this with the following code. We use the predict() function to predict the sentiment scores of our training data and see how many often we classify correctly. Figure 7.9 presents the corresponding output.

```
# Test Random Forrest

predictRF = predict(RF_model, newdata=testSparse)
table(testSparse$sentiment, predictRF)
```

```
                    predictRF
            negative positive
negative      330       70
positive       76      324
```

Figure 7.9 Confusion matrix

So, it turns out that we have correctly predicted negative sentiments in 330 cases and correctly predicted positive sentiment in 324 cases. We have 76 false-positive classifications and 70 false-negative classifications. To understand the quality of our model, we can compute the accuracy measure as follows:

$$\text{Accuracy} = \frac{\text{Number of correctly classified titles}}{\text{Total number of titles}} = \frac{330+324}{800} = 0.8175.$$

Thus, in 81.75% of classifications, our classifier obtains the correct result. This is already a rather good fit. Still, we can do better, as we will shortly see.

Vector-based bottom-up analysis

So far, we have relied on the pure occurrence of words in a document to infer sentiment probabilities. However, we saw before that the context in which a word is embedded also matters. The latest developments in NLP account for this. Instead of only looking at which words occur in a document, one may similarly investigate which other words co-occur with a word to infer meaning. Thus, instead of only looking at the single occurrence, we can treat a word as an embedded feature in a vector of words. Newer approaches such as word2vec and GloVe use neural net approaches to construct these word vectors and use them to conduct different types of analyses. Figure 7.10 gives an illustration of what word2vec embeddings can achieve.

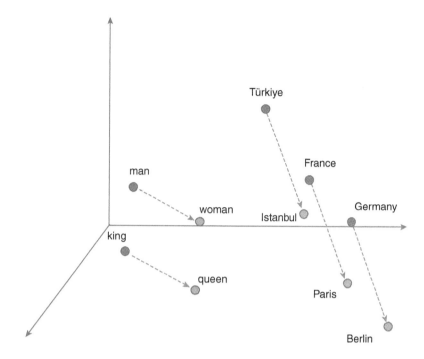

Figure 7.10 Word-embedding vectors

The word2vec approach is based on the fact that specific words co-occur with similar words. For example, 'king' and 'queen' co-occur with the same words as 'man' and 'woman'. This implies that the vectors representing the word embeddings of these words must be parallel, as shown in Figure 7.10. If this is the case, one can then apply basic mathematical operations to these vectors, which will lead to interesting and very useful results. Think of the following example: vector(King) – vector(Man) + vector(Woman). The result is, of course, Queen. We can similarly use an equation such as the following to determine the capital of any country: vector(Türkiye) – vector(Istanbul) + vector(France) = Paris. We can thus, by controlling for which other words frequently co-occur with a specific word and which other words share similar co-occurrences, infer much more meaning than by simply looking at the single occurrence of a word in a document. Building these co-occurrence vectors commonly takes some time and requires a lot of training data, and also requires a lot of computational power. We will thus not be able to explain in detail here how to build these vectors but instead refer the interested reader to Chapter 6 in Chollet and Allaire (2018), which gives a great introduction into how to train word vectors with the help of neural networks in R and conduct above vector calculations.

Luckily, R's text2vec package provides us with pre-trained word-embedding vectors, which we can use for our sentiment analysis and building a sentiment classifier that accounts for word co-occurrences. For more details on how these vectors have been estimated, we recommend looking up the great vignette and website of Selivanov et al. (2022), which feature not only more details but also interesting examples and use cases together with the corresponding R code.

We can access the package and start building our model with the following code.

```
#text2vec sentiment analysis

library(text2vec)
library(data.table)

Negative_Reviews = Airline_Reviews_Leviev %>% filter(overall_rating < 2)
Positive_Reviews = Airline_Reviews_Leviev %>% filter(overall_rating > 8)

set.seed(123)

Negative_Reviews_Sample = sample_n(Negative_Reviews, 2000)
Positive_Reviews_Sample = sample_n(Positive_Reviews, 2000)

BottomUpDF = data.frame(sentiment = "positive", text = Positive_
Reviews_Sample$title)
BottomUpDF = rbind(BottomUpDF, data.frame(sentiment = "negative",
text = Negative_Reviews_Sample$title))
BottomUpDF$id = 1:4000

index = sample(1:nrow(BottomUpDF), size = .80 * nrow(BottomUpDF))

train = BottomUpDF[index, ]
test = BottomUpDF[-index, ]
```

Similar to our random forest example, we again start by building a training and test dataset, which we can use for evaluating the accuracy of our sentiment classifier. To make things comparable we use the same number of randomly drawn review titles and an 80–20 split.

Furthermore, we again apply similar pre-processing steps and convert all words to lower case.

```
#Pre-Processing

prep_fun = tolower
tok_fun = word_tokenizer

it_train = itoken(train$text,
                  preprocessor = prep_fun,
                  tokenizer = tok_fun,
                  ids = train$id,
                  progressbar = FALSE)
```

```
vocab = create_vocabulary(it_train)

train_tokens = tok_fun(prep_fun(train$text))
it_train = itoken(train_tokens,
                  ids = train$id,
                  progressbar = FALSE)

vocab = create_vocabulary(it_train)
vectorizer = vocab_vectorizer(vocab)
dtm_train = create_dtm(it_train, vectorizer)
```

We can now start training the model with the following command.

```
# Train Model
library(glmnet)
NFOLDS = 4
glmnet_classifier = cv.glmnet(x = dtm_train, y = train[['sentiment']],
                              family = 'binomial',
                              alpha = 1,
                              type.measure = "auc",
                              nfolds = NFOLDS,
                              thresh = 1e-3,
                              maxit = 1e3)
```

We tell the `glmnet` function where it can find the training data (`dtm_train`) and which variable is the outcome variable of interest (`sentiment`). The other values in the function are tuning parameters, which can be ignored for now. In case you want to go into more detail here, we recommend consulting the vignette of the `text2vec` package (Selivanov et al., 2022).

To assess the accuracy of our model, we can again make a prediction for our test dataset and see how many correctly predicted titles we get. We can do this with the following code.

```
# Test Accuracy

it_test = tok_fun(prep_fun(test$text))
it_test = itoken(it_test, ids = test$id,progressbar = FALSE)

dtm_test = create_dtm(it_test, vectorizer)

preds = predict(glmnet_classifier, dtm_test, type = 'response')[,1]
glmnet:::auc(as.factor(test$sentiment), preds)
```

The output indicates that we achieve an accuracy of more than 91%, which is already impressive and indicates that our model is doing a great job in predicting sentiment.

To allow Leviev Air to now use this model, to predict customer sentiment in any sort of conversation, we can apply the following code and see how well our model predicts any sort of text we throw at it. Let us test the following six statements:

- 'I really hate this airline'
- 'Never again with Alitalia'
- 'They really suck in all dimensions'
- 'Great Service and Great Hospitality on Board'
- 'Awesome Experience and really nice staff!!'
- 'Best Airline ever! Will Fly Again with Qantas'

We need to again apply the same pre-processing to the new text as we did to our training data to enable the model to interpret it. Then we can simply apply the `predict` function and combine the prediction with the text. Figure 7.11 shows the corresponding output.

```
# Apply Model to new Text

NewTextData = c("I really hate this airline",
"Never again with Alitalia",
"They really suck in all dimensions",
"Great Service and Great Hospitality on Board",
"Awesome Experience and really nice staff!!",
"Best Airline ever! Will Fly Again with Qantas")

NewTextDataDF = data.frame(text= NewTextData, id = 4001:4006)
it_NewData = tok_fun(prep_fun(NewTextDataDF$text))
it_NewData = itoken(it_NewData, ids = NewTextDataDF$id,progressbar = FALSE)

dtm_NewData = create_dtm(it_NewData, vectorizer)

preds_NewData = predict(glmnet_classifier, dtm_NewData, type = 'class')[,1]
NewTextDataDF$SentimentPrediction = preds_NewData
```

Figure 7.11 Classification results of new text

Congratulations, our efforts really paid off! Our classifier correctly predicted the sentiments of all our new text input. You might like to play around a bit and try out other comments.

 Playing around with different input texts, what do you believe are the boundaries of the current classifier? How could Leviev Air extend it? Or if they do not wish to do so, for which use cases can this classifier be used, or not?

Topic modelling

So far, we have focused on the overall sentiment of a review. While sentiment analysis and classifiers play an important role when it comes to enriching or replacing classic brand health and mindset metric data, textual data offer more information than how well or how bad people like a brand, product, or service. While sentiment allows us to understand whether consumers are happy or not happy with us, this is rarely enough to fully grasp why they are happy or unhappy and what they specifically wish for. To get to this point, we 'unfortunately' have to read the full review, understand the different points within the review and come to a conclusion. Qualitative research has a rich tradition of content-analysing various text formats. Most of these content analysis techniques have in common that they try to identify reoccurring patterns or topics within their data.

Topic models such as latent Dirichlet allocation (LDA) and structural topic models have in common the idea that documents are composed of various (latent) topics. Topic models allow us to discover these hidden topics and to then classify each document to one or more topics. Think about different books you like. You will be easily able to assign them each to a specific genre by remembering the content. Topic models do the same. They rely on the content of various documents to first identify a (pre-set) number of topics or genres and then assign the documents to these. LDA models were among the first topic models and are today among the most widely applied models. Their starting point is that each document is composed of various words. Similarly, each topic has a set of common words which are specific to it. The ultimate goal of LDA is thus to identify the various topics a document belongs to, based on the words a document shares with a specific topic. LDAs belong to the group of unsupervised machine learning algorithms (for more details see Chapter 8) and are thus comparable to the cluster analysis algorithms we encountered in Chapter 2.

While we do not want to dive too deeply into the statistics behind it, let us briefly describe how the algorithm selects the words for each topic, before we try it out ourselves.

After we tell the algorithm how many topics we expect to be hidden in all documents, it goes through all the documents and randomly assigns each word w in each document d to one of the k topics. The algorithm then goes through each document d and computes the proportion of words in document d that are assigned to topic k. The assumption here is that if a lot of words from document d belong to topic k, it is more probable that word w also belongs to topic k. The algorithm then computes the proportion of assignments to topic k over all documents that are due to the presence of word w. If a word w has a high probability of being in a topic k, all other documents including word w will be more strongly associated with topic k as well. Similarly, if word w has a low probability of being in topic k, the documents which feature the word *w* will also have a very low probability of being in topic *k*, and the remaining words in document *d* will also have higher probabilities of belonging to some other topic. The probabilities will be updated iteratively until a certain threshold is reached or until the maximum number of iterations is reached. For more technical details we recommend consulting Büschken and Allenby (2016) who provide a detailed description of and code for various LDA applications and developments.

Let us now focus again on the application. R features multiple packages that enable us to conduct topic modelling. We recommend using the `topicmodel` package, as it offers the most versatile but still very approachable set-up and has many useful functions integrated, that, for example, allow us to parallelize processes, which will come handy if you face larger datasets and need to estimate multiple LDA models at the same time. We first reuse the data frame that only contains negative reviews (and which we constructed for the word2vec sentiment analysis). This will allow us to first focus on which topics consumers commonly dislike when flying and to then see which airlines are faced with which topics/complaints most. We again first create a corpus that contains the textual data from the reviews. We then apply the common text cleaning procedures that we have encountered before. Now the corpus is ready for the LDA.

```
# load packages and prepare data set
library(topicmodels)
library(ldatuning)

## Topic Models for Negative Reviews

Overall_corpus_Negative <- VCorpus(VectorSource(Negative_Reviews$review_text))

#Cleaning
Overall_corpus_clean.Negative <- tm_map(Overall_corpus_
Negative, content_transformer(tolower))
Overall_corpus_clean.Negative <- tm_map(Overall_corpus_clean.
Negative, removeNumbers)
Overall_corpus_clean.Negative <- tm_map(Overall_corpus_clean.
Negative, stemDocument)
Overall_corpus_clean.Negative <- tm_map(Overall_corpus_clean.
Negative, removeWords, stopwords(kind = "SMART"))
Overall_corpus_clean.Negative <- tm_map(Overall_corpus_clean.
Negative, removePunctuation)
Overall_corpus_clean.Negative <- tm_map(Overall_corpus_clean.
Negative, stripWhitespace)

#Adjust DF to match with dropped documents
Overall_dtm.Negative <- DocumentTermMatrix(Overall_corpus_clean.Negative)
ui = unique(Overall_dtm.Negative$i)
dtm.new.negative = Overall_dtm.Negative[ui,]
```

Remember the *k*-means cluster analysis we conducted in Chapter 2? There we needed to decide a priori how many clusters we suspected within the dataset. The same applies to LDA. We need to tell the algorithm how many latent topics we assume to be in the data. This is not always easy, as we might have an idea, but given that we usually cannot really read all the content, we often have a hard time finding an accurate number of topics. The good news, however, is that – as pointed out before – LDA is a sort of unsupervised machine learning algorithm, like *k*-means. And as with *k*-means, different approaches have been developed to determine the number of topics. Remember the elbow and silhouette plots which visualized the in-cluster homogeneity for different numbers of cluster solutions? For LDA the corresponding measures are a bit more complicated, but the idea is the same. We simply estimate a number of LDA models with a varying number of topics and try to compare the quality of the different models. The ldatuning package in R provides us with a straightforward means to do that. We simply have to determine the range of topics and the package will estimate all the different LDA models and compare them. Keep in mind that this of course will take some time and require sufficient computational power. We can try it with the following code. As you can see, we can specify in the FindTopicsNumber() function the range of numbers of topics we want to try out. Here we want to see anything between four and 12 topics. Feel free to try out different ranges. To speed up the process, the same function also allows us to parallelize the estimation, which means we can estimate multiple LDA models at the same time. This, however, requires our computer to also have multiple CPU cores available, as each core can take care of one model. You can adjust the mc.cores parameter to your specific setting. We set a default of 4 here, as most modern laptops have at least four cores or more available.

```
# Identify Topic Number
negative.result <- FindTopicsNumber(
  dtm.new.negative,
  topics = seq(from = 4, to = 12, by = 1),
  metrics = c("CaoJuan2009", "Deveaud2014"),
  method = "Gibbs",
  control = list(seed = 77),
  mc.cores = 4L,
  verbose = TRUE)


FindTopicsNumber_plot(negative.result)
```

The last part of the above code produces the plot shown in Figure 7.12.

Cao et al. (2009) show that the number of topics correlates with the topic distances and thus suggest a density-based topic selection criterion (shown in the upper part of Figure 7.11) that should be minimized. Alternatively, Deveaud et al. (2014) suggest focusing on semantic coherence and provide a score that needs to be maximized. This approach assumes that for models that are semantically coherent, all topic-specific words (indicated by their topic-specific occurrence probability) should also co-occur within the same type of documents. Both measures provide guidance, but rarely indicate the same solution. Here the Cao measure suggests the

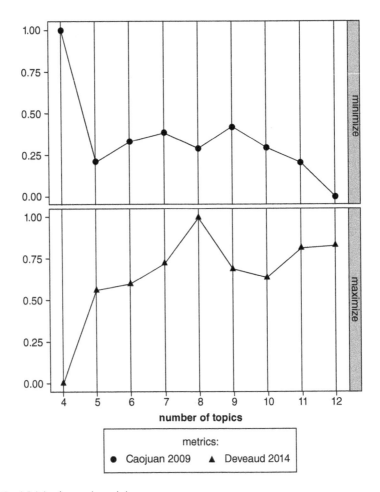

Figure 7.12   LDA topic number plots

12-topic solution, while the Deveaud indicator suggests an eight-topic solution (with the Cao also showing at least a local minimum for eight topics). We suggest that you do not base your decision on these indicators alone, but also on the interpretability of the LDA results. Therefore, it often makes sense to estimate different LDA models (here between eight and 12 topics) and to focus on the usability and interpretability of the output. Here it is convenient to focus on the eight-topic solution and to continue with an eight-topic LDA as follows.

```
# Run LDA
k=8
control_list_gibbs <- list(
  burnin = 2500, #set burn in
  iter = 5000,#set iterations
  seed = 1500,
```

```
   nstart = 5, #set random starts at 5
   best = TRUE, # return the highest probability as the result
   alpha = 50/k,
   delta = 0.1)


set.seed(1500)
negative_lda <- LDA(dtm.new.negative, k=8, method="Gibbs", control=control_
list_gibbs)
```

We can use the `control_list_gibbs` list to specify some of the LDA model characteristics such as the total number of iterations before the LDA stops or the seeding points for the random words. For more details, we recommend checking the help file of the `topicmodels` package and the accompanying vignette. Our suggested starting points turn out to be good for ordinary models, but if you would like to tweak the model further, you might try alternative `alpha` and `delta` values. Once the model converges we can focus on the output and try to understand which topics the model identified. To do so, we will first plot the top words for each topic with the following code. The corresponding output is shown in Figure 7.13. Figure 7.14 shows the corresponding output for the positive reviews. The code for this LDA can be found in the markdown for this chapter.

```
# Plot Top Terms per Topic


tidy_negative_lda <- tidy(negative_lda)


top_terms_negative <- tidy_negative_lda %>%
  group_by(topic) %>%
  top_n(10, beta) %>%
  ungroup() %>%
  arrange(topic, -beta)


top_terms_negative %>%
  mutate(term = reorder(term, beta)) %>%
  group_by(topic, term) %>%
  arrange(desc(beta)) %>%
  ungroup() %>%
  mutate(term = factor(paste(term, topic, sep = "__"),
                       levels = rev(paste(term, topic, sep = "__")))) %>%
  ggplot(aes(term, beta, fill = as.factor(topic))) +
  geom_col(show.legend = FALSE) +
  coord_flip() +
  scale_x_discrete(labels = function(x) gsub("__.+$", "", x)) +
  labs(title = "Top 10 terms in each negative review LDA topic",
       x = NULL, y = expression(beta)) +
  facet_wrap(~ topic, ncol = 4, scales = "free")
```

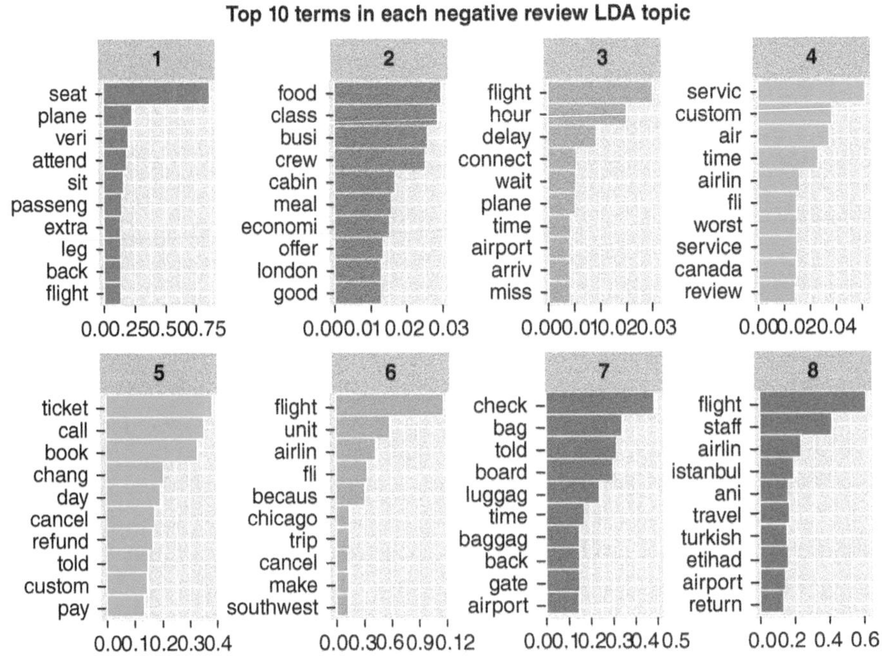

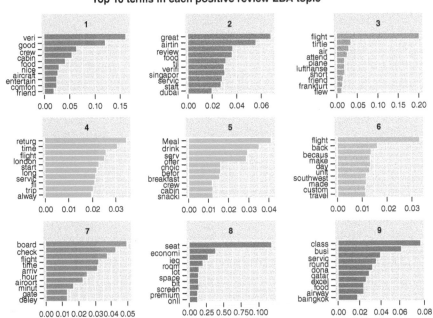

Figure 7.13   Words belonging to each topic (negative reviews)

Figure 7.14   Words belonging to each topic (positive reviews)

Looking at Figures 7.13 and 7.14, what kind of topics do you see here? Can you come up with meaningful topic names?

Airline insights

To assess which topics are associated with a specific airline, we first need to assign to each review the different topic probabilities, which we can do with the following code.

```
# Assign Topic Probabilities to Reviews

Negative_Reviews.Corrected <- Negative_Reviews[ui, ]
Negative_Reviews.wlables = cbind(Negative_Reviews.Corrected, negative_lda@gamma)
ldaresults.negative = as.data.frame(negative_lda@gamma)

names(Negative_Reviews.wlables)[13] <- "Topic1"
names(Negative_Reviews.wlables)[14] <- "Topic2"
names(Negative_Reviews.wlables)[15] <- "Topic3"
names(Negative_Reviews.wlables)[16] <- "Topic4"
names(Negative_Reviews.wlables)[17] <- "Topic5"
names(Negative_Reviews.wlables)[18] <- "Topic6"
names(Negative_Reviews.wlables)[19] <- "Topic7"
names(Negative_Reviews.wlables)[20] <- "Topic8"
```

We extract the topic probabilities (gammas) from the estimated LDA model and add them to the data frame with the reviews. Finally, we rename the columns.

We can now count the occurrence of each topic in each review. To do so we have to think about when we want to label a review, that is, when we believe the topic probability to be high enough to say that a review contains a specific topic. The advantage of this approach is that we allow reviews to contain more than one topic, compared to other common approaches, where one labels a review only with the topic with the highest probability.

What value should a topic probability exceed in this case to label a review with a topic?

```
# Build Dummies

CutoffDf.Negative <- Negative_Reviews.wlables %>% filter(Topic1 >=
0.25 | Topic2 >= 0.25|Topic3 >= 0.25 | Topic4 >= 0.25 | Topic5 >=
0.25 | Topic6 >= 0.25 | Topic7 >= 0.25 | Topic8 >= 0.25)

CutoffDf.Negative$Topic1Count <- ifelse(CutoffDf.Negative$Topic1 >=
0.25, 1, 0)
```

```
CutoffDf.Negative$Topic2Count <- ifelse(CutoffDf.Negative$Topic2 >=
0.25, 1,0)
CutoffDf.Negative$Topic3Count <- ifelse(CutoffDf.Negative$Topic3 >=
0.25, 1,0)
CutoffDf.Negative$Topic4Count <- ifelse(CutoffDf.Negative$Topic4 >=
0.25, 1,0)
CutoffDf.Negative$Topic5Count <- ifelse(CutoffDf.Negative$Topic5 >=
0.25, 1,0)
CutoffDf.Negative$Topic6Count <- ifelse(CutoffDf.Negative$Topic6 >=
0.25, 1,0)
CutoffDf.Negative$Topic7Count <- ifelse(CutoffDf.Negative$Topic7 >=
0.25, 1,0)
CutoffDf.Negative$Topic8Count <- ifelse(CutoffDf.Negative$Topic8 >=
0.25, 1,0)
TopicCount.Negative <- CutoffDf.Negative %>% group_by(Airline) %>%

summarize(
  Topic1 = sum(Topic1Count), Topic2 = sum(Topic2Count),
  Topic3 = sum(Topic3Count), Topic4 = sum(Topic4Count),
  Topic5 = sum(Topic5Count), Topic6 = sum(Topic6Count),
  Topic7 = sum(Topic7Count), Topic8 = sum(Topic8Count))
```

The resulting data frame is shown in Figure 7.15. We now have the information on how frequently certain airlines are faced with specific topics.

	Airline	Topic1	Topic2	Topic3	Topic4	Topic5	Topic6	Topic7	Topic8	sum
1	Air Canada	24	18	47	35	28	0	26	1	179
2	Air France	3	22	9	2	11	0	11	11	69
3	Alitalia	8	10	7	0	17	0	13	3	58
4	British Airways	25	192	18	4	45	0	15	0	299
5	Emirates	11	46	11	2	25	0	16	21	132
6	Etihad Airways	14	40	5	1	36	0	13	51	160
7	Iberia	3	8	9	0	32	0	4	0	56
8	Lufthansa	6	17	13	2	34	0	9	14	95
9	Qatar Airways	2	5	9	0	13	0	5	1	35
10	Singapore Airlines	6	16	1	0	10	0	2	2	37
11	Southwest Airlines	26	0	18	4	23	45	10	0	126
12	Swiss Airlines	6	4	3	1	12	0	2	6	34
13	Thai Airways	3	15	5	0	4	0	1	1	29
14	Turkish Airlines	14	21	27	2	50	0	23	43	180
15	United Airlines	59	33	160	21	51	157	83	2	566
16	Virgin Atlantic	12	47	0	0	5	0	2	1	67

Figure 7.15 Frequencies of negative topics, by airline

While the absolute numbers are already interesting, it may also make sense to look at the relative shares for each airline, which we obtain by dividing each value by the sum of reviews for each airline. We can do this with the following code. The resulting table is shown in Figure 7.16.

```
# Get Topic Share

TopicCount.Negative$sum = rowSums(TopicCount.Negative[,2:9])

WeightedTopics.Negative = data.frame(Airline = TopicCount.Negative$Airline,
            Topic1 = round(TopicCount.Negative$Topic1/TopicCount.Negative$sum,2),
            Topic2 = round(TopicCount.Negative$Topic2/TopicCount.Negative$sum,2),
            Topic3 = round(TopicCount.Negative$Topic3/TopicCount.Negative$sum,2),
            Topic4 = round(TopicCount.Negative$Topic4/TopicCount.Negative$sum,2),
            Topic5 = round(TopicCount.Negative$Topic5/TopicCount.Negative$sum,2),
            Topic6 = round(TopicCount.Negative$Topic6/TopicCount.Negative$sum,2),
            Topic7 = round(TopicCount.Negative$Topic7/TopicCount.Negative$sum,2),
            Topic8 = round(TopicCount.Negative$Topic8/TopicCount.Negative$sum,2))
```

	Airline	Topic1	Topic2	Topic3	Topic4	Topic5	Topic6	Topic7	Topic8
1	Air Canada	0.13	0.10	0.26	0.20	0.16	0.00	0.15	0.01
2	Air France	0.04	0.32	0.13	0.03	0.16	0.00	0.16	0.16
3	Alitalia	0.14	0.17	0.12	0.00	0.29	0.00	0.22	0.05
4	British Airways	0.08	0.64	0.06	0.01	0.15	0.00	0.05	0.00
5	Emirates	0.08	0.35	0.08	0.02	0.19	0.00	0.12	0.16
6	Etihad Airways	0.09	0.25	0.03	0.01	0.22	0.00	0.08	0.32
7	Iberia	0.05	0.14	0.16	0.00	0.57	0.00	0.07	0.00
8	Lufthansa	0.06	0.18	0.14	0.02	0.36	0.00	0.09	0.15
9	Qatar Airways	0.06	0.14	0.26	0.00	0.37	0.00	0.14	0.03
10	Singapore Airlines	0.16	0.43	0.03	0.00	0.27	0.00	0.05	0.05
11	Southwest Airlines	0.21	0.00	0.14	0.03	0.18	0.36	0.08	0.00
12	Swiss Airlines	0.18	0.12	0.09	0.03	0.35	0.00	0.06	0.18
13	Thai Airways	0.10	0.52	0.17	0.00	0.14	0.00	0.03	0.03
14	Turkish Airlines	0.08	0.12	0.15	0.01	0.28	0.00	0.13	0.24
15	United Airlines	0.10	0.06	0.28	0.04	0.09	0.28	0.15	0.00
16	Virgin Atlantic	0.18	0.70	0.00	0.00	0.07	0.00	0.03	0.01

Figure 7.16 Negative topic shares, by airline

There are many ways to visualize the shares (e.g. bar charts), but here we suggest a circular bar chart as shown in Figures 7.18 (negative reviews) and 7.19 (positive reviews). The code to produce this bar chart is also provided in the complimentary markdown together with the code to produce the positive topic shares for each airline as shown in Figure 7.17.

Looking at the topic shares of negative and positive reviews, and comparing these across airlines, which topics do you believe to be essentially important for high-class airlines?

	Airline	Topic1	Topic2	Topic3	Topic4	Topic5	Topic6	Topic7	Topic8	Topic9
1	Air Canada	0.00	0.10	0.00	0.32	0.02	0.41	0.07	0.00	0.07
2	Air France	0.03	0.14	0.00	0.59	0.03	0.03	0.07	0.00	0.10
3	Alitalia	0.67	0.11	0.00	0.00	0.11	0.00	0.11	0.00	0.00
4	British Airways	0.00	0.24	0.00	0.00	0.06	0.18	0.26	0.00	0.26
5	Emirates	0.07	0.16	0.25	0.00	0.00	0.09	0.16	0.00	0.27
6	Etihad Airways	0.00	0.13	0.00	0.00	0.00	0.09	0.04	0.48	0.26
7	Iberia	0.19	0.19	0.00	0.00	0.00	0.19	0.19	0.00	0.25
8	Lufthansa	0.02	0.23	0.00	0.02	0.28	0.17	0.16	0.00	0.12
9	Qatar Airways	0.03	0.04	0.00	0.00	0.01	0.14	0.12	0.41	0.24
10	Singapore Airlines	0.02	0.39	0.16	0.00	0.09	0.09	0.07	0.02	0.18
11	Southwest Airlines	0.00	0.00	0.00	0.00	0.01	0.83	0.16	0.00	0.00
12	Swiss Airlines	0.09	0.24	0.00	0.18	0.00	0.12	0.09	0.00	0.29
13	Thai Airways	0.08	0.36	0.00	0.00	0.00	0.04	0.08	0.20	0.24
14	Turkish Airlines	0.19	0.27	0.00	0.00	0.04	0.08	0.35	0.04	0.04
15	United Airlines	0.01	0.03	0.00	0.01	0.01	0.87	0.07	0.00	0.00
16	Virgin Atlantic	0.00	0.31	0.23	0.00	0.08	0.08	0.08	0.00	0.23

Figure 7.17   Positive topic shares, by airline

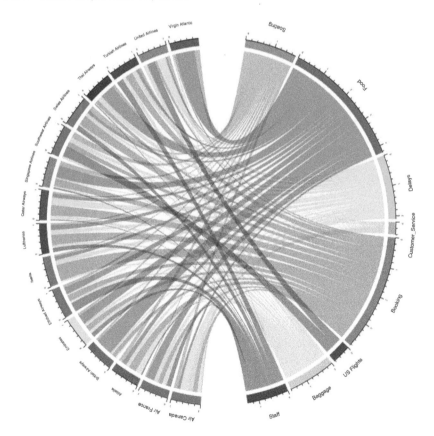

Figure 7.18   Negative review topics circular plot

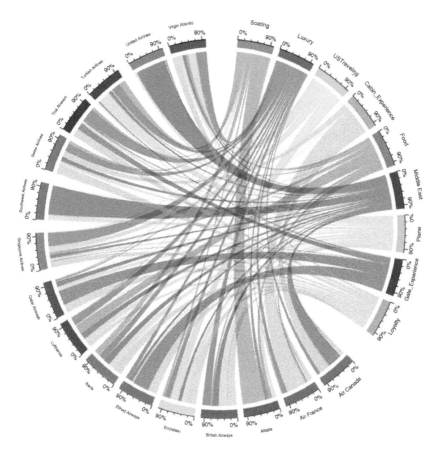

Figure 7.19   Positive review topics circular plot

CHAPTER SUMMARY

In this chapter, we discussed the large information potential of textual data for marketing managers. We developed a thorough understanding of different methods to help us extract meaning from text by encoding emotions and sentiment in text. We learned to differentiate between fast and easy top-down approaches – often also referred to as lexical approaches – and more precise but also more costly bottom-up approaches using machine learning and deep learning approaches. We developed an understanding of when to use which approach and how wrongly specified models may lead to fatal outcomes. Finally, we learned how topic models such as LDAs can help us identify latent topics within textual data and how we can classify text documents to belong to a specific topic, which again may be useful in many marketing applications such as consumer insight generation and customer relationship management.

REFERENCES

Archak, N., Ghose, A. and Ipeirotis, P. G. (2011) Deriving the pricing power of product features by mining consumer reviews. *Management Science*, 57(8), 1485–1509.

Berger, J., Humphreys, A., Ludwig, S., Moe, W. W., Netzer, O. and Schweidel, D. A. (2020) Uniting the tribes: Using text for marketing insight. *Journal of Marketing*, 84(1), 1–25.

Büschken, J. and Allenby, G. M. (2016) Sentence-based text analysis for customer reviews. *Marketing Science*, 35(6), 953–75.

Cao, J., Xia, T., Li, J., Zhang, Y. and Tang, S. (2009) A density-based method for adaptive LDA model selection. *Neurocomputing*, 72(7–9), 1775–81.

Chollet, F. and Allaire, J. J. (2018) *Deep Learning with R*. Shelter Island, NY: Manning.

Decker, R. and Trusov, M. (2010) Estimating aggregate consumer preferences from online product reviews. *International Journal of Research in Marketing*, 27(4), 293–307.

Deveaud, R., Sanjuan, E. and Bellot, P. (2014) Accurate and effective latent concept modeling for ad hoc information retrieval. *Document Numérique*, 17(1), 61–84.

Humphreys, A. and Wang, R. J.-H. (2018) Automated text analysis for consumer research. *Journal of Consumer Research*, 44(6), 1274–1306.

Hutto, C. and Gilbert, E. (2014) *Vader:* A parsimonious rule-based model for sentiment analysis of social media text. *In Proceedings of the Eighth International AAAI Conference on Web and Social Media* (pp. 216–25). Palo Alto, CA: AAAI Press.

Joung, J., Jung, K., Ko, S. and Kim, K. (2018) Customer complaints analysis using text mining and outcome-driven innovation method for market-oriented product development. *Sustainability*, 11(1), 40.

Kübler, R. V., Wieringa, J. E. and Pauwels, K. H. (2017) Machine learning and big data. In *Advanced Methods for Modeling Markets* (pp. 631–70). Springer: Cham.

Kübler, R., Pauwels, K. and Manke, K. (2020) How social media drove the 2016 US presidential election: A longitudinal topic and platform analysis. https://papers.ssrn.com/sol3/papers.cfm?abstract_id=3661846

Mohammad, S. M. and Turney, P. D. (2013) NRC emotion lexicon. *National Research Council, Canada* 2 (2013), 234.

Netzer, O., Feldman, R., Goldenberg, J. and Fresko, M. (2012) Mine your own business: Market-structure surveillance through text mining. *Marketing Science*, 31(3), 521–43.

Nofer, M. and Hinz, O. (2015) Using Twitter to predict the stock market. *Business & Information Systems Engineering*, 57(4), 229–42.

Russell, J. A. (1980) A circumplex model of affect. *Journal of Personality and Social Psychology*, 39(6), 1161.

Selivanov, D., Bickel, M. and Wang, Q. (2022) Package 'text2vec'. https://cran.r-project.org/web/packages/text2vec/text2vec.pdf

Skiera, B., Jürgensmeier, L., Stowe, K. and Gurevych, I. (2020) How to best predict the daily number of new infections of COVID-19. Preprint, arXiv:2004.03937.

Tirunillai, S. and Tellis, G. J. (2012) Does chatter really matter? Dynamics of user-generated content and stock performance. *Marketing Science*, 31(2), 198–215.

8

CHURN PREDICTION AND MARKETING CLASSIFICATION MODELS WITH SUPERVISED LEARNING

Chapter contents

LEARNING OBJECTIVES

At the end of this chapter, you should be able to:

- understand the importance of churn prediction in CRM
- identify classification problems in marketing
- understand the difference between unsupervised and supervised machine learning
- identify suitable machine learning models for marketing problems
- apply logistic regression, decision tree models, and random forest models to CRM data
- judge the quality of a supervised machine learning model.

This chapter focuses on predicting customer churn with the help of customer relationship management data. Like many other binary classification tasks in marketing, such as retargeting, real-time bidding, and fraud detection, churn prediction has become an essential part of operative, data-driven marketing. With access to large datasets of previous customer behaviour, marketers can today leverage the power of machine learning to develop prediction models which forecast customer behaviour and guide marketing decision-making. The present chapter will enable you to understand which classification tasks commonly exist in marketing and what kind of statistical and machine learning models you can apply to such problems.

To gain first-hand experience of developing our own machine learning prediction model, we provide a case study from an online gaming service which needs to better understand which customers are likely to leave the platform. We will discuss the importance of churn prevention and the costs of customer reacquisition. We will learn how churn prediction is similar to other binary classification tasks in marketing to develop a general understanding of the opportunities of binary prediction models. We then discuss classic statistical models such as logistic regression, which can be applied to address such problems. We also focus on state-of-the-art machine learning models, which can further be applied to classification problems in marketing, and we distinguish between unsupervised and supervised models. We develop a deeper understanding of the latter by applying decision tree and random forest models to our data. We learn how to judge the predictive power of our models and discuss relevant extensions such as bagging and boosting. Finally, we focus on possible issues and caveats and discuss overfitting issues in machine learning model development.

Case study

Logi.Tude

Logi.Tude is a famous game developer from Finland, founded in 2008, which offers a comprehensive online gaming platform with more than 15 million customers. The platform currently manages three major online real-time strategy games. Revenues are generated either through in-game purchases for avatars and mods or through a monthly subscription fee that may vary depending on which services and games a customer is using.

Logi.Tude has focused on platform development over the last 5 years by introducing new games and extending its current listings by introducing mods and unique games. The platform enjoyed substantial growth right after its launch. However, within the last 18 months, Logi.Tude has seen more and more customers becoming inactive and cancelling subscriptions.

It turns out that reactivating these lost customers consumes substantial resources and threatens Logi.Tude's cash flow, which is urgently needed to secure the development of future games. Therefore, the board of directors calls an emergency meeting to discuss measures. Dobs Bavis, the freshly appointed chief marketing officer (CMO) responsible for customer relations, has difficulty explaining the current developments and is facing harsh criticism. 'We cannot accept that we do not have a clear understanding of why customers are leaving us. Until we develop a better understanding and can take measures, we expect marketing to identify customers who may potentially leave the platform and to address these customers with adequate retention measures,' says Logi.Tude founder and current CEO Charles Selenski.

Right after the board meeting, Dobs contacts you as the head of the data science department and asks you to conduct a project that can predict which customers are likely to leave the company and understand from the available CRM database which factors best predict customer churn. For this purpose, Dob provides you with a dataset from the CRM system (Table 8.1).

Table 8.1   CRM data

Variable	Description	Measurement
customer_id	unique identifier for each customer	unique numerical identifier
churn	information if customer left company or stayed with service	yes/no
monthly_bill	payment data from customer based on returns from subscription and in-game purchases	spending in €
gender	customer gender	male/female
millennial	categorical information about age	Millennial or Gen Z
clanmembership	information if customer is a member of a gaming clan	yes/no
platformsince	time since customer was active on platform	number of months
avatar	information if customer has bought customized avatar	yes/no
internet_connect	average speed of internet connection	DSL, DSL16, Fiber
extrapro_account	information if customer is subscribing to a pro gaming account with bonus experience	yes/no
contract_length	type of subscription model	month-to-month, 1 year, 2 years
customer_support	information if customer has been in contact with support within the last 6 months	yes/no
payment_type	information on how customer pays invoices	pre-paid, electronic cheque, bank transfer, credit card

CUSTOMER CHURN AND REACQUISITION

While in the public mind marketing is often primarily associated only with acquiring customers, proper marketing aspires to manage and satisfy customer relations beyond the point of acquisition (Shapiro, 1988). Following the concept of market-oriented leadership, marketers need to continuously provide value to customers and understand whether existing customers are still satisfied with the product or service a company offers. The marketing literature tells us that longer customer relations are more profitable, as underlined by the customer lifetime value (CLV) concept. The CLV cumulates the total worth of a customer, or in other words, the total value he provides over his customer lifetime to the company (Gupta et al., 2006). The CLV is driven by increases in customer experience, such as loyalty or reward programmes, which help to keep customers satisfied and loyal. Repeated purchases and longer customer lifetimes often provide the company with high cross- and up-selling potential (Woodruff, 1997) and higher profitability rates through economies of scale. In addition, losing customers too early also means that high acquisition investments through marketing communication or discounts may become less profitable, as the company has lost the chance to generate cash in return for the investment through repeated purchases or enduring subscription rates (as in the case of Logi.Trade). Furthermore, to secure cash flow, companies need to compensate for leaving customers by acquiring new customers. Acquisition costs tend to be substantially higher than costs resulting from fostering and improving the customer experience. In the long run, it is thus more profitable for companies to successfully manage retention instead of losing customers and acquiring new customers. Not to mention that reacquiring customers who have previously decided to leave the company takes even more effort and consumes more firm resources than acquiring new customers. Companies are thus well advised to develop skills that help predict which customers are unsatisfied or likely to churn. This becomes even more important if a company decides to rely on CLV or net promoter score (see Chapter 5) values within their marketing strategy since these measures depend heavily on churn probabilities (Venkatesan and Kumar, 2004).

Churn prediction models are deeply rooted in the realm of CRM research. Churn models often use a mix of transactional and customer-specific data when trying to estimate the likelihood that a customer is terminating his or her relationship with a company. These models all have in common that CRM data with information about who has left and who has stayed with the company are used to model the likelihood of quitting. Input variables (in machine learning often referred to as 'features', in statistics often called 'independent variables') vary according to use cases. Rissellada et al. (2004) provide an overview of commonly used models and variables in churn prediction applications. According to their analysis, customer-specific data often include household size and income information, education levels, and other demographic and socio-demographic information. These data are enriched by customer relation-specific data such as relationship length (duration), breadth (number of extra products and services used), and depth (income generated).

Other binary classification tasks in marketing

It is worth mentioning that churn models are not the only application areas of binary classifiers in modern marketing. Especially in digital marketing, binary classification tasks play an essential role. In the case of real-time advertising, advertisers need to place a bid on how much they would pay to show their ad to an incoming website visitor (for more details, see Sayedi, 2018). To place a profitable bid, marketers must predict whether a customer will click on an ad and how likely it is that the customer will profitably engage with the landing page, or in other words, how much he or she will buy from the webshop. To find the optimal bid, marketers need to be able to infer from the available website visitor information (e.g. from cookies, pixels, or other identifiers) how likely the person is to click and engage. This can again be achieved with the help of binary classification models, which use past clicking data from previous website visitors to derive which features determine the likelihood of clicking and store this information in a model. Information from incoming customers is then used to make the model an individual prediction. As shown in Figure 8.1 the advertising company can decide based on the clicking prediction how much they want to bid to display their ad to the customer. If they deliver the highest bid, the ad will subsequently be shown to the website visitor.

Another similar but more downstream application field is retargeting. Here the customer is confronted with an ad that shows an article or product he or she has engaged with during a past website visit. Again, here marketers first need to predict whether a customer is likely to click on the ad; in addition, marketers may need to decide which type of product to include in the ad and whether they should show products to customers who previously have not bought, or other connected products. This decision may again be predicted with the help of customer-specific data fed into a previously trained model that has learned from clicking and shopping data how such customer information determines clicking and shopping likelihoods.

MACHINE LEARNING AND CLASSIFICATION MODELS

So far, we have often referred to models trained by data. We will now dive deeper into how we train models and how machines learn from data to make predictions.

While machine learning has seen a lot of interest and buzz during the last decade, the idea of making computers mimic human learning behaviour is by no means new, dating back to the 1950s (Solomonoff, 1957). Thanks to rapid technological advancement and the availability of large datasets today, what started as a theory is now a vivid and fast-growing area that connects informatics, computer sciences, management information systems, and marketing.

The critical idea in machine learning is that machines learn through observing similarities in a set of pre-labelled data. By seeing which similar features appear for all objects of one class, they learn how to predict class membership. Finally, they are able to classify new objects to belong to a class, observing whether the new data shares the class specific similarities (Kübler et al., 2017). Think of a child trying to understand what a cat is. Every time a grown-up shows a child an animal picture and tells the child what kind of animal is depicted, the child will try to find specific features which only occur with the particular animal so that it can later recognize the animal in another picture (or in reality) with the help of these features.

For example, the child will learn from repeated exposure that every animal with whiskers, four paws, and that meows rather than barks is a cat. Machines learn the same way. They will learn by observing from pre-labelled data. Such data resemble the cat pictures where the adult tells the child what kind of animal is depicted. The machine will then try to understand (e.g. by comparing frequencies or correlations) which features occur every time a cat picture is shown. While a child – needing only a minimal number of exposures to understand what a cat looks like – makes learning look easy, computers tend to need much more time and especially training data to come to similar results. This is especially true when we are interested in identifying customers who are likely to leave the company.

The idea behind machine learning is to use pre-labelled data to make a machine develop a function with which the machine can classify unlabelled new data. In marketing, this task is often referred to as a prediction or forecast model. You already encountered such forecasting tasks when fitting values to the regression model in Chapter 3. One commonly distinguishes between two forms of machine learning: *supervised* and *unsupervised* learning. So far, we have focused on supervised learning models, which all have in common that they follow the procedure depicted in Figure 8.2 and employ training data as input (CRM data) to make predictions for an output (churn).

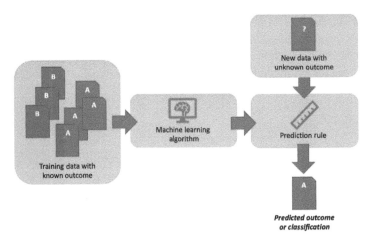

Figure 8.1 Supervised learning visualization

However, not all machine learning models follow this approach. Some machine learning applications do not focus on forecasts and predictions but aim to discover structure within data. These models do not need pre-labelled training data but try to reveal occurring patterns in data immediately. These models are commonly referred to as unsupervised machine learning models. Unsupervised accounts for the fact that the data does not need any supervision, that is, does not feature labels or codes, as shown in Figure 8.2. You already encountered unsupervised machine learning models when you worked with cluster analyses in the customer segmentation chapter. *k*-means cluster analysis belongs to the most widespread forms of unsupervised machine learning and, as you will remember, tries to identify subgroups (patterns) of similar (homogeneous) customers within CRM data.

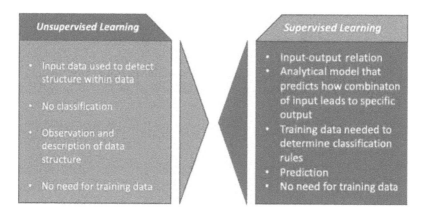

Figure 8.2 Supervised versus unsupervised machine learning

LOGISTIC REGRESSION MODELS

Logistic regression is one of the most frequently applied methods for analysing data with a binary outcome variable, such as churn. While logistic regression is often framed as a machine learning algorithm, it originates from classic statistics, where it has been used for decades to analyse data with a binary dependent variable. Therefore, it resembles traditional regression models as we have encountered them in Chapter 3. The main difference here is the type of dependent variable. While we had a continuous variable in the case of the marketing mix model (number of website visitors), we now face a situation where we are trying to explain whether a customer is leaving the company (churning) or staying with the company. The dependent variable can thus only take two different values: 1 (leaving) or 0 (staying). In this case, we cannot use a classic ordinary least squares regression model, as the nature of our dependent variable violates the key assumptions of the model, that the dependent variable is continuous.

The model aims to explain the impact of the independent variables on the probability that the dependent variable takes the value 1 or 0. In other words, we try to explain how the different customer- and usage-specific factors we observe in our CRM data sample affect the probability that a customer is leaving (or staying with) the platform. We can denote the probability that someone is churning by

$$P(y=1)=\frac{1}{1+e^{-z}},$$ (8.1)

where $P(y=1)$ expresses the probability of churn, and e is the base of natural logarithms. Z represents the logit function that accounts for the independent variables' influence in the model. We can write Z as another function somewhat similar to the one we already know from the OLS regression:.

$$z = \beta_0 + x_1\beta_1 + x_2\beta_2 + \cdots + x_n\beta_n .$$ (8.2)

We can then substitute the logit function from equation (8.2) into the probability function displayed in equation (8.1) to obtain the final model as shown in Equation (8.3),

$$P(y = 1) = \frac{1}{1 + e^{-(\beta_0 + x_1\beta_1 + x_2\beta_2 + \cdots + x_n\beta_n)}} ,$$ (8.3)

which we can estimate by maximum likelihood, where we try to find a function that maximizes the likelihood with the help of the best-fitting regression coefficients. We recommend checking Backhaus et al. (2021, pp. 267–354) for more details about maximum likelihood estimation.

Let us be more concrete and try to apply a logistic regression model directly in R and see if we can estimate the churn probabilities with the help of the data provided by Logi.Tude's CRM database. We first load the CSV dataset with the following command.

```
LogiTude_CRM_Data <- read_csv("LogiTude CRM Data.csv")
str(LogiTude_CRM_Data)
```

We can inspect the different variables in the imported data frame through the `str` command, as shown in Figure 8.3.

```
spec_tbl_df [13,043 × 14] (S3: spec_tbl_df/tbl_df/tbl/data.frame)
 $ X1               : num [1:13043] 1 2 3 4 5 6 7 8 9 10 ...
 $ customer_id      : num [1:13043] 115899 66486 87568 101850 66635 ...
 $ churn            : chr [1:13043] "No" "No" "Yes" "No" ...
 $ monthly_bill     : num [1:13043] 29.9 57 53.9 42.3 70.7 ...
 $ gender           : chr [1:13043] "Female" "Male" "Male" "Male" ...
 $ millenial        : chr [1:13043] "Gen Z" "Gen Z" "Gen Z" "Gen Z" ...
 $ clanmembership   : chr [1:13043] "Yes" "No" "No" "No" ...
 $ platformsince    : num [1:13043] 1 34 2 45 2 8 22 10 28 62 ...
 $ avatar           : chr [1:13043] "No" "Yes" "Yes" "No" ...
 $ internet_connect : chr [1:13043] "DSL_16MB/S" "DSL_16MB/S" "DSL_16MB/S" "DSL_16MB/S" ...
 $ extrapro_account : chr [1:13043] "No" "No" "No" "No" ...
 $ contract_length  : chr [1:13043] "Month-to-month" "One year" "Month-to-month" "One year" ...
 $ customer_support : chr [1:13043] "Yes" "No" "Yes" "No" ...
 $ payment_type     : chr [1:13043] "Electronic check" "PrePaid" "PrePaid" "Bank transfer (automatic)"
```

Figure 8.3 CRM data frame in R

Most of the variables were imported as characters, as R did not understand that these should be treated as factors so that we can easily include them in the analysis. We must thus recode these variables. We can do this by recoding every character variable with the `as.factor` function in R. However, this would take some coding effort and time. Instead, we can also tell R to recode all variables which are not numeric into factors with `sapply` and `lapply`. The example below first shows the basic code and then the code that transforms all other character variables into factors. Finally, we use the `str()` function again to inspect the data frame and observe the changes, as shown in Figure 8.4.

```
LogiTude_CRM_Data$churn = as.factor(LogiTude_CRM_Data$churn)

LogiTude_CRM_Data[sapply(LogiTude_CRM_Data, is.character)] <-lapply (LogiTude_
CRM_Data[sapply (LogiTude_CRM_Data, is.character)], as.factor)

Str(LogiTude_CRM_Data)
```

```
spec_tbl_df [13,043 x 14] (S3: spec_tbl_df/tbl_df/tbl/data.frame)
 $ X1              : num [1:13043] 1 2 3 4 5 6 7 8 9 10 ...
 $ customer_id     : num [1:13043] 115899 66486 87568 101850 66635 ...
 $ churn           : Factor w/ 2 levels "No","Yes": 1 1 2 1 2 2 1 1 2 1 ...
 $ monthly_bill    : num [1:13043] 29.9 57 53.9 42.3 70.7 ...
 $ gender          : Factor w/ 2 levels "Female","Male": 1 2 2 2 1 1 2 1 1 2 ...
 $ millenial       : Factor w/ 2 levels "Gen Z","Millenial": 1 1 1 1 1 1 1 1 1 1 ...
 $ clanmembership  : Factor w/ 2 levels "No","Yes": 2 1 1 1 1 1 1 1 2 1 ...
 $ platformsince   : num [1:13043] 1 34 2 45 2 8 22 10 28 62 ...
 $ avatar          : Factor w/ 2 levels "No","Yes": 1 2 2 1 2 2 2 1 2 2 ...
 $ internet_connect: Factor w/ 3 levels "Base DSL_16MB/S",..: 2 2 2 3 3 3 2 3 2 ...
 $ extrapro_account: Factor w/ 2 levels "No","Yes": 1 1 1 1 2 2 1 2 1 ...
 $ contract_length : Factor w/ 3 levels "Month-to-month",..: 1 2 1 2 1 1 1 1 1 2 ...
 $ customer_support: Factor w/ 2 levels "No","Yes": 2 1 2 1 2 2 2 1 2 1 ...
 $ payment_type    : Factor w/ 4 levels "Bank transfer (automatic)",..: 3 4 4 1 3 3 2 4 3 1 ...
```

Figure 8.4 CRM data frame with factors coded variables

We are now ready to inspect the data further to build our logistic regression model. To demonstrate how well we can predict churn, we further split our dataset into a training and a test set. We will run the logistic regression only with the training set and then use the test set to predict who is likely to churn and who is expected to stay with the company. As we already have this information, we can then compare how well our predictive model performs and how well our logistic regression model helps Logi.Tude predict which customers are likely to leave the platform. To have an adequate training dataset with sufficient variation and information, we use 80% of the dataset for the training set and save 20% of the data for our test set. We can achieve this with the following code. As you can see in the first line, we use 0.8 as a cut value. You can, of course, also try out other sample sizes, such as 75% training and 25% test data, a split which is also often used in machine learning practice. With the set.seed command, we ensure that the results are reproducible as it forces R to start with the same randomly chosen rows.

```
sample_size = floor(0.8*nrow(Logi.Data))
set.seed(777)
picked = sample(seq_len(nrow(Logi.Data)),size = sample_size)
train.LogiTude =Logi.Data[picked,]
test.Logi.Tude =Logi.Data[-picked,]
```

As with the ordinary regression models used in Chapter 3, logistic regression models are sensitive to correlations that may cause biased (i.e., inflated) estimates, as the model cannot assign causality to a specific independent variable. For example, suppose you constantly change your ad spending together with your price promotion activities. In that case, the model will not be able to understand whether the sales effect originates from the ad increase or the price promotion. We thus need first to see the correlations among our numeric variables.

```
install.packages("Hmisc")
library(Hmisc)
Logi.Data.Num = train.LogiTude %>% select(where(is.numeric))
correlation.matrix = as.data.frame(Hmisc::rcorr(as.matrix(Logi.Data.Num),
type = "pearson")$P)
```

We can inspect the correlation matrix and see that the correlation is 0, which means that both numeric variables (time on platform and spending) are not highly correlated, that is, they do not change together and do not show any relation. In other words, we cannot say that spending is somehow related to time with the platform. As a rule of thumb, you should be suspicious of any significant correlation above 0.6. We will soon see that we can approach this issue also with another test. However, let us first continue building our logistic regression model. We use the `glm` package in R to estimate the model with the following command.

```
LR.Logi.Tude = glm(churn ~ monthly_bill + gender + millennial + clanmembership +
                   platformsince + avatar + internet_connect + extrapro_account +
                   contract_length + customer_support + payment_type,
                   data = train.LogiTude, family = "binomial")
```

As pointed out above, correlations among all variables may lead to inflated estimates. Predictive models often ignore multicollinearity among the independent variables (or features), as solid correlations often do not bias the predictive power. As pointed out before, multicollinearity (i.e., the problem that we cannot assign causality to a pair of highly correlated independent variables) is an issue if we want to understand which variables cause churn. While we have focused solely on a correlation analysis among the numerical variables, we now conduct another test, which helps us ensure that we do not face inflated estimates and that we inspect effects across all – categorical and continuous – variables in our model. We do this with the help of the variance inflation factor (VIF) test, which is the standard test procedure for multicollinearity in regression models. We need to install another package with the following code to obtain the VIFs values for a logistic regression model.

```
install.packages("performance")
library(performance)
check_collinearity(LR.Logi.Tude)
```

The output is shown in Figure 8.5.

```
Low Correlation

                Term  VIF Increased SE Tolerance
              gender 1.00          1.00      1.00
            millenial 1.09          1.04      0.92
       clanmembership 1.12          1.06      0.89
        platformsince 2.12          1.46      0.47
               avatar 1.85          1.36      0.54
     extrapro_account 1.54          1.24      0.65
       contract_length 1.53          1.24      0.65
      customer_support 1.11          1.05      0.90
         payment_type 1.33          1.15      0.75

Moderate Correlation

                Term  VIF Increased SE Tolerance
         monthly_bill 9.36          3.06      0.11
      internet_connect 8.74          2.96      0.11
```

Figure 8.5   Variance inflation factors of our first logistic regression model

The performance package helps us with the interpretation and splits the variables into different groups. Here we see that for nine out of our 11 variables, VIFs remain well below 3, which is often defined as an acceptable threshold. Only monthly billing and the type of internet connection exhibit higher VIFs and are thus considered to be moderately correlated, with VIFs between 3 and 10. Note that a VIF over 10 would immediately be regarded as unacceptable for analysis. Still, as we want to be on the safe side here, we must decide which variable we would like to drop from our model. We drop internet connection from our model, as this variable originates from data obtained by an external service provider, while monthly billing has been recorded by our own company.

Which variable do you suggest dropping here? Why?

Let us develop our final model and see if dropping the variable improved the VIFs.

```
LR.Logi.Tudel = glm(churn ~ monthly_bill + gender + millennial +
                clanmembership +platformsince + avatar + extrapro_
                account +contract_length + customer_support + payment_type,
                data = Logi.Data, family = "binomial")

check_collinearity(LR.Logi.Tudel)
```

Figure 8.6 shows the VIFs, and as we can see, all VIFs are now well below 3, and we can thus trust our model not to show any inflated estimates.

```
Low Correlation

                    Term  VIF  Increased SE  Tolerance
            monthly_bill  2.04         1.43       0.49
                  gender  1.00         1.00       1.00
                millenial 1.08         1.04       0.93
           clanmembership 1.12         1.06       0.89
            platformsince 2.02         1.42       0.50
                  avatar  1.30         1.14       0.77
          extrapro_account 1.49        1.22       0.67
          contract_length 1.44         1.20       0.69
         customer_support 1.11         1.05       0.90
             payment_type 1.30         1.14       0.77
```

Figure 8.6   VIFs of corrected model

Figure 8.7 displays the results of the logistic regression model, which we obtain with the `summary` function of R:

```
summary(LR.Logi.Tude1)
```

```
Call:
glm(formula = churn ~ monthly_bill + gender + millenial + clanmembership +
    platformsince + avatar + extrapro_account + contract_length +
    customer_support + payment_type, family = "binomial", data = train.LogiTude)

Deviance Residuals:
    Min       1Q   Median       3Q      Max
-1.9044  -0.7043  -0.3165   0.7472   3.2827

Coefficients:
                                      Estimate Std. Error z value Pr(>|z|)
(Intercept)                          -1.209361   0.123888  -9.762  < 2e-16 ***
monthly_bill                          0.025047   0.001426  17.561  < 2e-16 ***
genderMale                           -0.001393   0.052210  -0.027   0.9787
millenialMillenial                    0.306510   0.066411   4.615 3.92e-06 ***
clanmembershipYes                    -0.095525   0.056510  -1.690   0.0909 .
platformsince                        -0.037771   0.001829 -20.646  < 2e-16 ***
avatarYes                            -0.797027   0.098232  -8.114 4.91e-16 ***
extrapro_accountYes                   0.266196   0.064268   4.142 3.44e-05 ***
contract_lengthOne year              -0.803962   0.084680  -9.494  < 2e-16 ***
contract_lengthTwo year              -1.603381   0.133136 -12.043  < 2e-16 ***
customer_supportYes                   0.366601   0.059253   6.187 6.13e-10 ***
payment_typeCredit card (automatic)   0.007389   0.091145   0.081   0.9354
payment_typeElectronic check          0.441301   0.075603   5.837 5.31e-09 ***
payment_typePrePaid                  -0.028475   0.090982  -0.313   0.7543
---
Signif. codes:  0 '***' 0.001 '**' 0.01 '*' 0.05 '.' 0.1 ' ' 1

(Dispersion parameter for binomial family taken to be 1)

    Null deviance: 12113.0  on 10433  degrees of freedom
Residual deviance:  8959.8  on 10420  degrees of freedom
AIC: 8987.8

Number of Fisher Scoring iterations: 6
```

Figure 8.7   Results of the logistic regression

Looking at the *p*-values, we can conclude that at the 95% confidence level, all variables but three show significant effects and thus influence the probability that a customer is leaving the platform. Only gender and credit card and pre-paid payments do not significantly affect the churning likelihood. For our categorical variables, we see that one category is always missing. In this case contract length (e.g. monthly payments) is not listed. This is because R is treating the factors as dummy-coded variables. One category is thus permanently excluded from the model. It serves as a reference category, which means that we can interpret the effects always in comparison to the missing reference category. In the case of contract length, we must thus conclude that longer contracts show a 'lower' probability of churning, as indicated by the negative coefficients for the two categories, One year and Two year, of our factor contract length. From the output above we can interpret the log-odds. We can say the log-odds for churn are –0.8 if someone has a one-year contract compared to a monthly contract.

Go through all the significant effects, interpret the direction of each effect, and suggest possible explanations for what you find.

Remember the functional form of the logistic regression model? We modelled the probability of a customer churning with the help of the logit function, which included all independent variables but was integrated into an exponential function. We thus cannot simply interpret the coefficients from the logistic regression but need to transform them into the odds that someone is churning, given a change of each variable. We can interpret it, but the log-odds is hard to grasp. Therefore, we can calculate exp(*b*), which is the odds ratio.

If exp(*b*) = 1: no influence of independent on dependent variable.

If exp(*b*) > 1: positive relationship.

If exp(*b*) < 1: negative relationship.

We can ask R to provide us with the odds of each variable with the following code; the resulting output is displayed in Figure 8.8.

```
exp(cbind(OR=coef(LR.Logi.Tude1), confint(LR.Logi.Tude1)))
```

The odds can now be interpreted as the corresponding likelihood of each variable for churning.

We can now finally make the predictions for our test dataset and see how well we can predict churn. We use the following code that first predicts our model with the data stored in our test data frame. We then transform the prediction into a yes/no format and check the accuracy of our prediction.

	OR	2.5 %	97.5 %
Waiting for profiling to be done...			
(Intercept)	0.2983879	0.2338164	0.3800322
monthly_bill	1.0253637	1.0225188	1.0282524
genderMale	0.9986082	0.9014828	1.1062363
millenialMillenial	1.3586754	1.1927653	1.5474892
clanmembershipYes	0.9088952	0.8136047	1.0153726
platformsince	0.9629332	0.9594690	0.9663752
avatarYes	0.4506666	0.3719180	0.5466702
extrapro_accountYes	1.3049905	1.1506380	1.4803316
contract_lengthOne year	0.4475521	0.3786097	0.5277123
contract_lengthTwo year	0.2012151	0.1540938	0.2598297
customer_supportYes	1.4428223	1.2848302	1.6208041
payment_typeCredit card (automatic)	1.0074166	0.8425254	1.2044414
payment_typeElectronic check	1.5547293	1.3411775	1.8039254
payment_typePrePaid	0.9719263	0.8133324	1.1619418

Figure 8.8 Odd ratios of independent variables

```
fitted.results.LR1 <- predict(LR.Logi.Tude1,newdata = test.Logi.Tude,
type = 'response')
fitted.results.LR1 <- ifelse(fitted.results.LR1 > 0.5,1,0)
fitted.results.LR1 <- ifelse(fitted.results.LR1 == 1,"Yes","No")
fitted.results.LR1 <- as.factor(fitted.results.LR1)
misClasificError <- mean(fitted.results.LR1 != test.Logi.Tude$churn)
print(paste('Logistic Regression Accuracy',1-misClasificError))
```

R will now return the logistic regression accuracy with a value of 0.8098. In almost 81% of our test data, we were able to forecast correctly whether a customer left the company correctly.

DECISION TREE MODELS

Let us now try to see how well we can predict churn with a decision tree model. Decision trees belong to the category of supervised machine learning methods. Conceptually, the decision tree algorithm starts with all the data at the root node and searches all the variables for a suitable variable to split the dataset. The goal is to develop a split that results in a pure subgroup, that is, only contains members of one of the two groups of our binary dependent variable churn. However, this may also imply that the second group is still impure and consists of more than one group. If this is the case, the algorithm continues to split this subgroup (leaf) with another variable to achieve the same outcome again. This continues until all resulting leaves only consist of either churners or non-churners. The nodes at the bottom of the decision tree are thus called the end nodes, and the majority of observations in those nodes determine how new observations that land at that end node are estimated. Let us simply give it a try so that you can learn the principle from our application. You will use R's `rpart` package to build your first decision tree. Figure 8.9 shows the output of the tree model.

```
install.packages("rpart")
install.packages("rpart.plot")
library(rpart)
library(rpart.plot)


my_1sttree.LogiTude <- rpart(churn ~
                            monthly_bill + gender + millennial +
                            clanmembership + platformsince + avatar +
                            internet_connect + extrapro_account +
                            contract_length + customer_support +
                            payment_type,
                            data = train.LogiTude,
                            method = "class", cp = 0.001, minsplit
                            = 400, maxdepth = 5)


rpart.plot(my_1sttree.LogiTude)
```

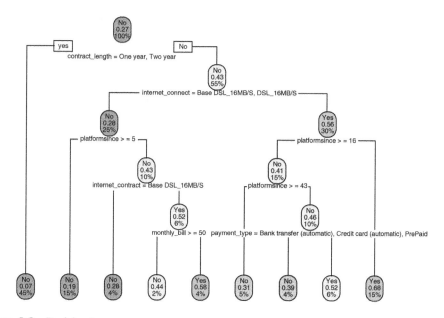

Figure 8.9 Decision tree

We start at the root, where contract length is the first variable for a split. The tree shows that if you have a one- or two-year contract, you are immediately moved to the non-churning leaf that takes 45% of the sample and in which only 7% of the members churned, at the bottom left. You are moved to the right leaf if you have a monthly contract that incorporates 55% of the sample. Here another variable is now used for the split: the type of internet connection. If you have fibre, the tree sends you to the left leaf, which consists of 25% of the sample; if you have base DSL or DSL16, you are sent to the right leaf, which consists of 30% of the sample. Here platform age is used for another split. If you have been with the platform for more than 16 weeks, you are assigned to the bottom leaf consisting of 15% of the sample, which indicates that you are a churner. We must thus assume that every user who has been with the platform for more than 16 weeks, using a medium or slow DSL connection, and having a monthly payment plan, is likely to churn and needs our attention. Checking the other bottom leaves, we can develop similar rules. Check, for example, the green leaf with churners in the middle of the bottom row that incorporates 4% of the sample. Going up from here, we can similarly conclude that all people who pay more than €50 per month, who use a base DSL connection, and have been with the platform for more than 5 weeks while having a monthly subscription plan, are also likely to churn. You may by now understand why decision trees are popular with managers. They are easy to understand, can be nicely visualized, and lead to actionable rules and insights.

Finally, we can check the tree's accuracy by making a prediction with the help of our test sample to see how many churning customers were correctly predicted by our tree model.

```
fitted.results.Tree1 <- predict(my_1sttree.LogiTude, test.Logi.Tude)
fitted.results.Tree1.bin = as.factor(ifelse(fitted.results.
Tree1[,1]>0.5, "No", "Yes"))

p1 <- predict(my_1sttree.LogiTude, train.LogiTude)
p1.bin <- as.factor(ifelse(p1[,1]>0.5, "No", "Yes"))

table1 <- table(Predicted = p1.bin, Actual = train.LogiTude$churn)
table2 <- table(Predicted = fitted.results.Tree1.bin, Actual = test.
Logi.Tude$churn)

print(paste('Decision Tree Accuracy',sum(diag(table2))/sum(table2)))
```

As you can see, the churn prediction accuracy is 80.57%, very slightly less than the accuracy of the logistic regression model.

 Why do you believe the decision tree model's accuracy to be slightly below the accuracy of the logistic regression? What key differences between the two models can you identify?

Model tuning

So, it turns out that our current model does not include all the variables of our dataset. The reason for this is that we limited the decision tree algorithm by different arguments such as `max.depth`, `min.leaves`, and `cp`. These arguments allow us to determine how detailed a tree becomes and how many decision rules the algorithm includes. There are more controls that can be deployed to affect the tree development process. If you write `? rpart.control` in the console, R will guide you to the package's help facility where you will find a detailed description of each control parameter and how it affects the tree development. Of course, all control parameters will have a large impact on the results and the predictive accuracy of the tree model and we must thus think about the best setting. This process is often referred to as *model tuning*. The key idea of model tuning is to find the best control setting, which maximizes the model's accuracy. This is commonly achieved through a so-called grid search, in which many models with different settings are estimated and their prediction accuracy compared. You can basically think of model tuning as a systematic trial-and-error approach in which the computer automatically tests all possible combinations.

Boosting and bagging

Even though tuning helps to improve the model's accuracy, decision tree models often lack precision. Thus, extensions have been developed to deliver more accurate and precise predictions. These extensions can be assigned to two major categories: *boosting* and *bagging*.

In boosting approaches, trees are sequentially advanced with the help of weights, and weights are determined by how well a decision tree model predicts. At each step, the new tree attempts to minimize the errors of the previous tree models by dropping variables or assigning higher importance to variables. The weights help to guide the tree models in a better direction. Contrary to expectations, the misclassified observations receive a higher weight in the next step of the boosting algorithm. The idea is that a stronger focus on the misclassified data points increases the accuracy of subsequent steps in the algorithm. The final classification is based on a weighted vote across the sequential classifications, where better classifications get a higher weight. Since trees are added sequentially, boosting algorithms learn slowly, but tend to be a powerful tool in developing predictive models. Most commonly boosting models such as AdaBoost, gradient boosting, or XGBoost dominate machine learning tasks and are thus frequently applied. Still, we want to warn against blindly using these models just because they seem to perform best. Given that one can apply different weight functions for sequential model development, finding the right model setting can be difficult and prone to error.

In contrast to boosting, bagging models do not work sequentially but develop many trees in parallel and construct an 'averaged' model from the results of many models. The key idea here is to randomly sample different training datasets from the main training dataset. The approach is very similar to 'common' bootstrapping approaches from statistics, where subparts from a large main dataset are used to build many smaller datasets used for analysis. By randomly sampling the subsets, one ensures that sets are never precisely the same. In bagging tree models, we use these randomly sampled subsets to build different tree models, which we then combine. The most commonly known bagging approach is random forest, where we create a forest from the different trees, which are trained with the randomly generated training subsets.

Random forest

Let us now try out this approach. We again need to install a new package so that we can use the `random.forest` function.

```
install.packages("randomForest")
library(randomForest)


set.seed(111)
my_1stforest.LogiTude <- randomForest(churn ~
                     monthly_bill + gender + millennial + clanmembership
                     + platformsince + avatar + internet_connect +
                     extrapro_account +  length + customer_support +
                     payment_type, data = train.LogiTude, importance = TRUE,
                     ntree = 5000)
```

Don't worry if this takes a while. With the `ntree = 5000` argument, we are basically forcing R to estimate 5000 different decision trees.

To compare the model's accuracy with the single tree model and logistic regression, we can further calculate the accuracy with the help of the test set and the following code.

```
forest.prediction <- predict(my_1stforest.LogiTude, test.Logi.Tude)
misClasificError.RF <- mean(forest.prediction != test.Logi.Tude$churn)


print(paste('Logistic Regression Accuracy',1-misClasificError.RF)
```

We obtain a slightly better accuracy (86.41%) than with the two previous models and have a model that can already be employed by Logi.Tude's CRM department to forecast which customers are likely to leave the company and thus need special attention.

While logistic regression allowed us to use odds ratios, and the decision tree allowed us to examine the different branches, to gain an understanding of which factors increase churning probabilities, the `randomForest` package provides us with the feature importance scores to determine the features which have the strongest impact on churn. We can access these – as shown in Figure 8.10 – with the help of the following code.

```
varImpPlot(my_1stforest.LogiTude)
```

my_1stforest.LogiTude

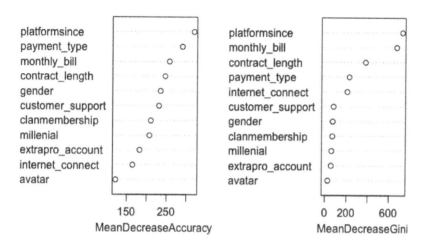

Figure 8.10 Feature importance plots

The accuracy plot shows how much worse the model would perform without the variables included. Thus, a large decrease (i.e. a high value on the *x*-axis) is associated with a variable of high estimation power. The second plot is the Gini coefficient. The higher the variable values here, the more important the variables are for the model.

 Which variables have the strongest impact on churn? What can Logi.Tude learn from that and perhaps improve?

Predictive power and overfitting

While we of course want to ensure that we always end up with the best prediction model, we also need to be careful about how we get there and how much we trust the accuracy values we obtain from our split samples. Especially with tree models, we are quickly developing a model that basically depicts the structure of our training data and delivers outstanding accuracy values. Once we apply it to out-of-sample data (i.e. data from fresh incoming customers) we may soon realize that the predictive power of our model is not as good as we initially thought. This issue is often referred to as *overfitting*. A common approach to avoid overfitting is to keep an eye on the increase in accuracy. If your model adaptions suddenly only lead to minor increases in accuracy, or even if accuracy stagnates, this is a common indication of overfitting. In addition, you should always monitor your model's predictive power with new data. For example, you might use a small number of classified churners as a control group. How many of these identified customers really do churn if you do not address them? Is this number comparable to the accuracy values of your model? If not, you may need to reassess your model's predictive power and retrain the model from scratch. Also, keep in mind that customer behaviour is not as steady as situational and market factors. The entry of new competitors in the market, new technologies, new pricing models, or other changes may affect customer preferences and thus affect churn behaviour. This may mean that you continuously need to monitor the predictive power of your model and question whether your training and classification data really incorporate all relevant variables. As a marketing analyst, you should not simply trust data and methods but also integrate classic marketing theory into your model building and variable selection. You will realize that existing theory and research insights will be tremendously helpful in finding the correct model formulation and deciding which variables you want to track and include in your CRM database so that you can be sure that you have the right data at your disposal when building your churn model. We especially recommend sources such as the *Journal of Marketing* seminar series, the American Marketing Association's webinar series and the Marketing Science Institute working paper series, which all bring the latest marketing research insights to marketing practitioners and ensure that you stay up to date.

CHAPTER SUMMARY

In this chapter, we discussed the essential role of churn prediction in marketing. We developed a clear understanding of why preventing churn is essential, given the high (re)acquisition costs companies face. Furthermore, we developed an understanding of the concept of customer lifetime value and that a customer's profitability increases with his or her time staying with the company. Gaining insights into which customers are likely to leave the company (i.e. churn) is thus essential to either address these customers and prevent them from leaving, or gain a better understanding of why these customers leave to address the underlying reasons to prevent further customers from leaving. We learned that we can employ different forms of supervised machine learning algorithms to make such predictions. Supervised machine learning relies on pre-trained data to make any sort of prediction. Like other predictive models, the quality of the prediction is again subject to the quality of the training data. We must thus ensure that training data and algorithms fit the task well and that we prevent models from being too specific to the training data (overfitting), as otherwise our models may not generalize well and only be able to predict the relations in the training dataset.

REFERENCES

Backhaus, K., Erichson, B., Gensler, S., Weiber, R. and Weiber, T. (2021) *Multivariate Analysis: An Application-Oriented Introduction.* Wiesbaden: Springer Gabler.

Gupta, S., Hanssens, D., Hardie, B., Kahn, W., Kumar, V., Lin, N., Ravishanker, N. and Sriram, S. (2006) Modeling customer lifetime value. *Journal of Service Research*, 9(2), 139–55.

Kübler, R. V., Wieringa, J. E. and Pauwels, K. H. (2017) Machine learning and big data. In P. S. H. Leeflang, J. E. Wieringa, T. H. A. Bijmolt, and K. H. Pauwels (eds), *Advanced Methods for Modeling Markets* (pp. 631–70). Cham: Springer.

Risselada, H., Verhoef, P. C. and Bijmolt, T. H. (2010) Staying power of churn prediction models. *Journal of Interactive Marketing*, 24(3), 198–208.

Sayedi, A. (2018) Real-time bidding in online display advertising. *Marketing Science*, 37(4), 553–68.

Shapiro, B. P. (1988) *What the Hell is Market Oriented?* Boston: HBR Reprints.

Solomonoff, R. J. (1957) An inductive inference machine. In *IRE Convention Record, Section on Information Theory* (Vol. 2, pp. 56–62). New York: Institute of Radio Engineers.

Venkatesan, R. and Kumar, V. (2004) A customer lifetime value framework for customer selection and resource allocation strategy. *Journal of Marketing*, 68(4), 106–25.

Woodruff, R. B. (1997) Customer value: The next source for competitive advantage. *Journal of the Academy of Marketing Science*, 25(2), 139–53.

9

DEMAND FORECASTING

Chapter contents

LEARNING OBJECTIVES

At the end of this chapter, you should be able to:

- define demand forecasting and explain why it is important in marketing
- understand some of the well-established modelling approaches to sales forecasting, including simple exponential smoothing (SES), the Holt–Winters method, and autoregressive integrated moving average (ARIMA) models
- gain hands-on experience by applying the analytical models in R to a real-world dataset.

This chapter is about demand forecasting. We begin with a small case study to illustrate the demand forecasting problem faced by a kitchen appliance company in an emerging market. Next, we lay the foundations of the topic. We review some of the well-established sales forecasting models (i.e. simple exponential smoothing, the Holt–Winters method, and autoregressive integrated moving average), using intuitive and easy-to-follow examples. We discuss in depth various data patterns that these models typically account for: seasonality, deterministic, and stochastic trend, and autocorrelations. Also, we explain the essential steps in building a good demand forecasting model, and describe some of the important modelling concepts such as model validation, forecast accuracy metrics, and prediction intervals in an accessible manner. Finally, we apply the demand forecasting models to the case study using R. The software application walks the reader through all the modelling steps from data visualization and model identification to model validation and model comparison. The application emphasizes the importance of model validation and shows that once a forecasting model is developed to fit past data well, it can be used to predict what may happen in the future.

======== Case study ========

Silverline

It was a sunny day in Istanbul. The chief marketing officer of Silverline, an award-winning Turkish supplier of built-in appliances for cooking, cooling, and dishwashing, was on a video call with the sales manager (SM) from his office. In a worried voice, the SM said: 'Look - we have great appliances. All of our retailers say that customers love them. But our favourite store in Istanbul complains about the same issue over and over again. They just can't get enough of our products - in particular, the extractor fans. So they end up pointing customers to competitors' products. This is a big opportunity loss for us. We should do something about this.'

A silence fell upon the room and the CMO said: 'You are right. My heart bleeds when I see our great products fail to take their deserved share in the market. We should keep good ties with all the retailers as they are the gatekeepers to the market. But perhaps we also need an analytical demand forecasting solution at store level. What do you think?'

The SM responded excitedly: 'What a great idea! As far as I know, the use of analytical approaches in our sector is not very common. If we had an automated demand forecasting tool and applied it for each store, it might well give us a huge advantage over our competitors. For stores with the stockout issue, we can try to predict future demand in a similar store in terms of demographics and other characteristics, and use that as an estimate.'

The CMO was pleased that her suggestion resonated with the SM: 'Perfect! Why don't we dive right into this? I will talk to the production team and try to find out how to build a data analytics team that can provide some data-driven solutions.'

The following day, the CMO had a meeting with the production team and towards the end of the meeting said: 'I am so excited! Let's build this analytics team together. The team can use some forecasting tools and tell us how demand will look like in the next several months. This way, we can support the stores that have stock issues in relation to our extractor fans.'

Not long afterwards, the analytics team started to work with a dataset from a similar store to the one highlighted. The data covered the historical monthly sales of an extractor fan over a time span of 122 months.

The question was straightforward: what would be the demand for this product over the next year?

To be able to address the question in the case study, we will introduce the concept of demand forecasting, discuss briefly why it is important for marketers, and then take a look at the techniques that firms commonly use. Finally, we will use R to apply the models to the case study.

WHAT IS DEMAND FORECASTING?

Demand forecasting focuses on the 'what' aspect of marketing. Instead of examining the potential mechanisms behind a particular phenomenon, the emphasis is placed on understanding *what will happen next*. Obviously, knowing the 'why' (e.g. why consumers behave in the way they do behave in a particular setting) and the 'how' (e.g. how price promotions or advertising work) provides valuable strategic guidance to marketers. However, there are some situations in which marketers need to concentrate more on the 'what'. For example, in retail, forecasting the future demand for perishable items at a large scale and in an automated way is very crucial – managers need to come up with scalable and automated demand forecasts for a large number of stock-keeping units (Franses and Legerstee, 2013).

Broadly speaking, demand forecasting in marketing is defined as the practice of predicting whether customers will buy, what they will buy, and how much they will buy.[1] This practice requires the use of past data to determine future demand for a product or service.

Why is demand forecasting important?

Demand forecasting is of utmost importance to marketing managers for several reasons:

---

[1]In this chapter, we use the term 'demand forecasting' to refer to 'sales forecasting'. However, demand forecasting is a broad term that is used for choice models in marketing as well. For a broad perspective on these models, we refer the reader to Chintagunta and Nair (2011).

Learning from the past. Looking at past sales dynamics, marketing managers can discern patterns (e.g. trends, troughs, spikes, seasonality) and project them into future. Also, they can develop associations between demand drivers (e.g. price) and realized demand. This kind of analysis helps them understand what happened in the past and make better plans for the future (Ord et al., 2017).

Keeping customers happy. 'Bricks-and-mortar' stores should make sure that they have enough products available on their shelves. If not, it is very likely that they will lose their customers to competitors, resulting in an increase in customer dissatisfaction. Moreover, online retailers need to determine the next purchasable products by a customer and fulfil their needs. Therefore, good demand forecasting leads to better planning and efficiency, and is an integral part of keeping customers satisfied.

Optimizing stock levels. Retailers may buy too much from their suppliers, leading to obsolete stock, or too little, leading to stock-outs. Forecasting future demand well helps retailers optimize inventory and significantly reduce costs (Ma and Fildes, 2021).

Cultivating a forward-looking culture. If implemented regularly and correctly, demand forecasting may force firms to think continually about the future and where they are headed. This fosters a forward-looking culture within their organization.

In what follows, we review some of the well-established demand forecasting models and tools in order to be able to answer the questions raised in our case study. It is worth noting that demand forecasting can also be performed using more sophisticated supervised machine learning models (e.g. neural networks, support vector machines, and decision trees). Having introduced some of the machine learning models with different marketing applications in previous chapters, we devote this chapter to the conventional demand forecasting techniques employed by practitioners. Although these models are developed much earlier than some of the sophisticated machine learning models, they are quite robust and not very sensitive to overfitting. For a comprehensive review of forecasting with machine learning models, see James et al. (2014) and Petropoulos et al. (2022).

Note that, although the predictive models that we will discuss in this chapter are useful in predicting future demand for some product types (e.g. perishable items and cleaning products in the consumer packaged goods category), their application may be less useful in other product categories (e.g. fashion-forward clothing products). For instance, it might be difficult to predict next year's demand for luxury or high-fashion items sold by brands such as Chanel and Burberry because consumer preferences for such products may change rapidly and show inconsistencies across time, implying that past purchase data may not be indicative of future purchases for this kind of products.

DEMAND FORECASTING APPROACHES

Let us begin with a simple example. Figure 9.1 shows the historical sales of a fast-moving consumer product from a retail store in London.

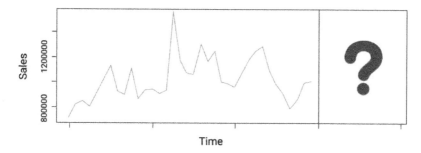

Figure 9.1 Historical sales of a fast-moving consumer product

Suppose that we want to forecast the future sales values for this product, represented in Figure 9.1 by a question mark. How should we approach this forecasting task? The most basic method perhaps would be to compute the arithmetic mean for the series using all the past data, and state that the forecast will be equal to the average or mean of the historical data (see Figure 9.2).

Figure 9.2 Arithmetic mean

The second basic forecasting method would be a naïve forecast. Using this method, we simply set all future forecasts to the last observation of the series:

$$\hat{y}_{t+1|t} = y_t , \tag{9.1}$$

where y_t is the observation at time t and $\hat{y}_{t+1|t}$ is the forecast at time $t + 1$.

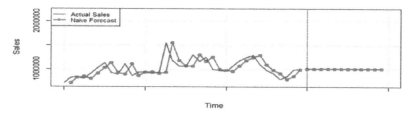

Figure 9.3 Naïve forecast

Figure 9.3 shows the naïve forecast. A slight variation of this method is the seasonal naïve method, which sets each forecast to the last observed value from the same season of the previous year.

The third intuitive forecasting approach would be to calculate the average of the last k observations in the series as a forecast for the next period. We call this method the simple moving average (SMA). It is calculated as

$$\hat{y}_{t+1|t} = \frac{1}{k}\sum_{i=t-k+1}^{t} y_i \, , \tag{9.2}$$

where k denotes the number of observations (also known as the length of the sequence), t is the time index, and y_i is the ith sales datum. For example, an SMA of length 3, denoted by SMA(3), is expressed as follows:

$$\hat{y}_{t+1|t} = \frac{1}{3}\sum_{i=t-2}^{t} y_i \, . \tag{9.3}$$

In equation (9.3), we simply take the arithmetic mean of y_{t-2}, y_{t-1}, and y_t, and designate it as our forecast for the next period, $t + 1$. Figure 9.4 shows the sales forecast for our fast-moving consumer product based on SMA(3).

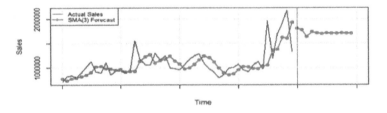

Figure 9.4 Forecast with SMA(3)

How do we determine k? The best length depends on whether we want to filter noise or capture the ups and downs in the series. SMAs with higher lengths will filter noise but will not fully capture the ups and downs. To find the optimal length, we can calculate the SMA with different lengths, and select the model with the smallest forecast error.[2]

To summarize, using the arithmetic mean, all forecasts are equal to a simple average of the observed data. This method assumes that all observations are of equal importance, that is to say, they are given equal weight. In contrast, the naïve method assumes that the most recent observation is the only important datum and all data points prior to that observation provide no information for the future. In SMA, only the last k observations matter and each of them carries equal weight. However, in some cases, it may be more appropriate to give larger weights to more recent observations of the data than to observations from the distant past (Hyndman and Athanasopoulos, 2018). The simple exponential smoothing (SES) model accommodates this feature. Below, we discuss SES in depth.

---

[2]We discuss the forecast errors later in detail.

Simple exponential smoothing

The model for SES is formulated as follows (Gardner, 1985):

$$\hat{y}_{t+1|t} = \alpha y_t + \alpha(1-\alpha)y_{t-1} + \alpha(1-\alpha)^2 y_{t-2} + \cdots ,$$

(9.4)

where y_t, y_{t-1}, and, y_{t-2} are the observed data at time t, $t-1$, and $t-2$, respectively. α is the smoothing parameter and $\hat{y}_{t+1|t}$ is the forecast for y at time $t+1$ given all the past information up to time t. Equation (9.4) simply suggests that the forecast for the next period will be a combination of the past values of y with decaying weights. For instance, if α is chosen to be 0.2, the weight for y_{t-1} will be 0.160. Similarly, the weight for y_{t-2} will be 0.128, and the remaining weights of the model will decay exponentially.

With repeated substitution, the model in equation (9.4) becomes

$$\hat{y}_{t+1|t} = \alpha y_t + (1-\alpha)\hat{y}_{t|t-1} ,$$

(9.5)

where $\hat{y}_{t|t-1}$ is the forecast for y at time t, given all the past information up to time $t-1$.

Although SES is a very simple model, in some cases it may outperform other sophisticated models. The downside of the SES is that it is not suitable for data with seasonality and/or trend patterns. When such patterns occur, we usually employ the Holt–Winters method.

The Holt-Winters method

A simple visual inspection of the sales data in Figure 9.5 (blue line) suggests that there is an upward trend (indicated by the straight red line) and a reoccurring peak pattern at fixed and known points, a form of seasonality (marked with circles).

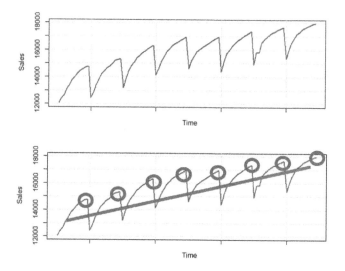

Figure 9.5 Sales data with trend and seasonality

Such patterns can be modelled by the Holt–Winters method. In essence, this method specifies a time series with three components: (i) level, (ii) trend, and (iii) seasonality. The level can be understood as the average of the data, which does not include trend and seasonality. The three components are formulated as follows:[3]

$$l_t = \alpha(y_t - s_{t-m}) + (1 - \alpha)(l_{t-1} + b_{t-1}), \tag{9.6}$$

$$b_t = \beta(l_t - l_{t-1}) + (1 - \beta)b_{t-1}, \tag{9.7}$$

$$s_t = \gamma(y_t - l_t) + (1 - \gamma) s_{t-m}. \tag{9.8}$$

Equation (9.6) models the level of the data (l_t), while equations (9.7) and (9.8) show the trend (b_t) and seasonality (s_t) components, respectively. In these equations, l_{t-1} is the previous level, y_t is the actual data, b_{t-1} is the previous trend, s_{t-m} is the seasonality component and m is the frequency of the data. Furthermore, α, β, and γ are the smoothing parameters for the level, trend, and seasonality equations, respectively. The smoothing parameters lie within the interval [0,1].

A closer look at equation (9.6) suggests that the level component is updated using the difference between the latest observation and the seasonal effect ($y_t - s_{t-m}$), adjusted by the previous level and previous trend ($l_{t-1} + b_{t-1}$). Equation (9.7) updates the trend component by using the difference between levels at time t and $t - 1$ (i.e. $l_t - l_{t-1}$), adjusted by the previous trend (b_{t-1}). Finally, equation (9.8) updates the seasonality component by using the difference between the actual data and the level (i.e. $y_t - l_t$), adjusted by the seasonal effect at frequency m (i.e. s_{t-m}).

Based on these components, the forecast equation of the Holt–Winters method is written as

$$\hat{y}_{t+h|t} = l_t + hb_t + s_{t-m+h}, \tag{9.9}$$

where $\hat{y}_{t+h|t}$ is the h-step-ahead forecast, h being the forecast horizon. To clarify the concept of forecast horizon, let us take an example. If $h = 1$, forecasts are called one-step-ahead (e.g. $\hat{y}_{2|1}$, $\hat{y}_{3|2}$, $\hat{y}_{4|3}$). If $h = 12$ and the last observation in the data is at period 48, then 1- to 12-step-ahead forecasts are written as $\hat{y}_{49|48}$, $\hat{y}_{50|48}, \ldots, \hat{y}_{60|48}$.

Note that Figure 9.5 and the model formulation in equations (9.6)–(9.9) are based on an example of additive (linear) seasonality. In some demand forecasting applications, seasonality can be multiplicative (i.e. nonlinear). The appendix to this chapter shows an example of a multiplicative seasonality pattern and how such a pattern can be modelled by the Holt–Winters method. In addition, it provides an illustration of how level, trend, and seasonality components are calculated.

Next, we introduce another popular approach to demand forecasting: autoregressive integrated moving average (ARIMA) models (Box and Jenkins, 1970; Box et al., 2015; Pauwels, 2017).

---

[3]In statistical models (e.g. multiple linear regression), trend and seasonality patterns are also modelled by using dummy variables.

ARIMA models

Unlike the Holt–Winters method, ARIMA models aim to uncover the past correlational dynamics in the data. These models are very useful for marketers who wish to forecast future demand because brand performance measures such as sales are often path-dependent, implying that their past values are indicative of future performance (Wang and Yildirim, 2022).

More specifically, ARIMA models consist of three components:

1. *Autoregressive (AR) component.* This component captures the past dynamics of the data. The process is summarized as AR(p), where p denotes the number of autoregressive terms.
2. *Integrated (I) component.* Some time-series data may exhibit non-stationary or evolving behaviour. In such cases, we should transform a non-stationary series into a stationary one.[4]. To put it differently, we should decide the order of integration (d), that is, how many times we need to perform differencing on a variable.
3. *Moving average (MA) component.* This component refers to the past random shock (e.g. Covid-19 pandemic). It is also known as the past dynamics of forecast errors. The process is summarized as MA(q), where q is the highest lag length of the error term of the model.

Putting all these components together, the generic model formulation of an ARIMA (p,d,q) process is expressed as follows:

$$y_t = c + \underbrace{\varphi_1 y_{t-1} + \ldots + \varphi_p y_{t-p}}_{AR(p)} + \underbrace{\theta_1 \varepsilon_{t-1} + \ldots + \theta_q \varepsilon_{t-q}}_{MA(q)} + \varepsilon_t, \tag{9.10}$$

where the time-series data y_t (e.g. sales) are modelled as a function of a constant term, c, its past values through the autoregressive term up to lag p, and past random shocks through the moving average term up to lag q. φ and θ are vectors of parameters for the AR and MA terms. The residuals, ε_t, are assumed to be white noise with zero mean and constant variance σ_ε^2.

For example, the ARIMA(1,0,1) model is written as

$$y_t = c + \varphi y_{t-1} + \theta \varepsilon_{t-1} + \varepsilon_t. \tag{9.11}$$

Here the parameter d is set to zero, meaning that y_t is assumed to be stationary. In addition, for the AR and MA terms, we use one lag (i.e. $p = 1$ and $q = 1$).

Seasonal ARIMA

In the case of seasonal data, the ARIMA (p,d,q) model is extended to ARIMA(p,d,q) (P,D,Q). This model is also called seasonal ARIMA or SARIMA. In SARIMA, the P and Q parameters capture the autoregressive and moving average components for the seasonal part of the model. The D parameter suggests how many seasonal differences are needed.

---

[4]A series can be weakly or strongly stationary. Here, we mean weak stationarity. A weakly stationary process is defined by the first two moments of a series (i.e. the mean and the variance). In a weakly stationary series, we assume that mean and variance are constant. Strong stationarity, however, implies that the whole distribution is the same as we shift in time.

So far we have provided the basis for ARIMA models. Next, we will explore the essential steps for building an ARIMA model. More specifically, we will discuss in detail how to determine the ARIMA parameters in practice.

Testing stationarity

The first step in developing an ARIMA model is to determine whether the series is stationary. We test this using either a visual inspection of the data or a statistical test. Figure 9.6 helps us understand the concept of stationarity.

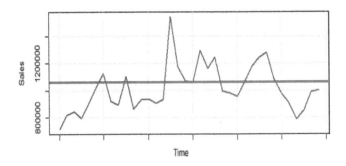

Figure 9.6   Mean reversion (stationarity)

The horizontal line in Figure 9.6 shows the average sales performance. We observe that sales (blue line) move up and down around this average over time. In other words, the deviations from the mean level of sales are temporary. The performance reverts to the average. Thus the sales performance is stationary, implying that marketing efforts do not lead to evolving sales performance, rather they create temporary deviations.

For instance, sales promotions run by a brand may induce a thousand consumers to switch to that brand. If these consumers return to their previous purchase habits once the promotion has ended, the brand's performance will not be altered as a result of this marketing effort (Dekimpe and Hanssens, 1995). Instead, we will observe stationary sales, and the fluctuations due to the promotion will be temporary in nature.

Figure 9.7 illustrates an example of a non-stationary sales performance (the thin solid line). An interpretation of this non-stationary behaviour would be that the marketing actions taken by the brand lead to an increasing sales pattern over time. Marketing efforts in this case have the potential to generate an evolving sales performance. In marketing, there are various ways in which this type of time-series behaviour can be observed. For example, after a new product trial, customers may stick with the brand. It is said that the new product introduction (NPI) has a persistent effect. In other words, the observed sales deviate permanently from pre-NPI levels. Hence, there is no mean reversion and sales performance evolves over time.

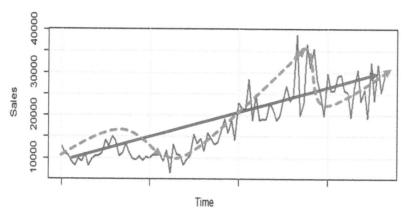

Figure 9.7 Non-stationarity

An important question to ask at this point is the following. Is the upward trend in the data deterministic or stochastic? In other words, is the trend in the data regular (the thick solid line in Figure 9.7) or irregular (the dashed line)?

Let us explain the difference between a deterministic trend and a stochastic trend in detail. A deterministic trend implies that the slope of the trend does not change over time. A series with a deterministic trend can be modelled by using nonparametric methods (e.g. moving averages) or parametric models (e.g. regression). A simple example of a parametric approach is a regression with a linear trend variable:

$$y_t = c + \beta t + \varepsilon_t ,$$ (9.12)

where y_t is a time-series vector, c is a constant, t is the deterministic trend, and β is the slope of the deterministic trend. ε_t can be modelled using a suitable data-generating process. For example, it could be white noise with zero mean and constant variance, or an ARMA process.

In contrast, a stochastic trend suggests that the slope of the trend line varies irregularly over time. A random walk process is the simplest example of a stochastic trend. Recall that a random walk is written as $y_t = \varphi y_{t-1} + \varepsilon_t$. With repeated substitution, we can write the random walk process as $y_t = y_0 + \sum_{t=0}^{t} \varepsilon_t$. Here, the sum of the white noise shocks represents the stochastic trend. Clearly, this model does not allow us to predict how the series will change over time. Instead, it tells us how much the series grew on average in the past.

Why are we concerned about non-stationarity?

The distinction between a deterministic and stochastic trend has important implications for demand forecasting. First, for a non-stationary dataset, sample statistics such as the mean and variance are unstable, and thus uninformative. Second, while data with a deterministic trend always return to the trend in the long run, data with a stochastic trend do not recover from shocks. An example of a 'shock' is the introduction of Coca-Cola Zero in the beverage industry. Following this new product introduction, consumers' tastes slowly evolved and the effects of the shock on consumers' preferences became permanent. Prediction intervals (explained later in this chapter) built from models with a stochastic trend tend to grow over time, allowing more uncertainty for the long-term forecasts. However, prediction intervals based on models with a deterministic trend have constant width, that is, they do not grow over time, so that long-term forecasts are less uncertain.

Over and above its impact on long-term forecasts and prediction intervals, the presence of a unit root (see below) leads to some issues if we want to test a relationship between variables. If non-stationarity is ignored, we are likely to find significant relationships when in fact there are none. These are known as *spurious relationships*. Since this chapter centres on demand forecasting, we do not delve into this issue. We refer the interested reader to Granger and Newbold (1974), Bass and Srinivasan (2002), and Pauwels and Hanssens (2007).

How can we deal with data that show an evolving pattern?

There are two methods that help us deal with non-stationarity.

If the trend is *deterministic*, we estimate the trend first, and then remove it from the data. Using equation (9.12), we can detrend y_t as follows:

$$y_t' = y_t - \hat{\beta}_t, \tag{9.13}$$

where y_t is the original data, t is the deterministic trend, $\hat{\beta}$ is the estimated coefficient, and y_t' is the detrended data. This method allows us to make the data *trend stationary*.

If the trend is *stochastic*, we apply differencing to the series until it becomes stationary. For example, when we take the first difference of a random walk series, it becomes stationary with constant mean and variance. For a random walk we have

$$y_t = \varphi y_{t-1} + \varepsilon_t, \tag{9.14}$$

$$y_{t-1} = \varphi y_{t-2} + \varepsilon_{t-1}. \tag{9.15}$$

Subtracting (9.15) from (9.14) gives us the first-differenced model:

$$y_t - y_{t-1} = \varphi (y_{t-1} - y_{t-2}) + (\varepsilon_t - \varepsilon_{t-1}), \tag{9.16}$$

$$\Delta y_t = \varphi \Delta y_{t-1} + \Delta \varepsilon_t. \tag{9.17}$$

In equation (9.17), Δ is the first-difference operator and Δy_t is the first-differenced data. This method allows us to make non-stationary data *difference stationary*.

How do we know that if there is a stochastic trend in the data? Although visual inspection of a time series helps us understand whether there is an evolving or stable pattern, relying solely on simple time-series plots to detect the presence of a stochastic trend sometimes may be misleading. The unit root testing procedure informs us more formally about the presence or absence of a stochastic trend.

Unit root testing

Unit root tests identify the presence or absence of a stochastic trend in the data-generating process (Dekimpe and Hanssens, 1995; Lütkepohl, 2005). Through unit root tests, a time-series dataset can be tested to see if it is stationary or not. Technically, a time series is said to be integrated of order d, denoted I(d), if it becomes stationary after differencing d times.

There are several unit root tests in the literature, including the augmented Dickey–Fuller (ADF), Kwiatkowski–Phillips–Schmidt–Shin (KPSS), and Phillips–Perron (PP) tests (Zivot and Wang, 2005). Each of these tests has some advantages and disadvantages. We will not go into details of these comparisons in this chapter. Instead, we will focus on the ADF test which is the most widely used method to test stationarity (Enders, 2004). The model used in the ADF test is given by

$$\Delta y_t = \alpha + \beta t + \pi y_{t-1} + \sum_{k=1}^{K} \gamma_k \Delta y_{t-k} + \varepsilon_t , \tag{9.18}$$

where Δy_t is the first-differenced time-series data, α is the intercept, t is the deterministic trend, and β is its coefficient. y_{t-1} is the first-lagged data and π is its coefficient. The term $\sum_{k=1}^{k} \Delta y_{t-k}$ denotes the sum of the first-differenced past data over k lags, and γ_k is the coefficient at lag k. Finally, ε_t represents the residuals of the model, which follow a white noise process.

To decide whether the time-series data is non-stationary or mean-reverting (stationary), the ADF test is conducted on the coefficient π:

$H_0 : \pi = 0,$

$HA : \pi < 0.$

The null hypothesis is that the series is non-stationary, $\pi = 0$. The alternative hypothesis implies that the series is stationary or mean-reverting, $\pi < 0$. Statistical testing is performed by comparing the test statistic for the parameter π with the Dickey–Fuller critical value.

The intuition behind the ADF test is the following. If the series is non-stationary, the lagged level of the series, y_{t-1}, should provide no relevant information in predicting Δy_t, besides Δy_{t-k}.

If we fail to reject the null hypothesis, we conclude that the series has a unit root, that is, the series is non-stationary and we need to difference it until we achieve stationarity. Luckily, most statistical software allow us to implement unit root tests very quickly. In our R application, we provide detailed guidance on how to use R to perform the ADF test.

Identification of AR and MA components

Once we have determined how many times we need to difference the data (the value of d), we need to identify the number of lags to be used for the AR and MA components (i.e. p and q) in order to complete the specification of the ARIMA(p,d,q) model. To do so, we typically rely on autocorrelation function (ACF) and partial autocorrelation function (PACF) plots. The formulae to obtain these plots are explained in Wei (2006) and many other introductory time-series books. Therefore, we will not repeat them here. Instead, we will focus on their visual interpretation for ARIMA model specification.

Suppose that we are given the weekly time-series data for a fast-moving consumer good to produce forecasts for the next 4 weeks. We perform unit root tests and find that the dataset is non-stationary. We take the first difference to make the data stationary (i.e. $d = 1$). Furthermore, using the first-differenced data, we obtain the ACF and PACF plots in Figure 9.8.

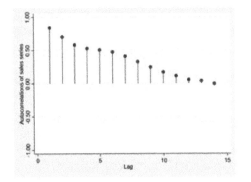 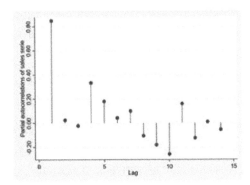

Figure 9.8   (a) ACF and (b) PACF plots (Wang and Yildirim, 2022)

How can these plots inform us about whether our ARIMA model follows an AR, MA, or ARMA process? The decision rule can be summarized as follows:

- If the ACF plot tails off and the PACF plot cuts off at lag p, the process is an AR(p) process.
- If the ACF plot cuts off at lag q and the PACF plot tails off, the process is an MA(q) process.
- If both the ACF and PACF plots tail off, the process is an ARMA process.

In our example plots, the ACF plot tails off and the PACF plot cuts off at lag 1. Therefore, the process is an AR(1) process. Provided that the original sales data only needed first-differencing, we can conclude that the model specification is ARIMA(1,1,0).

So far, we have introduced the intuition behind the ARIMA models and examined their specific components to be able to develop a good forecasting model. Next, we will discuss model estimation and diagnostics.

Model estimation and diagnostic checks

After we identify the model components and arrive at a potential model, we estimate its coefficients. Most software packages, including R, use the maximum likelihood estimation (MLE) technique to estimate ARIMA model coefficients. MLE finds the coefficients of the model that maximize the likelihood of obtaining the observed data. Once coefficients are estimated, we need to do some kind of health check, also known as *model diagnostics*. Essentially, we examine whether the assumptions that we made in the model hold in the data. In ARIMA modelling, we assume that residuals follow a white noise process. This means that residuals of the model are uncorrelated, have zero mean and constant variance. We can check these assumptions through residuals plots or statistical tests, which we describe below.

1. *Autocorrelation.* We look at the ACF plot of the residuals to see if they are free of auto-correlations. For a good model, we should not see a significant autocorrelation at any lag in the ACF plot (see Figure 9.9).

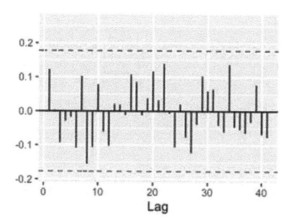

Figure 9.9   ACF plot of residuals

Instead of testing autocorrelation at each lag through the ACF plot, we can apply the Ljung–Box statistical test to check the overall autocorrelation in the residuals (Ljung and Box, 1978; Harvey, 1993). This test is a modified version of the Box–Pierce test.

2. *Zero mean.* The mean of the model's residuals should be zero, $E(\varepsilon_t) = 0$. If this assumption is violated, we may end up having bias in our forecasts.
3. *Constant variance.* The residuals should have a constant variance, also known as homoscedasticity. We inspect this assumption through the 'residuals versus fitted values' plot. The pattern that we should expect is randomly distributed data points (see Figure 9.10)

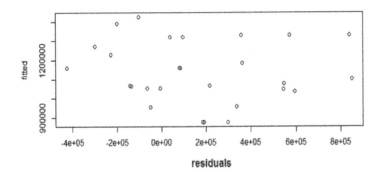

Figure 9.10 Residuals versus fitted values plot

4. *Normality*: We plot the histogram of the residuals to determine whether residuals are normally distributed.[5] For example, Figure 9.11 shows that the distribution of the residuals is (approximately) normal.

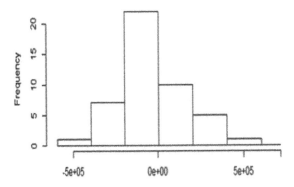

Figure 9.11 Histogram of residuals

It is important to note that in practice getting an exact bell-shaped distribution is difficult. Thus, some data transformation techniques (e.g. Box–Cox) may be needed to obtain better results. Another approach to test normality would be to look at quantile–quantile plots.

Suppose that our model passes all these model diagnostic checks and that we have produced some sales forecasts. How do we know if the model has produced a good sales forecast?

Forecast evaluation

No matter how good our model is, there will always be some errors in our sales forecasts. Hence, our objective should be to pick the model with the lowest forecast error. Next, how do we compute forecast errors?

---

[5]These plots are also helpful to detect outliers in the data. We address this issue in Chapter 11.

The process starts with splitting the data. We split the data into two periods: an estimation period and a validation period.

The *estimation period* is also known as the in-sample period (the blue line in Figure 9.12). We use the data that fall into this period to fit a model and estimate the parameters. This is referred to in the machine learning literature as the training set.

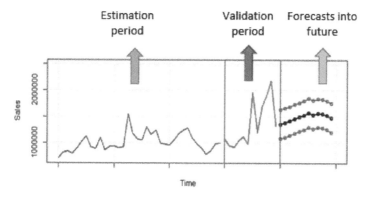

Figure 9.12 Data split

The *validation period*[6] is referred to in the machine learning literature as the holdout sample or test set (the red line in Figure 9.12). We have these data in our records, but we do not use them for model estimation. Rather, we use this sample to check how close our forecasts get to the actual data.

If we believe that our model is able to forecast the observations in the validation period well, we compute forecasts for the future periods, and release them as our final forecasts. The last window in Figure 9.12 shows future sales forecasts (the black dotted line) and the upper and lower bounds (the green dotted lines) based on a 95% prediction interval.

How many observations should be kept in the estimation period and validation period? Demand forecasting literature suggests an 80/20 rule if the time series is long enough. Hence, the first 80% of the observations should be used to estimate the model coefficients, while the following 20% should be used to validate the model.[7]

---

[6]In some machine learning applications, the validation set is further split into two parts: a validation set and a test set. The intuition behind this split is that in using the training set we pair the input and output. In the validation period, we look at different versions of the same model (e.g. using different sets of features) and select the best-performing model. Then in the test set we compare the prediction errors of alternative models.

[7]In machine learning, there are several ways of model validation (e.g. one-leave-out, *k*-fold cross-validation, cross-validation for time series). Since the applications of these validation techniques are beyond the scope of this chapter, we refer the reader to James et al. (2014).

How do we calculate the forecast errors? The forecast error (e_t) is the difference between actual sales (y_t) and forecast sales ($\hat{y}_t$):

$$e_t = y_t - \hat{y}_t .$$

(9.19)

We calculate these forecast errors for both the estimation period and validation period. We expect that the forecast errors from the estimation period will be close to those from the validation period.

Having introduced the relevant concepts around forecast errors, we will next discuss forecast accuracy metrics that help us compare the predictive ability of alternative models.

Forecast accuracy metrics

The first forecast accuracy metric is the mean error (ME), calculated as

$$ME = \frac{1}{n}\sum_{t=1}^{n} e_t ,$$

(9.20)

where e_t is the forecast error at time t (see equation (9.19)) and n is the number of observations in the holdout sample. Equation (9.20) simply shows that we calculate the average of all forecast errors. The ME suggests whether there is systematic under- or overforecasting. It is also called 'forecast bias'. This metric does not give much indication about the size of the error because errors can be positive and negative, and when we sum them they tend to offset one another.

The second forecast accuracy metric is the mean absolute error (MAE) given by

$$MAE = \frac{1}{n}\sum_{t=1}^{n} |e_t| .$$

(9.21)

Here we compute the average of the absolute forecast values, that is, ignoring sign. The MAE does not have the problem of positive and negative forecast errors cancelling each other. Also, it is easy for non-specialists to interpret. However, it depends on the scale of the data. For instance, we cannot compare forecast performances of two time-series datasets, one in British pounds sterling and the other in US dollars.

The third forecast accuracy metric is the mean squared error (MSE), calculated as

$$MSE = \frac{1}{n}\sum_{t=1}^{n} e_t^2 .$$

(9.22)

Equation (9.22) tells us to square each forecast error first, then compute the average. This metric gives greater emphasis to large forecast errors. Similarly to the MAE, the MSE does not have the problem of positive and negative forecast errors cancelling each other. Furthermore, it still depends on the scale of the data. Taking the square root of the MSE yields the root mean squared error (RMSE), which has the same units as the quantity being estimated. The RMSE is also known as the 'standard error of the forecast'.

The final forecast accuracy metric that we introduce is the mean absolute percentage error (MAPE). This is given by

$$MAPE = \frac{1}{n}\sum_{t=1}^{n}\left|\frac{e_t}{y_t}\right| \times 100.$$
(9.23)

This metric shows the size of the error in percentage terms. It is always easier to communicate the forecast accuracy in percentage terms. For instance, it is more meaningful to say that our forecast error is about 5% than that our average forecast error is 125 units. The MAPE is a scale-free metric that allows us to make a comparison across time series measured in different units, for example sales revenues in pounds sterling and US dollars. However, if the sales data contain small or zero values, then this measure is slightly problematic.

There are other various forecast accuracy metrics in the demand forecasting literature, such as Theil's U statistic and the mean absolute scaled error (Hyndman and Koehler, 2006), but they are beyond the scope of this book.

Up until this point, we have learned how to build various demand forecasting models, produce point forecasts (i.e. single forecast values), and evaluate the forecast performance using forecast accuracy metrics. But, how sure are we about the forecasts that we compute? The answer to this question lies in prediction intervals.

Prediction intervals

Suppose that our forecasting model generates a sales forecast of 1200 units for the next week. If the manager plans for the sale of exactly 1200 units and never considers the possibility of selling more or fewer units, this may have some cost implications. If actual sales fall short of the point forecast, the business must bear the holding costs. If actual sales exceed the point forecast, the business loses the opportunity of more sales, that is, the manager faces an opportunity cost. This example shows us that future demand is uncertain and we need to reveal how much uncertainty is associated with each point forecast.

A prediction interval (PI) is defined as a range in which the generated point forecast is expected to lie with a specified probability (Hyndman and Athanasopoulos, 2018). If we assume that forecast errors (residuals) are normally distributed, we can compute the PI as follows:

$$PI = f_{t+1} \pm z_{\alpha/2}\sqrt{MSE},$$
(9.24)

where f_{t+1} is the point forecast for time $t + 1$ and the square root of MSE, $\sqrt{MSE}$, is an estimate of the standard deviation of the forecast errors. $Z_{\alpha/2}$ is the alpha-level z-score or multiplier. For instance, for a 95% prediction interval from a normal distribution we take $\alpha = 0.05$, from which we obtain $Z_{\alpha/2} = Z_{0.025} = 1.96$.

Let us take a simple example here to clarify the concept of PIs. Suppose that our ARIMA model produced a sales forecast of 1200 units for the next week, and that the MSE is computed as 1600. Assuming that forecast errors are normally distributed, the PI is calculated as follows:

$$PI = 1200 \pm 1.96\sqrt{1600}. \qquad (9.25)$$

This gives us a range of [1121.6, 1278.4]. Therefore, we can conclude that with 0.95 probability, next week's sales will fall within this range.

MODEL APPLICATIONS WITH R

This section guides the reader through the R application. Although we present step-by-step instructions alongside software screenshots here, we encourage the reader to go through these notes together with the R Markdown file which is provided on the website of the book.

To address the question of the case study on Silverline, we will use three modelling approaches: ARIMA, SES, and the Holt–Winters method.

We start the process by opening an R Markdown file from RStudio. Once RStudio appears on the screen, select *File>New File>R Markdown* from the menu bar. Recall that the R Markdown file is where we write and run our code.

Click on the ▦ ▾ button and from the drop-down list and select the option 'R' (Figure 9.13).

Figure 9.13 Inserting a new code chunk in R Markdown

You should see an empty code chunk like the one below.

```
```{r}

```
```

Next, we will populate the chunk with our own code. The very first code chunk will be for downloading the R packages.

Downloading the R packages

The following code chunk shows how to download and load the R packages for the Silverline case study.

```{r, eval=TRUE, error=FALSE, warning=FALSE, message=FALSE}
# We download the packages needed for this R application.

if(!require(forecast)) install.packages("forecast",repos =
"http://cran.us.r-project.org")
if(!require(fpp2)) install.packages("fpp2",repos =
"http://cran.us.r-project.org")
if(!require(stargazer)) install.packages("stargazer",repos =
"http://cran.us.r-project.org")
if(!require(tseries)) install.packages("tseries",repos =
"http://cran.us.r-project.org")
if(!require(knitr)) install.packages("knitr",repos =
"http://cran.us.r-project.org")
if(!require(kableExtra)) install.packages("kableExtra",repos =
"http://cran.us.r-project.org")
if(!require(readxl)) install.packages("readxl",repos =
"http://cran.us.r-project.org")
if(!require(ggfortify)) install.packages("ggfortify",repos =
"http://cran.us.r-project.org")
if(!require(modelr)) install.packages("modelr",repos =
"http://cran.us.r-project.org")

library(tidyverse)
library(fpp2)
library(knitr)
library(kableExtra)
library(readxl)
library(forecast)
library(tseries)
library(stargazer)
library(ggplot2)
library(modelr)
library(vars)
library(ggfortify)
```

Next, we set up the working directory and load the dataset.

Setting up the working directory and loading the dataset

The following code chunk sets up the working directory and loads the dataset of the case study.

```
```{r include=TRUE}
# Run the following codes depending on the operating system on your
laptop/PC.

# If you are using iOS, you may want to set your working directory
to the 'demand forecasting' folder and download your dataset into
that folder:

setwd("~/Downloads/demand_forecasting")

# If you are using Windows, you may want to set your working direc-
tory to the 'demand_forecasting' folder of the H drive:

#setwd('H:/downloads/demand_forecasting')

data <- read.csv("silverline_data.csv")
```
```

Depending on the operating system of our computer, the code we need to use to set up the working directory changes. For example, if we use iOS, we may want to set our working directory to the *demand_forecasting* folder. If we use Windows, we may want to place our work in the *downloads* folder of the H drive.

To be able to load the dataset into R, first we need to download the data file (*silverline_data.csv*) from the website of the book to our working directory. Then, using the read.csv function in R, we can complete the data loading process.

Data visualization

We may want to have a quick look at how the dataset and variables look. As an example, by running the code chunk below, we can generate a table that provides a brief preview of the first 10 rows of our dataset. The output (Figure 9.14) shows that during the first month, the store mentioned in the case study managed to sell 116 units of extractor fan from Silverline.

```
```{r echo=FALSE}
data_view <- data [1:10, 1:2]

kable(data_view, table.attr = "style='width:50%;'" ) %>%
kable_classic(full_width = T, position = "center", )


```
```

Time	Sales
1	116
2	184
3	211
4	228
5	283
6	219
7	178
8	141
9	175
10	146

Figure 9.14 Preview of data

To get a feel for the data patterns, it is usually good practice to perform a visual inspection. We obtain the simple time-series plot of the raw data (Figure 9.15) using the ts.plot function, as shown in the following code chunk.

```r
```{r}
ts.plot(data$Sales, col="blue", main="Sales")
```
```

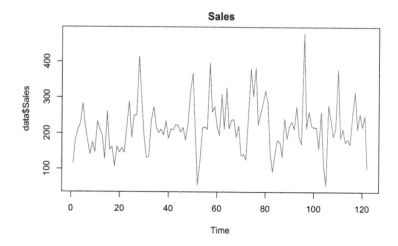

Figure 9.15 Sales performance over time

What is your interpretation of this plot? Is there a seasonal or trend pattern in the data?

Having conducted a short data visualization, we are ready to proceed to model estimation and prediction. We will perform the following steps for each of the models:

- Split the data into training and test set, and estimate a demand forecasting model using the training set.
- Predict sales in the test set and evaluate forecast accuracy via the RMSE.
- Re-estimate the forecasting model using the whole dataset and generate sales predictions for the next 12 months.

Finally, we will compare the models based on the RMSE metric and pick the best model.

ARIMA model

We will build an ARIMA model following the procedure summarized below:

- Perform unit root tests to check for non-stationarity in the data and perform differencing if necessary.
- Obtain the ACF and PACF plots to determine the order of lags and hence the specification of ARIMA.
- Split the data into training and test sets, estimate an ARIMA model using the training set and predict sales using the test set. We will evaluate forecast accuracy via the RMSE metric.
- Generate the sales forecast for the next 12 months.

Log transformation

A visual inspection of the sales plot suggests that there is some variation in the data. To reduce the variation, we will take the logarithm.

```r
```{r}

data$LSales <- log(data$Sales)

#If your variable contains zero values, you should add a small
number (e.g. 1) before you perform the log transformation:

#data$LSales <- log(data$Sales+1)

```
```

Note that our sales data do not contain zero values. However, in some datasets we may observe variables data that do take zero values. In such cases, we need to add a small number (e.g. 1) to each observation in the data before we perform the log transformation. In doing so, we avoid having log(0), which is undefined.

Stationarity test

As introduced in the chapter, there are multiple tests for testing stationarity, including the ADF, KPSS, and PP tests. In this application, we demonstrate the procedure with the ADF test. Recall that under the ADF test, the null and alternative hypotheses are:

H_0 : The data are not stationary,
H_A : The data are stationary.

If the p-value from the ADF test is smaller than a given significance level (e.g. 0.05), we should reject the null hypothesis and conclude that the variable is stationary.

To run the ADF test, we need to first let R know that our sales variable, LSales, is a time series. To this end, we use the ts function. The code below executes the ADF test and produces the output in Figure 9.16.

```r
```{r warning=FALSE}
LSales <- ts(data$LSales, frequency = 12, start = c(1, 1))

adf.test(LSales)

```
```

```
        Augmented Dickey-Fuller Test

data:  LSales
Dickey-Fuller = -5.2479, Lag order = 4, p-value = 0.01
alternative hypothesis: stationary
```

Figure 9.16   ADF test

We reject the null hypothesis because the p-value in the output, 0.01, is smaller than the significance level, 0.05. Therefore, the ADF test result suggests that the series is stationary.

ACF and PACF analysis

A systematic way to determine the order of lags for the autoregressive (AR) and moving average (MA) components of ARIMA model is to plot and inspect the ACF and PACF graphs. To this end, we use the R function ggtsdisplay, which can simultaneously generate the plot of the series over time, the ACF plot, and the PACF plot (see the following code chunk and the corresponding output in Figure 9.17).

```r
```{r}
Sales <- ts(data$LSales, frequency = 12, start = c(1, 1))
ggtsdisplay(Sales) #trend plot and ACF and PACF.

```
```

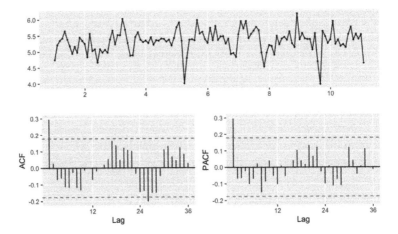

Figure 9.17 ACF and PACF plots

In the ACF and PACF plots, the dashed horizontal lines represent the upper and lower bounds of the critical region (i.e. at the 95% confidence level). The lag order of the AR and MA components is identified by the behaviour of the PACF and ACF plots. We find that both ACF and PACF have a cut-off at lag 1. This suggests that we should probably take a lag order of 1 for both MA and AR components. Given that we did not take the difference of the sales series, the specification of the non-seasonal part of our model is ARIMA (1,0,1).

Furthermore, the sales data show a recurring pattern and the ACF plot displays a sinusoidal wave. This kind of pattern suggests the existence of seasonality in the data. Therefore, the best specification would be seasonal ARIMA(1,0,1)(1,0,1). Note that at this point we assume the same number of lags for the AR and MA components in the seasonal part. However, we will explore this specification in more detail below when we discuss the model estimation.

Data split

To examine the ARIMA model's predictive ability, we need to split the data into training (in-sample) and test (out-of-sample) sets.

To do this, we apply the 80/20 rule, using the first 80% of the observations for the training set and the remaining 20% for the test set. Given that we have 121 observations in total, we should use the first 96 observations for the training set, and the remaining 25 observations for the test set. The following code chunk shows how we implement the data split in R.

```
```{r warning=FALSE}
#Splitting the data into training and testing sets

lag_Sales <- data$LSales[1:121]
Month <- ts(data$Time, frequency=12, start = c(1, 1))
data.prep <- data.frame(window(cbind(Month,LSales)))[2:122,]
data.final <- data.frame(data.prep, lag_Sales)
```
```

```
arima.train <- data.final[1:96,]
arima.test <-data.final[97:121,]

```

Model estimation

Recall that the ACF and PACF analysis suggests the seasonal ARIMA(1,0,1) (1,0,1) model specification. To estimate this model using the training set, we use the R function `Arima`. The code
below produces the model output in Figure 9.18.

```
```{r warning=FALSE}
#Estimating the ARIMA model using our training set:

fit_arima <- Arima(ts(LSales[1:96], frequency = 12),order = c(1,0,1),
seasonal = c(1,0,1))

summary(fit_arima)

```

```
Series: ts(LSales[1:96], frequency = 12)
ARIMA(1,0,1)(1,0,1)[12] with non-zero mean

Coefficients:
         ar1     ma1     sar1    sma1    mean
      0.2565  0.1854  -0.8234  0.9998  5.3310
s.e.  0.1963  0.1884   0.1187  0.5203  0.0524

sigma^2 = 0.09224:  log likelihood = -22.78
AIC=57.55   AICc=58.5   BIC=72.94

Training set error measures:
                     ME       RMSE       MAE       MPE      MAPE      MASE         ACF1
Training set 0.001161668 0.2956916 0.2238784 -0.3130141 4.262558 0.6350175 -0.004481622
```

Figure 9.18   ARIMA model estimation

The output shows:

- the estimated model parameters *p*, *q*, *P*, and *Q* (displayed as `ar1`, `ma1`, `sar1`, and `sma1`,
  respectively) and their standard errors. For example, *p* is estimated to be 0.2565 and its
  standard error is 0.1963
- the residuals variance σ^2 (displayed as `sigma^2`) and the model fit statistics (log likeli-
  hood, AIC, AICc, and BIC)
- the error metrics (ME, RMSE, MAE, etc.).

Although we relied on the ACF and PACF analysis for model identification, we may want to
estimate ARIMA models with different specifications and compare model performances based
on model fit statistics such as the AIC and BIC.
```

There are also other R functions that can automatically pick the specifications with the lowest AIC and BIC (e.g. `auto.arima`). However, we should keep in mind that model identification with an automated procedure may sometimes provide misleading results. For instance, some firms might operate within a certain cycle and would want to evaluate sales using a specific order of lags.

Next, we evaluate the forecast performance of the model using the fitted model parameters.

Forecast performance evaluation of seasonal ARIMA

The following code produces ARIMA model predictions and the time-series plot that displays the actual versus predicted sales in Figure 9.19.

```
```{r, message=FALSE, warning=FALSE}

# Predict sales based on seasonal ARIMA model estimations
predict_arima <- predict(fit_arima, newdata=arima.test, n.ahead = 25)

#Plot the actual and predicted sales on the same graph
data_plot <- data.frame(arima.test$Month,arima.test$LSales,
predict_arima$pred)

ggplot(data_plot, aes(arima.test.Month)) +
  geom_line(aes(y = arima.test.LSales, colour="Actual Sales")) +
  geom_line(aes(y = predict_arima$pred, colour = "Predicted Sales:
SARIMA"),linetype="longdash")

```
```

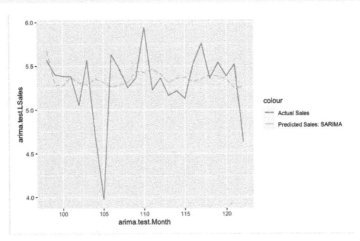

Figure 9.19 ARIMA model forecast evaluation

The plot in Figure 9.19 suggests that the predicted sales based on the seasonal ARIMA model can mimic (to a certain extent) the general pattern of actual sales in the test set. To determine which method does a relatively more accurate job, we will calculate and compare the root mean squared error of both predictions.

Sales forecast using seasonal ARIMA

The following code computes the RMSE metric for the seasonal ARIMA model. The output (not shown) shows that the RMSE of our seasonal ARIMA model is 0.386.

```r
```{r, message=FALSE, warning=FALSE}
# Calculate the RMSE metric based on the estimated ARIMA model above.

rmse.predict_arima <- (sum((arima.test$LSales - predict_arima$pred
)^2)/25)^0.5

rmse.predict_arima

```
```

Finally, we re-estimate the seasonal ARIMA model using the full dataset, and then generate 12-month sales forecasts, as shown in the following code chunk and the corresponding output in Figure 9.20.

```r
```{r, message=FALSE, warning=FALSE}
fit_arima_final <- Arima(ts(LSales, frequency = 12),order = c(1,0,1),
seasonal = c(1,0,1))

#Plot sales forecasts in the next 12 months or observations) using
SARIMA
fit_arima_final %>% forecast(h=12) %>% autoplot()

#Sales forecasts
forecast_arima_final<-fit_arima_final %>% forecast(h=12)

```
```

Description **df [12 × 5]**

	Point Forecast	Lo 80	Hi 80	Lo 95	Hi 95
	<dbl>	<dbl>	<dbl>	<dbl>	<dbl>
Mar 11	5.144578	4.725144	5.564011	4.503109	5.786046
Apr 11	5.236775	4.797373	5.676178	4.564767	5.908784
May 11	5.354785	4.914718	5.794852	4.681761	6.027809
Jun 11	5.364513	4.924424	5.804602	4.691454	6.037571
Jul 11	5.293233	4.853143	5.733323	4.620174	5.966293
Aug 11	5.402235	4.962145	5.842325	4.729175	6.075295
Sep 11	5.316132	4.876042	5.756222	4.643072	5.989192
Oct 11	5.365781	4.925691	5.805871	4.692721	6.038840
Nov 11	5.402957	4.962868	5.843045	4.729900	6.076014
Dec 11	5.284106	4.844068	5.724144	4.611125	5.957086

1-10 of 12 rows

Figure 9.20   ARIMA model forecasts in log-level

The output in Figure 9.20 shows the point forecasts for the next 12 months along with the prediction intervals. Lo 80 and Hi 80 show the lower and upper bounds of the prediction interval at 0.80 probability. Similarly, Lo 95 and Hi 95 show the lower and upper bounds of the prediction interval at 0.95 probability. For example, the first row suggests that with 0.80 probability, the next month's logged sales will fall within the range of [4.725, 5.564]. Similarly, with 0.95 probability, the next month's logged sales will fall within the range of [4.503, 5.786].

Using the code below, we can plot these forecasts and display the prediction intervals.

```{r}
#Plot sales forecasts in the next 12 months or observations) using
SARIMA
fit_arima_final %>% forecast(h=12) %>% autoplot()
```

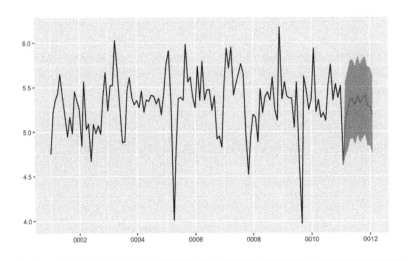

Figure 9.21 Logged sales forecasts and prediction intervals from ARIMA model

The plot in Figure 9.21 shows the sales forecasts in logarithms. Therefore, we need to convert the log-sales forecasts to sales forecasts proper. We do this by taking the antilogarithm of the forecasts, using exp() function in R The following code chunk performs this function and produces the output in Figure 9.22.

```{r}
forecast_sales_arima_final <- exp(forecast_arima_final$mean)

# If we add 1 to the raw data before we take the log, then we should
run the following code instead.
```

```
# forecast_sales_arima_final <- exp(forecast_arima_final$mean)-1

forecast_sales_arima_final
```

```
      Jan     Feb     Mar     Apr     May     Jun     Jul     Aug     Sep     Oct     Nov     Dec
11                171.4990 188.0627 211.6185 213.6871 198.9858 221.9018 203.5949 213.9582 222.0620 197.1778
12 196.1802 179.7391
```

Figure 9.22 Sales forecasts and prediction intervals from ARIMA model

These are our final sales forecasts using the seasonal ARIMA modelling approach. Now we proceed to the second method: Holt–Winters.

Holt-Winters method

Similar to ARIMA model building, in the Holt–Winters method, first we create a training set, as shown in the following code chunk.

```{r}
hw_train <- ts(LSales[1:96], frequency = 12)
```

Model fitting with the Holt-Winters method

Before we predict future values, we will need to fit the Holt–Winters model to the data. If we are dealing with many time-series data simultaneously, we may simply want to call the Holt–Winters function in R and let the software figure out the tuning parameters of the model on its own. We also have the opportunity to tune the fit manually:

- α, the parameter for the *level* equation. A higher alpha puts more weight on the most recent observations.
- β, the parameter for the *trend* equation. A higher beta means the trend slope is more dependent on recent trend slopes.
- γ, the parameter for the *seasonality* equation. A higher gamma puts more weight on the most recent seasonal observations.

For further information about these model parameters, see equations (9.6)–(9.8).

For model fitting, we may have two approaches: HW1 and HW2. *HW1* refers to the model where R automatically finds the optimal values for the alpha, beta, and gamma parameters. *HW2* refers to the model, where we specify α, β, and γ to be 0.2, 0.1, and 0.2, respectively. We plot the fitted values against the raw data to see the quality of the model fit. We may want to try different values for alpha, beta, and gamma to see how the fit changes.

The following R code obtains the model fit using both approaches and generates the plot in Figure 9.23. The black line in the plot is the log-sales data. The blue dashed line shows the model fit based on HW1, while the red dashed line represents the model fit based on HW2. How well does the Holt–Winters method capture the past patterns in the data?

```r
HW1 <- HoltWinters(hw_train)

# Custom Holt-Winters' fitting
HW2 <- HoltWinters(hw_train, alpha=0.2, beta=0.1, gamma=0.1)

#Visually evaluate the fits
plot(hw_train, ylab="Sales",xlim=c(1,9))
lines(HW1$fitted[,1], lty=2, col="blue")
lines(HW2$fitted[,1], lty=2, col="red")
```

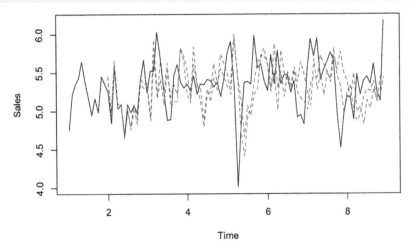

Figure 9.23 Model fitting with Holt-Winters method

Forecast performance evaluation using the Holt-Winters method

First, we generate the predicted sales in the test set based on the HW1 model fit. To this end, we use the following code and obtain the forecast plot in Figure 9.24.

```r
#Forecasting
HW1.pred <- predict(HW1, 26, prediction.interval = TRUE, level=0.95)
```

```
#Visually evaluate the prediction
plot(hw_train, ylab="Monthly Sales", xlim=c(1,11), ylim=c(2,9))
lines(HW1$fitted[,1], lty=2, col="blue")
lines(HW1.pred[,1], col="red")
lines(HW1.pred[,2], lty=2, col="orange")
lines(HW1.pred[,3], lty=2, col="orange")

```

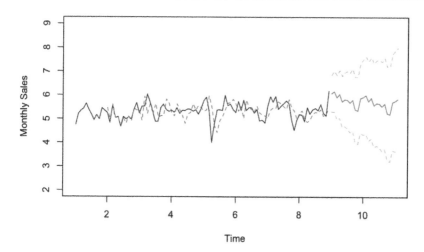

Figure 9.24 Forecast performance evaluation using Holt-Winters method

The black line in Figure 9.24 is the log-sales data. The blue dashed line is the estimated sales based on the HW1 model fit. The red solid line represents the predicted sales over the next quarter, while the orange dashed lines are the upper and lower bounds of the prediction interval with 0.95 probability.

Multiplicative seasonality

When we use the Holt–Winters method to fit the data, we may also want to tune the behaviour of the seasonality component. The standard Holt–Winters method uses additive seasonality, which assumes that the amplitude of any seasonality components is relatively constant throughout the series. However, if we use multiplicative seasonality, we allow the seasonal variations to grow with the overall level of the data. To see how that works, we will fit the model, generate forecasts, and compare the results to our additive fit of HW1. The following code produces the forecast plot in Figure 9.25 based on the choice of multiplicative seasonality in the Holt–Winters method. As the plot suggests, the confidence intervals spread wildly outward. For this dataset, multiplicative seasonality fitting does not appear to be the way to go.

```{r}
HW3 <- HoltWinters(hw_train, seasonal = "multiplicative")
```

```
HW3.pred <- predict(HW3, 26, prediction.interval = TRUE, level=0.95)
plot(hw_train, ylab="candy production", xlim=c(1,11), ylim=c(2,8))
lines(HW3$fitted[,1], lty=2, col="blue")
lines(HW3.pred[,1], col="red")
lines(HW3.pred[,2], lty=2, col="orange")
lines(HW3.pred[,3], lty=2, col="orange")

```
```
```

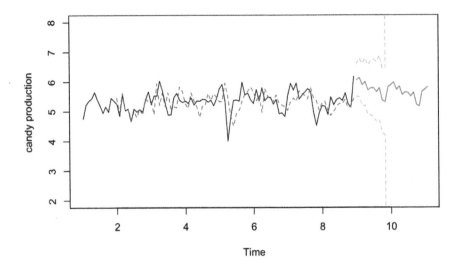

Figure 9.25 Holt-Winters method with multiplicative seasonality

An alternative to the above forecasting and visualization method is to use the `forecast` function and plot forecast values with multiple confidence intervals. See the following code chunk and the associated output in Figure 9.26.

```
```{r}
library(forecast)
HW1_for <- forecast(HW1, h=26, level=c(80,95))
#visualize our predictions:
plot(HW1_for, xlim=c(1,11))
lines(HW1_for$fitted, lty=2, col="purple")

```
```

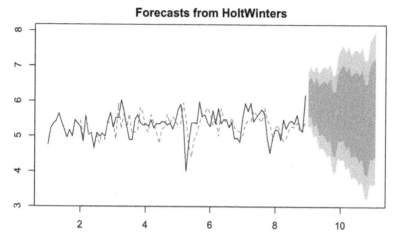

Figure 9.26 Log-sales forecasts and prediction intervals by the Holt-Winters method

Having conducted these explorations, we calculate the RMSE of predicted sales using HW1 approach, as shown in the following code chunk. The model's output (not shown) suggests that the RMSE is 0.623.

```{r}
rmse_HW <- (sum((as.numeric(HW1.pred[,1])-LSales[97:122])^2/26))^0.5

rmse_HW
```

We can also evaluate the quality of our predictions by compiling the observed values minus the predicted values for each data point. These are added to our forecast model as 'residuals'.

Next, we will illustrate how model diagnostics can be performed and interpreted to assess whether the chosen model does a good job of forecasting.

Model diagnostics

To best evaluate the smoothing functions we used in our model, we want to check whether there are autocorrelations in the residuals. Simply put, if neighbouring points in our fits continually miss the observed values in a similar fashion, our main fit line is not reactive enough to the changes in the data. To capture this, we use the `acf` function:

```{r}
acf(HW1_for$residuals, lag.max=20, na.action=na.pass)
```

Ideally, for a non-zero lag, the ACF bars will lie within the blue dashed lines, as shown in Figure 9.27.

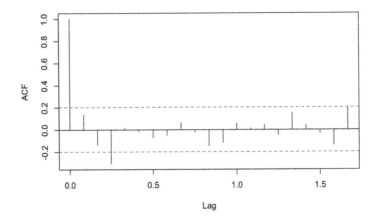

Figure 9.27   ACF plot of residuals

It is important to specify $na.action=na.pass$ because the last value of the residuals is always *NA*, and the function will otherwise give an error.

The ACF plot of the residuals shows that there is no significant autocorrelation at any lag, except for lag 3. We could strengthen the model even further by including the third lag for the AR component. Alternatively, we can check the Ljung–Box test results to assess the overall autocorrelation in the residuals. If we obtain a *p*-value greater than 0.05, we can conclude that residuals are not autocorrelated with 0.95 probability. The following code chunk runs the Ljung–Box test and generates the output in Figure 9.28. Since the *p*-value of the test is greater than 0.05, we can infer that the residuals do not show a significant overall autocorrelation pattern.

```r
```{r}
Box.test(HW1_for$residuals, lag=20, type="Ljung-Box")

```
```

```
        Box-Ljung test

data:  HW1_for$residuals
X-squared = 26.402, df = 20, p-value = 0.1529
```

Figure 9.28   Ljung-Box test

Finally, it is useful to check the histogram of the residuals to ensure that they follow a normal distribution. If the residuals are heavily skewed, our model may be consistently overshooting in one direction. The following code chunk obtains the histogram plot of the residuals.

```{r}
hist(HW1_for$residuals)
```

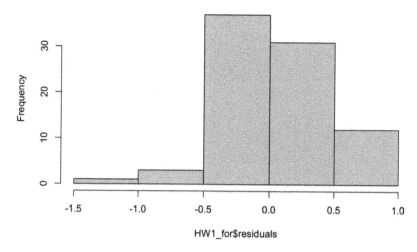

Figure 9.29   Model residuals' histogram

The histogram plot in Figure 9.29 suggests that residuals are slightly skewed or follow a close-to-normal distribution.

Once the model has passed the diagnostics checks, we can generate the forecasts.

Sales forecast using the Holt-Winters method

Using the Holt–Winters method with the HW1 approach, we will generate log-sales forecasts for the next 12 months. The following code chunk produces the output in Figure 9.30.

```{r}
# Estimate the finalized HW model using the entire data set and generate
12 forecasts
HW_final <- HoltWinters(ts(data$LSales, frequency=12))
HW_final_forecast <- predict(HW_final, 12, prediction.interval = TRUE,
level=0.95)

# List the forecasted sales for the next 12 months
HW_final_forecast[,2]
```

	Jan	Feb	Mar	Apr	May	Jun	Jul	Aug	Sep	Oct	Nov	Dec
11			6.209491	6.173280	6.081459	6.011090	6.151444	6.024966	6.103710	6.069358	6.118564	6.226339
12	6.238074	6.197930										

Figure 9.30   Logged sales forecasts with Holt-Winters method

Note that the forecasts in Figure 9.30 are in logarithms. Therefore, we need to convert the log-sales forecasts to sales forecasts proper. We do this by taking the antilogarithm of the forecasts using the `exp()` function in R (see the following code chunk). The output in Figure 9.31 shows our final forecasts based on the Holt–Winters method.

```{r}

# Note that we worked with the logged data. Therefore, we should
take the exponentiation.

HW_final_forecast_sales <- exp(HW_final_forecast[,2])

# If we add 1 to the raw data before we take the log, then we should
run the following code instead.
# HW_final_forecast_sales <- exp(HW_final_forecast[,2])-1

HW_final_forecast_sales

```

	Jan	Feb	Mar	Apr	May	Jun	Jul	Aug	Sep	Oct	Nov	Dec
11			497.4479	479.7572	437.6672	407.9278	469.3949	413.6274	447.5149	432.4029	454.2120	505.8997
12	511.8716	491.7302										

Figure 9.31   Sales forecasts with Holt-Winters method

Simple exponential smoothing

We repeat the above tasks using the simple exponential smoothing method. First, we split our data again into training and test sets as follows.

```{r}
ses.train <- window(data$LSales, end = 96)
ses.test <- window(data$LSales, start = 97)

```

Parameter tuning and estimation

To find the best alpha (smoothing parameter), we can ask R to take different values between 0.1 and 0.9 in steps of 0.01, estimate the SES model, and calculate the corresponding RMSE metric for each alpha. Then we can plot all the RMSE values against values of alpha. Finally, we can choose the alpha parameter that yields the lowest RMSE. The following code performs parameter tuning for the SES model and generates the output in Figure 9.32.

```{r warning=FALSE}
# Identify the optimal alpha parameter

alpha <- seq(.1, .9, by = .01)
RMSE <- NA
for(i in seq_along(alpha)) {
  fit <- ses(ses.train, alpha = alpha[i], h = 26)
  RMSE[i] <- accuracy(fit, ses.test)[2,2]
}

# convert to a data frame and identify min alpha value
alpha.fit <- data_frame(alpha, RMSE)
alpha.min <- filter(alpha.fit, RMSE == min(RMSE))

# plot RMSE vs. alpha
ggplot(alpha.fit, aes(alpha, RMSE)) +
  geom_line() +
  geom_point(data = alpha.min, aes(alpha, RMSE), size = 2, color = "blue")

```

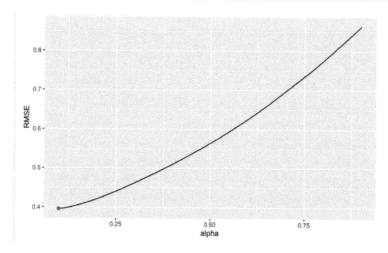

Figure 9.32 Parameter tuning with SES

The plot in Figure 9.32 shows that alpha should be 0.1. Thus, we will fit the SES model using the training set and setting the alpha parameter to 0.1. The following code performs this task and creates the output in Figure 9.33.

```r
```{r}
# refit the optimal model with alpha = .1
ses.opt <- ses(ses.train, alpha = .1, h = 26)

# plotting results
plot_ses <- autoplot(ses.opt) +
  theme(legend.position = "bottom")
plot_ses
```
```

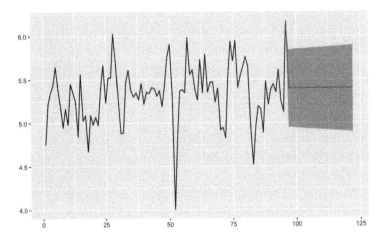

Figure 9.33 Model fitting with SES

Forecast performance evaluation using SES

To evaluate the forecast performance based on the SES method, we make use of the accuracy() function in R. The following code provides the forecast accuracy metrics from the SES model as shown in Figure 9.34.

```r
```{r}

# performance evaluation
accuracy(ses.opt, ses.test)

```
```

```
                  ME      RMSE      MAE        MPE     MAPE     MASE      ACF1 Theil's U
Training set  0.01865957 0.3435948 0.2510447 -0.06584821 4.801455 0.8960431 0.3415052       NA
Test set     -0.09959182 0.3949005 0.2453876 -2.49821389 5.059127 0.8758518 0.0634269 0.7236933
```

Figure 9.34 Forecast accuracy metrics from SES

This output shows that the RMSE in our test set is approximately 0.395. Also, the RMSE for the training set is 0.344. The comparison of RMSE values from the training and test sets suggests that there is no overfitting issue.

Sales forecast using SES

Finally, we will produce the log-sales forecasts for the next 12 months. The following code chunk yields the output in Figure 9.35.

```{r}

# Estimate the SES model using the entire dataset and generate fore-
casts for the next 12 months
ses_forecast <- ses(ts(data$LSales, frequency=12), alpha = .1, h = 12)

# List the forecaster sales for the next year
ses_forecast$mean
```

```
      Jan      Feb      Mar      Apr      May      Jun      Jul      Aug      Sep      Oct      Nov      Dec
11                   5.306542 5.306542 5.306542 5.306542 5.306542 5.306542 5.306542 5.306542 5.306542
12 5.306542 5.306542
```

Figure 9.35 Log-sales forecasts from SES

We need to convert these into sales forecasts proper. We do this by taking the antilogarithm using the exp() function in R.

```{r}
ses_forecast_sales <- exp(ses_forecast$mean)

# If we add 1 to the raw data before we take the log, then we should
run the following code instead.
# ses_forecast_sales <- exp(ses_forecast$mean)-1

ses_forecast_sales
```

Figure 9.36 shows the final sales forecasts from the SES model.

```
        Jan     Feb     Mar     Apr     May     Jun     Jul     Aug     Sep     Oct     Nov     Dec
11              201.6517 201.6517 201.6517 201.6517 201.6517 201.6517 201.6517 201.6517 201.6517 201.6517
12 201.6517 201.6517
```

Figure 9.36 Sales forecasts from SES

So far, we have executed three different models (ARIMA, Holt–Winters, and SES) and obtained three different forecasts. How should we decide which model to choose?

Model comparison

We compare the forecast performance of these models based on the RMSE metric. The following code summarizes the RMSE output and displays it in Figure 9.37. The RMSE metric is computed as 0.387, 0.395, and 0.624 for the seasonal ARIMA, SES, and Holt–Winters method, respectively.

```{r}
table_rmse_summary<-data.frame(
  Method=c("SARIMA", "SES", "Holt-Winters"), RMSE = c(0.387, 0.395,
0.624))

table_rmse_summary
```

Description: **df [3 × 2]**

Method <chr>	RMSE <dbl>
SARIMA	0.387
SES	0.395
Holt–Winters	0.624

3 rows

Figure 9.37 Model comparison

 Which of these models should Silverline choose, and why?

The RMSE values suggest that the seasonal ARIMA model outperforms the other two models. The following code produces the final forecasts from the seasonal ARIMA model and displays the output in Figure 9.38.

```{r}

table_forecast_summary<-data.frame(
   Future_Month=c(1,2,3,4,5,6,7,8,9,10,11,12), Forecast_SARIMA =
forecast_sales_arima_final)

table_forecast_summary

```

Description: **df [12 × 2]**

Future_Month <dbl>	Forecast_SARIMA <dbl>
1	171.4990
2	188.0627
3	211.6185
4	213.6871
5	198.9858
6	221.9018
7	203.5949
8	213.9582
9	222.0620
10	197.1778
11	196.1802
12	179.7391

Figure 9.38 Final forecasts

How should Silverline move forward with these point forecasts? (*Hint*: remember prediction intervals.)

All in all, using the seasonal ARIMA model's forecasts for this store, Silverline can try to predict the demand for the other store struggling with the stockout problems. Further investigation may be warranted, as there are doubtless other sophisticated models which include further significant drivers of store demand (e.g. price, promotion) that would improve these forecasts.

CHAPTER SUMMARY

In this chapter, we introduced a small case study of a kitchen appliance company from an emerging market on demand forecasting. To explore the question outlined in the case study, we reviewed some of the well-established demand forecasting models: simple exponential smoothing, the Holt–Winters method, and ARIMA. These models belong to the domain of predictive analytics. They make use of past data to predict the future. We discussed in detail different types of data features (e.g. seasonality, trend, autocorrelations, stationarity) accommodated by these models. An important assumption of these models is that past patterns and dynamics hold in the future, that is, no major changes occur. Furthermore, we outlined some of the important concepts around demand forecasting such as model validation, forecast accuracy metrics, and prediction intervals.

We then turned our attention to the case study. We demonstrated the application of the aforementioned models in R to the kitchen appliance company. More specifically, we emphasized the importance of model validation and showed that once a forecasting model is developed to fit past data well, it can be used to predict what may happen in the future.

These models are considered less sophisticated than some of the advanced machine learning models (e.g. regression trees, neural networks, support vector machines), but their performance sometimes may be surprisingly better (Makridakis et al., 2018). Therefore, our recommendation is that their predictive performance should always be compared with that of more complex models available to the user.

It is important to note that in using all these predictive models we make an assumption that consumers' past purchases are good indicators of future demand and that changes in purchasing context (e.g. shopping companions, consumer's mood) do not alter consumer preferences. However, research in consumer psychology often shows that in some situations consumers are inconsistent in their preferences (Israeli and Avery, 2017). For example, consumers sometimes may seek variety in their purchases and thus may not show consistent buying behaviour. In the same vein, consumers may make impulse purchases rather than planned purchases. This kind of behaviour may be difficult to predict based on past data. Moreover, social context (e.g. shopping in the presence of friends) may influence consumers' buying habits. Therefore, it is recommended that marketing analysts understand the conceptual underpinnings of consumer purchase behaviour prior to embarking on a demand forecasting task, and investigate the past data of the product accordingly.

REFERENCES

Bass, F. M. and Srinivasan, S. (2002) A study of 'spurious regression' and model discrimination in the generalized bass model. In *Advances in Econometrics* (Vol 16, pp. 295–315). Bingley: Emerald Group Publishing.

Box, G. E. P. and Jenkins, G. M. (1970) *Time Series Analysis: Forecasting and Control*. San Francisco: Holden-Day.

Box, G. E. P., Jenkins, G. M., Reinsel, G. C. and Ljung, G. M. (2015). *Time Series Analysis: Forecasting and Control*, 5th edn. Hoboken, NJ: John Wiley & Sons.

Chintagunta, P. K. and Nair, H. S. (2011) Discrete choice models of consumer demand in marketing. Working paper. https://www.gsb.stanford.edu/faculty-research/working-papers/discrete-choice-models-consumer-demand-marketing

Dekimpe, M. G. and Hanssens, D. M. (1995) The persistence of marketing effects on sales. *Marketing Science*, 14(1), 1–21.

Enders, W. (2004) *Applied Econometric Time Series*. Hoboken, NJ: John Wiley & Sons.

Franses, P. H. and Legerstee, R. (2013) Do statistical forecasting models for SKU-level data benefit from including past expert knowledge? *International Journal of Forecasting*, 29(1), 80–87.

Gardner, E. S. (1985) Exponential smoothing: The state of the art. *Journal of Forecasting*, 4, 1–28.

Granger, C. W. J. and Newbold, P. (1974) Spurious regressions in econometrics. *Journal of Econometrics*, 2, 111–20.

Harvey, A. C. (1993) *Time Series Models*, 2nd edn. New York: Harvester Wheatsheaf.

Hyndman, R. J. and Koehler, A. B. (2006) Another look at measures of forecast accuracy. *International Journal of Forecasting*, 22, 679–88.

Hyndman, R. J. and Athanasopoulos, G. (2018) *Forecasting: Principles and Practice*, 2nd edn. Melbourne: OTexts.

Israeli, A. and Avery, J. (2017) Predicting consumer tastes with big data at *Gap. Harvard Business School Case*, 517-115, May. (Revised March 2018.) https://www.hbs.edu/faculty/Pages/item.aspx?num=52590

James, G., Witten, D., Hastie, T. and Tibshirani, R. (2014) *An Introduction to Statistical Learning: With Applications in R*. New York: Springer.

Ljung, G. M. and Box, G. E. P. (1978) On a measure of lack of fit in time series models. *Biometrika*, 65, 297–303.

Lütkepohl, H. (2005) *New Introduction to Multiple Time Series Analysis*. Berlin: Springer.

Ma, S. and Fildes, R. (2021) Retail sales forecasting with meta-learning. *European Journal of Operational Research*, 288(1), 111–28.

Makridakis, S., Spiliotis, E. and Assimakopoulos, V. (2018) Statistical and machine learning forecasting methods: Concerns and ways forward. *PLoS ONE*, 13(3), e0194889.

Ord, J. K., Fildes, R. and Kourentzes, N. (2017). *Principles of Business Forecasting*, 2nd edn. New York: Wessex Press.

Pauwels, K. H. (2017). Modern (multiple) time series models: The dynamic system. In P. S. H. Leeflang, J. E. Wieringa, T. H. A. Bijmolt, and K. H. Pauwels (eds), *Advanced Methods for Modeling Markets* (pp. 115–48). Cham: Springer.

Pauwels, K. and Hanssens, D. M. (2007) Performance regimes and marketing policy shifts. *Marketing Science*, 26(3), 293–311.

Petropoulos, F., Apiletti, D., Assimakopoulos, V., et al. (2022) Forecasting: theory and practice. *International Journal of Forecasting*, 38(3), 705–871.

Wang, W. and Yildirim, G. (2022) Applied time-series analysis in marketing. In C. Homburg, M. Klarmann and A. E. Vomberg (eds), *Handbook of Market Research (pp.* 469–513). Cham: Springer.

Wei, W. W. S. (2006) *Time Series Analysis Univariate and Multivariate Methods*. 2nd edn (pp. 33–59). New York: Addison Wesley.

Zivot, E. and Wang, J. (2005) *Modeling Financial Time Series with S-PLUS*, 2nd edn. New York: Springer.

APPENDIX

Multiplicative seasonality

Figure 9A.1 suggests that there is an upward trend (indicated by a thick straight line) and a non-constant seasonal variation over time, that is, multiplicative seasonality (marked with circles).

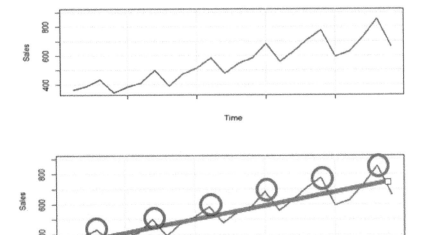

Figure 9A.1 Holt-Winters method (multiplicative seasonality)

The Holt–Winters method with multiplicative seasonality is formulated as follows:

$$l_t = \alpha\left(\frac{y_t}{s_{t-m}}\right)+(1-\alpha)(l_{t-1}+b_{t-1}),\tag{9A.1}$$

$$b_t = \beta(l_t - l_{t-1})+(1-\beta)b_{t-1},\tag{9A.2}$$

$$s_t = \gamma\left(\frac{y_t}{l_t}\right)+(1-\gamma)s_{t-m},\tag{9A.3}$$

$$\hat{y}_{t+h|t} = (l_t + hb_t)s_{t-m+h}.\tag{9A.4}$$

Equation (9A.1) shows how the level of the data is updated, while equations (9A.2) and (9A.3) update the trend (b_t) and seasonality (s_t) components, respectively. In these equations, l_{t-1} is the previous level, y_t is the actual data, b_{t-1} is the previous trend, s_{t-m} is seasonality component, and m is the frequency of the data. Furthermore, α, β, and γ are the smoothing parameters for the level, trend, and seasonality equations, respectively. The smoothing parameters lie within the interval [0,1].

Below we illustrate the calculations of Holt–Winters method with multiplicative seasonality using a simple example.

Suppose that we are given quarterly sales data with 24 observations, shown in column B of Figure 9A.2. We are asked to compute the one-step-ahead forecasts for periods 25–30 using the Holt–Winters method with multiplicative seasonality.

	A	B	C	D	E	F	G
1	Period	Data	Level	Trend	Seasonal	Forecast	
2	1	362	-	-	0.953	-	
3	2	385	-	-	1.013	-	
4	3	432	-	-	1.137	-	
5	4	341	380	9.75	0.897	-	
6	5	382	398.993	10.258	0.953	371.288	
7	6	409	404.679	10.007	1.013	414.636	
8	7	498	433.896	11.063	1.137	471.432	
9	8	387	433.699	10.444	0.897	399.292	
10	9	473	487.196	12.812	0.953	423.105	
11	10	513	505.211	13.098	1.013	506.588	
12	11	582	513.077	12.810	1.137	589.236	
13	12	474	527.798	12.915	0.897	471.915	
14	13	544	565.650	14.287	0.953	515.100	
15	14	582	575.420	14.039	1.013	587.568	
16	15	681	597.324	14.471	1.137	670.121	
17	16	557	619.118	14.874	0.897	549.006	
18	17	628	654.735	16.015	0.953	603.961	
19	18	707	693.000	17.239	1.013	679.575	
20	19	773	685.344	15.869	1.137	807.429	
21	20	592	667.095	13.993	0.897	629.247	
22	21	627	662.255	12.957	0.953	648.826	
23	22	725	708.398	14.782	1.013	684.096	
24	23	854	746.216	16.049	1.137	822.142	
25	24	661	741.167	14.889	0.897	684.032	
26	25	?			0.953	720.243	h=1
27	26	?			1.013	781.089	h=2
28	27	?			1.137	893.368	h=3
29	28	?			0.897	718.543	h=4
30	29	?				776.977	h=5
31	30	?				841.427	h=6

Figure 9A.2   Illustration of Holt-Winters method

To be able to compute the forecasts, first we should find the initial values for the level, trend, and seasonality components of the data. The equations to compute the initial values are given by

$$l_m = \frac{1}{m}(y_1 + y_2 + \ldots + y_m),$$

$$b_m = \frac{1}{m}\left[\frac{y_{m+1} - y_1}{m} + \frac{y_{m+2} - y_2}{m} + \ldots + \frac{y_{m+m} - y_m}{m}\right],$$

$$s_1 = \frac{y_1}{l_m}, \; s_2 = \frac{y_2}{l_m}, \ldots, s_m = \frac{y_s}{l_m},$$

for the level, trend, and seasonality, respectively. The initial value for the level will be

$$l_4 = \frac{362 + 385 + 432 + 341}{4} = 380 \quad \text{(see column C, row 5 in Figure 9A.2).}$$

The initial value for the trend will be

$$b_4 = \frac{1}{4}\left[\frac{382 - 362}{4} + \frac{409 - 385}{4} + \frac{498 - 432}{4} + \frac{387 - 341}{4}\right] = 9.75$$

(see column D, row 5 in Figure 9A.2).
The initial values for the seasonality component will be

$$s_1 = \frac{y_1}{l_m} = \frac{362}{380} = 0.953, \; s_2 = \frac{y_2}{l_m} = \frac{385}{380} = 1.013, \; s_3 = \frac{y_2}{l_m} = \frac{432}{380} = 1.137, \; s_4 = \frac{y_4}{l_m} = \frac{341}{380} = 0.897$$

(see column E, rows 2 through 5).
So, the one-step-ahead ($h = 1$) forecast for period 5 becomes

$$\hat{y}_5 = (l_4 + b_4) \times s_1 = (380 + 9.75) \times 0.953 = 371.288$$

(see column F, row 6).
Next, using equations (9A.1)–(9A.3), we update the level, trend, and seasonal components. To do so, we need to set the values for m, α, β, and γ. Since the given data are quarterly, $m = 4$. Furthermore, we assume that α, β, and γ are 0.822, 0.055, and 0.000, respectively.[8] For instance, for period 5 we obtain the values of 398.993, 10.258, and 0.953 for the level, trend, and seasonal components, respectively. Finally, at period 24, we compute forecasts $\hat{y}_{25|24}$, $\hat{y}_{26|24}$, $\hat{y}_{27|24}$, $\hat{y}_{28|24}$, $\hat{y}_{29|24}$, and $\hat{y}_{30|24}$ (see column F, rows 26–31).
Note that the ETS package in R, developed by Hyndman and Athanasopoulos (2018), allows users to do all these automatically. However, we believe that knowing the calculations behind such packages is also important.

---

[8]These optimal parameters can be found by either trying different values and comparing the model fits or using an optimization algorithm.

10

IMAGE ANALYTICS

Chapter contents

LEARNING OBJECTIVES

At the end of this chapter, you should be able to:

- understand the theoretical underpinnings of neural networks
- describe the key concepts of neural networks such as weights, bias, and activation function
- understand the intuition behind the feedforward and backpropagation algorithms that are used to train neural networks
- gain a working knowledge of convolutional neural networks
- apply convolutional neural network modelling to image data in R.

Social media users very often reference brands in their posts using images. By detecting the important elements of user-generated images (e.g. colour and design of a brand logo or product), marketing managers can monitor *visual conversations* on social media and other digital platforms, and boost their marketing impact further. This chapter focuses on *image analytics* through an advanced machine learning model: *convolutional neural networks*. We begin the chapter with a gentle introduction to neural networks and describe the core concepts behind this class of models such as weights, bias, and activation function. Then we provide intuitive explanations of the feedforward and backpropagation algorithms used to train neural networks. Next, drawing on the conceptual and mathematical background of neural networks, we discuss convolutional neural networks, which are a very effective deep learning tool for processing and classifying images. Finally, in our R application, we apply convolutional neural networks to a sample of consumer-uploaded images of Coca-Cola on Flickr to illustrate how these models can be applied to real-world datasets.

We found it! 🥤 🍓 strawberry Diet Coke 😍 I'm having this in the car with a Tesco Katsu chicken and Hosin Duck sushi pack (3.5 syns) ~ so so good 😋 I was trying to wait until we go out for lunch but it's not until half past 2! & I couldn't cope 🙄.

Figure 10.1 User-generated image on Instagram

INTRODUCTION

Over the past few years, technological advancements in mobile devices have allowed consumers to take, store, and share images very easily. This, in turn, has led to an increased number of user-generated images on digital platforms. Recent evidence suggests that Instagram users upload 1074 pictures every second (Omnicore Agency, 2022), while Snapchat users share 527,760 photos every minute (Marr, 2018). The use of images is also prevalent in firm-initiated digital marketing campaigns (Overgoor et al., 2021). For example, Figure 10.1 shows an Instagram post that contains a user-generated image of a strawberry Diet Coke product wih some text information.

Thanks to the volume of such image data and the availability of user-friendly analytics tools, marketers can gain some important insights into consumer behaviour and competitors' marketing activities (Ma and Sun, 2020). Later in this chapter, we will discuss in depth how marketers can leverage image data to guide their marketing strategies, from advertising and product design to branding and visual product presentation.

What is image analytics?

Image analytics involves the extraction of information from visual data through deep learning techniques (Ngai and Yu, 2022; Nielsen, 2015; Solomon and Breckon, 2011). The goal of image analytics is to process the features of an image and then classify it into a pre-defined category. For example, a dress image can be broken down into its essential features to determine whether it looks casual or formal. Similarly, a bike image can be analysed to find out whether it has a modern or vintage look.

Why use images?

Eighty per cent of the images with a brand's logo do not include any text mentioning the brand (Brandwatch, 2017). Therefore, relying solely on text searches, brands will not be able to fully hear the voice of their customers. Also, research in consumer behaviour shows that images are identified and understood much faster than textual information. According to Potter et al. (2013), it takes only 13 milliseconds to process an image. Thus, images are seen as effective tools to attract customers' attention and cut through the communication noise (Pieters and Wedel, 2004).

Images are considerably easier for people to process and recall than text-based information (MacInnis and Price, 1987). A study conducted by MDG Advertising (2018) shows that a brand with a picture in the search engine results is 60 times more likely to be remembered and contacted by customers than one without. Images, therefore, make it easy for consumers to retrieve a brand input from memory.

Images have the power to evoke consumers' emotions. Brands use images to touch consumers' hearts, disrupt the narrative, and build imagery brand meaning.

Also, it has been demonstrated that the use of images in social media marketing campaigns greatly increases user engagement (Li and Xie, 2020). In search engine marketing, content with images receives more clicks than that without. This is in part because (i) consumers do not always have the mental availability to read textual content, and (ii) images reduce search cost significantly.

From a customer perspective, image sharing is a crucial activity in staying connected in a social network. Users fulfil their social needs by sharing images with their peers. Moreover, in online shopping, it has become more common for users to leave feedback with pictorial content.

With such image-supported feedback, consumers typically feel the responsibility of informing other users and the seller about their product usage experience and product returns (Dzyabura et al., 2020).

Consumers also use images to initiate their online search process. For example, ASOS, a UK-based online fashion and cosmetic retailer, offers its customers a visual search tool called 'Style Match'. Shoppers take a picture of an item and do a search within ASOS's product catalogue for similar items.

Visual search supported by image analytics helps consumers explore product assortments and get inspired further.

Having emphasized the importance of image data from both a firm and a customer perspective, next we review some of the common and emerging trends in marketing that benefit from image analytics.

MARKETING APPLICATIONS OF IMAGE ANALYTICS

Marketers can use image data to guide their strategic decisions such as branding, advertising, product design, online and in-store product presentation, and customer segmentation (Dzyabura et al., 2022; Vilnai-Yavetz and Tifferet, 2015; Xiao and Ding, 2014). In this section we explain some of the common marketing applications of image analytics in these areas.

Branding

For brand managers, the logo is one of the most important strategic brand elements. It is a great tool that conveys brand identity and meaning to end-users, and helps firms increase the visibility of their brands. In today's digitalized world, consumers increasingly use brand logos in their social media posts. Identifying brand logos on digital platforms through image analytics, firms can figure out how much *visual mention* their brands get *vis-à-vis* their competitors. This approach allows firms to follow visual conversations continuously and establish the practice of *visual brand listening*.

In recent years, a significant number of digital logo makers have been established around the world (e.g. Tailor Brands). These online businesses use image and text analytics tools to produce affordable brand logos for small businesses. Advertising agencies also use image analytics techniques to design brand logos that are distinct, yet close to other award-winning logos in the marketplace.

Research by Liu et al. (2020) demonstrates the ability of image classification tools to determine a brand's perceptual attribute (e.g. does a product in an image look fun, energetic, or family-friendly?). Other research by Dzyabura and Peres (2021) shows that image analytics can also be performed to obtain visual representation of

brand associations and link it to brand personality and brand equity. These applications go beyond brand logo generation and allow firms to have a deep understanding of customers' perceptions and attitudes towards their brands.

Advertising

Analysing images from social media paid ads, marketing managers can understand which combination of visual elements (e.g. objects, colours, background) of an image drive higher user engagement. Although engagement is a key customer response metric, other emotional or cognitive metrics (e.g. warmth, fear, attention, ad recall and long-term memory effects) can also be used to evaluate the impact of different visual elements of an image. Moreover, image analytics can support firms' online recommender systems. Different visuals can be delivered to customers who are at different stages in their purchase journey (e.g. affect versus behaviour stages of the purchase funnel, or new versus repeat purchases). Also, advertising agencies can use image analytics to quantify the economic value of each visual feature and improve their pricing decisions.

Product design

Consumer perceptions are significantly influenced by product design (e.g. package materials, colours, fonts, graphics). The external look of a product is very helpful for consumers to understand at first sight what the product stands for (i.e. identity) and who typically consumes it (i.e. usage or user imagery). Image analytics can compare a large number of possible product designs with a firm's past designs, and recommend them as 'average' or 'innovative' to the design team. Also, using product package design images, competitors' best-selling products can be compared with a firm's new products to see how unique or standard the firm's new offerings would be.

Product presentation and identification

In online retail, product display plays a central role in consumer search behaviour. The combination of visual elements of an image as well as the location where the image is shown (e.g. next to similar or dissimilar items) have a huge impact on users' expectations, search activity, click behaviour, and purchase intentions. Image analytics can inform web designers and retail managers about the most appropriate presentation of their products that enhances user experience.

In bricks-and-mortar retail, monitoring store shelves and ensuring product availability is a crucial task to keep customers satisfied and prevent possible profit loss. Image analytics can help retailers detect and identify missing products on store shelves and replenish them very quickly (Tonioni and Di Stefano, 2017). Figure 10.2 illustrates an example of image recognition that detects empty shelves for fast-moving consumer products. This image recognition application in retail can also be extended to misplaced products.

Figure 10.2 Detecting empty store shelves through image analytics (www.kdnuggets.com)

Another important application of image analytics is self-checkout systems in cashier-free grocery stores. For example, Amazon Fresh stores use an array of cameras and some sensors to record customer purchases, then process image data to identify unique product codes, and then charge customers after they exit the store.

Image analytics has a myriad of applications in marketing, limited only by our imagination. What is the modelling background that lies behind these applications? Next, we introduce the neural networks modelling approach, a deep learning technique that is used for a wide range of marketing problems, including image recognition.

NEURAL NETWORKS

Suppose that we see the blurred image on the following page in Figure 10.3. Our brain processes the image cells, lists all the available digits from 0 to 9, and finally says 'the digit looks like a 3'. This is how humans do image processing. How can a computer guess what the digit is?

Figure 10.3   An example of image data

Neural networks (NNs) are a form of artificial intelligence that can help us with this kind of image recognition problems (Ghatak, 2019). If the pattern exists and enough information is provided, NNs can find the pattern on their own by *learning* it from the data. As in any other machine learning model, the ultimate goal of NNs is to make predictions.

NNs were first studied by McCulloch and Pitts (1943) and extended by Hebb (1949) in an influential book on brain theory. As the name suggests, NNs are neurons that are linked together. A neuron in biology is defined as a nerve cell that carries information between the brain and other parts of the body. In the context of image recognition problems, a neuron is defined a little differently. A neuron can be thought of as a circle that contains a number inside (see Figure 10.4).

Suppose that the image in Figure 10.3 is a 25 × 25 matrix. Inside this matrix, there are 625 neurons. Each cell in the matrix, therefore, is a neuron. The number inside the neuron is called its *activation* (see Figure 10.4). The activation number lies in the range [0,1]. Each neuron has a greyscale. The black neurons have a very small number (e.g. 0.01), the grey ones have intermediate numbers (e.g. 0.56), and white ones are close to or equal to 1. A neuron is lit up when its activation number is large. For example, in Figure 10.4, the third neuron is lit up as its activation number is 1.

Figure 10.4   Neurons and activation numbers

Figure 10.5 shows how neural networks are formed. Following our example, 625 neurons make up the first layer of the network, also called the *input layer*. The last layer, also known as the *output layer*, has 10 neurons, each representing one of the possible digits. The activation in these neurons is a number between 0 and 1. Each activation number represents how much the system thinks that a given image corresponds to a given digit.

Figure 10.5   Layers in neural networks

There are also other layers between the input and output layers. They are called *hidden layers*. Hidden layers basically carry the information from the input layer to the output layer.

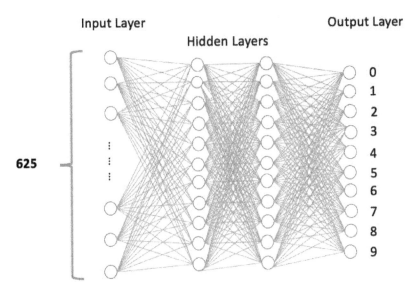

Figure 10.6 A neural network

Figure 10.6 shows how all the layers form the structure of the network. The input layer passes the information to the first hidden layer, then to the second hidden layer, and then finally to the output layer.

Hidden layers help us understand which combination of subcomponents from the image of '3' corresponds to which digits. For example, the first hidden layer captures the little edges, and the second hidden layer captures the bigger patterns. Finally, the output is formed (see Figure 10.7).

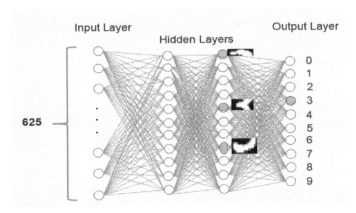

Figure 10.7 Pattern capturing in neural networks

Our hope is that each neuron in the hidden layers of the network corresponds to various relevant patterns of the image. How does one layer influence another layer? What is the mechanism that forms the interrelationship between the layers? We will explore this next.

Weight, bias, and activation function

To understand how the layers of NNs influence one another, we will dig into the mathematical background of NNs. The relationship between layers is determined by the weights, biases, and activation functions.

Each input in the NN is multiplied by its weight. Following our introductory example, Figure 10.8 shows that neurons from the input layer, $x_1,...,x_{625}$, are multiplied by their corresponding weights, $w_1,...,w_{625}$. Thus, *weight* tells us which pattern the first neuron of the first hidden layer (h_1) captures from the input layer.

Bias informs us about how high the weighted sum needs to be before the neuron becomes active. As an example, we may want the neuron to be active only when the weighted sum is higher than 10. This implies that we need to add a bias to the weighted sum to make the neuron (in)active.

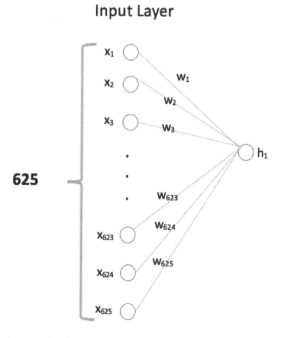

Figure 10.8   Weights in neural networks

Equation (10.1) shows how the output h_1 is calculated using the weighted sum and the bias:

$$h_1 = \underbrace{w_1 x_1 + w_2 x_2 + \ldots + w_n x_n}_{\text{weighted sum}} + \underbrace{b_1}_{\text{bias}}. \tag{10.1}$$

Here n is the number of neurons in the input layer, and b_1 is the bias for the first neuron of the first hidden layer. The output h_1 shows the activation number; it can take any value. In the classification context, we require the activation number to be between 0 and 1. To achieve this, we use an *activation function*. Different activation functions are used depending on the problem at hand. At this point, we discuss the application of the sigmoid function, one of the widely used activation functions for classification problems in machine learning. Later in this chapter, we will use the rectified linear unit (RLU) function in an image processing problem.

The sigmoid function, also called the logistic curve, sends very negative numbers close to 0, and very positive numbers close to 1. The following equation shows how the sigmoid function is applied to h_1:

$$h_1 = \sigma(w_1 x_1 + w_2 x_2 + \ldots + w_n x_n + b_1), \tag{10.2}$$

where σ denotes the sigmoid function. Recall that $\sigma(z) = 1/(1+e^{-z})$, where z is the input.

To summarize, to compute the output of the network, we take the weighted sum, then add the bias, and then pass the result through the activation function. We can express this mechanism in a neat matrix–vector form:

$$\begin{bmatrix} h_1 \\ \vdots \\ h_k \end{bmatrix}_{\text{output vector}} = \underbrace{\sigma}_{\substack{\text{sigmoid} \\ \text{function}}} \left(\underbrace{\begin{bmatrix} w_{11} & \cdots & w_{1n} \\ \vdots & \ddots & \vdots \\ w_{k1} & \cdots & w_{kn} \end{bmatrix}}_{\text{weight matrix}} \underbrace{\begin{bmatrix} x_1 \\ \vdots \\ x_n \end{bmatrix}}_{\text{input vector}} + \underbrace{\begin{bmatrix} b_1 \\ \vdots \\ b_k \end{bmatrix}}_{\text{bias vector}} \right), \tag{10.3}$$

where n is the number of neurons in the input layer and k is the number of neurons in the first hidden layer. This mechanism can be easily extended to the other layers of the network. Equation (10.3) can be written in a more compact form as

$$\mathbf{h} = \sigma(\mathbf{Wx} + \mathbf{b}). \tag{10.4}$$

How many parameters?

The NN model is parameter-heavy. Consider the 25×25 input matrix from our introductory example. Suppose that we have 11 neurons in each hidden layer, and 10 neurons in the output layer. Then, we will have 625×11 weights from the input layer to the first hidden layer; 11×11 weights from the first hidden layer to the second hidden layer; and 11×10 weights from the second hidden layer to the output layer. In addition, we have 11 biases for the first hidden layer, 11 biases for the second hidden layer, and 10 biases for the output layer. In total, there are 7138 parameters to estimate. NNs, therefore, are quite sensitive to overfitting. When building an NN model, our task should be to find a model which is simple enough, yet reliable in terms of predictive performance.

Model training

As in any machine learning model, an NN should be trained and tested before the final predictions are released. There are two algorithms that are used to train NNs: feedforward and backpropagation.

As its name suggests, in applying the feedforward algorithm, we feed the model forward. In other words, we get the input in, pass it through the hidden layers, apply the activation function, and finally obtain the prediction ($\hat{y}$), as shown in the upper part of Figure 10.9.

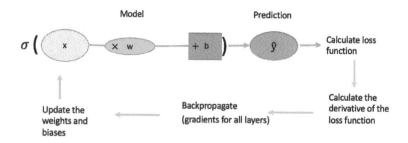

Figure 10.9   Feedforward and backpropagation algorithms

Next, we apply the backpropagation algorithm. Backpropagation, in layman's terms, sends feedback to the neural net. Through backpropagation, we aim to get better and better at predicting the target or observed value (y).

The lower part of Figure 10.9 shows the sequence of steps in the backpropagation algorithm. Once we get the prediction, we compute the error, $y - \hat{y}$. The error shows how far our model prediction is from the target or observed value. Then we compute the loss function. Typically, the loss function is the sum of squared errors, $\sum_{i=1}^{n}(y_i-\hat{y}_i)^2$. Next, we take the partial derivatives of the loss function with respect to weight and bias parameters, and propagate the error back through each layer to find a finer-tuned error. We do the backpropagation by applying the chain rule of partial derivatives. The details are beyond the scope of this book. But understanding the intuition behind the concept is essential. Therefore, for a more technical overview of backpropagation, we refer the interested reader to James et al. (2021). Finally, we update the weight and bias parameters, using the well-established gradient descent optimization algorithm (Chong and Żak, 2013). We run the model again and obtain the updated prediction. We iterate this process until the improvement in model prediction becomes marginal or we reach a certain number of iterations.

To summarize, the model training steps for a neural network are the following:

1. We apply the feedforward algorithm, using the training data and random values for weight and bias parameters to compute the output.
2. We calculate the error and the loss function, and get the derivative of the loss function with respect to the parameters of the last layer in the neural network.
3. We propagate the error back through the chain rule, and get the derivatives for all the layers.
4. We update the weights and bias parameters. We perform gradient descent to update each parameter.
5. We iterate this process until we achieve convergence, that is, until we are satisfied with the error level or reach a pre-set maximum number of iterations.

Model validation

Sometimes, model predictions are very good with training data, but very poor with unseen (test) data. As mentioned in various chapters of this book, this phenomenon is known as *overfitting*. NNs are sensitive to the overfitting issue because the number of parameters grows rapidly as one increases the number of neurons and hidden layers in the model. To make sure that the model is robust or can predict future or unseen data well, we should validate it using cross-validation techniques such as *leave-one-out cross-validation* and *k-fold* cross-validation. We refer the reader to James et al. (2021) for an in-depth explanation of these concepts.

So far, we have laid the foundations for NNs. Next, we will introduce the convolutional neural networks (CNNs). CNNs are a suitable modelling tool for processing and classifying images.

CONVOLUTIONAL NEURAL NETWORKS

Having laid the foundations for neural networks, we introduce *convolutional neural networks* (CNNs). CNNs are a special type of neural network and a suitable modelling tool for processing and classifying images (Goodfellow et al., 2016).

An image is made up of pixels – the smallest unit of an image. The word 'convolutional' refers to the process of filtering pixels. Put simply, an image, a highly complex piece of data, is simplified and classified by a CNN.

Let us explain the basics of CNN through an example. Suppose that we wish to identify a brand using its logo as shown in Figure 10.10. Clearly, the brand logo belongs to Puma, a German manufacturer of footwear, apparel, and accessories.

In this example, there is only one image. If we wanted to track visual conversations about

Figure 10.10 Puma brand logo

Puma in social media, how might we process and classify the brand's logo from thousands of pictures? Obviously, doing it manually would not be possible. CNN modelling powered by artificial intelligence replaces the manual process of image detection. Here, we explore how a CNN model works.

A CNN consists of multiple layers: a convolutional layer, a pooling layer, and a fully connected layer (see Figure 10.11).

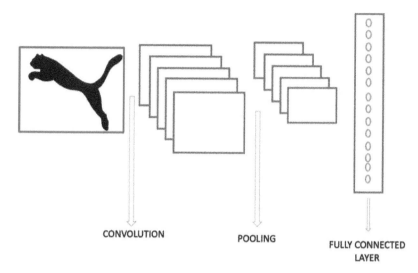

CONVOLUTION   POOLING   FULLY CONNECTED
                                        LAYER

Figure 10.11   CNN model structure

The *convolutional layer* does the filtering for separate square patches of pixels in an image. Filters are also known as kernels in CNN. Figure 10.12 visualizes the convolutional layer. The upper left part of the picture is a specific feature that is filtered. Once this filtering is done for all the pixels, we get the convolved feature map.

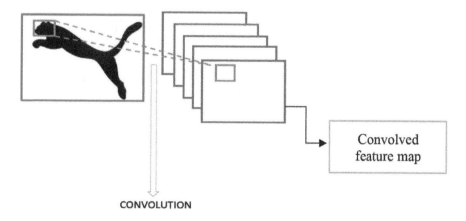

Convolved
feature map

CONVOLUTION

Figure 10.12   Convolutional layer

The *pooling* layer reduces the sample size of the convolved feature map. Figure 10.13 illustrates this process. This layer allows us to get the predominant features of an image in lower dimensions. The pooling layer is very important because it helps the model reduce the computation time by taking the most relevant features of an image. There are two ways pooling is done: maximum and average pooling. Maximum pooling takes the maximum input of a particular convolved feature. while average pooling just takes the average. The output of the pooling process is a *pooled feature map*. Thus, maximum and average pooling lead to feature extraction.

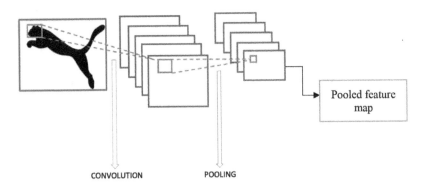

Figure 10.13 Pooling layer

Finally, the pooling layer is converted to a one-dimensional *fully connected layer* comprised of multiple neurons (see Figure 10.14). Using this layer, we perform the classification task. The relevant neurons are activated, and we pick the neuron with the largest activation number. Turning to our example, the CNN predicts that the brand logo is from Puma.

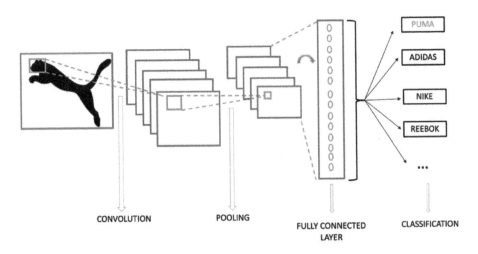

Figure 10.14 Fully connected layer and classification

Note that in real-world applications, the number of layers can be extended. Later in this chapter, the software application shows an example of image analytics with more layers.

Mathematical background of CNNs

Now to get into the nitty-gritty of how layers are interconnected in CNNs. How do we construct the convolved feature map from an image? We can think of images as numerical matrices based on colour intensity, as shown in Figure 10.15.

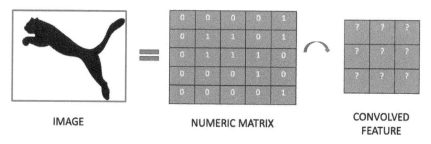

IMAGE　　　　　**NUMERIC MATRIX**　　　　　**CONVOLVED FEATURE**

Figure 10.15　Convolved feature map

Using this matrix, we get the convolved feature map. But how exactly do we operationalize this extraction? Suppose that convolved feature map is a 3 × 3 matrix. From the top left of the numerical matrix, we take the 3 × 3 sub-matrix and compute the sum of the element-by-element product of this sub-matrix. Figure 10.16 shows an example of how the convolved feature map is computed.

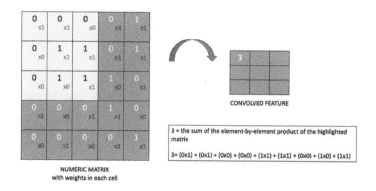

NUMERIC MATRIX
with weights in each cell

CONVOLVED FEATURE

3 = the sum of the element-by-element product of the highlighted matrix

3= (0x1) + (0x1) + (0x0) + (0x0) + (1x1) + (1x1) + (0x0) + (1x0) + (1x1)

Figure 10.16　Computation of convolved feature map

Then, we stride across the numeric matrix until we populate all the cells of the convolved feature map (see Figure 10.17).

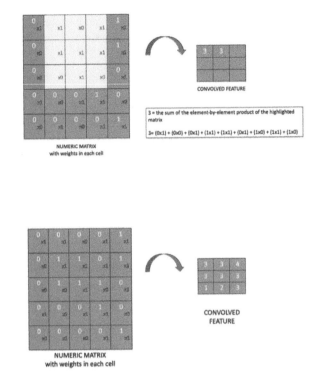

Figure 10.17 Completion of the convolved feature map

To get the pooled feature map, we stride across the convolved feature and do either maximum or average pooling. Figure 10.18 shows that we take the maximum of the top left 2 × 2 sub-matrix and put it at the top left of the pooled feature. We do this until we have filled all the cells of the pooled feature. Figure 10.19 shows how the completion of the pooled feature is done.

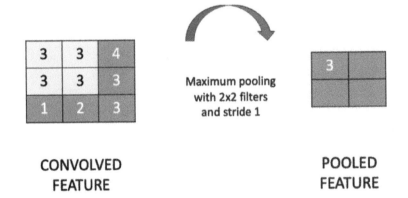

Figure 10.18 Computation of pooled feature

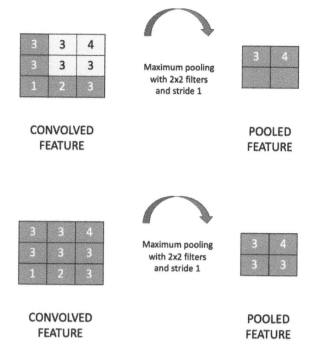

Figure 10.19   Completion of the pooled feature map

In our Puma logo example, we may have pooled features like the ones in Figure 10.20.

Figure 10.20   Pooling layer: feature extraction

Finally, we take the pooled layer, convert it to a one-dimensional fully connected layer through vectorization, and do the classification. Figure 10.21 illustrates this stage. In the classification layer, the relevant neurons are activated, and we pick the neuron with the largest activation number. These are the basic principles of CNNs. Next, we briefly discuss model training for CNNs.

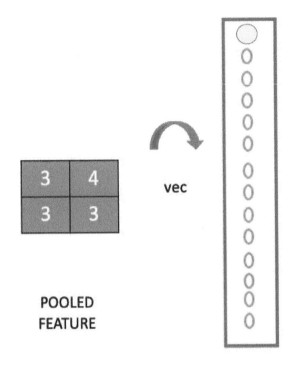

POOLED
FEATURE

Classification layer

Figure 10.21   Classification layer

CNN model training

There are different ways in which a CNN model can be trained. If we have unlabelled data, we can use unsupervised machine learning methods (e.g. autoencoders). These turn our data into a low-dimensional space. Once we have done the unsupervised learning, we create additional layers to our data and train our model as such. Another method which is slightly more complicated is generative adversarial networks. We leave CNN model training to our software application in which all the steps are explained in depth with an illustration to a real-world image dataset.

All the principles discussed regarding NNs (i.e. weights, activation function, loss function, backpropagation) apply to CNNs as well. In CNNs, the activation function we use for the output layers is the RLU.

We next show the CNN model application in R. Our objective is to classify consumer-uploaded images of Coca-Cola on Flickr. Through the software application, we explore what brand attributes of Coca-Cola lead to higher popularity among consumers.

MODEL APPLICATION IN R

The marketing team at Coca-Cola would like to perform visual listening by investigating the images taken and shared by consumers on Flickr.com. The user-generated images reflect consumers' impression of the brand (or marketing campaign) more truly than self-reported statements. The members of the team are aware that they can create better future ad copies by learning which images would and would not become popular. Furthermore, by studying the link between image attributes and their popularity, the team can have a better idea of (i) which ad features are appreciated by consumers, and (ii) how to design more appealing advertisements in the future.

In this software application, our objectives, therefore, are to use CNNs to classify consumer-uploaded images of the Coca-Cola brand on Flickr, and to illustrate which ad features of Coca-Cola lead to higher popularity among consumers, using a small sample of images.

Preparation and set-up

For a better understanding of the R code provided in this section, the reader is encouraged to go through the associated R Markdown file which is available on the book's website.

Before we roll out the analyses, we need to make sure that all our files are organized and our R environment is set up. To do so, we execute the following steps:

- Create a folder and set a working directory to that folder on our device.
- Download the data and all the other files needed for this session onto our working directory.

We create a folder on our desktop and name it *image_analytics*. Next, we launch RStudio and open a new R Markdown file. From the RStudio menu bar, we choose *File>New File>R Markdown*.

Next, we set the working directory in our R Markdown file. The code chunk below shows how to set the working directory. Depending on the operating system of our device, we run only part of the code. To avoid running code that is not applicable and receiving error messages, we add # before each line of non-applicable code. For example, if we use a Mac computer, we need to put # before the code setwd("H:/downloads/image_analytics").

```
```{r warning=FALSE}

# Run the following codes depending on the operating system on your
laptop/PC.

# If you are using iOS, and your *image_analytics* folder is created
under the 'Downloads' on your Mac, you will need to first set your
working directory to the 'image_analytics' folder as follows:
```
```

```
setwd("~/downloads/image_analytics")

# If you are using Windows, and your 'image_analytics' folder is
created in your H drive, you will need to first set your working
directory to 'image_analytics' folder as follows:

#setwd("H:/downloads/image_analytics")

```
```

Install and load R packages

The next step is to install and load the R packages, as per the code below. It is important to note that installing and loading packages for this chapter may take more time than usual since we are working on image data. Therefore, it is recommended that the reader looks at their console. For instance, when the console says Update all/some/none? [a/s/n]:, we type a and press the enter button. When it asks Do you want to install from sources the packages which need compilation? (Yes/no/cancel) we choose the option no.

```
```{r, eval=TRUE, error=FALSE, warning=FALSE, message=FALSE}
# It is important to note that installing and loading packages for
this session take more time than usual since we work on image data.
Therefore, it is recommended that the reader looks at their Console
in case there are some commands to put in.

# For instance, when it says "Update all/some/none? [a/s/n]:", type
'a' and press the enter button.
# When it asks "Do you want to install from sources the packages
which need compilation? (Yes/no/cancel), choose the option 'no'.

if (!require("raster")) install.packages("raster", repos =
"http://cran.us.r-project.org")
if (!require("e1071"))install.packages("e1071", repos =
"http://cran.us.r-project.org")
if (!require("rgdal")) install.packages("rgdal", repos =
"http://cran.us.r-project.org")
if (!require("keras")) install.packages("keras",repos =
"http://cran.us.r-project.org")
if (!require("readxl")) install.packages("readxl",repos =
"http://cran.us.r-project.org")
if (!require("stringr")) install.packages("stringr",repos =
```

```
"http://cran.us.r-project.org")
if (!require("graphics")) install.packages("graphics",repos =
"http://cran.us.r-project.org")
if (!require("systemfonts")) install.packages("systemfonts",repos=
"http://cran.us.r-project.org")
if (!require("kableExtra")) install.packages("kableExtra",repos =
"http://cran.us.r-project.org")
if (!require("BiocManager")) install.packages("BiocManager",repos=
"http://cran.us.r-project.org")
if (!require("tidyverse")) install.packages("tidyverse",repos=
"http://cran.us.r-project.org")
if (!require("ggplot2")) install.packages("ggplot2",repos=
"http://cran.us.r-project.org")
BiocManager::install("EBImage")
BiocManager::install("pbapply")

library(pbapply)
library(readxl)
library(keras)
library(EBImage)
library(stringr)
library(rgdal)
library(e1071)
library(graphics)
library(raster)
library(kableExtra)
library(graphics)
library(ggplot2)
library(kableExtra)
library(tidyverse)

```
```

Data

We obtain the image data on Coca-Cola ads from Flickr, a famous online portal where people share photos that they take themselves. We searched for all images about Coca-Cola shared by users during the first quarter of 2021. Although we use a small sample of data (20 pictures), the R code we present here can easily be extended to large datasets.

The basic information about the images is summarized in the data file *flickr_data.xlsx*. We load the Excel file to explore the variables of this dataset. The following R code loads the data into R and Figure 10.22 shows the features of the data.
```

```{r}
data<- read_excel("flickr_data.xlsx")

kable(data)

```

Original Image ID	No. of Views	No. of Favourites	No. of Comments	Index for Analysis	Popular	Colour Image	Human Centric	Direct Logo Exposure	Direct Product Exposure
20	9535	52	5	Popular 1	1	1	1	1	0
18	2702	165	12	Popular 2	1	1	0	1	1
3	2427	144	3	Popular 3	1	0	0	1	1
5	2374	62	6	Popular 4	1	1	1	1	0
15	1770	9	1	Popular 5	1	1	1	0	0
4	1539	35	2	Popular 6	1	1	0	1	0
21	1512	46	16	Popular 7	1	1	0	1	0
13	1272	20	2	Popular 8	1	1	0	1	1
19	1043	140	7	Popular 9	1	1	0	1	0
14	1009	35	9	Popular 10	1	1	0	1	1
7	699	11	0	Unpopular 1	0	1	0	1	1
17	631	5	0	Unpopular 2	0	1	0	1	1
12	11	0	0	Unpopular 3	0	1	0	1	1
11	613	8	0	Unpopular 4	0	1	1	1	1
1	570	27	5	Unpopular 5	0	1	0	1	0
6	538	40	11	Unpopular 6	0	1	1	1	1
8	414	33	0	Unpopular 7	0	1	0	1	0
16	94	1	0	Unpopular 8	0	1	0	1	1
10	83	0	0	Unpopular 9	0	1	0	1	1
9	43	0	0	Unpopular 10	0	1	0	1	1

Figure 10.22 Data features

The `Popular` column shows whether the image is considered 'popular' or 'unpopular'. To classify (or pre-label images) into the 'popular' and 'unpopular' classes, we use the number of likes as a proxy for popularity, randomly select 20 images, and rank them by the number of likes. We label the top 10 images as 'popular', and the rest as 'unpopular'.

We summarize the descriptions of the other variables by running the code below. Figure 10.23 shows the output.

```{r echo=FALSE}
var_exp <- data.frame(Item = c("Original ID", "No. of Views", "No.
of Favourites", "No. of Comments", "Index for Analysis", "Popular",
"Color Image", "Human Centric", "Direct Logo Exposure", "Product
Exposure"), Description = c("Original ID of each image in the database",
"Total number of views of each image", "Total number of Favourites
received of each image", "Total number of comments of each image",
"Image index (i.e., after labelling) used for analysis", "Image label
(Popular = 1, Unpopular = 0)", "Dummy variable indicating if an image
```

is color (1) or black-and-white (0)", "Dummy variable indicating if
a image is human-centric (1) or not (0)", "Dummy variable indicating
if the Coca-Cola logo was displayed in the image (1 = Yes, 0 = No)",
"Dummy variable indicating if the product (i.e., coke) was displayed
in the image (1 = Yes, 0 = No) "))

kable(var_exp)


```
```

Item	Description
Original ID	Original ID of each image in the database
No. of Views	Total number of views of each image
No. of Favourites	Total number of favourites received of each image
No. of Comments	Total number of comments of each image
Index for Analysis	Image index (i.e., after labelling) used for analysis
Popular	Image label (Popular = 1, Unpopular = 0)
Colour Image	Dummy variable indicating if the image is colour (1) or black-and-white (0)
Human Centric	Dummy variable indicating if the image is human-centric (1) or not (0)
Direct Logo Exposure	Dummy variable indicating if the Coca-Cola logo was displayed in the image (1 = Yes, 0 = No)
Product Exposure	Dummy variable indicating if the product (i.e., Coke) was displayed in the image (1 = Yes, 0 = No)

Figure 10.23 Variable descriptions

Next, we create a list of images using the code below. The output can be seen in the global
environment, in the upper right-hand corner of RStudio.

```r
```{r}
#Save image names in a vector
pics <- c("popular_1.jpeg","popular_2.jpeg","popular_3.jpeg",
"popular_4.jpeg","popular_5.jpeg", "popular_6.jpeg","popular_7.jpeg",
"popular_8.jpeg", "popular_9.jpeg", "popular_10.jpeg", "unpopular_1.jpeg",
"unpopular_2.jpeg", "unpopular_3.jpeg","unpopular_4.jpeg", "unpopular_5.jpeg",
"unpopular_6.jpeg", "unpopular_7.jpeg", "unpopular_8.jpeg", "unpopular_9.jpeg",
"unpopular_10.jpeg")

mypic <- list()

#Load files into list using a for loop
for(x in 1:length(pics)){
  mypic[[x]] <- readImage(pics[x])
}

```
```

Take a quick look at the code chunk below, which produces two of the images in Figure 10.24 that will be used for the analysis.

```r
```{r}
popular_sample <- brick("popular_4.jpeg")
unpopular_sample <- brick("unpopular_6.jpeg")
plotRGB(popular_sample)
plotRGB(unpopular_sample)

```
```

Figure 10.24 Image examples

Training and test sets

We use the first eight images in each group as our training data. Hence, our training set consists of 16 images (eight popular, eight unpopular) and our test set contains four images (two popular and two unpopular). The following code chunk does the sample split.

```r
```{r}
#training set of 16 images
trainX <- list(1:16)

#select first 8 images of each group
for(x in 1:8){
  trainX[[x]] <- mypic[[x]] #popular
  trainX[[x+8]] <- mypic[[x+10]] #unpopular
}


#test set of 4 images
testX <- list(1:4)

#select last two images in each group
for(x in 1:2){
  testX[[x]] <- mypic[[x+8]] #popular
  testX[[x+2]] <- mypic[[x+16]] #unpopular

}
```
```

Now we go through a few image inspection steps. We run the following code to understand the image sizes.

```r
```{r}
#Inspect the structure for resizing
str(trainX)
str(testX)

```
```

```
List of 16
 $ :Formal class 'Image' [package "EBImage"] with 2 slots
  .. ..@ .Data    : num [1:737, 1:517, 1:3] 1 0.933 0.784 0.784 0.827 ...
  .. ..@ colormode: int 2
  .. ..$ dim: int [1:3] 737 517 3
 $ :Formal class 'Image' [package "EBImage"] with 2 slots
  .. ..@ .Data    : num [1:800, 1:541, 1:3] 0.00392 0.00784 0 0.02353 0 ...
  .. ..@ colormode: int 2
  .. ..$ dim: int [1:3] 800 541 3
 $ :Formal class 'Image' [package "EBImage"] with 2 slots
  .. ..@ .Data    : num [1:516, 1:637, 1:3] 0.0471 0.0471 0.0471 0.0471 0.0471 ...
  .. ..@ colormode: int 2
  .. ..$ dim: int [1:3] 516 637 3
 $ :Formal class 'Image' [package "EBImage"] with 2 slots
  .. ..@ .Data    : num [1:801, 1:525, 1:3] 0.969 0.796 0.765 0.745 0.741 ...
  .. ..@ colormode: int 2
  .. ..$ dim: int [1:3] 801 525 3
 $ :Formal class 'Image' [package "EBImage"] with 2 slots
  .. ..@ .Data    : num [1:500, 1:500, 1:3] 0.988 0.988 0.988 0.988 0.988 ...
  .. ..@ colormode: int 2
  .. ..$ dim: int [1:3] 500 500 3
 $ :Formal class 'Image' [package "EBImage"] with 2 slots
  .. ..@ .Data    : num [1:736, 1:552, 1:3] 0.259 0.251 0.247 0.255 0.259 ...
  .. ..@ colormode: int 2
  .. ..$ dim: int [1:3] 736 552 3
 $ :Formal class 'Image' [package "EBImage"] with 2 slots
  .. ..@ .Data    : num [1:637, 1:436, 1:3] 0.9176 0.0706 0.0275 0.0745 0.3529 ...
  .. ..@ colormode: int 2
  .. ..$ dim: int [1:3] 637 436 3
```

Figure 10.25 Image sizes

The output in Figure 10.25 suggests that the images are three-dimensional but have varying lengths and widths. Looking at the data category of the structure of the list of images, we can see that the first two numbers (width and height) are different for each image and all images are colour ('3' stands for numbers in RGB format that indicate a colour image).

To further prepare the data for training and testing, we want to keep all image dimensions consistent. To do this, we resize all images so that they are 400 × 400 pixels using the resize() function. Here, we pick 400 × 400 because it is smaller than the smallest height of all the images in the imported data. Images must also have equal width and height (square dimensions) because we want to end up with square matrices. The following code chunk resizes the images.

```r
```{r}
#Resizing Images (Train)
for(x in 1:length(trainX)){
    trainX[[x]] <- resize(trainX[[x]], 400, 400)
}

#Resizing Images (test)
for(x in 1:length(testX)){
  testX[[x]] <- resize(testX[[x]], 400, 400)
}
```
```

```
#Display new dimensions
#str(trainX)
str(testX)
```

` ` `

```
List of 4
 $ :Formal class 'Image' [package "EBImage"] with 2 slots
 .. ..@ .Data     : num [1:400, 1:400, 1:3] 1 1 1 1 1 1 1 1 1 1 ...
 .. ..@ colormode: int 2
 .. ..$ dim: int [1:3] 400 400 3
 $ :Formal class 'Image' [package "EBImage"] with 2 slots
 .. ..@ .Data     : num [1:400, 1:400, 1:3] 0.986 0.991 0.985 0.997 0.999 ...
 .. ..@ colormode: int 2
 .. ..$ dim: int [1:3] 400 400 3
 $ :Formal class 'Image' [package "EBImage"] with 2 slots
 .. ..@ .Data     : num [1:400, 1:400, 1:3] 0.208 0.21 0.212 0.212 0.212 ...
 .. ..@ colormode: int 2
 .. ..$ dim: int [1:3] 400 400 3
 $ :Formal class 'Image' [package "EBImage"] with 2 slots
 .. ..@ .Data     : num [1:400, 1:400, 1:3] 0.0608 0.0569 0.0588 0.0549 0.0608 ...
 .. ..@ colormode: int 2
 .. ..$ dim: int [1:3] 400 400 3
```

Figure 10.26 Image resizing

The output in Figure 10.26 shows the size of the images of the resized test set. We can see that the images now have the same dimensions.

We now look at the resized images in the training set and test set. The following code chunk yields the images for the training set in Figure 10.27.

```{r}
#Display resized images (train)

trainX <- combine(trainX)
dis <- tile(trainX, 4)
display(dis, title = "Images in training set")
```

` ` `

The next code chunk yields the images for the test set in Figure 10.28.

```{r}
#Display Resized Images (test)
testX <- combine(testX)
dis2 <- tile(testX, 2)
display(dis2, title = "Images in test set")
```

` ` `

Figure 10.27   Resized images for the training set

Figure 10.28   Resized images for the test set

Denoting popular by 1, unpopular by 0, we label the images in the training and test set. The following code produces the output in Figure 10.29.

```r
```{r}
#Response variable for the two categories
trainY <- c(rep(1, 8), rep(0, 8))
testY <- c(1,1,0,0)
```
```

```
trainLabels <- to_categorical(trainY)
testLabels <- to_categorical(testY)

#Display matrix
kable(testLabels) %>%
  kable_styling() %>%
  scroll_box(width = "100%", height = "200px")

```
```

0	1
0	1
1	0
1	0

Figure 10.29   Labelling images

The output in Figure 10.29 shows the matrix of test labels. The first two images are in the popular category, and the next two are in the unpopular category. The same encoding was also done for training labels.

CNN model set-up

Having explored the general features of the images in our dataset, we are ready to implement the CNN modelling approach. The following code sets up the CNN model. We explore the model input below.

```
```{r warning=FALSE}

#Model with a linear stack of layers
model <- keras_model_sequential()

#Layers within the model(as listed above)
model %>%
  layer_conv_2d(filters = 32, kernel_size = c(3,3), activation =
'relu', input_shape = c(400, 400, 3)) %>%
  layer_conv_2d(filters = 32, kernel_size = c(3,3), activation =
'relu') %>%
  layer_max_pooling_2d(pool_size = c(2,2)) %>%
  layer_dropout(rate = 0.25) %>%
```

```
  layer_conv_2d(filters = 64, kernel_size = c(3,3), activation =
'relu')%>%
  layer_conv_2d(filters = 64, kernel_size = c(3,3), activation =
'relu') %>%
  layer_max_pooling_2d(pool_size = c(2,2)) %>%
  layer_dropout(rate = 0.25) %>%
  layer_flatten() %>%
  layer_dense(units = 256, activation = 'relu') %>%
  layer_dropout(rate = 0.25) %>%
  layer_dense(units = 2, activation = "softmax") %>%
  compile(loss = "categorical_crossentropy", optimizer =
          optimizer_sgd(lr = 0.001, momentum = 0.9, decay = 1e-6,
nesterov = T),
          metrics = c('accuracy'))

#View the model
summary(model)
```

Layers

In this model, layers are abbreviated. There are five different layers used:

- Convolutional layers (4). The first two convolutional layers use 32 filters with dimensions 3 × 3. The last two convolutional layers use 64 filters. The primary function of these layers is to extract features from each image. The first two layers extract initial features, and the last two layers include more filters.
- Pooling layers (2). Pooling layers follow convolutional layers in the visual geometry group (VGG) architecture. The VGG is a CNN architecture with multiple layers. The function of these layers is to reduce the number of parameters in the network by operating on each feature map with a 2 × 2 filter. This helps save space and abstract features to avoid overfitting and is located after two convolutional layers for effective parameter reduction. The type of pooling used is maximum pooling.
- Dropout layers (3). The function of these layers is also to decrease the number of parameters to avoid overfitting. In this section, a dropout rate of 0.25 is used, which is 25% of the input units (which are considered the weakest predictors) from the previous layer. The input units are set to zero after a pooling layer, thereby reducing parameters even further and freeing up some memory space.
- Flattening layer (1). This layer 'flattens' the 2 × 2 matrix from the preceding layer into a vector that can be fed into the next layer (a fully connected neural network classifier).
- Dense layers (2). These are the fully connected neural network classifiers. The first has 256 neurons, and the last has three neurons.

Activation functions

A rectified linear unit (RLU) is used as an activation function in convolutional layers and in the first fully connected layer. A softmax activation function is used for the final fully connected layer to produce a probability distribution in output as per the VGG16 architecture.

Model architecture

The 12 layers of the model architecture are as follows:

- Layer 1: input layer – convolutional layer with 32 3 × 3 filters, RLU activation function and input dimensions of 400 × 400 × 3
- Layer 2: convolutional layer with 32 3 × 3 filters and RLU activation function
- Layer 3: pooling layer with 2 × 2 filter
- Layer 4: dropout layer with rate 25%
- Layers 5 and 6: convolutional layer with 64 3 × 3 filters and RLU activation function
- Layer 7: pooling layer with 2 × 2 filter
- Layer 8: dropout layer with rate 25%
- Layer 9: flattening layer transforms matrix into a vector for fully connected layer
- Layer 10: fully connected layer with 256 neurons and RLU activation function
- Layer 11: dropout layer with rate 25%
- Layer 12: output layer – fully connected layer with two neurons (because we have two categories) and a softmax activation function for probability output.

Hyperparameters

Using the `compile()` function, we configure the CNN and specify the following parameters:

- Loss function: `categorical_crossentropy` is used because each image can only belong to one category.
- Optimizer: `optimizer_sgd()` is a stochastic gradient descent optimizer that is currently the best choice for computer vision problems.

There are four hyperparameters this function takes that can be changed to optimize the model:

1. `lr` indicates the learning rate, which is set to 0.001.
2. `decay` indicates the adjustment to the learning rate after each iteration. This is set to e^{-6}.
3. `momentum` indicates the moving average of our gradients, which is set to 0.9 (i.e. standard setting).
4. `nesterov` indicates the type of momentum function.

Running the code at the beginning of this subsection gives us the model configuration output in Figure 10.30.

```
Model: "sequential_1"
_____
 Layer (type)                        Output Shape                        Param #
================================================================================
 conv2d_7 (Conv2D)                   (None, 398, 398, 32)                 896
 conv2d_6 (Conv2D)                   (None, 396, 396, 32)                 9248
 max_pooling2d_3 (MaxPooling2D)      (None, 198, 198, 32)                 0
 dropout_5 (Dropout)                 (None, 198, 198, 32)                 0
 conv2d_5 (Conv2D)                   (None, 196, 196, 64)                 18496
 conv2d_4 (Conv2D)                   (None, 194, 194, 64)                 36928
 max_pooling2d_2 (MaxPooling2D)      (None, 97, 97, 64)                   0
 dropout_4 (Dropout)                 (None, 97, 97, 64)                   0
 flatten_1 (Flatten)                 (None, 602176)                       0
 dense_3 (Dense)                     (None, 256)                          154157312
 dropout_3 (Dropout)                 (None, 256)                          0
 dense_2 (Dense)                     (None, 2)                            514
================================================================================
Total params: 154,223,394
Trainable params: 154,223,394
Non-trainable params: 0
_____
```

Figure 10.30   CNN model configuration output

From Figure 10.30, we can see each layer in our model and the number of parameters that each layer introduces. With each layer, the shape of our output changes until we have an output with three units.

Before we can train and test our model, we need to convert the images back into the dimensions needed for input into the CNN. Looking at the structure, instead of having a list of images, we have one matrix with dimensions $400 \times 400 \times 3 \times 16$. The additional 16 comes from the 16 images we combined above in our training set; for the test set, we have dimensions $400 \times 400 \times 3 \times 4$. We can reorder the dimensions (number of images, width, height, and colour) using the `aperm()` function. The code chunk below reorders the image dimensions. The purpose is to have the training set organized with dimensions $16 \times 400 \times 400 \times 3$, while the test set is $4 \times 400 \times 400 \times 3$.

```{r}
trainX <- aperm(trainX,c(4,1,2,3))
testX <- aperm(testX, c(4,1,2,3))

``
```

Now that we have built the architecture of the model and the image data have been processed, we are ready to integrate the two. To do this, we use the `fit()` function from the `keras` package with the training data and training labels.

```{r}
history <- model %>%
   fit(trainX, trainLabels, epochs = 30, batch_size = 16,
validation_split = 0.2)
plot(history)

```
```
```

Some of the hyperparameters defined in the model fit are as follows:

- `epochs` = 30. This indicates the number times the data are passed through the CNN for optimization (this can be changed to optimize the model).
- `batch_size` = 32. This indicates the subset of the dataset that will be passed through the CNN at any one time.
- `validation_split` = 0.2. This indicates the proportion of training data used for validation source.

As the model trains epoch after epoch, cross-entropy (loss) should be minimized in both training and validation splits. If there is an apparent increase in the validation split after a certain epoch, then the plot is suggestive of slight overfitting. Figure 10.31 shows the model fit output with the loss and accuracy metrics. Accuracy, inversely proportional to cross-entropy, stalls at around 95% and 75% in the training and validation splits, respectively, which are decent results on the fly.

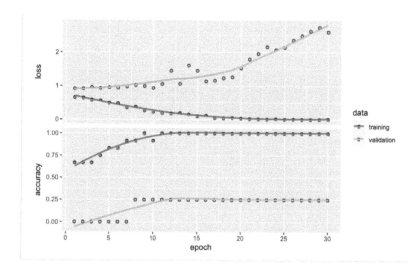

Figure 10.31   CNN model fit output

Model performance evaluation

We use the `evaluate()` function to calculate loss and accuracy metrics. The code chunk below evaluates the model performance and generates the output in Figure 10.32. The model we trained above needs to be run more than once to get the highest accuracy.

```r
```{r}
evTrain <- model %>%
```
```

```
   evaluate(trainX, trainLabels)


evTrain
```

```
1/1 [==============================] - 1s 742ms/step - loss: 0.6538 - accuracy: 0.8125
      loss    accuracy
0.6537572 0.8125000
```

Figure 10.32   CNN model performance evaluation

Here we observe that the prediction accuracy is 81.25%. On the third try, this model has a 93.33% accuracy for predicting the training set with a loss of 30.16%.

Before going to the test set, we can make a prediction for the training set and create a confusion matrix. We can then evaluate the model by looking at the probability that the model assigns a certain category to each image. The following code chunk generates the outputs in Figures 10.33 and 10.34.

```{r}

#make a prediction of the classes
predTrain <-model %>% predict(trainX)

pred_class<-rep(0,16)
for (i in 1:16) {
  if(predTrain[i,2]>0.5) {
  pred_class[i]<-1
}else{pred_class[i]<-0}
}

probability_popular<-round(predTrain[,2],2)
# visualize the results

col1 <- data.frame(matrix(unlist(probability_popular),
nrow=length(probability_popular), byrow=TRUE))
col2 <- data.frame(matrix(unlist(pred_class), nrow=length(pred_
class), byrow=TRUE))
col3 <- data.frame(matrix(unlist(trainY), nrow=length(trainY),
byrow=TRUE))

results_summary<-as.data.frame(cbind(col1, col2, col3))
```

```
colnames(results_summary)<-c("predict_probability_1","predicted_class",
"actual_class")
results_summary

# visualize the confusion matrix
table(pred_class, trainY)
```

```
```
```

| | R Console | data.frame 16 x 3 | | | ↗ x |

Description **df [16 × 3]**

| predict_probability_1<br><dbl> | predicted_class<br><dbl> | actual_class<br><dbl> |
|---|---|---|
| 1.00 | 1 | 1 |
| 1.00 | 1 | 1 |
| 0.97 | 1 | 1 |
| 1.00 | 1 | 1 |
| 1.00 | 1 | 1 |
| 1.00 | 1 | 1 |
| 1.00 | 1 | 1 |
| 1.00 | 1 | 1 |
| 0.00 | 0 | 0 |
| 0.00 | 0 | 0 |

1-10 of 16 rows                                                    Previous  1  2  Next

**Figure 10.33** Prediction of classes for the training set

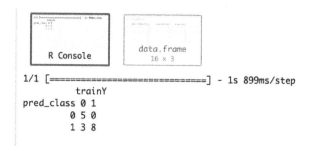

```
1/1 [==============================] - 1s 899ms/step
             trainY
pred_class 0 1
         0 5 0
         1 3 8
```

Figure 10.34 Confusion matrix for the training set

In Figure 10.33, the first column refers to the probability that an image is classified as class '1' (i.e., popular). The next two columns show the predicted and the actual class of each image, respectively.

The confusion matrix output in Figure 10.34 summarizes the model predictions. Class '0' refers to the unpopular images while class '1' refers to the popular images. The diagonal entries in
```

this matrix show the number of correctly classified images. For example, there were eight popular images in the training set, and the model predicted the class of all these images correctly. Three out of eight unpopular images were classified incorrectly.

Now we turn to the test set and obtain class predictions.

Prediction using the test set

We repeat the above procedure for the test set. The following code produces model predictions and generates the outputs in Figures 10.35 and 10.36.

```{r}
evTest <- model %>%
  evaluate(testX, testLabels)
evTest
#generate the predicted probability
predTest <- model %>%predict(testX)

pred_class<-rep(0,4)
for (i in 1:4) {
  if(predTest[i,2]>0.5) {
  pred_class[i]<-1
}else{pred_class[i]<-0}
}

probability_popular_test <- round(predTest[,2],2)

col1 <- data.frame(matrix(unlist(probability_popular_test),
nrow=length(probability_popular_test), byrow=TRUE))
col2 <- data.frame(matrix(unlist(pred_class), nrow=length(pred_
class), byrow=TRUE))
col3 <- data.frame(matrix(unlist(testY), nrow=length(testY),
byrow=TRUE))

results_summary<-as.data.frame(cbind(col1, col2, col3))

colnames(results_summary)<-c("predict_probability_1","predicted_class",
"actual_class")
results_summary

# visualize the confusion matrix
table(pred_class, testY)

```

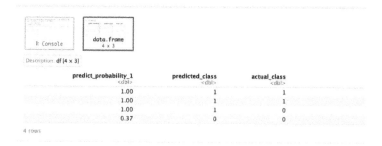

predict_probability_1 <dbl>	predicted_class <dbl>	actual_class <dbl>
1.00	1	1
1.00	1	1
1.00	1	0
0.37	0	0

4 rows

Figure 10.35 Model predictions for the test set

```
1/1 [==============================] - 0s 301ms/step - loss: 1.4601 - accuracy: 0.7500
     loss accuracy
1.460055 0.750000
1/1 [==============================] - 0s 243ms/step
          testY
pred_class 0 1
         0 1 0
         1 1 2
```

Figure 10.36 Confusion matrix for the test set

The output in Figures 10.35 and 10.36 suggests that the accuracy of prediction based on the test set is 75%. Specifically, the model failed to predict the class for one of the images in the test set. With larger datasets, we may train the CNN model further to improve model predictions for the test set.

In this software application, we show that the keras package provides a simple way to implement multiple types of CNN architectures and facilitates easy fine-tuning of hyperparameters. To find a CNN model that produces robust predictions, we need to find a good balance of accuracy and loss for both training and test sets. To build such a model, there are a few things we can do:

1. Increase the number of images in our training and test set. This would also require a graphics processing unit. Otherwise, it just might take a very long time to run.
2. Add more diverse images with varying colours, tones, and backgrounds.
3. Decrease loss by adding more convolutional layers and fully connected layers.
4. Decrease the learning rate.

What makes an attractive image?

Assuming that our CNN is the most accurate that we can possibly have, what managerial conclusions can we draw from the model? Focusing on the images that are classified as 'popular' in the test set, we can investigate the features of those images. In doing so, the brand can design its marketing communications more effectively. Note that the test set here is very limited, consisting of only four images with three classified as 'popular'. The interpretations will be much more accurate and convincing if you have a larger test set.

The following code chunk examines four features in the images: (i) colour, (ii) human-centricity, (iii) direct logo exposure, and (iv) direct product exposure. The output is shown in Figure 10.37.

```{r}
# Get the data from the test set that is predicted as "Popular"
testset<- data[c(9,10,19),]

testset$`Colour Image` <- as.factor(testset$`Colour Image`)
testset$`Human Centric` <- as.factor(testset$`Human Centric`)
testset$`Direct Logo Exposure` <- as.factor(testset$`Direct Logo
Exposure`)
testset$`Direct Product Exposure` <- as.factor(testset$`Direct
Product Exposure`)

p1 <- testset %>% ggplot() + geom_histogram(aes(x=factor('Colour
Image')), fill="blue", alpha=0.6, stat="count", binwidth=1) + labs(
y = "Count", x="Colour image") +
theme(text = element_text(size=6))

p2 <- testset %>% ggplot() + geom_histogram(aes(x=`Human Centric`),
fill="green", alpha=0.6,stat="count") + labs(y = "Count", x="Human
Centric")+
theme(text = element_text(size=6))

p3 <- testset %>% ggplot() + geom_histogram(aes(x=`Direct Logo
Exposure`), fill="red", alpha=0.6,stat="count") + labs(y = "Count",
x="Direct Logo Exposure")+
theme(text = element_text(size=6))

p4 <- testset %>% ggplot() + geom_histogram(aes(x=`Direct Product
Exposure`), fill="yellow", alpha=0.6,stat="count") + labs(y = "Count",
x="Direct Product Exposure")+
theme(text = element_text(size=6))

p1
p2
p3
p4

```

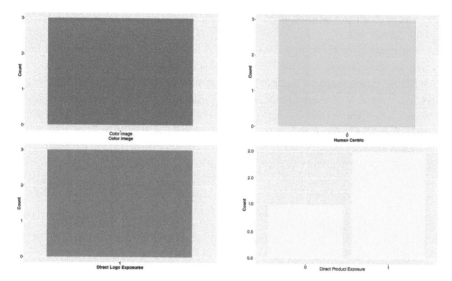

Figure 10.37   Popular image features

The output in Figure 10.37 shows the number of times these features appear in the popular images from the test set. Judging from the results above, consumers, in general, will be engaged by images that are in colour, with humans, with the brand logo displayed and probably with the product also displayed.

Here, we have followed an intuitive approach to analyse image features. A more comprehensive approach would be to run a conjoint analysis using the extracted image features from the CNN model. However, one should note that model-based image features may not always be interpretable (Zhang et al., 2022).

CHAPTER SUMMARY

Consumers increasingly take, store, and share images on social media and other digital platforms. In parallel, marketers have more analytical tools than ever. Both the abundance of image data and the recent developments in deep learning modelling techniques open new opportunities for marketers to plan and execute their branding, advertising, product design and presentation strategies (Dzyabura et al., 2022). For example, by identifying the key features of user-generated images (e.g. colours, objects, logos) shared on social media, marketing managers can monitor visual conversations, follow trends, and increase the effectiveness of their marketing mix decisions. In this chapter, we focused on image analytics through convolutional neural networks (CNNs), a cutting-edge deep learning model that has recently gained popularity among marketing practitioners and academics. CNNs are used to process and classify images. We applied the CNN modelling tool to a sample of consumer-uploaded images of Coca-Cola on Flickr to illustrate how these models can be applied to real-world datasets.

Although CNNs are very useful for image classification problems, their applications are sometimes challenging. For example, important objects in user-generated images may appear partially or distorted, which complicates the model learning. Also, images that contain brand images may be shown as a combination of text and visuals rather than just visuals. In such cases, extracting image features becomes very complex. Moreover, brand images may appear in different contexts. A user may share an image with a famous football player who wears a Nike T-shirt. Understanding the consumer motives behind such an image sharing behaviour is difficult if we rely only on image classification algorithms. Therefore, practitioners are recommended to complement deep learning techniques with behavioural research methods.

REFERENCES

Brandwatch (2017) What is visual listening and why do I need it? https://www.brandwatch.com/blog/what-visual-listening/

Chong, E. K. P. and Żak, S. H. (2013) Gradient methods. In *An Introduction to Optimization*, 4th edn. Hoboken, NJ: Wiley.

Dzyabura, D., El Kihal, S., Ibragimov, M. and Hauser J. (2020) Leveraging the power of images in managing product return rates. https://papers.ssrn.com/sol3/papers.cfm?abstract_id=3209307

Dzyabura, D., El Khial, S. and Peres, R. (2022) Image analytics in marketing. In C. Homburg, M. Klarmann and A. E. Vomberg (eds), *Handbook of Market Research*. Cham: Springer.

Dzyabura D. and Peres R. (2021) Visual elicitation of brand perception. *Journal of Marketing*, 85(4), 44–66.

Ghatak, A. (2019) *Deep Learning with R*. Singapore: Springer Singapore.

Goodfellow, I., Bengio, Y., Courville, A. and Bengio, Y. (2016) *Deep Learning*. Cambridge, MA: MIT Press. http://www.deeplearningbook.org

Hebb, D. O. (1949) *The Organization of Behavior: A Neuropsychological Theory*. New York: Wiley.

James, G., Witten, D., Hastie, T. and Tibshirani, R. (2021) *An Introduction to Statistical Learning with Applications in R*, 2nd edn. New York: Springer.

Li, Y. and Xie, Y. (2020) Is a picture worth a thousand words? An empirical study of image content and social media engagement. *Journal of Marketing Research*, 57(1), 1–19.

Liu, L., Dzyabura, D. and Mizik, N. (2020) Visual listening in: Extracting brand image portrayed on social media. *Marketing Science*, 39(4), 669–86.

Ma, L. Y. and Sun, B. H. (2020) Machine learning and AI in marketing – Connecting computing power to human insights. *International Journal of Research in Marketing*, 37(3), 481–504.

MacInnis, D. J. and Price, L. L. (1987) The role of imagery in information processing: Review and extensions. *Journal of Consumer Research*, 13(4), 473–91.

Marr, B. (2018) How much data do we create every day? The mind-blowing stats everyone should read. *Forbes*, 21 May. https://www.forbes.com/sites/bernardmarr/2018/05/21/how-much-data-do-we-create-every-day-the-mind-blowing-stats-everyone-should-read/?sh=3b85010560ba.

McCulloch, W. and Pitts, W. (1943) A logical calculus of ideas immanent in nervous activity. *Bulletin of Mathematical Biophysics*. 5(4), 115–33.

MDG Advertising (2018) It's all about the images. https://www.mdgadvertising.com/marketing-insights/infographics/its-all-about-the-images-infographic/

Ngai, E. W. T. and Wu, Y. (2022), Machine learning in marketing: A literature review, conceptual framework, and research agenda. *Journal of Business Research*, 145, 35–48.

Nielsen, M. A. (2015). *Neural Networks and Deep Learning*. Determination Press. http://neuralnetworksanddeeplearning.com/

Omnicore Agency (2022), Instagram by the numbers: Stats, demographics, and fun facts. https://www.omnicoreagency.com/instagram-statistics/

Overgoor, G., Rand, W., Van Dolen, W. and Mazloom, M. (2021) Simplicity is not key: Understanding firm-generated social media images and consumer liking. *International Journal of Research in Marketing*, 39(3), 639–55.

Pieters, R. and Wedel, M. (2004) Attention capture and transfer in advertising: Brand, pictorial, and text-size effects. *Journal of Marketing*, 68(2), 36–50.

Potter, M. C., Wyble, B., Hagmann, C. E. and McCourt, E. S. (2013) Detecting meaning in RSVP at 13 ms per picture. *Attention, Perception, & Psychophysics*, 76(2), 270–9.

Solomon, C. and Breckon, T. (2011) *Fundamentals of Digital Image Processing: A Practical Approach with Examples in Matlab*. Chichester: John Wiley & Sons.

Tonioni, A. and Di Stefano, L. (2017) Product recognition in store shelves as a sub-graph isomorphism problem. In S. Battiato, G. Gallo, R. Schettini and F. Stanco (eds), *Image Analysis and Processing – ICIAP 2017*, Lecture Notes in Computer Science, vol. 10484. Cham: Springer.

Vilnai-Yavetz, I. and Tifferet, S. (2015) A picture is worth a thousand words: Segmenting consumers by Facebook profile images. *Journal of Interactive Marketing*, 32, 53–69.

Xiao, Li and Ding, M. (2014) Just the faces: Exploring the effects of facial features in print advertising. *Marketing Science*, 33(3), 338–52.

Zhang, S., Lee, D., Singh, P. V. and Srinivasan, K. (2022) What makes a good image? Airbnb demand analytics leveraging interpretable image features. *Management Science*, 68(8). 5644–66.

11

DATA PROJECT MANAGEMENT AND GENERAL RECOMMENDATIONS

Chapter contents

LEARNING OBJECTIVES

At the end of this chapter, you should be able to:

- understand common database standards and know when to use which standard
- assess, improve, and foster data quality through various controls and check-up procedures
- use parallel computing to speed up analysis
- integrate R projects into other analytical frameworks such as Python
- understand key principles of storytelling with data
- understand how to implement data-driven insights into marketing practice
- ensure key ethical principles in data analysis.

In the previous chapters, we have focused largely on analytical methods and how the right method together with the right data can help you find the right answers to your marketing questions. We hope that you have developed by now a profound knowledge of how analytics can help you take more informed decisions in marketing. However, we also suspect that by now you have also realized that answering questions with the help of analytics takes more than the right method and an R markdown. Often the most painful process in marketing analytics is not the analysis, but the different steps needed to get to the point where you can apply analytics. As you will certainly know, relevant data are rarely immediately available but need to be taken and combined from various sources within and outside the company. Identifying and controlling data sources, checking data quality and reliability, as well as managing data are thus also essential tasks in marketing analytics and often take more time than the analysis itself. In fact, many data scientists believe that 90% of the time and resources of a marketing analytics project are taken up with data collection, data preparation, and quality control, with only 10% used for analytics and reporting. Textbooks and courses often neglect this important matter. Many tutorials thus only provide students with perfect, ready-to-use datasets, while later in marketing practice, data handling and data preparation tasks can become as challenging as analysis and interpretation.

This chapter will alert you to common issues when managing marketing analytics projects and discuss how to spot and address these issues.

DATA ANALYTICS PROJECT STAGES AND ISSUES

While the analysis often seems to be the most essential part of a project, it is commonly not the part that takes the most time and resources. Figure 11.1 depicts the common process with the different stages of a marketing analytics project.

Projects commonly start with problem identification and the refining of the research question. The researcher is tasked with and responsible for identifying the relevant variables and data sources needed to answer the question. This leads to the data gathering stage. In the case of projects relying on primary data, surveys need to be created, managed, and handled.

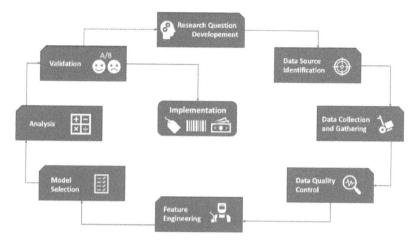

Figure 11.1   Stages in an analytics project

In the case of secondary data, data sources (i.e. databases) need to be identified and accessed. Projects often combine data from multiple sources, which may be located inside and outside the company. Data may come at different aggregation levels (such as weekly or daily), or in different measurement units (e.g. from different time zones, grams or ounces, Celsius or Fahrenheit, etc.), as well as from different distributions or sample groups (e.g. in the case of surveys, samples may significantly differ in terms of covariates such as age, income, education, and involvement). In all these cases the researcher is responsible for correctly assessing the pros and cons of merging datasets and has to ensure the highest data quality.

Data may also be corrupted by other issues such as missing observations or outliers, which may later compromise the analysis and findings. Again, the researcher is responsible for identifying and addressing potential issues. When it comes to choosing the right method for the problem analysis, the researcher is similarly responsible for verifying that the data meet the formal requirements of the chosen method (e.g. some tests require normally distributed data).

In the case of machine learning applications (or any other model in a prediction context), the role of training data becomes essential, as these models suffer especially from the 'garbage in, garbage out' (GIGO) problem. If the training data are already compromised, the model will never be able to correctly predict the outcome variable of interest. Researchers are thus responsible for either checking the training data or creating suitable training data. It is also often the case that a specific outcome variable is extremely unbalanced. For example, the number of fraudulent ad clicks may only constitute a small proportion of all clicks, or churn may only occur very infrequently. This imbalance may similarly pose a challenge to models and must thus be taken into consideration by the researcher.

While we generally believe more data to always be better, we often see that large datasets may also create new problems. While storing large datasets is already challenging, analysing them can be even more of a hurdle, as the lack of working memory and computational power often creates substantial barriers, which can be addressed by either subsampling or parallelization. This, however, may create additional challenges, as researchers may be forced to move the analysis outside the main analytical framework (i.e. R) and employ additional analytical frameworks and languages such as Python or C++. Data transfer and analysis integration can then quickly become a new potential source of errors and obstacles if transfers between environments and frameworks do not go well.

Once the results are in, the job is far from done. While many data scientists believe that their main task is analysis, they neglect their responsibility to transfer insights to marketing practice and decision-makers. Here the key challenge revolves around how to tell easy-to-grasp stories, building on the estimates and numbers from the output tables within R. Visualization as well as data storytelling are thus key challenges that need to be mastered to turn insights into value-creating decisions. Often researchers will have difficulties in deciding which details are essential for decisions and which information can be omitted to make the core story come to light – especially as results often do not indicate clear go-to solutions but often involve 'it depends' answers.

This may similarly require managers as well as data scientists to run additional tests, either by collecting more data and redoing analyses, or by conducting experiments. For example, the initial results from a secondary data analysis may be validated with the help of test market experiments or online A/B tests where creatives or products get first tested in smaller sub-markets, and only if these test markets support or confirm the initial findings will campaigns or products be rolled out at a larger scale.

Finally – and still too often overlooked – researchers should always critically assess the consequences of their analyses for individuals, subgroups, or minorities. Inappropriate research questions, incorrect training data, misspecified algorithms, and incorrect conclusions can quickly turn a well-intended model into a 'weapon of math destruction' (O'Neil, 2016). The ability to critically assess the impact of an analysis on a larger scale is thus just as essential as the initial analytical skills, if not more so.

In the following, we will discuss some of the above-mentioned issues alongside the analytical value-creation chain and briefly discuss potential solutions. Keep in mind that this list is far from complete and will only alert you to potential issues and give you some starting points for finding solutions to your problems. In many cases, this will require you to do further reading and to use the different packages' vignettes and tutorials to explore fixes in more detail.

DATA STORAGE AND DATABASE MANAGEMENT

To our surprise, we still often see companies solely relying on spreadsheet software such as Microsoft Excel to store large datasets. While this is certainly possible for smaller datasets, one should remember that MS Excel only allows 1,048,576 rows and 16,384 columns per spreadsheet. Larger datasets thus require other storage forms such as tab-separated CSV files which can theoretically store an infinite number of rows and columns. In practice, however, storage is commonly limited by computational power and other restrictions. To ensure that data can be quickly checked and examined, we recommend storing larger datasets in database formats. Here the common standard in the industry today seems to be SQL. SQL databases can be easily stored on web servers and allow quick access by multiple users. While SQL itself is its own programming language, one can also access and work with SQL databases through R, which provides multiple packages to integrate SQL data into R. The dbGetQuery function in the DBI package allows the user to directly access an SQL database and use SQL code within the R environment. Similarly, the dbplyr package allows the user to apply the classic dplyr language from R to SQL data, ensuring a quick integration of SQL data into a project. For more details we recommend installing both packages and accessing the help files to learn how to integrate SQL into your analysis, as shown below.

```
install.packages("DBI")
install.packages("dbplyr")

library(DBI)
library(dbplyr)

?dbGetQuery
```

A common shortcoming of SQL is that it requires data to be structured (i.e. to be in a spreadsheet format). Often, however, data come – and are stored – in an unstructured format. For example, a webpage may provide different reviews, with each review consisting of different variables. A classic spreadsheet format would thus require us to have in each review cell another spreadsheet for the different variables of the particular review so that we end up with a hierarchy of different tables and spreadsheets integrated into each other. The benefit of the unstructured format is its high degree of flexibility; however, this commonly comes at the cost of complex and often untransparent structures, which make it hard to stream and parse information into a classic analytical model that again requires a plain spreadsheet format. The most common storage format for semi-unstructured data is the JSON standard. Especially in the case of social media and web scrapping, researchers will quickly encounter JSON files. But also, many companies nowadays employ JSON-like databases (e.g. MongoDB) to collect and store data from various sources in an semi-unstructured format. R is perfectly able to cope with JSON formats (and R lists are comparable to the JSON file format). To stream (i.e. load) JSON files into R and to manipulate JSON files, R's jsonlite package has become the common standard. Similarly, the tidyjson package allows the user to apply the popular dplyr and tidy language from R to data stored in a JSON file. The following code will allow you to access the corresponding vignettes and to explore the potential of both packages to transfer data from a JSON file into R for subsequent analysis.

```
install.packages("jsonlite")
install.packages("tidyjson")
```

```
library(jsonlite)
library(tidyjson)

browseVignettes("tidyjson")
browseVignettes("jsonlite")
```

DATA SUITABILITY AND DATA HANDLING

When selecting or constructing datasets, researchers should always question the suitability of data. Availability does not automatically mean suitability. Before including observations or variables in a dataset, the researcher should carefully check whether it truly makes sense to do so. A key task here is to ensure that the data contain relevant information that is suitable for answering the chosen research question. While this sounds obvious, we often witness in marketing practice analytical models which incorporate all sorts of available data sources a company has access to, without first questioning whether the variables really provide any explanatory power and can truly contribute to explaining a phenomenon or answering the question of interest. Such a 'throw in everything we got' approach may sometimes turn out to be helpful, but in most cases only threatens the quality of the analysis. Unobserved or uncontrolled multicollinearity (i.e. a strong correlation among multiple variables included in the analysis) may either inflate findings and thus lead to wrong conclusions or even prevent the model from finding anything at all. Similarly, too many variables in the model may prevent model conversion or lead to other irritations. To select suitable data, we recommend two approaches: theory and explorative analysis. Previous research in the field can often provide valuable information on which variables should be included in an analysis and which variables and variable combinations may create problems (e.g. through multicollinearity or other effects such as endogeneity). The many available conceptual frameworks that have been developed and tested by marketing research in the last three decades commonly offer excellent guidance when it comes to identifying necessary data and variables. In addition, one can use the many publicly available studies (accessible through Google Scholar or networks such as ResearchGate, SSRN, or arXiv) as a benchmark for one's own research results. For example, by comparing the effects one has found from search engine advertising and social media ads with the effects found in academic studies, one can quickly see how well one's own model is doing. Similarly, if one's model delivers opposite effects to the majority of previous studies, one may take this as a serious warning signal and check the model specifications or the data quality.

Meanwhile, for some variables or questions, previous research may not yet provide sufficient knowledge. For example, in the case of new media channels or dynamic effects across multiple new channels, deep knowledge may be scarce. Here we recommend relying on an explorative approach. By trying to understand how variables relate to each other and exploring causal relations among pairs of variables (with the second variable in the pair being the performance/outcome variable of interest), one may gain a better understanding of which variables to include and which not to include in a dataset and analysis. Pauwels (2014) provides a great step-by-step guide on how to identify key performance indicators and how to exploratively combine these into a performance measurement model.

Such an explorative approach may, however, be challenged by the size of the dataset, as running even a simple correlation analysis may take a lot of time in the case of datasets with hundreds of millions of observations. Here random subsampling may be an alternative, where the researcher randomly draws observations from the main dataset to create a smaller dataset (assuming that this set will follow the same distribution for all randomly drawn observations), as shown by the code below. Here we use the `sample_n` function from `dplyr` to create the data frame `subsample_DF`, which contains 10,000 random rows from the initial data frame `MainDF`.

```
library(dplyr)
subsample_DF = sample_n(MainDF, 10000)
```

In the case of predictive models, where our main aim is to forecast some outcome (e.g. customer churn or demand), the role of training data becomes even more important. As we try to predict future behaviour with the help of past observations, we have to ensure that the data we have at hand is not compromised by changes in preferences or market environment which we do not observe in the past data. For example, if we are aiming to forecast demand for an online streaming service such as Netflix in 2022 with data from 2018–19, we may ignore the effect of Disney+ on demand, as that service only entered the market in 2020. Similarly, other shocks such as the Covid-19 pandemic or weather phenomena may lead to effects which may bias our predictions, if not included or accounted for in the data. Again, the researcher is responsible for critically assessing the suitability of the data, by either theoretically identifying possibly confounding events, or by checking the data with the help of suitable, empirical analyses.

Especially in the case of time-series data, one may start with a visual inspection of the dataset to see if things substantially vary across time. Breaks like those shown in Figure 11.2 may indicate radical changes caused by unobserved events in the dataset. This should at least motivate the researcher to try to understand why these breaks occur and think about whether the data

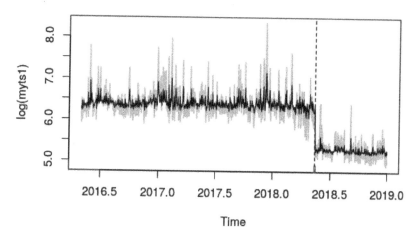

Figure 11.2   Structural break example

are still suitable for training a predictive model (which is unlikely). Similarly, trends (as shown in Figure 11.3) or seasonal effects (as shown in Figure 11.4) may also be easily identified with a visual inspection. In these cases, models could then be enriched by variables accounting for each season or a variable that captures the general market trend. Similarly, an evolving time series (such as a growing number of followers) can be corrected by using daily growth (operationalized as the difference in followers between day $t-1$ and day t) instead of the total number of followers by day (for more details see, for example, Pauwels et al., 2004).

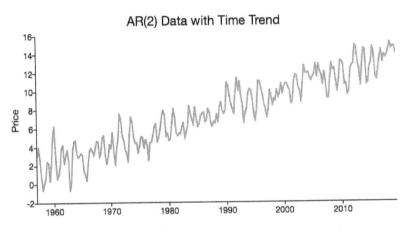

Figure 11.3 Example of a time series with trend

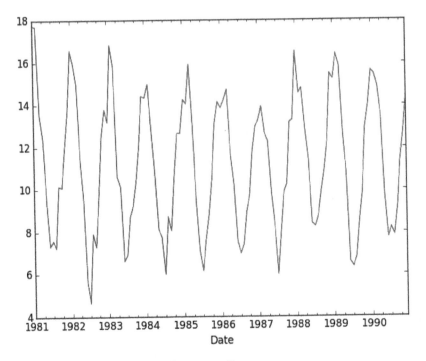

Figure 11.4 Example of a time series with seasonality

While in the above examples a visual inspection is enough to clearly determine changes over time, in many cases the image may fail to give confirmation. Here structural break analysis with the help of statistical tools as integrated in R's strucchange package maybe helpful. For more details, we recommend studying the package's vignette, which can be accessed through the following code.

```
install.packages("strucchange")
library(strucchange)

browseVignettes("strucchange")
```

DATA QUALITY

Once suitable, relevant, and timely data have been identified, researchers need to confirm the quality of the data. Often we will realize that datasets – despite being relevant and suitable – face limitations. For example, when observing the number of daily tweets which mention a company, some observations may be missing, as the corresponding crawler was offline on some days. Or the company failed for a period to record complaints or leads in the CRM database. Such temporarily missing information may again be easily identifiable with the help of a visual inspection. Especially in the case of time series, plots are a powerful tool for inspecting data. Histograms or distribution tables can also help spot NAs within the dataset. You may simply use the code below to count for each variable in your dataset the number of missing observations. Here we use the sum function from base R to count the number of NAs in the column col of data frame df.

```
sum(is.na(df$col))
```

In the case of cross-sectional data, NAs may not create too many problems. Still, many models react sensitively to missing observations and mostly (without telling us in R) drop these from the estimation. In the case of time-series analysis, an NA may even prevent us from estimating the model. So, we are in both cases well advised to find ways to replace the NAs with suitable values, which is commonly referred to as *data imputation*. Let us assume we have a time series of followers of a social media account. Unfortunately, our webcrawler was down for 2 weeks in the summer, so for 14 days the numbers of followers are missing. A simple way to address this issue could be to look at the number of followers before the missing period and after the blackout. We can now take the difference (i.e. the total growth within the time of the blackout) and distribute it equally over the 14 missing days. This approach may, however, create other issues as we assume that growth is linear. We know, however, that specific events (such as being featured by another account), time effects (on weekends there is more social media engagement), and other effects cause nonlinear growth effects. In such a case, we recommend using other, more sophisticated imputation approaches as implemented in R's mice package. The package's imputation function, for example allows you to predict the daily growth of followers with the help of a regression model that uses the previous daily growth rates to impute the missing data.

For more information on how to use `mice` to impute missing data, we recommend investigating the package's help file, which can be found with the following code.

```
install.packages("mice")
library(mice)

?mice
```

Even when all observations are present, some observations may create issues. For example, by including the extreme behaviour or extreme reactions of a single customer to certain marketing actions in a dataset, one may end up with confounded results which are inflated by a single outlier. Think of calculating the mean of the income distribution of an apartment complex. While most people in the building make a close to average income, the two people sharing the rooftop apartment make a seven-digit income. By including these in the building's average income calculations, we would distort the mean, which would be much higher compared to a case where we simply ignore the two top floor residents (of course you are also well advised in this case to use the median instead of the mean, but we hope that you understand the main issue outliers can create). Outlier identification is far from simple, and by removing observations from the dataset one may substantially change insights. We thus recommend being really careful about simply dropping the top or bottom observations. To identify potential outliers, one may first visually inspect the data to get an understanding of how extreme a certain observation is compared to other observations in the same dataset. This may help one gain an understanding of why this observation is so extreme and whether the specific case is representative of the sample or not (and can be dropped). Visual inspections may be conducted with the help of simple boxplots, as shown in the code below and in Figure 11.5.

```
library(ggplot2)
dat <- ggplot2::mpg
boxplot(dat$hwy, ylab = "hwy")
```

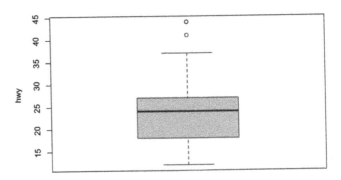

Figure 11.5 Example of the use of a boxplot to identify outliers

In this example, we use the `mpg` dataset that is integrated in the `ggplot` package. The dataset features information on different car models. We focus on the 'highway miles per gallon' variable and try to see with a boxplot if the variable contains outliers. Boxplots commonly provide information on five important locations within the distribution of a variable: the minimum (bottom line), the median (line within the box here), the first and third quartiles (the box), and the maximum (line on the top). The two circles in Figure 11.5 represent the two observations the boxplot function suspects to be outliers. For this purpose, the function relies on the interquartile range (IQR), which is a common identification method for outliers. The IQR is defined as the distance between the first and the third quartile (represented by the box in our figure). Any observation that is outside the interval composed of the first quartile minus 1.5 × IQR and the third quartile plus 1.5 × IQR is considered to be an outlier. In our case these are the two large observations with `hwy` values of 41 and 44. Beside visual inspection, one can rely on various other statistical tests to identify outliers, as underlined by the two example vignettes in the `outliersTests` package, which can be accessed with the following code. The package also provides valuable suggestions for further reading on the treatment of outliers.

```
install.packages("outliersTests")
library(outliersTests)

?outliersTests::example1
?outliersTests::example2
```

COMPUTATIONAL POWER AND PARALLELIZATION OF TASKS

We have already discussed that an increase in the amount of data may result in the need for more computational power or cause models to take a long time to provide results. For example, think of classic dictionary-based sentiment analysis, which we encountered Chapter 7. Here the computer needs to check, for each comment we submit, whether the particular comment contains a specific set of words featured in the sentiment dictionary. Of course, computers can do this in a much shorter time than humans, but think of a dataset with billions of comments. One computer will of course take quite some time to check all comments (an average laptop will take hours to check a dataset of 50 million comments). We could, however, help the computer by splitting the dataset into two sets and using a second computer. We could give each set to one of the computers and have them work in parallel. As both computers are now working at the same time but only have to assess half of the comments, we would also be able to cut the analysis time in half (in fact splitting the dataset and merging the results after the analysis also takes time, so we cannot exactly do things in half of the time, but almost). If we had three computers at hand, we could probably come close to a third of the initially required time by splitting the dataset into three parts, etc. But don't worry about having to buy more laptops or computers. It turns out that for most tasks your computer relies directly on your

CPU's core. Luckily, today's computers all feature more than one core. At the time of writing, most standard laptops have at least four – many eight – cores. This means that with a normal home market laptop you can already use the majority of your cores to parallelize tasks. While it sounds tempting to use all your cores for your analysis, keep in mind that your computer of course also needs to do other stuff (like showing you the pdf of this book) in the background and that you are well advised to at least reserve one core for tasks other than the analysis.

In R you can use different packages to parallelize tasks. The most commonly used packages are `parallel` (which is part of base R) and `doParallel` (which is most commonly also integrated into other packages which allow parallel computation). We recommend having a look at both packages' vignettes to familiarize yourself with the code. The vignettes can again be accessed with the following code.

```
install.packages("doParallel")
library(doParallel)

browseVignettes("doParallel")
browseVignettes("parallel")
```

An important thing to keep in mind is that parallelization of course only works if the data analysis or data manipulation does not require you to look at the whole dataset at once (as it does in the case of creating a term frequency matrix) or if tasks are conducted in a sequential way, where each step requires the results of the previous step (as we saw in case of the iterative process of the *k*-means cluster analysis). In these cases, parallelization does not apply.

DATA STORYTELLING AND VISUALIZATION

While marketing analytics is often believed to focus solely on analysis, the job ain't over until the results of the analysis are shared with the relevant managers and used by them to adjust marketing actions to come to a more effective or efficient solution. This implies that marketing analysts should not only have excellent analytical skills but also be able to translate their statistical findings into a more managerial lingo to facilitate and drive insight adaption and change within the company. Given the space limitations and the focus of this book on the methodology, we cannot give too much detail here and recommend readers to seek the help of the many available resources in the field of data visualization. Nevertheless, we want to share some important experiences from our own careers.

We strongly believe that selling your analytics is not too different from selling products. In other words, put your target group's interests first! This may require you to also gain an understanding of the management and decision-making style of your peers. While some managers may be more comfortable with relying on clear analytical results, others may feel more comfortable with intuitive or experience-based decision-making (for more details, see Blattberg and Hoch, 1990). Hanssens and Pauwels (2016) suggest communicating with both groups in separate ways. They suggest that, as the first group may focus more on numbers, one should address analytically oriented managers with the model output and guide the discussion more towards the question of optimization. Here, presenting elasticities – which enable managers to quickly forecast the outcomes of their own decisions and strategies – may turn out to be especially suitable. In the case of the latter group – with the more intuitive managers – visual presentations relying on graphs and figures can be more effective. When preparing graphs, Midway (2020) recommends first choosing the right form of diagram, suitable for answering the key question or delivering the key message of your data story and recommended actions. For example, clustered barplots can facilitate the understanding of effects for different customer segments, while heatmaps give a better understanding of favourable and unfavourable approaches. Furthermore, one may use colours to highlight differences among groups or observations, which should be used consistently throughout a presentation. Include detailed information in legends, which facilitate comprehension and remove ambiguity. Sometimes your results will not provide a clear story. In these cases, try to transparently address ambiguity, uncertainty, or risk, by including error bars or highlighting the confidence intervals with the help of shaded areas in your plots. You might even turn a classic graphic into an infographic, by adding more textual elements, which verbally support the interpretation of the graph.

No matter which type of approach you use, a key rule is to focus on the essentials. Even though you feel the urge to tell everyone how much you did and how many tears and hours went into your project or what kind of challenges you needed to master to obtain your results, most managers will only be interested in your final recommendations and what they need to do to be more successful. Keep this in mind when preparing your presentation. Try to first understand what your key message will be. Based on this message, start crafting your story, by asking yourself questions such as 'What kind of information is essential for taking the decisions?', 'What kind of information supports the decision?', 'What kind of information will enhance trust and confidence in my recommendations?', and 'What kind of additional information is essential to understand the context of the analysis?'. By keeping in mind your key message and guided by the answers to the above questions, you will be able to develop a suitable story.

IMPLEMENTATION OF ANALYSIS RESULTS IN MARKETING PRACTICE

Previous research (see Hanssens and Pauwels, 2016), as well as many implementation examples, emphasize that analyses and forecasts do not guarantee that predictions always fully materialize. Albers (1998) identifies four major sources of error which may explain the deviation between a forecast and the real market situation: (1) planning variance, which results from incorrect estimates due, for example, to data issues or misspecified models; (2) execution variance, which results from management not fully implementing the solution suggested by the initial analysis; (3) reaction variance, which results from any sort of competitive reaction that has not been anticipated by the initial model; (4) unexplained variance, resulting from all other omitted factors which may possibly affect consumer behaviour such as unobserved trends or random effects which are hard to observe and include in the analysis. All these potential error sources require marketing researchers as well as marketing managers to carefully assess the quality of their initial analysis results and to invest more time and effort in validating findings in a smaller test setting, before changing marketing actions at a large scale. As wrongly informed marketing actions can become very expensive for companies, with not only the company's fortune at stake but also the fortune of all involved stakeholders – such as employees and suppliers – at risk, managers are well advised to include a second parachute in their marketing analytics. Let us assume that a company has conducted a thorough marketing mix analysis and realized that the current allocation of the marketing budget in various channels is inefficient. The results of the analysis suggest moving the budget from traditional media channels such as radio and TV towards digital channels such as search engine advertising and specifically targeted campaigns on social media. Wiesel et al. (2011) present a two-step iterative process to achieve this. The process allows one to first confirm the positive impact of the new allocation in a small field test setting, before moving the whole budget. Field experiments can easily be created and administrated by, for example, selecting sales territories that are similar in terms of buying power and other relevant consumer criteria and systematically changing the marketing actions in these chosen sales territories as recommended by the model for a short time (e.g. 3 months) to see if consumer reactions move in the predicted direction. Wiesel et al. (2011) present a 2 × 2 approach in which they use four sales territories to test the impact of the different changes. In our case, this would lead to the following four territory implementations. In territory 1, we do not alter traditional media or digital media and use this territory as a business-as-usual base (i.e. benchmark) setting. In territory 2, we lower traditional media spending (e.g. by half) but keep digital at the same level. In territory 3, we do not alter traditional media spending but increase digital spending. Finally, we use territory 4 as a 'full' manipulation territory in which we increase (e.g. double) digital spending and cut (halve) traditional spending. We can now compare effects as displayed in Table 11.1 and see how profits changed in the different scenarios, to see if our model's initial predictions are confirmed by the field experiments.

Table 11.1 Visualization of field experiment results

Changes to net profit		Digital ad spending	
		Base	Double
Traditional ad spending	Base	+ 0	+ 55K
	Half	+ 80K	+ 140K

In the case of the business-as-usual scenario with no reallocation of ad spending, profits – obviously – remain unchanged. If we only double the digital ad spending, profits increase by €55,000, as sales react, but of course we have to pay more for our advertising (as we have not yet cut traditional spending). If we leave digital ad spending at the base level, and only cut our traditional advertising, we profit mostly from the savings, which increase our profits to by €80,000, while shifting these savings to digital channels allows us to realize a €140,000 increase in profits. Given that the field experiments further validate our model findings, we can now start slowly adapting the allocation change to all other sales territories. Again, we recommend carefully monitoring the effects and only slowly moving towards the intended solution, instead of rushing things by suddenly changing the budget in a one-time move.

CRITICALLY ASSESS THE ETHICAL DIMENSIONS OF YOUR DATA ANALYSIS

Algorithms and predictive models as we have encountered them in many chapters in this book (e.g. think of churn prediction or the other machine learning skills you have acquired) have conquered the business world within the last decade and now touch many people's daily lives. Often this happens without consumers even noticing that they have been analysed, targeted, and judged by an algorithm, as computers decide in milliseconds in the background how a website we are visiting is composed or what kinds of products we are going to see when visiting an online store. Predictive algorithms also judge what content we see on social media. Similarly, they decide who is going to see our own content on social media and how much reach our content gets. Latest research shows that some social media platforms assess the attractiveness of people's faces in a video or image and only show these to a larger audience if people are classified as more attractive (Sherpa, 2020). But algorithms not only decide what content we see, but are also used to assess our interest and willingness to pay for products and services. Dynamic pricing, where websites adapt price tags to the estimated interest and buying power of each website visitor, has become a frequent practice in the travel industry, with airlines and train companies varying prices based on factors such as the visitor's operating system, IP address, or type of access device, assuming that people using more expensive devices are browsing from a higher-income address and are more likely to accept higher prices. Similarly, we see customer predictions also affect companies' offline marketing communication activities, as underlined by the widely discussed Target campaign for pregnant women. Target – interested in securing future mothers as customers – intended to send out specific catalogues to pregnant customers. To do so, the company used machine learning to identify pregnant customers through changes in their buying behaviour. The programme garnered a lot of public attention when the company targeted a 16-year-old pregnant girl before she had a chance to tell her own parents about the pregnancy. But machine learning applications are not unique to marketing applications. Machine learning models are also used in finance to assess the repayment likelihood of a mortgage or line of credit. Based on the estimated probability that a person may not be able to repay the credit, the system recommends a higher interest rate. More extreme applications can be found in the insurance industry, where companies try to explore the personal traits of applicants using data and information obtained from social media to assess the health risks of an application. That said, machine learning-based predictions are not exclusive to the business sector. In the case of predictive policing previous crime data are used to predict the occurrence of future crimes with the help of structural and socio-economic factors to send police officers to areas where the model predicts most crimes will happen. By now you will have realized, from your own growing discomfort, that investigating – and using – personal trait information with the help of predictive models can quickly cross comfort zones, especially in cases where consumers are not actively involved and do not give consent. Relying on (even anonymous) data from other people to predict someone else's personal interests and traits can often be perceived by customers as a violation of privacy standards (even if the specific operation is within legal boundaries), as underlined by the previously mentioned Target case. Researchers are thus well advised to question themselves if the intended measurement or prediction might upset consumers or cause irritation. If so, they may be well advised to refrain from predicting the variable of interest.

And even if you can answer the question 'should I really...' with an honest 'yes', other problems may arise while designing and using analytical models. O'Neil (2016) discusses many areas of application where misspecified and ill-trained models can ultimately cause tremendous consequences. Think of the mortgage example. If a model overestimates the personal credit default risk, the interest rate for that person increases, making it even more likely for that person to default, as the interest is ultimately too high. While the model will see the default as a confirmation of the initial prediction, and move more in that direction with future recommendations, it ignores the fact that the cause of the default is the model's false prediction. The model became its own false prophecy, with fatal consequences for the creditor. Researchers must thus control at all times how models learn. This also involves understanding why models make predictions and why certain predictions come true and others do not. This, however, requires researchers to develop a profound understanding of statistical methods. Simply applying some code or package from the internet without clearly understanding it and knowing that it fits the data and application's needs and circumstances can easily produce such a false prophecy situation.

O'Neil (2016) shows, however, that fatal inaccuracy does not only result from faulty modelling applications or people naively applying code. Using incorrect training data – as discussed earlier – can similarly lead to incorrect conclusions, resulting in sometimes fatal consequences for some of the stakeholders involved. In the mortgage case, the model's inability to correctly predict the default risk may come from the fact that not too many successful mortgage applications from minorities are within the initial training set. Due to this imbalance, the model's prediction error is larger for this specific group. With the model learning from its own incorrect predictions (i.e. seeing that people with low income and a minority background have a higher default risk and thus should be given higher interest rates, which leads again to higher default numbers) the GIGO effect is further amplified. In many cases, we do not realize that training data commonly contain average information that can perfectly address average questions and predict average behaviour. However, as soon as we try to predict extraordinary behaviour (such as credit defaults by minorities) the training data must fail as there are not enough instances to learn from. As a researcher you are thus required not only to be sure that your training dataset contains enough information to answer your research question, but also to think about what happens if your training dataset creates wrong or biased predictions.

CHAPTER SUMMARY

In this chapter, we discussed the many different issues and problems which arise from using real-world data alongside the research process. For each stage of the research journey we identify common pitfalls and issues and discuss how to entangle and address them. We start with the question of how much data we need and how database management can help us to ensure proper data access and fast and easy data handling. Having developed an understanding of the importance of data quality when it comes to making decisions and predictions, we have now furthered our knowledge of how to check data for outlier issues, trends, and seasonality effects, and how to remove potential confounds from our data. Given the increase in available data, we furthermore learned how parallelization can be used to speed up analytics and how we can either combine the cores of our own computers or various computers together to analyse parts of our dataset in parallel. While all these steps ensure the highest data quality and reliability of our analysis, taking decisions based on the results of our analysis is still a challenge. We therefore also learned how visualizations can facilitate decision-making, especially for managers not familiar with the analytical procedures. Furthermore, we learned that one should not immediately trust the analysis and put all one's eggs in one basket, but carefully assess the quality of the analysis by conducting field experiments based on the initial findings of the analytical insights generated. Last but not least, we discussed the serious potential negative effects of misspecified models and incorrectly executed analyses, not only for companies but also for all stakeholders and for society in general.

REFERENCES

Albers, S. (1998) A framework for analysis of sources of profit contribution variance between actual and plan. *International Journal of Research in Marketing*, 15(2), 109–22.

Blattberg, R. C. and Hoch, S. J. (2010) Database models and managerial intuition: 50% model + 50% manager. In *Perspectives on Promotion and Database Marketing: The Collected Works of Robert C Blattberg* (pp. 215–27). Singapore: World Scientific.

Hanssens, D. M. and Pauwels, K. H. (2016) Demonstrating the value of marketing. *Journal of Marketing*, 80(6), 173–90.

Midway, S. R. (2020) Principles of effective data visualization. *Patterns*, 1(9), 100141.

O'Neil, C. (2016) *Weapons of Math Destruction: How Big Data Increases Inequality and Threatens Democracy*. New York: Broadway Books.

Pauwels, K. (2014) *It's Not the Size of the Data – It's How You Use it: Smarter Marketing with Analytics and Dashboards*. New York: Amacom.

Pauwels, K., Currim, I., Dekimpe, M. G., Hanssens, D. M., Mizik, N., Ghysels, E. and Naik, P. (2004) Modeling marketing dynamics by time series econometrics. *Marketing Letters*, 15(4), 167–83.

Sherpa (2020) How normal am I? www.hownormalami.eu

Wiesel, T., Pauwels, K. and Arts, J. (2011) Practice prize paper – Marketing's profit impact: Quantifying online and off-line funnel progression. *Marketing Science*, 30(4), 604–11.

INDEX

Page numbers followed by f indicate figures.

APPLIED
MARKETING
ANALYTICS
USING R